# Heaven Was Not Enough

"Now, Constance, do not dramatize yourself: you are not a black sheep; merely an unattractive, dirty gray."

SISTER JULIE DU SAINT-ESPRIT, S.N.D.

# HEAVEN WAS NOT ENOUGH

By Constance O'Hara

*Philadelphia and New York*
J. B. LIPPINCOTT COMPANY

FIRST EDITION



*Printed in the United States of America*
*Library of Congress Catalog Card Number 55-6308*

To the Memory

of

My Friend

RIGHT REVEREND

MONSIGNOR HENRY T. DRUMGOOLE, D.D., LITT.D

*This was the noblest Roman of them all*

# BOOK ONE

## 1

FEBRUARY 11, 1911, AND the great bell of St. Patrick's Church in Philadelphia, is tolling for His Grace, the Most Reverend Archbishop, Patrick John Ryan.

The solemn bell is calling me from the warm obscurity of infancy into the demanding world of self. The tolling of a bell is my first memory. It is a lonely sound, but it has grandeur. I reach over and touch my cousin Frances, and look into her grave blue eyes. She has a round pretty face. I see her for the first time with my new vision. I can remember.

An adult voice calls, "The Archbishop is dead."

Archbishop! A name to match the bell. The tears spill out of Frances' eyes, and she cries, "Aunt Constance."

I am aware that I am in my grandfather O'Hara's house at Twentieth and Locust Streets. We are in the old sitting room overlooking the garden of the Convent of Notre Dame. The room is filled with Victorian litter and stuffiness—a bedlam of mahogany and tapestry and marble statuary. There are copies of masterpieces framed in alarmingly bright gilt. Sets of books in rich leather fill the bookcase at the back of the room. Deep carpets suck all sound from footsteps; at night gaslights whistle in ornate chandeliers. A coal fire burns red as roses in the grate, this February afternoon. The curtains, in superimposed layers of velvet, silk and Brussels lace, shut out the pale eastern light.

My grandfather's house always swarmed with family and visiting cousins and clergy, and rang with the rich laughter of colored servants. I can see the family now as they were that afternoon in 1911, and there is a sunlit loneliness in my mind, as if I keep them safe from harm in the memory of a child. They were such gentle, fantastic people, compounded of Philadelphia provincialism and untrammeled Celtic lunacy. The child I was could understand them perfectly, for they were like the familiar magic and homely fact of all the fairy tales I knew.

Aunt Constance came into the room. John Singer Sargent called her "the Irish beauty," when he met her at Dr. De Forest Willard's. She was probably pushing a lock of unruly red-brown hair from her wonderful forehead. Her eyes were too generous for the uncompromising spinster she was to become. She should have been courted and loved, should have married and produced children. She became instead an unknown saint.

Uncle Tom leaned against the mantel, his mouth sullen. He was a handsome man, with deep-set eyes and a Roman nose, a scholar and an eccentric, given to speaking in the tongue of Aeschylus and Homer to his bewildered patients. All the women were mad about him. In many ways, even then, he was absent from himself.

His brother Theobald was in the room now. Uncle Thé, the romantic one, sent violets every day to the woman he adored, paid for out of his fast dwindling inheritance; so far he had had no encouragement. This made his mouth droop, and he was given to bilious attacks.

Aunt Francie tripped in, the mother of my cousin Frances, flashing a mischievous smile toward the little girls. Even with a bell tolling for an archbishop, she was capable of singing a few bars from *The Merry Widow*. She had then been widowed for almost five years, but from the cradle to the grave Aunt Francie could never be indifferent to men. Soon now she would be married a second time, for she'd found a man courageous enough to live with the turbulent O'Haras. She wouldn't dream of leaving home again.

There must have been cousins besides Frances in the room. The servants, Lizzie, Mary and Robert were certainly in the doorway, for this was an occasion. Lizzie had cooked those famous terrapin dinners for His Grace; Mary had polished the brasses and the silver, washed the Haviland dinner service and rubbed the cut glass till it sparkled, while Robert had helped Jesse serve, and had led His Grace to his carriage.

But Jesse Coxe, who had been my grandfather's body servant in the Civil War, in 1911 was sleeping the last long sleep beside him in the family plot at Old Cathedral. Dying he had made sure of that: "Send for the priest, Doctah O'Hara, sah. Ah's been through with sin for a long time. Ah wants to be suah to spend all time with mah family."

And the bell tolls, and Aunt Constance commences the Rosary.

I did not know it then, but we were praying for more than the soul of Archbishop Ryan that February afternoon. The days of our fame as one of the great Catholic families were ending on the slow rhythm of a bell. Already we were living on capital, and the family concept of a mortgage was a paper that stretched and added a few needed thousands each year. Now our friend at court was dead.

The encroaching years would yield every retributive grief that life brings to the proud, wilful and sensitive. These people were richly endowed with talents, grace of mind, and virtue, prodigal with love and wit and ready sympathy—and they never had a particle of common sense. The house was to go, and the furniture and the pictures and the silver, scattered in a dozen auction rooms. Today didn't matter. It was gray, meaningless. But tomorrow would be bright.

I think I saw them with a child's complete divination that day. I never thereafter tried to dwell on the normal and the unexceptional when I thought of them. As the years went on they seemed waiting to be absolved of mortality, yet they were never gloomy or fearful. There was a bond between all of us that can never be severed, the terrifying bond of weakness. It is in our blood to wait for tomorrow. What did they achieve, these charming men and women? Nothing. Nothing in the huckster's view, or the view of the bank-clerk mentality. Yet they were extravagant, generous, loyal, and the Catholic tradition gave them a live and vital faith.

Sell the stocks and bonds in the safe-deposit vault—and trust in God. Light a candle to His Mother when things go wrong. They drove ambitious people mad, but if they scorned thrift they also abhorred craftiness, and somehow, like the lilies of the field, they endured. In ruin they were never humdrum or pitiful, but picturesque and memorable.

When I was older I commenced to believe that my fiery grandfather had drained the life force from his family. He died before I was born, and yet his presence still dominated the house. In his pictures he is razor-thin, with a spare ascetic face; no flesh could linger on that frame supercharged with energy.

He had been medical director of St. Agnes Hospital, and he quarreled violently with Sister Borromeo on cleanliness. "Infection is always our fault," he'd thundered. "It's wilful murder." When he was dying Sister Borromeo, his ancient enemy, came to call. He opened one cold blue eye and said, "Dear Lord, I thought that damn Borromeo was in the room." She replied, acid sweet, "Poor Doctor, he's delirious."

In the house on Twentieth Street you could still feel him charging in the door, with a new cause in tow. It might be the Temperance Society, perhaps, when G. Washington Logue and he engaged in mighty battles over a fountain in the park. My grandfather won, and the black marble monolith of Moses in Fairmount Park, erected by the Catholic Total Abstinence Society, is as stern, uncompromising and depressing a piece of statuary as there is in the country.

Old Dr. O'Hara had an interesting life. He had seen the world as a doctor in the Army and in the Navy and found it sinful. He was opposed to sin for everyone else—after he gave it up. Irascible, a bully, a brilliant satiric wit, he was a mighty marksman, and he regarded as the bull's-eye God had commanded him to hit, all Protestants, all heretics; in fact, everyone and everything that wasn't Catholic.

Though I never saw him in the flesh, I see him sitting at the dining room table, dropping the silver in frantic exasperation if it wasn't *warmed*. I can see him quelled, as his gentle wife would remark sternly, "Doctor O'Hara. Now, Doctor O'Hara." She was the only one who could calm him, and shamefacedly he would murmur, "I beg your pardon, France."

His friend Miss Mary Kerevan would often risk argument with him and, I am told, the walls shook as Grandfather blasted: "Alexander Pope ruined English poetry. Facts are not the stuff of poetry. And as for your Tennyson . . . pap, Mary Kerevan. Pap, for infants to ruin their bowels. I tell you poetry's dead in England."

There was another story told of my grandfather when his brother, Bishop O'Hara, was Rector of St. Patrick's. My grandfather left the Navy, after serving in the tragic first expedition to Atrato on the Isthmus of Panama, and in the Civil War was an Army surgeon attached to the famous Bucktails, stationed in Washington. He borrowed money from his brother to buy a horse. The Bishop, then plain Dr. William O'Hara, sent the money with this note, "I take this from church funds over which I am only the custodian. When the war is over, I wish the horse in payment."

My grandfather rode the horse home from the battle of Gettysburg. He was slightly wounded, but what smarted was Willie's shrewdness. Horses had doubled and tripled in value. This was a fine horse, and now it was Willie's. My grandfather was scrupulous about his debts, but he paused at many inns along the road to reflect on his grievance. He planned to practise medicine in Philadelphia and he needed a horse. He could never afford to buy one. It was Willie's Roman education that made him drive such a hard bargain. Why, he was like a Jesuit! Major O'Hara rode his white horse at a wild gallop down Twentieth Street, drove it up on the steps of St. Patrick's rectory, bellowing, in the hope that every fine upstanding Catholic in the vicinity would hear him, "*Here's your church property, come and get it and be damned to you, Willie.*" Grandfather was not a Temperance man at that time.

It is hard to remove the embellishments from memory and recover the bare fact, but I know that Aunt Constance must have said to me that afternoon, in 1911:

"Your father was with the Archbishop."

I am sure she said it, because I remember that with memory dawned pride. My father, Dr. Michael O'Hara, Jr., is with the Archbishop! That meant—and only a Celt will understand—that all our axes were ground long ago. We do not have to lower others to gain height ourselves. It means we O'Haras do not have to ask for things; they are ours by right. It is my father's privilege to stand with a dying archbishop. We are special. . . .

The bell tolled on, as we prayed for a witty and gracious churchman, His Grace, Archbishop Patrick John Ryan. The measure of a man cannot be taken till he is gone. Not democratic, His Grace, but if he believed in social privilege he never divorced it from social responsibility; and he represented the spiritual power of the Church in an age of transition in a way that gave Catholicity in Philadelphia unity and dignity.

"The eyes of the world are upon you," he would tell his priests sternly. His Grace made many converts. He understood that the divine and the human can come together within the limits of a sacred tradition. It was his genius to know how to define those limits.

On February 11, 1911, the bells ringing mournfully on the still air gave me memory. Perhaps, when I had come to middle age, they thundered through my closed and bitter mind and brought me to my knees again.

# 2

On an April afternoon in 1907 they dressed me, a two-week-old infant, in the christening robes made by the Sisters of the Good Shepherd for their doctor's daughter. Yards of batiste, lace and hand embroidery; over my own, the ancestral christening dress worn by my father, then a coat of corded silk with a padded cape, and a bonnet of duchesse lace. It was no wonder I was sound asleep when they carried me into St. Patrick's Church for my baptism. Uncle Thé was my godfather, and he frowned during the ceremonies at his sister Francie who persisted in giggling at the sleeping infant. Monsignor Kirlin tried to arouse me in my pretty godmother's arms, but the vanities of the world had done me in and the solemn ceremonies proceeded without my vocal response.

Albert Dutrieulle, the caterer, was readying the christening feast, and it was hoped that Archbishop Ryan would drop in. My close relatives would be there, a goodly representation of the cloth, and the touch of purple that was so necessary to the family honor. The immediate family were present at the baptismal font. My mother's beautiful sister Caroline wore a velvet picture hat, the latest thing in feminine attire. The men were in cutaways, for the Sacraments were solemn occasions.

Afterward, there was a spirited argument whether a child that didn't cry at its own baptism might not grow up a heretic. That set off Monsignor Kieran, Rector of St. Patrick's, into a flood of Latin quotations, while Uncle Tom tried to top him and lead him into a labyrinth of obscure heresies. My mother's relatives applied themselves to the supper, with the unspoken reservation that all O'Hara parties eventually became forums for the clergy; there was no opportunity to have a good family gossip. Cousin Mary congratulated the fiery Dr. Garvey, Rector of St. Charles Seminary, when he arrived, on having recently been raised to Monsignor.

"Stop, stop!" he boomed. "What use have I for these red rags from Rome?"

At that exact moment His Grace Archbishop Ryan was framed in the doorway, and Dr. Garvey without a quiver of embarrassment genuflected and kissed the episcopal ring, murmuring, "Your Grace."

It was said a long, long look passed between the two eminent churchmen. Dr. Garvey had expected a bishopric—as well the Archbishop knew.

It was a good party, for the world of the middle classes was standing virtually still on its axis. It was an age of immense security and serenity. A child born in this era was cradled in an atmosphere of emotional and mental safety. Europe and its involvements were far away. The Spanish-American War had settled that nonsense. It was true the man in the White House, Theodore Roosevelt, might stir up a certain amount of social unrest; but basically the upper middle class could not be touched, and a man with a profession—a doctor like my father—had nothing to do with politics. It was an age without fear, a tight comfortable world.

There was not a priest present at my christening party who did not know it was a hollow world.

The word "security" on American lips, uttered with such desperate longing, comes from those who were living before 1914 in that tight snug little world. Few priests ever say it, for they know that America was never secure, and the artificial peace of the early years of the twentieth century was the mother of murderous wars and gross exploitation of human beings.

There was an American dream of freedom, close to the *Utopia* of St. Thomas More, which brought my ancestors across the Atlantic in small unsafe sailing vessels, through gales and days of calm, with two thoughts in their minds: "Freedom for the faith. Education." It would have been fitting if they had been present in spirit at the Catholic baptism of their latest descendant, for from the counties of Ireland they had brought the faith safe from persecutions, and the hard ancient wisdom of a historic and stormy past.

James Gartland, my great-great-grandfather on my mother's side, entered this in his diary:

> The year one thousand eight hundred and eight. April first. On Palm Sunday, sailed self and family, except Eliza, from Dublin in the Ship Diana. Captain Nathaniel R. Macy Master for America. Arrived in New York after a prosperous voyage on the 5th. of May following.

James had brought his family of ten, save Eliza his two-year-old daughter. The diary did not mention that Eliza had succumbed to a children's disease and was left behind in the care of a nurse till the next year, but till her burial in her ninety-first year in the vault at St. John the Evangelist Church, Philadelphia, she never wearied of her grievance, for she came to America second class in charge of the ship's captain. Auntie Eliza made up for that by being the haughtiest member of a haughty family.

James had married Mary Conroy, who was more than a Conroy, for her mother was Mary Carlisle, daughter of the Earl of Bellew. The Irish must have a title, for an aristocrat in the family tree keeps their heads up in heartbreak. It is true the Celts have an unfortunate habit of acting as if they created their own ancestors, and unquestionably they embellish them. So Patrick, Lord Bellew, sustained James and Mary in the new world; when the first son, the beloved Simon Gartland, my great-granduncle died in the Jesuit novitiate in Georgetown, James tidily wrote, "He was the great-grandson of . . ."

The afternoon in 1819 when they lowered Mary, in religion Sister Jane Frances de Chantal, into her grave at Emmitsburg with Mother Seton standing with them, Francis Xavier Gartland, another son and a candidate for the priesthood, entered in the family log, "My beloved sister at St. Joseph's Vale, Emmitsburg,

Maryland. She was the great-granddaughter of . . ." Francis could not be accused of pride, for he was a gentle saint, destined to be first Bishop of Savannah, and die a martyr in the yellow fever epidemic, selflessly nursing the most despised and rejected of men—the Negro slaves; yet more than once he mentions Lord Bellew. . . .

In July, 1808, James Gartland came to Philadelphia, and on December thirtieth that same year he enters in his diary:

> Made a declaration of my intention of becoming a citizen of the United States in the Supreme Court.

He lies now in St. John's graveyard under this simple lettering, "The Family Vault of James Gartland." A decent, godly man asleep in the Lord in the shadow of the Church, to which he gave his money, his sons, and his entire devotion. He left his beloved Dublin, and the house by the sea in Drogheda with a view of the green hills, to give his sons and daughters a Catholic education. No one ever looked down on a Gartland in Dublin, nor yet in London, Irishman and Catholic though he was, and in Philadelphia he demanded that right for his sons and daughters. The Quakers liked his ways, the Episcopalians honored him; but he preferred the society of the Jesuits, and the good Fathers at St. Mary's. Too much a Dublin gentleman for the other Irish of Philadelphia, James Gartland was not a cheerful man; and Mary, granddaughter of the Earl of Bellew, must often have tired of clerical society.

James never caught the due balance between his spiritual and temporal position, and except among the clergy never met anyone better informed, or more the perfect gentleman than himself. This tended to a corroding and bitter piety that exalted the man but never humbled his soul. He was a born leader of his own people in the new land, but he was too proud to lead, so the Irish took him down a peg or two on every occasion. He did not desert to the Christ Church party during the Trustee troubles of the 1820s; that never entered his head. He just became more pious, more learned—and pitifully lonely; but the boys went to Georgetown and the girls to Emmitsburg. James's class consciousness gave his descendants a bitter battle, for we inherited it—so the Irish keep on taking us down a peg or two.

Another boat comes up the Delaware in the eighteen thirties. A giant of an Irish lad in broadcloth, with the unspeakable elegance of gloves, welcomes his widowed mother Abigail Horan—gentle Abigail from Seven Churches, with the soft Gaelic on her tongue, and no use for those she could not love. But who was there in the world from a poor beggar to a king that was not in need of love? Abigail's heart was a hearthfire casting warmth and light on all those frightened by the storm.

She had lived through a dreadful winter when Thomas, her eldest, had ridden the only horse on the farm to Queenstown for America. Poor fatherless boy, there was no living to be wrung from the worked-out land, and he had dreams of gold in America. He promised to send for her, and here they were, all ten of them, with the deep green seas and the strong winds and half a world between them and Ireland.

My maternal grandfather, the first Hubert Horan, clinging to her hand, must have seen with his two-year-old eyes a strange world as the packet ship docked at Water Street; beyond the low gray line of the wharf, the Delaware was a forest of high-masted sailing boats at anchor, with gulls dipping lazily into the clean blue river. Great teams of horses passed on the cobbled streets. He would have caught a glimpse of stately houses, and the silver spire of Christ Church still rising high over Philadelphia, a city that would reward him and his family with much good fortune.

Abigail saw her son, and the ready laughter bubbled on her lips at the shoneen in his broadcloth straining over his splendid shoulders and his strong hands bursting from the seams of those kid gloves. She saw the shame in him at the wretched band of immigrants huddling on the pier, and his firm decision to get away as soon as possible. A few priests were there, and kind men with the brogue still on their tongues. Thomas explained they were the Friendly Sons of St. Patrick who met every ship and saw to the people.

He led her to a hired carriage standing on a side street. The pretty sisters in their shabby dresses stepped after him like queens, and Abigail as proud. After all, her own uncle was Hubert Devereux, once physician to Empress Josephine. Had anyone told her that Hubert's French education had given him liberal views and that Josephine was lax about her marriage vows, Abigail would have answered, "Acushla, keep the black spite from the tongue. I'll hear no evil of an empress. She had many temptations, God save her, that we'll never know."

And now Abigail was riding up Market Street, like a queen herself, with quarterings on her hired carriage, trying gently, oh, so gently, to learn what Thomas had in hard cash apart from the elegant broadcloth on his back. She wasn't afraid, for the Horans were strong men and proud men and they would not be defeated.

My father's family were different, for they had a hunger of the mind. Thomas O'Hara, my great-grandfather, was from the far North of Ireland, where the wild winds of the Atlantic blow and the fierce ocean beats at the puny acres of men. His father had been a mercenary soldier, but Thomas wanted the priesthood. The parish priest, Father O'Neil, was delighted, for the young man had a great aptitude for studies and the qualities from which good priests are made. In the wars of Ulster the O'Haras had been lost to the Church, the boy's own uncle, James O'Hara, had been knighted by an English king, fought in George Washington's army, and built a Presbyterian church in Pittsburgh, Pennsylvania.

There was no money left for the Catholic O'Hara, but Father O'Neil aspired higher than Maynooth for young Thomas. He would be entered as a scholastic in Paris, and Rome would come next.

But there was a girl in Tyrone who had other ideas; a Presbyterian girl, who had a queer passion for knowledge, whose people had come from England with Cromwell's men. What could she know of Ireland, a bright light in the dark ages, glorious when Rome was rotting? What could she know of a land that knew Patrick and Augustine, whose monasteries were houses of study when barbarian hordes settled England? What could she want with this lad who was straining toward the sanctuary? Louisa Miller had this passion for learning and she, an orphan girl and an heiress, was bound and determined to have the brilliant Thomas O'Hara.

She got him, and Father O'Neil knew even more deeply the lonely agony of a priest's soul in the dead of night, trying to determine what was right: break a girl's heart when Thomas had pledged himself to her, and pack him off to Paris; or let him marry this Presbyterian girl who had made him teach her Latin. A new wrinkle in courtship surely. He examined his conscience and they were married the next morning.

There was no tolerance extended to them; her dour brothers quarreled with Thomas, and she saw the wretchedness in his eyes as he walked lonely miles to Mass. Louisa demanded her inheritance, and Thomas and she set sail for America.

It was a tidy fortune, for her pounds sterling came to twenty thousand dollars, and prudently it waited for her in Philadelphia, with a furnished house ordered, not a grand house but a suitable one, for the money was to be spent educating the children.

On the high seas with a winter gale tearing at the little ship, Louisa lay down in her berth and drew the green curtain. She never groaned once, though the winds shrieked and the seas pounded; toward morning the old granny who helped the silent and agonized girl went for Thomas to tell him he had a son.

And that is how it came down in family legends: "The Bishop was born on the high seas." True, the official record places the Bishop's birthplace in County Derry, Ireland, but to be born at sea in a ship plowing through the broad sweep of the Atlantic is much more satisfactory.

She called him William and there is no one to say that she was not thinking of Prince William of Orange, this indomitable woman from Ulster. He went to Georgetown at twelve, and from there to the Urban College in Rome, where he was consecrated to the priesthood by Cardinal Franzoni in the Basilica of St. John Lateran. In God's time, hurried on a bit by Louisa, he was made first Bishop of Scranton.

She knew or guessed none of these things when she carried

the infant William through the streets of Philadelphia, in the year 1816, with a good bit of that twenty thousand dollars still reposing in Mr. Girard's bank. I am sure there was no carriage for Louisa, and the house was plain, for she set to work that first day to cook a dinner for Thomas. She gave him no time to dream or present his letters to the priests at St. Mary's, but reminded him there was an accountant's job open at the United States Mint, where they coined the money, and he had better go see to it.

It was on Louisa's capital, carefully hoarded, that William went to Rome, and my grandfather Michael O'Hara went to the University of Pennsylvania for his medical degree. Louisa said not a word when Thomas led his family to daily Mass at St. Mary's, each holding a tallow candle against the darkness. Louisa said not a word on a Sunday morning when William was celebrating Mass in his own fine church, St. Patrick's, and she rose from her pew and knelt at the altar rail to receive First Communion from her startled son. The Jesuits had instructed her—and kept her secret. Louisa was a stern woman who knew the meaning of sacrifice for the learning she craved. This Ulster woman knew the freedom of discipline, but often she must have remembered the dreamy Irish lad who taught her Latin in the County of Tyrone.

The fiery Father Hughes, pastor of St. John the Evangelist in Philadelphia, was writing a letter, and his assistant Father Gartland was waiting to deliver it personally to the captain of the fastest packet ship afloat. Father Gartland looked at his watch anxiously, for Father Hughes was in a great hurry, and taking a long time. Father Hughes had started a Catholic free school for boys in 1829 and he was sending for a professor from Dublin. That was like Father Hughes, the great innovator, but it would lead to a row with the trustees when the bill had to be paid.

Father Hughes paused often as he wrote to Richard McCunney. Richard, after studying in Salamanca and Paris, had returned to Ireland without a sovereign in his pocket and accepted a post as schoolmaster in Donegal. Father Hughes could see it in his mind's eye: the ragged children clustered around Richard in the poor broken-down apology for a school; Richard fighting against the persistent, relentless persecution of education by the English in Ireland, with a burning faith in the cultural genius of the Irish people. The English had put a price on his head, and then they'd offered him a professorship in Trinity College—if he'd just give up the faith.

America was the place for young Richard now he was seasoned. He'd show these Philadelphians what an Irish scholar and patriot was like. Father Hughes remembered Mother Seton when he had been the gardener at St. Joseph's Vale. He'd like to tell Mother Seton how it felt to write to a McCunney sending him the passage money to America. But then Mother Seton had taught her gardener to shackle his wild arrogance, that awful hurt pride, and fling them at the feet of God in tempestuous humility. It would be the free school for Catholic boys that Mother Seton would applaud. Hadn't she made him a priest? Hadn't she taught him to reconcile the discordant elements within himself, in all humanity, with the ineffable sweet harmony of the Godhead? Those who knew Father Hughes, later to be made first Archbishop of New York, never could be sure how well he knew the lesson, or just when he would forget.

That is how my paternal great-grandfather Richard McCunney came to America with his little portable desk, ready and willing to be a schoolmaster in Philadelphia. The trustees warred, Father Hughes stormed, and Bishop Kenrick found the young Irish scholar temporary employment as a bookkeeper. In some way he met Bridget Kearny who knew her worth, and Richard made himself worthy. It was as a rising young capitalist that he married the daughter of Francis Kearny, the engraver, in the Cathedral of St. John the Evangelist, with Bishop Hughes officiating.

Here he was, a schoolmaster lately out of Dublin, now a real estate broker, marrying into the famous Tory family, the Kearnys of Perth Amboy, New Jersey. In all the sagas of Ireland there is not the name of a commoner mentioned, so this son of Donegal shared his wife's pride of family. Jane Gale, her widowed mother, remembered the aged General Washington. Then there was her uncle, Anthony Gale, one time professor of romance languages at the University of Pennsylvania, friend of Benjamin Franklin, and later the first colonel of the newly organized Marine Corps. Richard often heard them speak of Cousin Sharpe Delaney, first collector of the port of Philadelphia, and his wife Hannah Baldwin, sister-in-law of Mad Anthony Wayne; and of General Stephen Kearny, a hero of the war of 1812.

Bridget Kearny was very beautiful, and she presided graciously over the houses Richard bought her, and bore her many children without undue effort. She was a generous wife to a generous husband. He left her a rich widow with all the hierarchy in America to send her messages of condolence—the young Cardinal Gibbons, Cardinal McCloskey, and her close friend Archbishop Wood. All was well till one of her wild sons in a frenzy of speculation sold his equities, forcing her to sacrifice her home at the corner of Nineteenth and Sansom Streets, as well as property at Eighth and Market. And then he married, in her words, "beneath him," a girl from "out Schuylkill."

They tell of her that when she lay dying this son came to her bedside and said, "Mother, forgive me." She had raised his motherless children tenderly—in what for her was poverty, though to many of her descendants it might seem affluence—but she had never seen him again. They tell of her that she kept her eyes sternly on the black iron crucifix standing on a table at the foot of her bed. The son knelt beside her, weeping. "Forgive me, forgive me." There was a horrified gasp from those around her bedside as she turned her face away from him and died.

There is some strange element in the Irish soul that makes us horrified at the crawling seeker after sanctuary and forgiveness. We could be proud of the son if, head high, he had said, "I am not sorry, Mother, but I love you."

And so my great-grandmother, who, in a moment of dying, negated the Christian values of a lifetime, stirs up something very deep in me, something wrong and evil that has crisscrossed my life with savagery. My great-grandmother who had to face her God and ask forgiveness and could not forgive her own son. I think I know that everything in her was straining toward that man's hand. I think I feel the fierce pride that would not let her yield. I have often looked at that black iron crucifix, which still stands at a family deathbed, and felt the cold fingers of fear grip me.

Back at my christening supper, Archbishop Ryan has uttered one of those inimitable jests for which he was famous, but no one now remembers the jewel of wit from my baptism. My father, the young Dr. O'Hara, is a handsome man, but there is some strange melancholy undertone the Archbishop cannot understand. He does not have his father's fire, or simplicity.

A baby's fierce cry penetrates the dining room of the Twentieth Street house. I am a Christian child now, and my ancestors have led me to this warm cradle and wrapped me around with a scarf of enchantment—the Celtic imagination—by which one forgets time and what is to be done with a life. They had done well, these simple, hardy men and women. They had given me the right to be as happy as a king's daughter, and many gifts. And I cried out in the night, as if I guessed the cruel century in which I had been born.

Archbishop Ryan (just the year before, he had said in Baltimore with that uncanny prescience of Catholic clergymen, "*What we have to fear is divorce and Communism*") now makes a great sign of the cross in blessing as all the guests kneel, "In Nomine Patris, et Filii, et Spiritus Sancti. Amen." Thus he commenced the biography of a soul that for a few years was to live in absolute grace.

And the Archbishop rode away from my christening supper with the twin lamps on his carriage shining, like jeweled eyes, on the blue shadows of an April night in Philadelphia, when the century was young.

# 3

The first home I remember was a narrow house on the south side of Pine Street, near Twentieth, all red brick and white marble trim. In Pine Street the colored maids came out early every morning with their buckets and scrub brushes, and sand-soaped the three white steps; then with a bit of chamois rag polished the doctor's sign on the window of nearly every house. On winter mornings they worked swiftly, sullenly, their black fingers turning blue, but when spring caused the trees to bud they sang as they worked and their laughter rang out on the quiet street. The housemen on the north side of Pine, where the houses had four stories and the people were more prosperous, called out to the girls and they screamed insults at each other. Often Mrs. Windsor's butler would open the front door to stare with icy indignation at the spring and the singing colored people; or Mrs. Biddle's bedroom window would lower suddenly, and the cacophonous medley would stop on the instant and explode in whispering and giggling.

That's the way it was on a good morning on Pine Street. We'd go into the dark dining room with its two windows opening on a narrow side yard. The Welsbach burner would be lit in the ornate gas chandelier, and we'd have breakfast. My father, freshly shaved and handsome, ready to perform his neat operation with his egg—a gentle knock at the top, an exquisite finesse with the pepper and salt, then his spoon would go into the shell and sometimes a drop adhered to his mustache. That always made me feel a little ill, but he'd dab the damask napkin just so, and I'd continue trying to find lumps in my Cream of Wheat so I could stop eating it. My grandmother, Mary Gartland Horan, with her boned net guimpe as immaculate as her white pompadour, kept one eye on the *Morning Ledger* at my father's plate.

"Would you care to see the paper, Mrs. Horan?" he asked with stately courtesy, but the twinkle would appear deep in his eyes as she replied:

"No thank you, Doc. I wouldn't dream of taking it from you." Her long, blue-veined hand twitched yearningly toward the paper.

My father always rose and handed it to her at this point. Nana gave what can only be described as a little pounce, but not for worlds would she concede a favor. "Well, as long as you're finished."

Nannie Johnson brought in my mother's breakfast tray, an effete habit that drove Nana mad, but she never expressed her opinion to her son-in-law, though my mother and she frequently had acrimonious words on the subject. My father passed the early morning patients in the office, bearing his wife's breakfast tray, as Nana settled down to the paper.

In 1911-1912 the world was rapidly heading for dissolution. My grandmother in spite of a long line of Irish forebears felt the Queen's death had caused it all. Even I knew she meant Queen Victoria. Nana worried about Victoria's grandson the Kaiser. The Edwardian age filled her with dismay. And as for the United States of America, the domestic news appalled her; occasionally as she read of strikes her gray eyes behind her bifocals became dark with tragedy. The news could only mean that her properties would fall idle. That struck terror in my infant breast. Nothing could be as dreadful as idle properties. Sometimes the news in the papers was so dire she'd throw it from her in an abandonment of shock and, drumming her fingers on the table would utter a fearsome indictment:

"Democrats and corner-loungers!"

In the morning everyone was busy and no one could read me a story. My mother would have a creation freshly cut from a *Delineator* pattern, and the sewing machine on the third floor would whir and whir: in the afternoon her sister Caroline would come to visit and they'd sit in the second-story front bedroom, and debate whether to add a piece of passementerie. Uncle

Frank, Caroline's husband, was a banker with the Quakers and Aunt Caroline had her clothes made by Madam Josephine. She had sables and diamond rings and a crescent bar pin, and traveled to such places as California.

I'd look out the window as Mrs. Windsor's landau drove up; her butler opened the door and led her to the carriage, a little old lady in a bonnet with strings. She'd speak to the coachman with suitable graciousness and away they'd go for a round of calls. Sometimes Mrs. Biddle, with a scarf over her head, leaned out the window and took great gulps of air. Mrs. Biddle was different; she did what she pleased.

It was more interesting in the back of the house. There were rows of box-houses divided from our yard by a high fence. There the colored people lived, you could see right in their tiny houses. In the spring and fall they lived in their backyards, some of them even planted flowers which sprouted timidly in the midst of the steaming wash boilers and the clothes always hanging on lines, for the women on Waverly Street took in washing for the white folks. In winter they all moved into the kitchens, and the smoke rose thick from the wood stoves. They were poor, but there was no despair on Waverly Street, only a curious deep fatalistic melancholy that made something stick in my throat when Bill Schenk's accordion would sound and little colored children danced.

There was other music on Pine Street. Dr. Leopold Stokowski and Madame Olga Samaroff lived one door away. Hour after hour she'd practise scales in her studio. The monotony of it was maddening, till the swelling strength of her fingers penetrated your deadened senses, and she commenced to strike chord after chord. Then it was like the measured tread of glory.

My father resting between calls would play the gramophone. A nasal voice sang:

"Come, Josephine, in my flying machine.
Going up . . . Going up. . . ."

It was not because of its gayness that it embedded itself in my memory, but because it fixed a tone, a mood of change and rootlessness that haunted me. It was dissolution, forces hammering at the walls of snug little houses on Pine Street, forces that were evil and frightening. My father seeing my distressed baby face put on a Red Seal record, perhaps Madame Schumann-Heink singing Schubert's "Ave Maria." Nana came over from the front room and sat there quietly with her arm around me, as if we could hold off the surge and thunder of the modern world in the ancient "Hail Mary."

Nannie Johnson and I walked to the Square on nice afternoons. Rittenhouse Square was pleasant in those days, bordered with stately houses. The children would roll their hoops around the circle while the nursemaids sat on the benches and gossiped. A few French governesses kept to themselves, excluding the lone Fräulein. The Irish maids constituted the real autocracy of the Square, keeping the colored girls firmly in their place. The Irish nursemaids were fearful snobs—a Celtic characteristic—and their aristocratic young charges, who were often horrid little brats, were bragged about shamelessly to the other maids, as well as the heathen doings of their parents.

Mostly I played with other doctors' children, on the safe theory that the diseases our fathers brought home might as well be spread among ourselves; but one afternoon I approached a group of little girls.

"May I play with you?" I asked.

They backed away from me, and one small girl whispered. I looked at my hoop. It was just like theirs. We all had on white stockings and shoes and broadcloth coats with wide Irish lace collars. No one had ever rejected me before. I stood there with the loneliness and the shame consuming me. One of the children came back to me.

"It's not your fault. But we can't play with you, you're a Catholic."

The strangeness of it stunned me. What else was there to be? Catholic? That meant St. Patrick's Church, and Monsignor Kieran stopping to speak to me. It meant the Convent of Notre Dame de Namur on the west side of the Square, where I would go to school one day. Catholic? That meant the pictures in

Nana's room, the sad wonderful picture of Our Lord crowned with thorns, and the other picture of His Mother holding Him in her arms when He was a baby. Her eyes always seemed to be looking at the one where He wore thorns. Catholic? That was going to the Cathedral of SS. Peter and Paul with my father and mother, with all the flowers on the altar and the choir singing. It was my night prayers, and the little blue crucifix over my bed which had been brought to me from Rome by Mrs. La Farge. And now I had been told that it was a bad thing to be. I felt my lip trembling.

An Irish nursemaid stood beside me, and she was firmly smacking one of the children.

"Do you know who herself is?" she asked, and whacked mightily. "That's own grandniece to the sainted Bishop O'Hara, and her grandfather had his hands blessed in Rome by the Holy Father himself. And you'll not play with an O'Hara? Shure and you will not, for she'll have nothin' to do with *such* Protestant trash." The faith had won, and an illustrious Episcopalian bottom was stinging.

She led her frightened charge away, saying to me these ominous words: "Poor little thing. It's a quality child y'are. You're too good for your own, and called not good enough for such as these. You with the blood of the kings and queens of Ireland in your veins—and wisha child, *here* you're neither fish, fowl, nor good red herring."

It puzzled me for a long time, and I never asked another strange child if I might join their play. Even my own best friends were not Catholics. Maybe Freddy and Gurney Williams didn't know what I was; that besides being a girl—an overwhelming handicap—I was also a Catholic. Gurney Williams became an editor and a celebrated humorist, but he had no lightness of touch to console me that day. He stood before me, a seven-year-old Solomon in a Buster Brown collar, studying the problem with heavy seriousness.

"You tell the Park guard on those little snots," he said. "He won't let them hurt your feelings."

"Why won't he?" I asked.

"He's a Catholic, that's why." Gurney was away on his roller skates, with his little brother Freddy astride his velocipede pedaling after him.

They had enlightened me. The Park guard was a Catholic; the red-faced Irish nursemaids were Catholics; so were the poor people from "out Schuylkill." The children in Rittenhouse Square were not Catholic. It was clear I did not belong, that I was, in fact, an outcast. It was a very big problem. Servants were Catholics. (I did not know that the Popes assigned to themselves the title of the Servant of the Servants of God.) I felt sorry for poor people, but not friendly toward them. The first active alienation of my spirit from the Church took place in Rittenhouse Square. My security was lost. I became what all insecure people are: a snob. The world drifted its first mists over my eyes. I could not realize then that possessors of the faith must be like swords, and that it is the edge and temper of the blade that makes a good sword, not the richness of the scabbard.

I loved the early spring nights in Philadelphia when I was a child. The dusk came with a soft blue alleviation as if not to blot out the beautiful day in darkness. There were still a few gas lamps on Pine Street, and the lamplighter would come along with his ladder and torch, and the lamps would sizzle and sputter for a while and then come on brightly. The lamps in the long salon parlors across the street would be lit. Mrs. Windsor had wax candles in the candelabra on the mantel and each candle gleamed with a little flame. The butler locked and bolted the shutters against an intrusive world and the little girl across the street who was fascinated by all this stateliness.

When it grew quite dark by the window I'd go upstairs to Nana's rooms on the third floor. My little grandmother was an extraordinary woman. It is marvelous how a child's mind can encompass the past, so that things told become real. I almost felt I had been there when they carried her dying husband back to a twenty-four-year-old wife with three children. I knew how Hubert Horan, my grandfather, felt when his horse bolted in the Park, and he held on to the reins as tight as he could, till the carriage tipped over on that huge boulder and blotted out everything forever.

I knew all about her son Simon, who had been an infant when his father was killed. I knew how the Irish nurse dropped him from her arms, frightened at the heavy tread of men's feet carrying an unconscious man upstairs. I knew how the baby looked when Nana took him with the two little girls, home to her mother, his head all swollen, and heard his weak cries of pain.

I understood all about the three long years in which he never learned to walk or talk, and the trips to Dr. S. Weir Mitchell and the best doctors in town. I could fill in the story when Nana's little sister Josie, who went to Notre Dame Convent, asked the Sisters for prayers, and they started a novena to Our Lady of Lourdes. That was her statue on Nana's bureau, the same statue they had bought during the novena prayers. Here was the little medicine bottle that held the Lourdes water they put on the baby's head. I knew this part by heart, and shivers ran up and down my spine when the Angelus bell commenced to ring at St. John's Church and the family rose to say the prayer. It was the ninth day of the novena. I could see them standing in the front room of the Thirteenth Street house. There would be Cad. I knew my great-aunt Cad. And Lily. I knew my great-aunt Lily well. Then there would be Jane; that was Great-aunt Jen. My mother and her sister Caroline, little girls answering the responses in piping voices, with the helpless child lying in a carriage with his withered legs in braces, and his head too heavy to hold up.

My great-grandmother had sat down in the rosewood armchair, the very one I had often seen at Great-aunt Jen's, and said quietly:

"Come here to me, Simie."

And the little boy got up from his carriage and walked across the long room. I could see them holding their breath as those faltering footsteps came on and on.

Nana would take off her bifocals and clean them vigorously as she told the story.

"Your grandfather old Doctor O'Hara and Doctor Atlee said it was a miracle. Doctor S. Weir Mitchell said the same. A miracle—"

The picture on Nana's wall of the boy in the dress suit and the amused eyes was Uncle Si. He had never had a sick day again till he died at twenty-seven of pneumonia. I used to love to listen to Nana's account of how on horseback he led the Second City Troop down Twentieth Street, past the boy's department of the Convent of Notre Dame, so that Sister Vincent, his old teacher, could see him in his splendid blue dress uniform, laced with scarlet and gold, with the cockade of feathers on his high beaver hat, and the gleaming sword at his waist.

I seemed to know all the friends he brought home from Georgetown Prep—Jim Cook, and Malin Craig who was to become Chief of Staff of the United States Army, and those homesick Mexican boys the Peraltas, who stayed and stayed.

There was the picture of Nana's uncle, Bishop Gartland, who had baptized her in St. John's with water from the river Jordan. My burgeoning sense of drama insisted on being fed the accounts of his death in Savannah, Georgia. The dreaded yellow fever broke out, and Bishop Gartland and his assistant, Bishop Barron, worked night and day. The illness fell heaviest on the colored slaves and Uncle Francis had a tent city built, and nursed them himself. But there was more to come. A hurricane struck the stricken city, and the Bishop opened the Cathedral of St. John to the care of the ill, both Negro and white. A brave thing for Georgia in 1854.

She remembered the Civil War, and the draft riots, and the panic when Mr. Lincoln was shot. Nana would say, "But he should not have gone to the theatre on Good Friday." Her father had had the Thirteenth Street house draped in mourning and so was St. John's next door. She often told me of walking from the Convent of the Holy Child to see the dead President Lincoln lying in state at Independence Hall.

There were other wonderful stories told me up in that little sitting room crowded with all the things Nana loved—her oil paintings, and the marble clock with musical chimes. Nana was reassured when she was in the midst of time. She was always sending for the clock man, for the slightest slowing or hastening of time was unbearable. There were gentle ticks in that room, and noisy ticks. There were clocks that chimed sweetly and clocks that rang solidly and firmly with a resonant boom. There was the tiny beat of the gold watch she wore on her breast; snuggled against her you could hear it.

Time passed and passed. It did strange things. It swept people away.

I knew all about that, for sometimes Nana and I went by street car to Marble Park. This was a different sort of park from Rittenhouse Square. It was quiet and there were no trees, just marble shafts rising into the sky, and little fences around patches of green grass. Some of the patches were lovely and well tended. We had a white iron bench on our lawn and urns with flowers growing. But there were parts where the grass was wild and weeds grew and the shafts tilted forward at crazy angles. Nana explained, "There is no one left of the family." That made me immensely lonely, for I knew that Marble Park was where people went when they were dead. Nana would read on our monument: "Sacred to the Memory of Simon and Caroline Gartland." These were her parents. And then she'd read, "Josephine Gartland, aged sixteen years." That was her little sister. It made me feel sad, as if I shouldn't play with my ball. Nana sat on the bench looking at the place where Uncle Si was sleeping. Instead of bringing flowers, we stopped at St. John's Orphanage and Nana handed some money to the sister at the door saying, "Pray for my son."

I knew as I walked up and down the paths that Nana had in her hand the rosary that her godmother, Mrs. Reynolds, had bought for her husband who died on their wedding trip. And now Nana had it and was praying for all the people who were asleep under the warm ground.

Marble Park had names for the paths that crisscrossed each other. On St. John's Avenue were Grandfather and Grandmother O'Hara, and across from them were the graves of the Sisters of the Good Shepherd who gave me beautiful dolls and white dresses. Just at the corner was an imposing shaft of granite with the names "Richard McCunney–Bridget Kearny–his wife." There were no living children in Marble Park, and occasionally there would be a great raw wound in the earth with the clay piled and flowers wilting.

One day when I was sitting quietly beside Nana, filled with a gentle melancholy as the breeze lifted and turned the leaves on the bushes with a faint swishing sound, a tall woman came along the path, swathed in mourning, a crepe veil to her waist.

My grandmother and she embraced and the woman lifted me in her arms. I sat on her lap. She had great dark eyes and a skin that was like a moss rose. I liked her very much. In no time at all I knew she was my father's Aunt Maggie. She showered me with compliments. My eyes were beautiful, and my hands. It seemed that Aunt Maggie was sensitive to hands, and mine were perfect. She kissed every finger. My grandmother pursed her lips. She didn't believe in indiscriminate flattery.

In a moment Great-aunt Maggie was weeping on my grandmother's shoulder. "Mary Gartland, what's to become of me, now that I've buried two husbands?"

It wasn't at all sad, for she wept beautifully and was thoroughly enjoying herself.

"Two husbands, Mary. I had an eye for your Hubert, then I met Tom Dooner. You know what he said?–'I like a big horse and a big woman.' That was Tom for you."

I slid down from her lap and watched her in fascination. It was plain Nana did not approve of the conversation.

"And now Joseph Gassline's over there. Poor Joseph! I don't mind telling you I set my cap for him. Mary, wasn't he the image of Lord Byron? I was always the great one for poetry. Childe Harold led me to Gassline. It wasn't all poetry. But just the same I'll miss my poor Joseph."

In no time at all, with the tears still twinkling like diamonds on her face, Aunt Maggie was reminiscing. Her laugh rang out like silver bells, and my grave little grandmother was smiling too. Aunt Maggie gestured as she talked, and leaned back against the bench when she laughed. The stillness of Marble Park was broken in her great gusts of drama. I was fearful the dead people would not like it.

"And you, Mary Gartland," Aunt Maggie's gestures were sweeping, "why did you not marry again after Hubert? A beautiful little thing like you, and your mother's money coming to you and all. For a while there I was sure you'd marry—"

"Maggie, be still." My grandmother's face was a fiery crimson.

"He still wants you, Mary." Aunt Maggie, the perpetual romantic, collapsed with laughter. "Look at Nana now, Constance, blushing she is."

"Maggie McCunney," my grandmother's thin lips were determined, "I swear you're nothing but a butterfly."

And Aunt Maggie commenced to sing a rollicking tune that I've never forgotten:

"There's nothing to marry but men. Nowhere to go but bed."

I swayed to the music, but stopped, frightened at Nana's face. She'd called this fascinating Aunt Maggie "a butterfly," and, since the tall woman with the capacious bosom didn't resemble a butterfly, I thought it was a pet name and that Nana liked her as much as I did. Now Nana was in a tantrum.

"Aunt Maggie," I explained carefully, not wanting to lose a minute of this entrancing creature's society, "nobody sings in Marble Park. Everybody's dead."

"Marble Park?" Aunt Maggie's arms were around me. "Mary Gartland, what nonsense! This is Old Cathedral Cemetery, child. There's not a soul here, darling baby girl, but the workmen and us. The people under the ground have all gone to Heaven."

The sadness left me. The sky was bright with sunshine. The soul was victorious over all the evil which life could send it. The birds wheeled in freedom, upheld by a loving hand. I felt exalted and filled with love for Aunt Maggie who wept and laughed and sang naughty songs.

"Maggie!" My grandmother was jealous of this sober child, now all smiles and giggles, so prodigal with affection to the stranger. "How do you know everyone here is in Heaven? Did they come back to tell you so?"

"Dot the i's and cross the t's, Mary Gartland," said Aunt Maggie, now leading me by the hand. "Everyone we know is in Heaven or *nearly* so." Purgatory was taken care of by an undertone. "After all, there's not a soul in Old Cathedral who left the Church. Every grave here is blessed. If people just don't leave the Church, it's my belief they've every chance to be all right."

Aunt Maggie tossed my ball to me, and I tossed it back; her widow's bonnet with the white pleated facing came a bit awry, and her crepe veil streamed in the wind. Finally she bounced the ball against the granite monument of the McCunneys'. Nana was horrified.

But Aunt Maggie only said: "My poor sister Nan paid five thousand dollars for that silly nonsense, but then she was an old maid, and nothing to do with her money but waste it on the dead."

We parted at the corner, Aunt Maggie again kissing my hands and exclaiming over their beauty.

"She's frivolous," my grandmother said, gently rapping at my knuckles as I admired my hands. "Maggie's very frivolous."

The day in Marble Park that was not a park—Nana just called it that to make me think I was having a treat—was still fresh in my mind as I leaned against my grandmother begging for a story. She got one of the books from the bookcase and put me on her lap in the old rocker and read. Often it was *Child's Stories from Dickens*, and I lived in that enchanted world of Dombey and Son, the Marchioness, Pip, David Copperfield, and that lugubrious child Little Nell. The dinner bell sounded mutely. Nannie only rang it once on account of the patients.

We went down the stairs past the office, not looking in. The patients sat there in the light of the green glass globe on the center table and read the magazines, or looked at the pictures of Dr. John Deaver, Sir William Osler, and the engraving of John Martin's fearsome "Joshua Commanding the Sun to Stand Still"; or they just sat, looking worried and miserable.

Mother sat at the foot of the dining room table with her red-gold hair shining in the candlelight. Sometimes, if she had been to a five hundred party, she would look very stylish in an afternoon dress; often, hopefully, she was in full dress. She always knew she was going to be late for her engagement. Dinner was eaten quietly with the dining room door closed. We'd hear the front door open and shut as the patients came and went. Sometimes when my mother had a particular engagement, she'd say with angry resignation:

"Did you count the priests in there tonight?"

My father came in for dinner between patients. He always cut it to one course. His face was dead white, and he was exhausted. He would look hopefully at the beefsteak to see if it was rare; life offered him no such boons, but he never gave in to a sense of defeat. Some night the beef would be rare. He ate hastily, giving snatches of his day.

"Was that Father Turner I saw in the office?" Mother asked.

He nodded. "About a boy in the Seminary. Wants me to see the Archbishop."

"Why doesn't he go himself?" Mother inquired acidly.

"Father Turner always relied on Papa for things." My father shrugged wearily as he rose from his half-eaten dinner. "Get Nannie to save my dessert."

"Doc," my mother called at the half-open door, "unless it's Father John [Father John Crowley was his cousin], don't send any priests upstairs."

Nana frowned. "Don't say such things. She's old enough to get ideas."

Sometimes Mother exploded. "Every priest in the diocese taking advantage of him!"

"They'll bring a blessing," Nana assured her gravely.

"If they don't put us in the poorhouse first," my mother observed tartly.

Most nights it was like that. We went up to the sitting room with the painting of St. Cecelia over the mantel and the upright piano in the corner. My father came upstairs, usually with a priest, and sat in the Morris chair, with his face ashen, rolling a cigarette. The talk droned on about Archbishop Prendergast and his fear of Rome. Someone named Cardinal Gibbons was old. That was too bad. There was no one to replace him. It was worried talk. We needed new hospitals, new schools.

My mother took me to bed. I remember my little mahogany bed with the panels and the carved urns for posts. Over the bed was the picture I loved—"The Child Jesus Teaching in the Temple." My crucifix hung under it and beside the bed was a holy water font. My guardian angel was presenting it to me, all in blue, with great white wings flecked in gold.

At this hour I longed for my lovely mother to throw her arms around me, and she longed for me to stretch out mine. Neither of us, so craving each other's love, could express it, so we were cold and businesslike with each other. She'd wanted me to be a boy, I knew, and once she said teasingly, but meaning it for I felt the truth coming through: "I didn't want you at all. We were married five years when you came."

She loved me better than anyone on earth, and that is the way I loved my mother, and she hadn't wanted me. My mother didn't want me. There was nothing we could do to break down the barriers between us. She'd kiss me good night after I'd said my prayers and my cold little mouth was rigid, but my heart beat fast. Maybe just once she'd hold out her arms, and laugh, and pretend I was a baby again.

My father came in tiredly before the light went out, and sometimes with him the visiting priest to pull my rag hair-curlers. My father was never demonstrative with me. He had some sensitive awareness that I did not want it. But I could be capricious and shower him with affection and teasing. We understood each other. The priest would bless me, and I liked the feel of those firm hands on my head. Come to think of it, I liked priests, even if they were sending us to the poorhouse.

I'd lie awake for a long time. The moon tilted toward my side window, and I'd stare at the little pool of pale light on the floor. The colored people on Waverly Street sometimes sang or fought, or their rich voices called from house to house. The Pine Street cats howled on the fences. A train whistle sounded a long way off—a lonely sound that made me feel restless. A tug on the river gave deep mournful hoots. I'd drift off to sleep.

At night I'd often be wakened by the ringing of the doorbell. My father called out the second-story front window. I'd hear him say, "Some poor soul out Schuylkill."

"Oh, Doc," my mother protested, "you're not going? It's dangerous."

"No one ever hurts a doctor," he'd reply.

The gas went on with a sputter. I could hear his tired sighs as he dressed. Mother continued protesting, mentioning all the other doctors who wouldn't go. But my father went down the stairs, stopping in his office for the black bag he carried. Sometimes I'd rush to the window and see a poor ragged man waiting under the trees for the doctor who never refused night calls "out Schuylkill."

I was afraid there in the darkness, with my father out of the house. I never got used to it, though night calls were no rarity. The old house would creak and rustle. The noises outside weren't friendly. It was all sound and echo. The old sinful city of Philadelphia slept, but out in the darkness was my father. Someone needed him who was ill and poor. My father hated "money grubbers." I'd often heard him say so, and I was glad he did. I was proud of my father going those long blocks "out Schuylkill," where everyone was poor and wretched.

"God is everywhere," I'd whisper. He was "out Schuylkill." He was in the colored people's houses. He was in my room. He was in St. Patrick's Church in the sanctuary with the little red lamp burning through the lonely night. He was . . . The problem wearied St. Thomas Aquinas and it was too much for one little girl.

It was the deep of the night on Pine Street. My mother slept. I heard my father's key in the door and then slow weary footsteps coming upstairs. I called gently, "Daddy." He was in my room. He lit the night light, and sat on the side of my bed. His eyes were shadowed by what he had seen. He'd say odd things.

"Baby, the world needs some new saints who will do something about conditions."

"Are conditions bad, Daddy?" I savored the word.

"Conditions couldn't be worse. And people get rich on them. Now Daddy's girl must go to sleep." His mustache tickled pleasantly as he kissed me.

Conditions? Didn't God care about "out Schuylkill?" Daddy's remark stirred up a deep uneasiness. Mrs. Windsor was rich, but surely if she knew how bad things were she'd be worried. Nana said she was just like the Queen. It was very fine to be rich. Everyone said so. Aunt Caroline and Uncle Frank were going to be rich. But you couldn't enjoy fine houses if that caused "conditions." Come to think of it, my little bed was very comfortable. I had seen the cold hungry children from "out Schuylkill" on their way to St. Patrick's school. Something had to be done. Maybe I was the one to do it. Sleep whirled around me. I was in Mrs. Windsor's carriage and she was listening to me politely as I explained "conditions." The darkness blanketed me. I slept—a secure, well-fed, middle-class child in a starched cambric nightgown.

## 4

THE SINKING OF THE *Titanic* in 1912 came like a thunderclap of doom to the bourgeois world. It was the dramatic disaster that fixed our mind on the fact of death.

The *Titanic* on its maiden voyage, sliding down into the inscrutable sea, was to remain a haunting ghost. Men were shattered out of their mood of rationalism. This was tragedy and death. The *Titanic* was a warning and a portent.

The newsboys called out extras all day long and far into the night. Adult conversation buzzed like the sound of wasps. The papers passed from hand to hand. All social distinctions were at an end on Pine Street. When the boys called: "*EXTRA! EX-*

*TRA! READ ALL ABOUT IT—*" doors opened up and down the street to disclose Mrs. LeLand and Mrs. Biddle frantically shouting, "*Boy! Boy! Here!*"

Nannie Johnson was by far the best runner. Gurney Williams and the James boys, followed by the Wirgmans' Irish terrier, did a thriving trade getting papers from the boys all day. The colored people ran around from Waverly Street holding their pennies. Papers were even being sold "out Schuylkill," for in the business of dying things were evened up. Millionaires had gone down to anonymous graves in the dreadful sea, and poor women with shawls on their heads could read of this and pity.

Aunt Caroline said, "A fortune in jewels went down with the ship."

Over and over I heard the name, John Jacob Astor. He had given up his own life-preserver—an Astor who was worth millions—and stood at the rail watching his young wife in the lifeboat far below. He was lost, and countless other brave men, who had everything to live for, for they had money, houses on a place called Fifth Avenue in New York, houses in Newport. There wasn't a thing in the world they didn't have—and now they were dead.

Uncle Frank told Aunt Caroline by telephone from the Provident Trust Company, "It could cause a panic in the street."

I rushed to the window, but only a yellow trolley rumbled past. They were saying things I couldn't understand.

"I wonder how Ava Willing feels?" My mother wanted to know.

This caused much dramatic conjecture, with my grandmother firmly against the possibility that Ava Willing had any tender feelings toward her divorced husband, Mr. Astor.

Nana was being old-fashioned and her daughters were irritated. More interesting information was forthcoming: the brave Mr. Astor was on his honeymoon with someone called Madeleine Force, who was only a child. A child? It became more confusing by the moment.

The house was rocked by a new rumor that Nannie Johnson brought by the servants' grapevine. The desperate seamen had clawed and fought their way to the lifeboats, pushing women and children aside. These seamen from Scottish and Irish and English slums who hadn't a single good reason to cling to life, had behaved like cowards. The ship's officers had had to stand by the railings with drawn revolvers as the boats were made ready for launching. One of the sailors had even beaten off a man with an oar, and smashed at his hands clinging to the lifeboat.

"*That* class of people," Nana said, tapping her foot.

My father, returning for his evening office hour, brought sanity into the whole business. Some of the millionaires had behaved very badly indeed, screaming and crying like hysterical girls as they pushed their way into the lifeboats. And some of the seamen had been real heroes. Human nature evened things up. Some of the rich and some of the poor had magnificent reserves of courage and had died like brave men; others, both rich and poor, had survived by infamy. But the quality my father brought from that night in mid-Atlantic was that certain men remembered they were brothers, and American millionaires and men from the Clyde and the docks of Liverpool died happier because of it.

Monsignor Kieran, who had an Irishman's sense of drama, sat in the rectory of St. Patrick's preparing a sermon on the will of God. In the lamplight his profile looked more than ever as if it had been cast on a Roman coin. He paused often as he filled the pages of foolscap, for he was a good priest and reflected on this awe-inspiring creation, man, his presence on the earth, and the infinite possibilities of his destiny. He was a holy man and he thought perhaps the *Titanic* would call men back from their mad rush toward materialism.

"What does it profit a man . . . ?"

Monsignor William Kieran was intensely human, and he read the names of the lost again. We needed to get people like this in the Church. Important people. Monsignor Kieran yearned for such an apostolate so he prayed for their souls and preached a fine sermon the next Sunday, rich with classical allusions and splendid imagery that got off the subject only once or twice when he thundered at the French for their anti-clericalism. He always got that in—despite Agnes Repplier, the bluestocking, looking at him coldly from her pew, and thinking no doubt scornful thoughts about Irish Catholics.

"What does it profit a man . . . ?"

Not all the later diabolic inventions of men, the atoms they split, the bombs they rained from the sky—stirred up more deep uneasiness than a shipwreck in 1912. It set the tone of our dissolution.

## 5

MY FATHER WAS DOCTOR of the Seminary. Tuesday and Friday were his visiting days. I was about five years old when I first went with him, riding the steam-cars to Overbrook Station. Patrick Conway, the gatekeeper, gardener, coachman and general factotum of the Seminary, was waiting for us in the shabby buggy drawn by the old gray horse that plodded docilely along the road bordered with enormous pine trees. Every bit of this land belonged to the diocese.

Patrick's conversation differed in content, but never quantity:

"Many's the time I brought your father, the Old Doctor, along this very road. May God have mercy on his soul! He was always in a hurry, your father. Well, now there's another O'Hara at the Seminary, and that's the way it should be. Too many changes in this world—too many entirely. Bishop McCort drove up the road in one of thim motor-cars, stinkin' up the place it was. It's all right for Main Line swells, but a bishop should think twice afore he gets in one of thim things. I'd like to see McCort if it broke down and someone took the news to the old one at the Cathedral. Archbishop Prendygast is a kind man, he is that, but they've all got it in for him he ain't Ryan." Patrick chuckled. "Prendygast 'ull niver put the fear of God in thim. There's many a priest needs a tight hand on the reins, as well you know. My name isn't Patrick Conway if there's not big doin's plotted at the Seminary. Stand up for yourself, Doctor Michael—don't let thim put it upon yez."

The horse turned in the big double iron gates and the wide lawns stretched as far as the eye could see. Priests and seminarians in their black gowns walked to and fro. The statue of St. Charles Borromeo towered over everything. The students smiled at me and priests looked up from their breviaries and waved. There was some tremendous strength that seemed to flow in this place as if the prayer before Office were heard: "Open, O Lord, my mouth that I may praise Thy Holy Name."

"Shall I drive herself around to the convent now?" Patrick asked.

I held tight to my father's hand. I had no intention of going to any convent. I liked masculine society.

"No, she's going to assist me." My father smiled.

Patrick helped me down. "Takin' her to the Rector? All dressed up, ain't she?"

I was quite indignant and wanted to assure this man I had on my usual clothes, though I knew perfectly well that fresh blue satin ribbon had been threaded in my panties and I had on my very best white dress, not to mention my pale blue broadcloth coat and white beaver hat. I even had my little white kid gloves with the pearl buttons. Still, this Patrick had no right to comment that I was dressed up. He was being rude.

He was grinning broadly. "The Rector will know she's his sort of Catholic. Glory be to God, Doctor, he's givin' the b'ys demerits for their table manners." He talked quickly back of his hand. "You ain't heard who's here? No, not McCort." Priests were approaching, Patrick's eyes rolled. "*Dougherty*. On his way to Rome. Under the same roof as *thim* two."

"Umph! Bishop Dougherty." My father was interested. I took his hand and tried to pull him away from this garrulous old man. Priests surrounded us, the wind flapping at their black gowns. I had been told to curtsy, but it seemed the wrong thing to do. I was a princess surveying my subjects, picking out my favorites.

Then my father took me to the Rector's study. It was very quiet, looking out on the terrace with the splendid lawns and the pine trees. There was no one in the room. The walls were filled with pictures, many of them familiar to me. There was Bishop Gartland who had been a professor at the Seminary, and an oil painting of Bishop O'Hara. My father read me the inscription: "*Rector of the Seminary of St. Charles Borromeo. 1853-1861.*" It had a splendid sound.

"The Rector's not here," my father said. "I'll take you to the convent. I have to see the students."

Someone entered the room with a light graceful step. His soutane glistened. His eyes were the bluest things I had ever seen, and they spoke a wonderful language with extraordinary gaps. I came to know that in those gaps lay the true character of the Reverend Doctor Henry T. Drumgoole. The eyes were amused and gently ironic, they were sad, they were compassionate—but the blue was always soft and when he was stern the twinkle was ready to break through. Even in the face of disaster and apparent defeat this man could not have the steel of cruelty in his eyes. His hands were beautiful and he used them without self-consciousness in a variety of graceful gestures. He was short and stocky, and his face was ruddy, more from fine vintage wines than fresh air, though he knew how to handle all God's good gifts. He had the most delightful giggle, rather like a high-spirited, boarding-school girl defying the Reverend Mother, but it was not at all incongruous. His hair on this long ago day had not yet become the beautiful silver-white we were all to know, though streaks of it had already appeared.

My father made the wrong remark. "Don't touch her, Father, she doesn't make friends quickly. Just let her sit there and I'll ask one of the nuns to take her to the convent."

Father Drumgoole understood my resentment perfectly. He even blushed for my father's lack of tact. That enchanting blush! I was coming across the room slowly, with my hand outstretched, and he was waiting for me. I was in love. I put my hand in his and it wasn't taut and muscular but soft and gentle. Why, we loved each other! One of my father's eyebrows cocked in the most provoking way.

"I will stay here, Daddy," I said precisely, "with Father Drumgoole."

There was a typewriter on the table, and before I knew it Father Drumgoole had made the chair high with three volumes of an encyclopedia, put a sheet of paper in the machine, and lifted me up before it.

"Now, Constance," he said, and his voice was like music, "you are a writer."

And so he condemned me to slavery and tyranny, at St. Charles Seminary. That is how Monsignor Drumgoole, part diplomat, part teacher, and all priest, entered my life.

I was to say to him when he was old and ill and worn, "Monsignor, you are my Catholic Church. When you go, there will be no other."

"Foolish child," and all gentleness came into that exquisite voice. "I—Cardinal Dougherty—specks in the dust of two thousand years. All that can matter for both of us is that our dust touched souls with the gold of the spirit. The spirit! Don't grieve for me—don't hate for me—look up at the Church Triumphant."

O my friend! how can I write of you?

And so this afternoon, my first at the Seminary, Father Drumgoole put my small hands on the keys.

I was a writer. I was happy.

Looking up at my amused father, he said, "You can go now, Michael. We're friends. Bosom friends!" He laughed as I struck a key, and added wryly, "By the way, Bishop Dougherty is in residence." His eyes were amused.

Father Drumgoole wasted no time in childish nonsense. He taught me to pick out letters that would make beautiful words. "Hail, Holy Queen, Mother of Mercy . . ." That is how I learned the "Salve Regina" when I was five at St. Charles Seminary, the prayer I never forgot.

When I grew tired of my high perch, I was lifted down, sat

on another chair and given a picture book of Rome. I could only hold the book by sticking my legs straight out in front of me.

"Here, Constance, are all our origins," said Father Drumgoole.

Origins! I liked that word. We looked at St. Peter's and the Vatican. We looked at the reigning Pope, Pius X, and Cardinal Merry del Val. We looked at the Sistine Chapel. God the Father on the ceiling was very angry, and Adam was very naked. Father Drumgoole used such names as Michelangelo. He said over and over, and it sounded like the long roll of drums. "*One. Holy. Catholic. Roman. Apostolic.*"

I ached all over from the heavy picture book, and my head was bursting from the knowledge that was going into it. Father Drumgoole put on my coat and told me to go walk on the terrace.

"I know you won't lean over the railings," he said, and airily returned to the typewriter.

I walked in the exact center of the porch. Close to the railings a priest sat. He wore a black hat pulled down on his head, and was wrapped in a plaid blanket. He was the homeliest man I had ever seen in my life, fat and squat, his face a sick yellow. He looked stern and then as I came nearer his face creased in smiles.

"Come here, Constance O'Hara," he said.

I drew near, amazed that he knew my name. He had magnificent eyes, startling in this homely face. They looked through things and people. These were the eyes of reason and truth, terrible eyes for a fool or a liar to face. In those days I could look in them unafraid.

"Why are you so yellow?" I asked impolitely.

He explained that he had got malaria in the Philippines. I saw with a child's uncanny perceptions that he didn't like being ugly, and I had hurt his feelings. I climbed on his lap without an invitation. He put his great arms around me and his whole body shook with laughter. I saw the ring on his stubby ugly hand.

"You're a bishop," I said.

"I'm Bishop Dougherty," he explained. "I knew Bishop O'Hara

and your grandfather and grandmother. I know and like all your family."

"Read me from your book," I ordered.

The most superb Latinist in the Church complied. The rich words flowed on. The holy Latin tongue was all around me.

"And now," he said, "I'll tell you a story."

It was a very sensible story, perfectly attuned to the understanding of a child. I did not have to reach or grasp at meanings. I was so interested I forgot everything else. He was talking to me in a child's own language, simple and profound. The little homilies did not bore me. I leaned against this man in utter contentment. His smile was innocent and gentle.

He was reaching the end of the story. I know that the climax did not startle my highly geared nervous system. It was just right, but I could not guess the ending and was intent on the tale. I felt his body stiffen, and he turned to stare, his underlip sticking out. Standing together on the porch were my father and Father Drumgoole with a third priest who wore, not a soutane, but trousers and a velvet smoking jacket. Now I could feel anger like a strong current coming from Bishop Dougherty. I did not like him, I was frightened.

Father Drumgoole had his head tossed back, and he looked amused. He held out his white well-tended hand. Bishop Dougherty took up the thread of his story, holding me tight as my father came toward us. I suddenly slid down from his lap and ran toward Father Drumgoole. I grasped his hand and he laughed, but there was no dislike in him, only a mocking triumph like one boy teasing another. The priest in the velvet smoking jacket took my other hand.

Just as we turned in the door, I got one hand free and waved at Bishop Dougherty. My father was talking to him, but those strange eyes were following me. I felt across the terrace his hurt that I hadn't waited for the end of the story.

Years later I stood on the street and watched him pass by in an open car wearing a wide red hat, a prince of the Church—His Eminence Denis, Cardinal Dougherty, Archbishop of Philadelphia. His thunderous edict had gone forth: "There shall be no caste in the fellowship of Catholics under the fatherhood of God." The Right Reverend Monsignor Henry T. Drumgoole and the aristocratic ideal were to go into eclipse, and the long martyrdom of my friend commenced. The great discipline of the Church and its acceptance by a beautiful and radiant soul is the true measure of its glory.

I never spoke to Denis, Cardinal Dougherty, again till I had come to middle age and he said, "Come here, Constance O'Hara." And I came, for he was a great man.

But when I was five I made my stand with Father Henry T. Drumgoole, and the delightful man in the velvet smoking jacket who was Dr. Hugh Henry, professor of music.

My father came into the room. "Bishop Dougherty is an extraordinary man."

There was a deep silence and Father Drumgoole unquestionably said, with that silvery giggle, "He saved the Philippine clergy from the concupiscence of the flesh." He loved to say that, in those days, he called himself "the Cardinal's gadfly."

At five I could not know that Bishop Dougherty had warred against seizure of church property by the Aglipayan schismatics in the diocese of Jaro in the Philippines, had taken the cases into the law courts of the United States, and affirmed the Catholic principle of legality in government, by which God's will works in the temporal affairs of men. He was called a dictator, but there was no more passionate exponent of American democracy. Some of the cases had gone to the United States Supreme Court, but both in Nueva Segovia and Jaro every piece of property had been returned by legal means to the Church.

There might have been a book that day in his pocket called *The Story of a Soul*, which the Reverend Mother of the Carmelite Convent in Philadelphia gave him that year—a book that was to send him to France, to the Carmel at Lisieux and then to Rome to champion the sanctity and to advance to sainthood the Little Flower—the saint of the atomic age. That strange man who never finished the story for a little girl at the Seminary, wrote finis to the story of the spiritual childhood of a Carmelite nun who died when she was twenty-four, afraid she had lost her faith.

They called him the Cardinal of the Little Flower, this man, into whose eyes only children could look in comfort.

I forgot all about Bishop Dougherty that afternoon because Father Drumgoole was doing the most extraordinary thing. It was a virtuoso performance. He had a little gold box in his hand and from the sleeve of his moiré soutane came a handkerchief that, as he shook its snowy linen folds, gave off a faint essence of lavender. In each nostril, so quickly that the eye could not follow it, went a pinch of snuff—his handkerchief caught the sneeze. He was proud of his sleight-of-hand. In a drawing room he could do it so swiftly no one noticed.

In 1915 Father Drumgoole became the Right Reverend Monsignor Henry T. Drumgoole. A red monsignor, and his sash was the most sumptuous shade of red-purple, and his pomponed biretta would have made a French cardinal's seem drab. On his surplices now there were bands of duchesse lace. There was no doubt that he graced the office, and that he was destined for high position in the Church.

At least once a week, for years, unless I had caught a children's disease, I went with my father to the Seminary. I always sat on the chair beside Monsignor's desk. Sometimes he would leave me quite alone with a book and if I got bored I could turn down the hall and visit Dr. Herman Heuser, whose name now ranks as one of the great scholars of the Catholic Church. I knew he taught theology, and as I stood at his door, he would greet me in German, and put everything aside to entertain me. Once he took out his water-color box and in a tiny sea shell painted a little ship with brave white sails skimming over a wave, under a clear blue sky; on the prow he lettered *Constance.* On the other side of the shell he painted an altar and a priest in white vestments holding aloft the Host; in letters almost too tiny for the naked eye to read it said: *For CONSTANCE.*

Monsignor Hugh Henry's room was comfortable with wide leather chairs and beautiful pictures. His violin lay on a table and occasionally he would put it under his chin and the most glorious music would pour forth. Sometimes he read me his own poetry.

It was best when I sat quietly with Monsignor Drumgoole, who went ahead with his work just as if I weren't there. Often we had visitors. Once a man glided into the room with a great cross on a chain around his neck and a heavy ring on his finger. He wore a scarlet zucchetto. His face was like parchment, with just a faint touch of pink. His voice was very high and sweet. It left a trailing echo. His old eyes were keen and piercingly blue. I curtsied and kissed the ring of His Eminence James, Cardinal Gibbons.

Once again, on one of the last sad days before Monsignor left the Seminary in 1920, a magnificent figure in scarlet came in the room. He was very tall, and a little stooped. I curtsied and kissed the ring of His Eminence Désiré, Cardinal Mercier.

How they troop back in memory! Shane Leslie, John Ferrick, Father Basil Maturin, Monsignor Joseph McMahon, the towering figure of Archbishop Prendergast. Monsignor Barry Doyle like a superb actor. Archbishop Downey of Liverpool. All these men, some of them from the far corners of the earth, all centered in the Catholic Church. They come before me like a Magnificat. Ambassador Paul Claudel and famous Anglican converts like Monsignor Hugh Benson and Gilbert Chesterton. Great scholars from the Catholic University. Exiles from Mexico, exiles from France. Monsignor Drumgoole raising a wine glass with his lovely toast:

"To the glory of God."

All human ideas sacred and profane were discussed in the Rector's room. I heard there of Cardinal Merry del Val, who had revived the Pan-Germanic dream that would restore the pre-Reformation Church and finish the British Empire. The Pan-Germanic illusion was to haunt the clerical mind through two world wars, and for its sake they made their most tragic mistakes.

So often I heard Monsignor Drumgoole say, "Pan-Germanism is a myth. Merry del Val will lead the world to war."

I heard the Industrial Revolution discussed. I heard the name Marx. Over and over sounded the name of Monsignor's hero, Leo XIII. He lived to the Right, this priest in his glistening soutanes with his French wines and his English snuff; but his heart was to the Left. He saw a new day for the Church, a spring coming after a dreadful winter.

I heard Monsignor say, "The Church has always been in a bad light. What we have to fear is total darkness."

It was in the Rector's room I first heard the word "apostasy"—abandonment of the Church.

"It's always our fault," Monsignor said. "It's always been our fault."

He was rather slow about putting a new roof on the Seminary, because he was busy sending for professors and lecturers from all the universities of Europe. He was rather slow about paying for the roof once it was on—but what priests he trained in St. Charles Seminary!

And I would go away from St. Charles Seminary and Patrick Conway would chat garrulously all the way to Overbrook Station. It did not matter, for my mind was stretched with great thoughts and my being was filled with quiet glory. The day came when I could not go again to the Seminary, but my heart and the clean soul of a little girl are in the Rector's study.

## 6

MY EXPANDING WORLD included visits to my relatives. Mother and I would visit the Horans on Arch Street. It was very confusing, for Great-uncle Hubert was my grandfather Horan's nephew, and Great-aunt Lily was grandmother Horan's sister. The Gartlands and the Horans had mixed up the blood in such a manner that we were double cousins, and the whole thing seemed faintly incestuous.

The Arch Street house was enormous. On my first remembered visit I refused to enter the double doors, and lay on the pavement, screaming in terror. The fright never left me. Great-uncle Hubert was a huge man who looked like Tolstoy, with his shock of white hair. He was the soul of friendliness, without a subtlety to his name, so all the way up the long dark staircase he pinched my legs and said:

"Match sticks! Don't they feed you enough?"

I hated my Uncle Hubert and his blond son Hubert, Jr., who teased me. I liked Gartland, the younger son, who from some unknown ancestor had inherited a splendid sad Hebrew face.

The sitting room was always overheated, with a coal fire burning in the grate. I sat on the green velvet couch with my heart in my mouth, looking up at the harrowing engraving of "The Slaughter of the Innocents."

Great-aunt Lily was exquisite. Her features were like a cameo and she had deep violet eyes. Her high-pitched laugh would ring out with delight, and her long white hands moved like flowers in a field with the wind blowing. She talked incessantly, yet she was never dull, for she loved to dramatize every incident and exaggerate it in repetition, so that nothing she said was ordinary. Aunt Lily wove romances, but nothing she said was mean and only the unimaginative could take exception. Women sometimes did, for men loved Aunt Lily; but she loved her stormy cossack Hubert, and never once did he stop her in the middle of one of her stories, or betray the slightest skepticism.

Uncle Hubert was a positive man. In the changing times he had found the solution, the hope of the twentieth century—the Republican party and the high tariff. He was a flour broker, and everyone except my father listened with the utmost respect to Hubert's opinions. There would be outlets for the accumulation of capital, said Uncle Hubert, inventors would create novelty upon novelty. Permanent employment would be found for laborers as befitted their merits and diligence. Articles of comfort and convenience would be sold with the help of advertising, which was the finest educational medium in America. Everyone would have motor-cars, bread from the baker's, because business was solid.

"There never can be an honest government," I heard Uncle Hubert shout at my father.

The family were rather annoyed at Doc for disputing such matters with Hubert. Why did he keep on insisting that the homeless must have their shelter, and the hungry their bread, and private philanthropy was not sufficient?

Once I heard Uncle Hubert roar at my father. "Wrap yourself in the American flag, Doc, and rave on about our Founding Fathers. Good God, man, this is the twentieth century, and Roosevelt's a fool."

He was referring to Theodore Roosevelt and the Progressive party. My father's face was white with anger, which I shared. I didn't even forgive Uncle Hubert when he took us riding in his new motor-car.

I felt that my mother's family did not like me, and I was quite right. I was "the alien corn." It made me unhappy then, and was to bring genuine sadness into my later life.

When I went to Grandfather O'Hara's house on Twentieth Street, I wasn't the same sullen little girl. Robert opened the door, all his teeth gleaming as white as his starched jacket, and I called: "Aunt Francie, I'm here."

The office door opened. What was the presence of a patient to my Uncle Tom? Often he brought me right in. My cousin Frances appeared, carrying a book. Frances went to school and could read. So could I, for by some feat of magic I had taught myself to read by an alphabet card and pestering every adult with my constant request: "What's that word?"

My father's family were immensely proud of me. They would have me stand with my little book and read to visitors who were expected to show amazement and delight. It was unfortunate for those who were restrained in their praise, for the family put it down to "black jealousy," and among themselves sinned all the sins against charity as they discussed the tepid one, while I listened blissfully. It was small wonder I loved my father's family, who told me to my face I was unusually bright.

Aunt Francie was still gay and could still sing lilting songs, though by this time she had married Mr. Matthews, the lawyer, started a family with twin daughters, and was to increase the population every year till there were seven little Matthews all born in the big double bed that Grandmother O'Hara bought at the Centennial Exhibition of 1876.

"Look at my little patterns," Aunt Francie would say of her flock of Matthews babies. She was pleased with her fecundity.

Times were changing. Aunt Constance, to economize (as if an O'Hara ever could) and save the old family home, which Mamma had requested on her deathbed, had become a career woman. She worked at Dr. Burton Carnett's doing the same things she had done for "Papa." "Papa" and "Mamma" were the deities in Grandfather's house, for though they were dead, they lived. They were quoted as oracles at least a hundred times a day.

The doorbell rang and rang. It was Aunt Sallie Moore and the girls. They were invited to dinner. It was France McCunney and her little girl. It was the Hepburns. It was . . . It didn't matter, everyone was invited. Often eighteen would sit down to dinner and the portrait of Great-grandfather McCunney by Sully looked at family and guests with jolly brown eyes dancing approval.

Uncle Tom said wistfully, "If I had under my vest what he had, I'd have a twinkle in my eye too."

There were those who said Uncle Tom was no longer a Temperance man. Next to atheism, taking a drink was the worst evil that could come to Grandfather's house.

Aunt Constance glared at him from the head of the table. Father John Crowley, our cousin, sat at her right; at her left Uncle Thé, finally rejected by the lady of the violets, had married pretty young Lillian Balderston, part Quaker, part Methodist, and all Spartan, taking this unusual family in her stride. Grace was said. Robert stood by Aunt Constance's side as she ladled the soup from the great tureen.

Each talked about his own pet subject, and they all talked at once—a play at the South Broad Street Theatre; what this new man Stokowski, whom I saw every day of my life, was playing at the Philadelphia Orchestra, Uncle Tom talked about Plato's *Republic;* Mr. Matthews announced that the times were not fair and good, the Republican party was all wrong. Aunt Lou and Uncle Augustine Peale came through the door, Uncle Gus with edging on his vest and a black ribbon on his glasses. Aunt Lou's voice soared over all the rest. Uncle Gus, who was a descendant of the famous portrait-painting Peales, had one great interest—the Academy of Fine Arts. Uncle Gus lived in the eighteenth century, but he was enmeshed in the economic laws of the twentieth. He could never extricate himself, but the edging on his vest was always immaculate, his manners beautiful, and when he talked about the fine arts his mind was fastidious and distinguished.

Sometimes Aunt Constance let me do my imitations for the company.

"The child's a born actress," they all exclaimed.

"She's going on the stage," Aunt Constance said. She had very advanced views.

The theatre was the supreme experience of my life. It was both luminous and poetic; only a child and a mystic can feel that pure sense of mystery which is the soul's natural element. Drama reaches a deeper consciousness than any other art. In the sensible order the primary magic of the theatre is the magic of the spoken word; but the exaltation of drama can only be achieved when the life presented makes one strain upward in spiritual exercise to its tragedy or glorification. It is not for nothing that the great dramatists of the world make the figures of their plays a little larger than the average man. The great buffoons of comedy and the great victims of tragedy have always been heroic in their measure.

I can remember the old South Broad, all gilt and red plush. It was what a theatre should be—artificial, apart from life. It had a certain smell that intoxicated me. People kept coming in, and there was a deep buzz of conversation. Suddenly there was a hush and the musicians appeared. They played mannered and tuneful airs, and then the lights went down. The curtain went up. Here was the heart of the mystery, a world with no more "I" in it. It was the emotion of Epiphany. . . .

One afternoon a man in a priest's collar stood in the lobby of the Garrick. He had white hair and uncanny dark eyes. Someone said, "Mr. Belasco." The name connected in my mind with theatre. We looked at each other, this strange Jew—part charlatan, part genius—and a little girl. He made a move toward me, but Nana led me quickly along by the hand. The crowds swirled around me and blotted him out.

I saw light operas and Nana bought the sheet music and played it for me. Nana in her boned guimpe and her sweeping black skirts was not Miss Ina Claire, but she did her best. I imitated Miss Ruth Chatterton, the sad orphan child of *Daddy Long-Legs.* I dreamed of Ruth Chatterton, for I yearned to find a perfect being whom I could love perfectly. I wanted to see an actress away from the stage. We did not know any actresses.

My wish came true one summer in Chelsea, New Jersey, where we always took a cottage. I loved the seashore; the roar of the surf was the most glorious of music. At three I would charge out into the sea, at four and five I was swimming in the breakers, quite unafraid. Chelsea was an enchanting place, though I understood from my father it was second-rate ocean; for only in Cape May was the marriage of land and sea perfectly realized. The one ideal summer cottage was Grandfather O'Hara's on Jackson Street in Cape May.

My father was quite right about Cape May, as I was to realize when we finally went there, but Chelsea was then all the seashore I knew. One Sunday afternoon my father and I walked on the boardwalk. The rolling chairs passed us as we went by the Ostend almost to the Chelsea Hotel, which was the best and where Aunt Caroline and Uncle Frank stayed. I knew if they were on the porch they would be proud and wave at us, for I was dressed to kill and my father wore white flannel trousers, a blue jacket and carried a cane. I cannot remember when I did not know that my mother's family cared passionately for appearances.

It happened by the Chelsea Hotel. In a rolling chair, turned with its back to the sea, sat a commanding woman in a white dress, her ringed hands resting on a tall parasol. She wore a leghorn hat with yards of veiling streaming from it.

A deep voice said, and it was sonorous, and somehow thrilling, "Why, Doctor, how are you?"

My father's hat was swept off. I had never seen him so pleased.

"Miss Russell," and he was bending over her outstretched hand, and she was laughing in the most tantalizing way. "This is my little girl. Constance, this is the famous Miss Lillian Russell."

I could not curtsy. I could not speak. This was Lillian Russell. Everyone spoke of her—Great-aunt Jen had her picture—and my father knew this fabulous woman. My heart beat so fast I was choking. Miss Russell no doubt saw a little girl with freckles and no manners. She looked at me sidewise and her eyes were provocative. Her face looked as if it were held in a vise and even I could notice the thick coating of powder. She had a huge diamond pin on the front of her gown.

My father and she uttered a few pleasantries, and we continued our walk. I could scarcely live with the wonder of it. How did my father know an actress, and none of us know a word about it? I bedeviled him with questions. He looked secretive, proud of himself, and very handsome.

"When I was a medical student I was a super in Miss Russell's operas." He explained: "I was theatre-crazy in those days."

My father not only knew an actress, he had been on the stage. I was suffused with pride. We were "of the profession." And Uncle Hubert presumed to argue about politics with my father. Why, there was no one in the family to touch his eminence. I was the daughter of an actor. I forgot my miserable showing before Miss Russell. The story in my own mind became very interesting. I heard Miss Russell say in that tremendous voice: "Doctor, your little girl belongs on the stage."

Gertrude Conaway, whose cottage was across the street from ours and who had through a long summer suffered my rapt worship of her dark curls, sweet face and lovely dresses, was annoyed no more. When she walked down to look at the bay in the evening with her mother's arm around her, there was no small adorer at her heels. I had even reversed the time track to keep her interest, inventing prodigious stories as to what I had done when I was a "big girl." My imaginary experiences in the world of maturity worried Mrs. Conaway, who entertained grave reservations about my sanity. Now they were free of me, but Gertrude was a gracious child and afraid she had hurt me, or maybe she actually missed an emotional nature who made the objects of its devotion perfect. She came across the street to our porch to learn what was the matter.

"Gertrude, I know Lillian Russell," I said.

She was not at all impressed. I dismissed her imperiously. I had loved her in my fashion, but that was before I met Lillian Russell. Gertrude grew up and married Harold Vanderbilt, and I am sure has no reason to remember her rejection for an aging queen of the stage.

These things I remember, and how everyone spoke of the changing times. We were on the threshold of marvels to some; to others order and graciousness were going from life. I grew up to change.

Monsignor Kieran stood at our open window on Pine Street on a warm June night and said ominous things. He spoke of divorce and the acceptance of it, of apostasy. Monsignor was tremendously sad. St. Patrick's Church had been cheated of two distinguished parishioners.

Dr. Leopold Stokowski and Madame Olga Samaroff his wife, should have been Catholics. Why, Dr. Stokowski was the son of a devout Irish mother and Polish father! And here they were fallen away from the Church—people with magnificent talent.

"What an acquisition they would have been." Poor Monsignor Kieran! Every time he was about to claim someone distinguished, in the name of the one true Church, the modern world and its evils stepped in.

It was said that Catholic women smoked cigarettes, though Nana did not believe it. We had all been present at Kugler's restaurant at Fifteenth and Chestnut Streets when a gay and beautiful girl lit a cigarette. I was fascinated; this was even more interesting than the goldfish pond in the lobby. Nana was horrified. The head waiter walked over with measured tread and asked her to put it out. She argued and so did her laughing male escorts, but finally she gave in under the petrified stares of the other diners. Kugler's was definitely for the family trade.

Despite the streets now thronged with motor-cars, and moving picture palaces on Market Street, there was one thing, I was told, that never changed. That was the Catholic Church. It had come down through two thousand years subtracting nothing from its eternal doctrine, adding only glories, such as cathedrals and ceremonies and new saints.

I loved to go to the Cathedral of SS. Peter and Paul to Solemn High Mass on great feast days. The usher always led us to the top of the church. The glories of Bishop O'Hara were dimming, but we were still considered among the prominent worshippers at the Cathedral. Murillo's lately restored Crucifixion shone out in all its magnificence over the main altar. The music was solemn but joyful. Archbishop Prendergast in his cope and mitre carrying the tall crozier entered through the side door and proceeded up the middle aisle with the bishops and the monsignori and the priests following him. He traced the blessing over and over. The altar was banked with flowers.

As the sublime ritual of a Pontifical Mass took place I was at peace. No one explained that peace to me; for this Mystery was surrounded by a dramatic form such as no theatre ever could emulate. The Archbishop on his faldstool sat like some great patient image, his ring gleaming on his gloved hand. And then the jeweled mitre was removed, and he ascended the altar steps. . . . The Gloria soared from the choir. . . . Golden bells rang out, and the cathedral was swept by a great rustling as the congregation knelt. . . .

Through all my life with all its dissonance the music of devotion remained in my ears; and my consciousness was linked up with the sense of something following me—the memory of absolute perfection—and the ringing of golden bells in the Cathedral of SS. Peter and Paul.

# 7

THE CELEBRATION OF CHRISTMAS made me a neurotic, a materialist, and a pagan. I was showered with handsome toys. All the convents for which my father was doctor vied with each other to send me gorgeously dressed dolls. Sentimental women patients, of which there were many, even presented me with jewelry. Nana, not to be outdone, closed the doors in her rooms so I could not get in (which set me kicking and screaming against them) and dressed dolls that would put everyone else's to shame. No one in the family was immune from the fever of seeing to it that Christmas left me limp with satiety, entirely bereft of the high and holy meanings of the day.

"She's an only child," they explained to visitors who stood appalled before the lofty tree and the great mass of presents.

Everyone doted on this young pagan who never destroyed anything. My dolls were still beautiful and new when the holy season was over, not a dish was cracked; and the games were in the playroom closet, more often than not, untouched. Nana didn't tell that when I had a little friend coming to play with me, I arrived in Nana's room laden down with my best dolls and toys, so that no harm could be done to them. She, the most generous woman on earth, boasted of my carefulness. No one guessed that I was a monster of selfishness, save my contemporaries, who probably only visited me under duress.

The adults even quoted with fond pride my remark after a children's party was over, and I was alone with all my possessions: "I like *myself* best."

The desire to spoil me completely by giving me every material thing in the world even infected my father, and nearly took his life.

My father suffered from modern man's most crippling alienation of the spirit—the unfulfilled desire to work with his hands. He had a tool chest and room in the cellar where he stole an hour or so each day from the patients and made things—cabinets, window screens, flower-boxes, all created with exquisite precision.

He decided, the Christmas of 1912, to build me a dollhouse that would be his masterpiece. It was, for it stood as tall as I, with six rooms, bath, and a curving staircase. The front came off, so that I could play with it. The rooms were papered, the floors carpeted, for the whole family co-operated. Box after box of doll furniture came from an expensive toy store. Nana dressed a family, with a colored maid in lawn apron and cap. It was to be a magnificent sight, for coming along the porch there was to be a bridal party ready to move in, with a cook already in the kitchen, a baby upstairs in the cradle, and a little boy and girl in the wedding party. Nana was opposed to the literal facts of life for children. Tiny lamps were even wired for electricity. The plan was to have them on, shining out through the curtained windows, and the miniature mechanical piano playing a tinkling tune when I was brought in to see it on Christmas morning.

Instead, on Christmas morning, there was a sheet shrouding the dollhouse, for my father had worked with the playroom windows wide open. He was lying in the second-story front bedroom gasping his lungs out with pneumonia.

I lived on the third floor with Nana while my father was ill. His illness went on for weeks. I slipped upstairs past my father's room where it was so quiet and the door was closed. I was afraid of the male nurse who had my little room and slept in my bed. I lay on Nana's box-couch and the ticking of the clocks grew louder, slower and made words: "Lord Jesus Christ, have mercy upon us. . . ."

It always hurt my pride and puzzled me that when they spoke of my father at Grandfather's house someone was sure to sigh and say, "Poor Michael." It dimmed the present man in sadness, and in his place I was given a legendary father I had never known. The dramatic instinct of the O'Haras brought before my eyes a brilliant, handsome young man who held every gift of life in his hands. I sensed that all Grandfather and Grandmother O'Hara had ever suffered, hoped to be, or longed for was crystallized in my father as he had been. Aunt Constance often described his graduation from the University of Pennsylvania Medical School, and as she told it tears welled in her eyes.

"They called the name, Doctor Michael O'Hara, Junior. The applause roared out in the Academy of Music. I heard cheers. Then the doctors rose to their feet in tribute to Papa. Doctor Leidy called out, 'Stand up, man.' I can see Mamma yet, it was the proudest moment of her life when Michael in cap and gown went up on the stage to get his diploma. He was an honor man and handsome as a Greek god. Papa wasn't one to play to the grandstand, but he sat down and took Mamma's hand, 'There's our boy, France.' Your Aunt Lou made her First Holy Communion that very morning. Papa and Mamma didn't even go to it, though there was ample time. It hurt Lou, but we were all used to the fact that your father was the favorite. Mamma used to say, 'Michael was gentle with me coming into the world, and he's never given me a pang since.'"

I resented putting my living father in the past. He seemed to me as other men; perhaps his voice was slower, his footsteps more measured. Why were the family so mournful about him? It had something to do with surgery. I heard them speak of a forceps; Mother, too, mentioned it with combined pride and regret. Doctors from all over the world had written to him, I knew. Later I was to hear that my father had perfected a forceps for intestinal anastomosis, a tremendous technical leap forward which revolutionized abdominal surgery, just one step behind the Murphy button.

His surgical career had been ended by peritonitis from a ruptured appendix. Dr. John Deaver operated on the man he considered the most promising young surgeon of his day, and my father spent nearly a year at the old Lankenau Hospital. The family love of drama was satisfied, in those long ago events, for my mother had been a bride when it all happened.

"I spent most of my honeymoon in the German Hospital," she used to say with humorous resignation.

Aunt Constance, the family historian, drenched these events in emotion. "Your mother and father were just back from Atlantic City. Mamma warned us not to rush in on the bride and groom. The first we knew Doctor Willard called Papa, and he went right to the hospital. He came back and sat here at the dining room table after the operation. 'Deaver did the best he could,' he said. 'How can I tell your mother? Michael will not live out the night. And if he should live he'll never have a day's health.' Then he slumped over the table in a faint. Jesse and Robert carried him to bed. He was raving in delirium by morning. We didn't expect Papa to live and Michael between life and death for months. That was trouble!"

"Poor Michael," his family sighed now, "he's had his share of suffering." Later I came to wonder if this relegating him to the past was a compensation for the years they had lived under the splendid shade of the favorite son. I hated their resignation; it seemed to say that life had buffeted my father too much and now he was leaving it without regret.

One morning I watched men spread tanbark on Pine Street to deaden the noise of the yellow trolley and the occasional teams of horses that passed under our windows. It was for my father, and one part of me tingled in appreciation of this public proclamation of our woe; the other fought against it with all my strength. My father had no right to be called, "Poor Michael," and given over to death. I loved my father. I needed him. He could not die. And yet there was something in me that enjoyed the dramatic notoriety of being stared at when I went out the door of the Pine Street house, of hearing the servants whisper, "Poor little thing! How pale she is!"

I enjoyed the visitors coming up the stairs, my own good-little-girl pose, the flowers. I remember feeling like a prima donna when I was taken down to my father's waiting room which was filled with priests and was led by Father Whittaker to one who seemed apart. "Constance, this is Very Reverend Abbot Obrecht who knew your grandfather." There was something about this man with his remote but piercing eyes that brought the healthy touch of realism to a stricken house, that blasted through the weak, self-pitying resignation.

This was Dom Edmund Obrecht of the Abbey of Our Lady of Gethsemani in Kentucky, in the East to beg for his Trappist monks. I liked the name—Trappist. It made me think of woods and men who were not afraid. I liked hearing of the perpetual silence of the monks. I wondered if they ever forgot how to talk. Dom Edmund's accented voice was strong. He put his hands on my head to bless me. As those strong hands touched me, I knew that death was not a way of escape, not a thing of funeral flowers, or solemn sentimentalities in Heaven. It could be friend—it could be foe. Dom Edmund would know how to handle it.

"I always start my begging trips in Philadelphia," he said.

Monsignor Drumgoole came upstairs to my playroom. He pulled the sheet from my dollhouse, and he and I sat there putting the furniture in the rooms. He turned on the batteries so the lights would shine out. The dollhouse seemed to belong to a greedy little girl who was dead. It made me feel guilty. Things were valueless. . . .

Monsignor held me in his arms. I felt the strong, steady beating of his heart. "Constance," he said, "do you know what my right name is? The only name for a priest. It's Father—"

Then he did not baby me any longer. "The only thing we can ever keep is Our Blessed Lord. Everything and everyone else goes."

Aunt Caroline took me to Dr. Ralph Butler's every morning, for something had gone wrong with my ears.

The lessons I was learning were too tremendous. I had to be patient when the doctor ran his instrument in my ears. I did not feel it as keenly as Aunt Caroline who sat beside me, her handsome dark eyes filled with anguish.

Dr. Butler probed and his hands ran skilfully over the glands in my neck and the place back of my ear where it never stopped hurting.

"I must say I don't like the look of this. I don't like the look of it a bit."

Aunt Caroline always had a package in her hands, a present for me. She would give it to me when we were in Nana's room. A beautiful hair ribbon and a sash to match, or a little vial of perfume from Paris. I tried to smile to show her I liked my surprise. It hurt her when I didn't show pleasure, and she scolded because I wasn't grateful.

When she went away my grandmother covered me with her cherished eiderdown, and got me the bound copies of *Harper's* to look at, or would produce the new copy of *St. Nicholas.* I could read the stories in that myself.

One night was different from all the others. I woke up because a pain was roaring through my head. I saw the blue votive light flickering before the statue of Our Lady of Lourdes. Nana was talking in a low hushed voice to my mother at the door. My mother was weeping in little shuddering gasps.

"He's dying, I tell you—"

Nana was scolding, but I knew she didn't mean it. I remembered that Mother was Nana's child. I heard my mother go away from the door, and Nana turned toward me. All the tragedy and bitter pain of living were on her face. I never forgot it. I knew in a split-second of time what it means to have sorrow come to someone you love. In some way my child's understanding grasped what it means to stand at the foot of the cross.

I sat up in bed, holding my ears that were filled with torture, a scream rising in my throat.

"Quiet." Nana said. "Not a sound. You'll disturb your father."

A woman, not yet six years old, could not be free of the terrible urgencies of this night. Nana put down the window and led me into her sitting room. She lit the Welsbach burner, and her little gas stove. She put a pan of water on to heat, and then wrapping me in her eiderdown held me in her arms in the old rocking chair. It made a comfortable squeaking noise. The warmth of her body eased the agony momentarily. My eyes looked up at the picture of the Ecce Homo. I could not turn away. There were deep shadows on the face one minute, the next it was clear and living.

"You must not cry," Nana said, over and over.

The clocks ticked and ticked. The pain grew. It was like some enormous thing outside me, then I was in the center of it, it came from all directions.

"Nana, Nana," I sobbed.

"Offer it up," she said. "Offer it up."

She sang a soft little song. Pain coiled like a spring. It rang like the chiming of clocks. It ticked like the clocks. Time was taking away my father. The thorns pressed down on the head of Christ. I felt them. They were in my ears. I could not bear the pain any more, but I had to, for my father was downstairs dying. In the business of dying women had to be brave. And then in the most completely selfless prayer of my entire life, I reached out beyond it, to that agonized Face. I was giving Him my pain —for my father.

"You're such a good girl," Nana breathed against my head.

She stood up, holding me in her arms, her nightgown soaked with blood and matter. It clung to her hands. She laid me down on the couch, and her face was white with terror. I could scarcely see her, but I did not want her to leave me. She was out the door, going downstairs. The clocks ticked on, those dreadful clocks, and everything around me grew dim.

My father and I convalesced together in the sitting room. He was thin and worn, and his cough racked him. He would not let me kiss him.

I had my sixth birthday party beside him—a child gone all legs and eyes, dressed in a flowered challis dressing gown, with brier stitching and pink ribbons. I blew out the candles on my cake but it made me feel childish and silly. I was grown up and aware. My father played Sousa's marches on the gramophone, and Mother and I smiled at each other knowingly for we understood the martial music made him recapture the stirring rhythms of hardy manhood. We pitied him. He was no longer my god, my tower of strength, but a man who was my father and needed the security of my love. I learned what all women have to know sooner or later: we are the stronger sex.

And so a man who from then on always had flecks of blood on his handkerchiefs, and a six-year-old child who loved him enough to hang on a cross of pain, drank milk punches together and played checkers. But nothing was ever the same after my father built the dollhouse.

# BOOK TWO

## 1

SISTER MARY FLORA takes me by the hand, and leads me up the wide staircase of the Convent of Notre Dame. Life is about to commence. I am in school. Sister Mary Flora is the first professional politician I have ever met, and I am intensely interested. She is the leading parlor nun of the convent, and her contacts with the world outside have given her a certain suave insincerity that is faintly repellent. She is shrewd and understands me perfectly as she turns me over to Sister Mary Immaculata, teacher of the first grade.

"Constance," says Sister Mary Flora, "is a highly imaginative child."

The two nuns exchange glances, and I am placed. My Irish ancestors have given me too much imagination, which could mean unusual gifts, or that the nuns have a little liar on their hands. The Irish imagination is always a great danger when it comes to religion and accounts for the fact that there are so few Irish saints.

Sister Mary Immaculata in her black habit and stiff white bib is both timid and kind; her face framed in her starched coif is dovelike, and her blue nearsighted eyes blink in nervous apprehension at this unpredictable thing—a child. It was her task to water down great truths for the first grade, and she faced it each year with religious stoicism; fortunately she had no imagination, which fact alone saved her reason.

Sister Mary Immaculata leads me into the classroom which houses the primary department. My cousin Frances, in the third grade, sits looking at me with an enigmatic expression on her face. In this corner room, with the high windows looking out on Rittenhouse Square, are my future classmates. I am interested, and not at all shy. I stand before them, and then I realize I am much taller than the others, and that box-pleated white piqué dresses trimmed with Irish lace are not the fashion for schoolwear. The others do not have long curls. I stand and am judged and giggles break out, which spread to the second and third grade; behind her reader my cousin Frances turns traitor and is laughing too.

I go to the seat Sister Mary Immaculata assigns me, and I do not cry. She shows me my books. I have interrupted a reading lesson. I turn to the place, and superiority returns to me.

"I can read everything in this book," I tell Sister Mary Immaculata.

The Sisters of Notre Dame have on their hands that most pitiful and objectionable of creatures—an only child. I can read fluently in the fourth reader, I can memorize every poem in the third grade poetry book, I can spell, I can write my name—and I have never been to school. The infant prodigy is taken from room to room, as an incentive to the ambition of older pupils, by Sister Superior Adela du Sacré Coeur. Sister Superior was devoted to my father, and had no idea of the tortures his child was enduring as I was led through the school reciting poetry, and even reading the newspaper to the eighth grade; by that time I was loathed by every child in the place, and when recreation came they made me feel it.

I stood alone, apart, dressed in the beautiful clothes Mother made me, which were the mode for Rittenhouse Square but not for the Convent of Notre Dame. The children trod heavily on my white buckskin shoes, and ran away with shouts of glee. There was one thing in the world I wanted, an Anderson gingham dress and brown shoes. I did not want to be different. There was only one way I could bear it—to assume I was the social superior of these children, who were having a marvelous time racing up and down the paths past the Lourdes grotto.

Only one thing saved me; I could not do sums. Sister Mary Immaculata could make me memorize the addition tables, but I could not apply the principle, one and one makes two, to the problems in my arithmetic book. My stupidity in this direction was absolute, it bordered on idiocy; it made me human and faintly, ever so faintly, endurable to the other children.

Gradually the rhythm of the school settled over me, and I was content to be apart. I liked the elaborate manners we were taught; that raise of the hand when we had to leave the room, and recognized, standing and saying, "Pardonnez-moi, s'il vous plaît." Sister Mary Immaculata's head nodded furtively as if bodily functions were somehow embarrassing. Clasping our soap and towel we left the room, pausing at the door to give a deep sweeping curtsy, counting four to get down, four to rise. We walked down the corridor, dipping our hand in the holy water font, making a sign of the cross, genuflecting at the chapel door, and then descended the long flights of stairs to the basement. It is true all this elaboration in the face of a simple human need frequently led to accidents in the baby grade and Sister Mary Immaculata in abashed modesty had to do more than minister to souls.

The discipline and the order of convent school life eventually reaches every child, for it is protective; it is clinging to the apron strings of Holy Mother the Church. I liked the long file of little girls mounting the stairs after recreation. I loved the line sweeping into that impressive curtsy as Sister Superior appeared. I liked the click of signals that governed all our actions and the convent bell that rang every half hour, and a room of little girls pausing to say, "Coeur Sacré de Jésus, j'ai confiance en vous." I liked the Litany of the Blessed Virgin by which we began the afternoon session with those majestic chanting words, "Tower of Ivory," "House of Gold. . . ."

One day Sister Saint Mary, the mistress of the younger boarders, saw my forlorn state at recreation. She took me up to the Holy Guardian Angels, the playroom of the boarders. These were cosmopolitan children who came from all over the United States and even Cuba and Mexico. Most of them went abroad every summer as casually as I went to Chelsea, New Jersey. Some of them even had mothers on the stage; and in the Holy Guardian Angels I made my first friends. I was assured that in this very room Ethel Barrymore had played as a child.

The first nightmare was over, and I settled down to school. I took elocution with Sister Julie du Saint Edward, and learned to recite with gestures: "A big golden sunflower grew so tall. It peeped right over the garden wall." Every priest who came to my grandfather's house had to hear me recite that piece, to which I added an encore: "Ten Little Tin Soldiers on the Nursery Floor."

Sometimes Sister Saint Mary prevailed upon my mother to let me spend the afternoon with the boarders, and I was received as someone not at all strange. They too had seen plays and heard concerts, and surpassed me by being able to hold conversations in two and even three languages. Occasionally their families visited them, a mother in Philadelphia with a play, or a mother on a concert tour. It was interesting to watch their radiant faces when they were sent for to come to the parlor; they often came upstairs after these visits and sat in the corner of the Holy Guardian Angels crying their eyes out; it seemed there were bitter penalties attached to being a cosmopolitan child.

My religious sense was fed by the chapel services on Friday afternoon. We came in two by two with our black veils, our hands held in an attitude of superhuman piety. The organ played in the back, and the nuns chanted in the nineteenth century manner never letting their voices out to reveal they were women. It was sexlessness in its worst sense. It was neutrality, a spiritual Temperate Zone. The carefully trained children sang a hymn; everyone from the youngest child to the young ladies of the

Graduating Class knelt bolt upright, a nun in every second bench to see that there would be no wickedness such as distraction at prayers or a child slumping, part on knees, part with a derrière touching the bench.

There was something Sulpician in those early religious services of my convent days; a pretty unreality for the most vibrantly real adoration in Catholicism—the Eucharist. It was too sweet, too cloyingly feminine, and there was a strange undertone of cruelty. We were overdisciplined, no doubt about it.

I think the one great lack of my beginning convent days was that I never heard that glorious phrase, "God so loved the world. . . ." We knew about "fear of the Lord," and, before we were even ready for First Communion Class, had a tragic consciousness of sin. We were made aware of the lurking presence of Lucifer long before we understood the Redemption. The Redemption was the most neglected dogma in my religious education; perhaps knowledge of the Redemption would have led us to love and courage, and we would have thrown off all the sticky fears and class consciousness that so obsessed the minds of convent school girls in my youth.

The bourgeois tradition haunted the French religious mind, and Notre Dame Academy, though its motherhouse was in Namur, Belgium, was intensely French. I can well understand how much of France was lost to the faith when I remember six-year-old children trembling before sin, their minds heavy with fear. It was amazing how many occasions of sin were found in that placid convent. We were made to feel guilty for the Cross on which our unspeakable sins had made Him hang, but never awestruck at how madly in love He was with the human race—including the children at the Academy of Notre Dame, West Rittenhouse Square, Philadelphia.

In that sense Nana was a far better teacher of religion than Sister Mary Immaculata; though she, dear nun, was innocent and good and it was conformity to her times that made her convey a certain joylessness in religion to the baby room.

Now that I went to school I was taken regularly to Mass with my father and mother. We went to the ten o'clock Low Mass in St. Patrick's Church basement. It was crowded and hot. Bathing was not yet a general practice, in fact indoor plumbing was unknown "out Schuylkill," deodorants were not a commonplace; as we waited and waited for the priest, who was always late, a sickening odor would assail my nostrils. It was my first great lesson in mortification of the senses, and I did not take to it at all kindly.

I might have been able to forget that, if Low Mass had been said with any reverence; but whatever went on was a deep mystery between the priest and his server. After the Latin Gospel, the sermon would commence, apparently in hog-Latin for it was nearly always quite unintelligible. The sacerdotal attitude in those days seemed to mean that Catholics had to accept what was given them; the faith would endure mumbling and unprepared sermons.

The beauty of the Offertory—that great moment in the Mass for which Paul Claudel wrote:

> The Lord is with you, my brothers. I pray you, be with me. Here is more than the paten, more than the chalice and the wine;
>
> Here you are, my little ones, held and supported in my hands.

—was never evoked in St. Patrick's basement at Low Mass. Only spiritual fortitude could bring the ecstasy of belief to the congregation. What took place in that basement chapel was enough to alienate anyone, and it was no wonder the congregation pushed and shoved at the doors to get away from this sorry re-enactment of Calvary. I began to hate church unless surrounded by "pomp and circumstance."

It is not surprising that so many middle-aged Catholics regard church as a painful necessity, a commandment, and find anyone peculiar who expects to enjoy Sunday Mass. "To see; to hear," is a perfectly legitimate demand on the part of the faithful; for the faithful were meant to be participants at Mass, instead of victims of clerical effrontery.

There was a flaw somewhere, as school, the Church and the world warred within me, and rebellion grew in my heart.

Monsignor Drumgoole listened to my complaints with suitable gravity, though a smile tugged at the corners of his mouth.

"You know, I agree with every word of it; but you'll be able to bear it much better when you make your First Communion. That will change everything, I promise it will."

The baby grade of the Academy of Notre Dame is led downstairs to St. Aloysius. On our heads we wear white veils, for we are now the First Communion Class. We sit on little blue chairs with our catechisms in our hands, and the fierce first spark of a conception that could blaze into glorious light is ignited. We are to hear of the bread and wine that was body and blood, that was Bethlehem and Calvary, and light eternal. We lean forward, little lambs ready to leap among the stars, and instruction begins.

Fear entered like a knife, for we must be cleansed of our enormous wickedness in First Confession before First Communion. I dramatized the blackness of my crimes till I felt the Devil's hot breath on my neck. I woke up at night and leaped from bed, endeavoring to make a perfect Act of Contrition. One midnight the Devil himself looked in the second-story back window. I saw him with his horrible green eyes shining, all in red, with smoke coming from his snout. My screams shattered the peace and quiet of Pine Street.

"What are they doing to that child?" Mrs. Biddle's autocratic voice sounded from her open window.

Mrs. Biddle could not know that the Devil was loose on Pine Street; neither could the Isaac Starrs next door, or Dr. Rhein on the other side who pounded on the bedroom wall. Lights went on up and down the street. The telephone shrilled. All our neighbors were well-bred Episcopalians or nice quiet Deists, so the Devil, in the century that was to say he didn't exist, probably enjoyed the commotion he created on Pine Street.

I learned how to go to confession, how to examine my tortured conscience in the light of the Ten Commandments given Moses, the Six Commandments of the Church, and no doubt the Four Sins that cry to Heaven for vengeance.

We were drilled on modesty. It seemed little convent girls in

France and Belgium even wore a chemise while in their bath, so that their own eyes would not be defiled with a sight of their bodies. The glorious vitality of Catholicism—its joyous affirmation of the body—was being lost in trails of a puritanism more deadly than Cotton Mather's; for the Church is the eternal contradiction of a doctrine that consumes spirituality as lime eats into human flesh and bones.

We were taught how to keep our purity in these solemn days before the reception of the Sacraments by undressing only to our underwear, then slipping our nightgowns over our heads, working the nether garments loose beneath this shelter. A Freudian psychoanalyst would have predicted neuroses galore, frigid wives, and all sorts of horrors, but it didn't happen that way. The convent, despite its mistakes, was giving us so much more than the best secular education was to give our contemporaries, that it should have been for all of us, particularly those who strayed into the modern world, a mighty bulwark against disaster. A few scruples never hurt any woman who had to live in the twentieth century; so it is not with unkindness I dwell on the First Communion Class of 1914.

My infant ears drank in the information that at the Seminary—at Father Drumgoole's and my Seminary—candidates for the priesthood studied sin. There were certain sins so dreadful that only the Pope could absolve them, sins that had to be mulled over by bishops, sins that candidates for Holy Orders studied about in books so they would recognize them.

And then there was the confessional seal, so absolute that it had never been broken. I heard of priests stretched on the rack and tortured just to reveal if a certain penitent had confessed a particular sin. I heard of them thrown into dungeons in chains, but the confessional seal was kept inviolate. The safety of the seal was my only protection. Suppose my confessor were to enter the convent and tell what a little liar I was—an inspired little liar, precocious enough never to be caught!

The day came when we were prepared to receive the Word Made Flesh. Sister Superior Adela du Sacré Coeur, with Sister Agnes des Anges at her side, sat on the dais in study hall and examined us. We were letter perfect even to the recitation of the long First Commandment.

"And Whom do you receive in Holy Communion?" Sister Agnes des Anges asked.

"Our Lord and Saviour Jesus Christ," each child answered.

We were intellectually prepared. Now came the actual rehearsals under the supervision of Sister Superior. It was to be the most impressive of all First Communions in the Academy of Notre Dame. We were to wear full-length dresses with three layers of veiling over our faces. The mothers protested, and our dresses were abbreviated to just below the knee, but they must have long sleeves and high necks; and Sister Superior would then consent that only two layers of protective veiling should cover our faces.

The First Communion Class of the Boys' Department, still under Sister Vincent (once she put a lad named John Barrymore in penance with Dante's *Inferno*, and he always claimed the Doré illustrations guided the conduct of his future life) joined us in Assembly Hall. Sister Marie des Anges and Sister Angelina from the Music Department drilled us in the hymns.

> "Jesus, Thou art coming
> Holy as Thou art.
> Thou, the God who made me,
> To my sinful heart."

My voice was loud, clear and tuneless. The nuns were in despair. There was nothing for it but to tell my father, who was doctor of the Convent of Notre Dame, as gently as possible, that his child would have to remain mute on her First Communion Day.

Then something else happened. I was half a head taller than any child in the class. Sister Superior Adela du Sacré Coeur approached me as if to cut off a few unwanted inches. It was clear I didn't match. . . . Ah! but we were an uneven number, so I was to enter alone at the end of the line. It was a rather churlish way to treat a bishop's grandniece, the granddaughter of a papal knight, and the Doctor's daughter; so as the great moment for reception came I was to walk up the center aisle with the little girls standing still on one side, the boys on the other, being careful to keep my feet on the brown marble blocks and move in perfect time to the singing; as I stood halfway between the front pews and the altar rail, the other children were to resume the procession and move fanwise toward me. Then we little girls were to lift one tier of veiling, approach the altar rail, and kneel, lift the last tier, point our hands toward Heaven, close our eyes, and as the priest came to the child beside us, open our mouths, flatten our tongues against our lower lips, and receive Our Lord in the form of unleavened bread—being careful not to use our teeth near the Host.

Oh, it was most elaborate! Exactly like the First Communion of the royal children of Belgium, Crown Prince Leopold and Princess Marie José.

There was First Confession to be got through. We knelt in the chapel examining our consciences. I can still see the faces of those deadly sinners, carefully counting their sins on fingers. Then I was in the dark confessional kneeling on the bench; behind the grating was the priest, who alone could save me from the ravenous fires of Hell.

"In the name of the Father, and of the Son, and of the Holy Ghost. Amen. This is my first confession. Bless me, Father, for I have sinned exceedingly in thought, word and deed. Through my fault, through my fault, through my grievous fault." I beat my breast in frantic Mea Culpas.

Then my sins burst forth in one vivid flash of dramatic imagination, with such astronomical totals that a strangled moan of quickly suppressed mirth came from gentle Father Deering. Maybe I couldn't be forgiven after all! I knew nothing of the deadly monotony of human nature and was sure that such iniquities as the time I kicked Nana, and stole a dime from my mother, were those secret sins they studied at the Seminary. No other child my age was ever so wicked. St. Augustine looked down from Heaven in happy approval as the tears gushed from my repentant eyes.

"Say a good Act of Contrition," came the kind voice from behind the screen.

I was going to be absolved. I was saved . . . saved. My voice, aching with sincerity, intoned the words, ". . . I dread the loss of Heaven and the pains of Hell. . . ." (The modern says, ". . . . thy just punishments," but we came to grips with the awful reality.)

The voice said, "Now you're a good child, and the Infant Jesus will be so happy to come to you tomorrow morning."

I walked out, with my penance, three "Hail Marys," for a life defiled with sin. I felt uplifted, shining white, as I went into the blessed silence of the chapel to atone. Tears streamed from my eyes in joyous release. The little boys waiting to be cleansed looked at me in sick terror. What was going to happen to them?

We left the chapel and gathered around Sister Superior for final instructions. Her splendid ugly face was transfigured with joy. "Tomorrow is your First Holy Communion Day. The Emperor Napoleon Bonaparte said, 'My First Communion was the happiest day of my life.' "

I had seen pictures of Napoleon. An emperor would not say such a thing if it were not true. Tomorrow would be the happiest day of my life! I was suffocating with the glory of anticipation.

I heard Sister Superior say, "Every child will be here at eight-thirty sharp. You will come to St. Aloysius. Your parents will be taken directly to the chapel. I know that none of the mothers of our children will wear a hobble-skirt."

I went home determined to avoid mortal sin. Perhaps I had better not open my mouth; my imagination might tangle with some bare fact and I would tell a lie. Yes, it was best for me to be silent. I did not sleep all night. There was so much to remember. I must not forget to walk on the brown blocks in the chapel. In the event the priest dropped the Sacred Host, we were not to touch it, for that would be the deadly sin of sacrilege, but wait quietly till his consecrated hands picked it up. There was that child in Paris, France, who knelt all day at the altar rail guarding the dropped Host. Should such a thing happen we were to follow the example of this unfortunate child. Was I perfectly sure I had committed no mortal sins since the absolution was pronounced over me?

A May dawn streaked the sky, and still I lay awake. It was here. It had come. "The happiest day of my life." I was twitching with nerves as the moment came to dress. The Sisters of the Good Shepherd had made my First Communion clothes. There was never such lace, such embroidery, such a froth of white satin ribbons. My white silk rib stockings were on and my buckskin slippers, my curls were brushed over Mother's fingers.

Nana and I walked to the convent together. She held my veil carefully. Nana looked so nice in her long black silk dress with her embroidered guimpe and her jet jewelry. She even had marcel waves in her white pompadour that showed under her best toque from Schmoles. Her kid gloves were brand new. The Sisters of Notre Dame de Namur would thoroughly approve of Nana. In a few minutes my father and mother would follow us. I knew my father was going to wear his cutaway and his high silk hat and carry Grandfather O'Hara's cane with the gold knob and initials. I wasn't sure of Mother; her new hat with the dashing osprey looked a bit too stylish. But then everyone said my mother was "a stunning dresser."

My spiritual emotions were somewhat anaemic, to put it mildly, when Nana turned me over to Sister Mary Immaculata, who with the help of Sister Helen Josephine would adjust our veils. Nana gave me my white silk gloves, my new white prayer book, my new pearl rosary. I was so tired I could scarcely stand as my veil was put on, and the two tiers of thickness fell over my face.

"Look at the circles under her eyes," Sister Helen Josephine said worriedly.

It was May, 1914, and a day as blue as morning-glories. It was the last tender spring of peace; and none of the little boys and girls entering the chapel of the Convent of Notre Dame would ever know a world of such serenity and security again.

The adults wept as this exquisite procession of children came through the main door, genuflected in perfect unison, went into the pews—little girls to the left, little boys to the right. Bishop McCort, with his chaplains, came up the aisle in a pure white cope and mitre, and took his place on the throne on the Gospel side of the altar. Father Deering in white vestments, with his acolytes in white cassocks like little popes, commenced our Mass.

The children's hymns soared forth . . . the Offertory . . . the Consecration— He is here! Here in the chapel with the little children in May, 1914. He is here in His Mother's month, and never was a spring to be so beautiful again, or the world so good and green.

The moment comes. Our gloves are removed. . . . Slowly, slowly, we move from the pews as a little bell rings. Bishop McCort ascends the altar steps. I start up the center of the aisle as the others sing the lovely hymn, "Jesus, Thou Art Coming." I could reach each brown block only by a jerking motion. Beauty lies shattered around me as I stand still, and, perfectly, the others spread out fanwise, and we kneel on the chapel floor. The words, "Corpus Domini nostri Jesu Christi . . ." pierce the silence.

Then we are at the rail. Holy Communion is coming to us. My mouth is dry and hot. I feel the Host on my tongue, it cleaves to the roof of my mouth. I cannot swallow. Then it is consumed. I wait for the ecstasy. The heavy perfume of the flowers assails me. Over and over I hear the words, "Corpus Domini nostri Jesu Christi. . . ." We return to the pews for the Thanksgiving. I am still in the chapel. I am still the same. Nothing has changed. It is time to say the Act of Love aloud. It is all over.

We are filing out of the chapel now. I see Nana, and she is looking sadly at the little boys, for this is where Uncle Si made his First Holy Communion. The yesterdays live in today; even the nuns are yearning toward us. We go down to the refectory, and stand to drink a glass of water first.

We are given café au lait and a buttered roll. Pandemonium breaks out in the room where our parents are having breakfast. I wait for the happiness to commence, but my head aches. I yearn to go to bed and sleep. Children with mysteries in their eyes drink the sweet hot mixture; at every place is a First Communion certificate, tied with bright red ribbon, and holy cards from Sister Mary Immaculata.

We are taken into the dining room where our parents wait. In the center of the room my mother is standing. She not only wears a hobble-skirt, but it is slit and a long expanse of her silk-stockinged leg can be seen. I close my eyes in horror at the disgrace she has brought upon us, but Sister Mary Flora is treating her in the manner she usually reserves for the Drexels, Bishop McCort stands beside her, and they are all laughing heartily. Mother looks very worldly in her hat with the osprey. Sister Superior Adela du Sacré Coeur joins the group around her, and she seems pleased with my fashionable mother. I lean against Nana. When does the happiness start?

We leave the convent and Mother has invited Mrs. Delaney to join us with her children, Regina and Florence. It is very gay at home and Regina and Florence dash up and down. Their nerves are not shattered by this tremendous day. I have a heap of presents, but they do not make me happy. The gramophone blasts out a one-step, and my father and Mrs. Delaney are imitating Mr. and Mrs. Vernon Castle. Regina and Florence are dancing. My father is going to mix cocktails.

I go into my bedroom and bolt the door. I yearn to retrace my steps, once more to have God upon my tongue for the first time. But it is past, it is over, and I ache with desolation.

## 2

It was time for my second confession. Frances and I knelt together in St. Patrick's basement examining our consciences. She was a happy, well-adjusted little girl who understood clearly the difference between mortal and venial sins. She did not cower in deadly fear before the inevitability of original sin. She waited patiently for me to awaken proper feelings of contrition. This time I was determined to be sorry because I had offended God.

I searched my soul to find love for Christ. I closed my eyes against the statue of the Sacred Heart, for this man with the woman's pink and white face to which a beard had been incongruously added inspired me with childish contempt. God knows how much harm has been done to religion by that image of a sugar-sweet effeminate Christ which lurks in the back of Catholic minds. I sought Him in the tabernacle, and then I was ready to take my place in line.

There is a great tranquility in Catholic churches when confessions are being heard. Atonement becomes at-one-ment. The people come and go out of the narrow boxes, and there is no sound at all but sibilant whispers. Sacramental confession that waits for the despairing and the hopeless, the sinner and the saint, the broken and the victorious, is the only force that can cure and heal the broken-hearted and the heartless men and women of our tragic century; only there can we be forgiven.

Forgive us our failures, Lord God of the Universe. Forgive us our unforgivingness, O, gentle Jewish Christ. Our incarnate God!

Frances' confession was heard, and she knelt saying her penance. I was in the box in the deep dark, an unknown sinner, confessing to a priest who took the place of Christ. This secrecy was absolute, only God knew my shame. It was over. I had made a good confession. The Act of Contrition was said, and a voice familiar to me as Monsignor Kieran's spoke:

"You're the little O'Hara girl, aren't you? Will you tell your father to stop up at the rectory tonight?"

I was in the center of a whirlwind of doubt and confusion. I rushed from the box, out of the church, like a soul possessed. I tore across the street, unmindful of automobiles or the yellow trolley that ambled along Twentieth Street. I reached the dining room where the family always assembled at this hour for a cup of tea and conversation.

"Aunt Constance!" I dashed for her protective arms, unmindful of the presence of Miss Jeanette Tomkins, the daughter of Dr. Floyd Tomkins, Rector of Holy Trinity Church. "It's all a lie—they told me lies! Monsignor Kieran knew me. My sins will be all over the parish."

Frances stood in the doorway, her face flushed with anger. "She ran out of the church screaming! Everybody looked at us."

Aunt Constance had the whole story from me by now. Robert was summoned to get me a glass of milk. Lizzie appeared with chocolate cake.

"Aunt Constance," I held my arms around her neck, "let's not be Catholics any more, let's go to Miss Jeanette's church where there aren't so many people."

Uncle Tom exploded in mirth. "It's the Protestant drop coming out."

"It could be the example of an uncle who didn't make his Easter duty." Aunt Constance withered him with a glance.

Uncle Tom lowered his eyes. He was having one of his temporary spells of agnosticism and they always made him miserable. Everyone knew he was not really going to leave the Church, but would eventually go to the Jesuits at St. Joseph's and the next day, with a look of burning shame on his handsome face, march up St. Patrick's aisle to Communion. But at least once in every year Uncle Tom left the Church; he was given to quoting Huxley during these periods.

Aunt Constance, with a look of grim determination on her face, was putting on her hat. "It's five to six," she said, ramming in the hat-pins, "they're almost through hearing. I'm going to the rectory and speak to Monsignor Kieran. It's an outrage, that's what it is. One fallen-away Catholic is bad enough for any family." Uncle Tom flushed. "I'll just remind Monsignor Kieran who we are. He may have forgotten Bishop O'Hara and the respect due his family, but I haven't. Tell a child in confession for her father to come to the rectory. There are telephones—"

Mr. Matthews frowned. "You're making a mountain out of a molehill."

"Monsignor Kieran," said Aunt Constance in her most militant suffragette mood, "will respect the Sacrament of Penance when I am through. The fright he gave that child—"

"I don't see why she can't act like other people!" Frances pouted.

"She's not other people. She's an O'Hara." Aunt Constance was really working herself up into a fine state. "Monsignor Kieran has done a very serious thing—very. . . . Jeanette, have dinner with us." It never occurred to Aunt Constance that we were having a remarkable conversation before the daughter of an Episcopal minister. Her voice could still be heard in the hall. "Tell her father to come to the rectory. I'll give Monsignor Kieran my opinion of him. For two pins I'll go to the Archbishop." The front door slammed.

"You didn't say your penance," Frances observed primly.

"Uncle Tom, what's my Protestant drop?" I asked.

"Now, see here." Mr. Matthews was indignant. "Constance is a reasonable child, and instead of all this fuss a calm, logical explanation should have been given."

"What's my Protestant drop?" I persisted.

"Oh, I don't know." Uncle Tom was sullen and ashamed.

"Constance, come upstairs with me," Mr. Matthews said quietly.

Mr. Matthews resembled Abraham Lincoln, and had a profound and reasoning intelligence. He had small tolerance for the modifications and counterstatements that make the legalistic mind, too often, shifty. He was an exponent of the dignity of the Catholic intelligence—a born Thomist—and what he said had a comprehensiveness and penetrating clarity that shone out like pure crystal in the midst of a family that had an impassioned devotion to the illogical.

He quickly cleared up my misconceptions of Monsignor Kieran's violation of the confessional seal. My sins were still protected under its shelter, though Monsignor Kieran had deviated from the strict pattern of orthodox behavior.

"Now," Mr. Matthews continued, "we take up the main problem: *Truth*. The Catholic Church is wholly true, not partially true, but truth entire. A reasonable person cannot live away from truth because of the action on the part of another human being that may shock, or anger us. That would not only be unreasonable—but sheer lunacy." Mr. Matthews lit an abbreviated cigar.

"We talk of the love of truth, but we cannot love it unless we know it, and that means the light of reason. The ultimate meaning of reason is God."

I felt as if Mr. Matthews were attempting to teach me arithmetic. "Don't we have to love and fear God?"

"How can we love what our minds do not know?" He stretched his long, lanky frame as if to tighten some loose bolts. "All important things like truth pass into the intellect. I am, for instance, telling you what is true, but you must convince yourself by reason. The more you learn, the closer you come to knowledge. That is the goal of life."

"Mr. Matthews," I was troubled, "Heaven is the goal of life. Sister said so."

"And how do you expect to go to Heaven without reason that makes you understand the justice and truth of the laws which govern good behavior? 'Sister says so,' is respect for authority, but your own mind must convince you of that truth. Our finite intelligence leads us to the infinite, and that is Heaven."

"The logos of Heaven!" Uncle Tom stood in the door. "Don't forget, Frank, that Hell is filled with muddled metaphysicians."

The house reverberated with Aunt Constance's voice. She had certainly given Monsignor Kieran a proper dressing-down. It was obvious she had also met several people and brought them home to dinner.

"I explained to Monsignor that she is a very gifted child, more like Papa than any of us. I said to him that he had shaken her faith." Aunt Constance was being highly dramatic. "Then I came right out and said, 'Bishop O'Hara's grandniece deserves better of St. Patrick's Church.' He turned beet-red at that. . . ."

The next morning I received Communion quietly, calmly, with the blessed conviction that God was truth, the source of all being. It was true He was in the Host. I willed in my mind to make Him welcome in my heart. Everything had changed. I lived in truth, in ever-widening circles of light.

That summer we were going to a hotel for July and August, so were home during the warm month of June. (Most of the houses on the north side of Pine Street were boarded-up and empty, as their owners had gone to the country.) Nana, who believed in fresh air with only slightly less fervor than she believed in God, took me on trolley rides. We started out on these journeys with a certain amount of heavy equipment, which included an umbrella, a coat for me and a sweater, this at ninety-eight degrees in the shade, a box of peppermints against car sickness, as well as religious medals that would protect us from the dangers of travel.

The best ride was the open trolley through Fairmount Park. Nana gave two nickels at the platform window. The trolley waited a long time for passengers, but finally we were off between banks of trees. The smell of the honeysuckle was intoxicating. There was a view of Lake Chamonix, with people rowing up and down in boats. Sometimes on the ride back we stopped at Belmont Mansion, where we ate vanilla ice cream on the wide veranda. It not only tasted like ambrosia, but it was wonderful to look at, served in a perfect geometrical mound. I tried to eat it from the bottom up to the point on top, but it always collapsed. It was like me to try to reverse Euclid every chance I got.

Sometimes we rode through the town, up into the impenetrable wilds of North Philadelphia. Once it was growing dark when we returned, and as we passed Baldwin's locomotive works, by the light of a blast furnace, I saw a man naked to the waist, his face twisted in apparent agony as he rammed a great block of steel into the roaring flames. I gasped in horror.

"Oh, Nana, why does he have to do that, the poor man?"

"God ordained it," Nana explained.

"God did not ordain it." I was furiously angry. My clear voice filled the streetcar, and people were smiling.

"Now, you hush." Nana ordered. Her lips were drawn tightly together.

I took up the argument as we got off the streetcar. She walked along Pine Street in cold silence, for Nana, like the Philadelphia Quakers, "believed in God and eight percent compound interest." She was a complete conservative and the workingman was divided from her by a tremendous gulf, which she fixed with her conscience by referring piously to "their station in life" and "God's holy will." Nana's favorite reading was history, she had an amazing knowledge of kings and queens, and she was passionately devoted to the arts, particularly the theatre; but despite her fine intelligence she believed till the day she died that no one should be permitted to vote unless he owned property. She was a firm advocate of charitable works for the poor, but she had no belief in equality; her brilliant friend and contemporary Agnes Repplier had identically the same views. Nana got around the social status of Christ by announcing that He belonged to the "Royal House of David"; in short, Jesus of Nazareth, being well born, in her mind belonged to "the genteel poor," which must have been an immense comfort.

"How," said Nina in disgust, "do you expect to have locomotives if that man doesn't do the heavy work?"

"Nana," I was thoughtful, "does he own the locomotive when he's finished building it?"

"Certainly not. The Baldwins own it, and the stockholders. How would the man get his wages if we didn't invest our capital?"

"The people who do the work should own the locomotive," I declared stubbornly.

"Tom O'Hara," and Nana was really annoyed, "has been talking socialism in front of you."

Nana led me weeping into the house. The world was comfortless and a place of peril. I was reacting to industrialism in a most Catholic way. I was appalled by the human entity reduced to its most marketable commodity–strength–and harnessed to a machine. I was demanding the immediate reconstruction of God's social body.

"I have never criticized Doc's family," Nana assured Mother, "but she's been listening to ideas. It's anarchy, that's what it is."

The first of July I was introduced to the re-paganization of society. We were at the Savoy in Chelsea, a tall, narrow frame hotel that overlooked the ocean. There were tremendous events going on in Europe–so tremendous that Aunt Caroline and Uncle Frank had canceled their annual passage, for war was believed inevitable. Americans turned their eyes away from a Europe which had lost its faith and its strength and now prepared to commit mass suicide.

It was a gay summer and we walked the Atlantic City boardwalk endlessly. The shops were filled with Rose O'Neill's Kewpie dolls; every child was making a collection of those angelic imps. The rolling chairs passed and repassed. The music of "Alexander's Ragtime Band" blared out on the boardwalk, salt-water taffy was made before our eyes, sand artists created masterpieces as we lined the boardwalk rails and threw money at them. There's something so stimulating to the human ego in tossing money.

The Savoy Hotel was filled with amusing people, and we were accepted at once. The ringleader in the fun was a tall, willowy Baltimore beauty, christened Maria, who had acquired the unique nickname of Ryde. She had a husky caressing voice and cold blue eyes. She smoked cigarettes openly and her talk was peppered with stories of other summers in Europe. I was devoted to her and used to sit quietly in a chair during auction bridge games—at the fearful stakes of a tenth of a cent a point—drinking in everything she said. I did not understand all of it for she had a way of dropping her eyes and drawling remarks that must have been outrageous, judging by the shrieks of laughter.

She was always talking about someone named Boothe. Once she regaled the group with a description of a dinner given for Maxine Elliott and Nat Goodwin, complete to a solid gold service. It seemed Boothe was the only man in Baltimore to own such a treasure.

"Maxine Elliott," I explained, delighted to have a piece of interesting information, "went to the Convent of Notre Dame in Boston."

"Yes, kiddo," Ryde said, lighting a Melachrino cigarette.

"She came to see Sister Mary Flora," I went on, "and Sister went in the chapel to pray about it, because Maxine Elliott was one of her favorite pupils. It broke her heart to do it, but she sent word to the parlor, 'I cannot see you, Maxine, because Mr. Goodwin is a divorced person, and you are living in sin.' "

I had indeed made a sensation. Ryde was extremely red, so were two of the other women. My mother looked daggers at me.

"Get your bucket and shovel and go down to the beach at once," she ordered, "and stop hanging around when we're playing cards."

I joined Pud, Jimmy and Alice Elzey in a sullen frame of mind. What had gone wrong with my story? I didn't want to play in the sand with children, and take bossing from Mary, their nursemaid. I wanted to listen to Ryde.

That night Mother explained my banishment. Everyone at the card table except herself was divorced and remarried. Mr. Boothe was Ryde's first husband.

"Mother, are all our friends living in sin?" I queried.

"No, certainly not. Divorce is all right for them. Catholics don't believe in divorce, that's all," she explained, a trifle worried.

"Mother, if it's a sin for us, it's a sin for them," I protested, finding myself in sympathy with the sinners.

"Now, you're only a little girl," Mother said. "Living in sin—you don't even know what that means."

I didn't, but the phrase was pithy with drama, and I liked to use it. I could not realize it, but it was apparent that people who were not Catholics were racing toward a new set of laws and customs, incompatible with all that I had been taught. A whole new social tissue was being built up in the world, which of necessity we had to reject. We had to live in this new society, and yet not be of it. The magnitude of the coming quarrel between Catholicism and the modern world dawned upon me (though I couldn't express my awareness) and I rebelled. I certainly didn't want to give up these fascinating people. I loved their gaiety, their bright worldliness.

Catholic Europe was suffering the same pangs. The inheritance of moral sanctions was dwindling. The old religious ideals that held society together were disintegrating. Men had lost their souls, and now were losing their wits. Sir Edward Grey was expressing more than a valedictory when he stood on an August night at a window of his room in the Foreign Office: "The lamps are going out all over Europe."

## 3

IN SEPTEMBER I RETURNED to the Convent of Notre Dame, an overgrown child, who was no longer a solitary. I said goodby to my companions of the previous year, for I had skipped a grade. My lopsided mind with its overdevelopment in certain areas and stunted growth in the more exact sciences, was to prove a great trial to Sister Helen Josephine. As I said, I could not do arithmetic; there was no human way she could penetrate my density. When all else failed I was frequently put in penance, which meant I had to stay after school and clean the blackboards, or I had to sit alone in the Holy Guardian Angels asking the Holy Ghost to enlighten my mind and strengthen my will. Once when the situation was desperate I was made to stand one half hour in front of my schoolmates, in the hope humiliation would inspire me to master short division. It did not, nor did a medal of St. Thomas Aquinas. My stupidity was absolute, impregnable; but in time it was ignored as my showy recitations of all other lessons helped my dear teachers out of many a tight spot when the supervisors came on their annual visit.

The war that had been only an echo in Chelsea—the war that was not America's business—was a crushing reality in the Convent of Notre Dame. The motherhouse at Namur had been captured by the invading German army on August twenty-fourth. Our small voices sang "La Brabonçonne," and "God Save the King," with passionate intensity. We were forbidden by Sister Superior to sing the stirring "Marseillaise," because it was a song of the anti-clerical rabble. It once had in it, we were told, the line, "May the blood of the aristocrats flow in the gutters of Paris."

"That is what Voltaire, the renegade Catholic, brought upon France—the 'Marseillaise,' and the infamous Danton," Sister Superior Adela du Sacré Coeur said with unusual venom. "Lose your faith, mes petites, and you destroy not only yourselves, but a world. Bad Catholics are the most dangerous people on earth." Her dark eyes blazed. "It is the bad Catholics all over Europe who make this cruel war. Pray for the faith. *Pray.*"

We started a spiritual bouquet for their Most Catholic Majesties King Albert and Queen Elizabeth of the Belgians, hoarding our prayers and good works, for it was to be sent to them by Christmas. Bazaars took place for the suffering Belgians. We heard of German atrocities and our infant fury knew no bounds. I fear if the Emperor of Germany had appeared in the hallway of the Convent of Notre Dame, the third grade children would have become assassins.

"Down with the Kaiser," we shouted at our play.

We went to the chapel every day now. Sister Superior in her stall called out the intentions: "We will pray for their Most Catholic Majesties King Albert and Queen Elizabeth and the royal children." "We offer this prayer in thanksgiving for our great American Ambassador to Belgium, Mr. Brand Whitlock." "We offer this prayer for a brave young American Catholic, Mr. Hugh Gibson, secretary of the American embassy, who at the risk of his own life, saved our sisters in Namur." "We offer this prayer . . ." And then came her final petition: "We offer this prayer for the German people of our own faith, and for all the Germans who suffer from this most cruel war." I was very young when I heard that gracious affirmation of the Church Universal and the divine precept, "Love your enemies," spoken in broken English by an Alsatian nun who remembered 1870 and, in a convent chapel in Philadelphia, prayed for the German people.

It was strange that with entirely Irish ancestry I should have been consumed with such passionate devotion to the Allied cause. My grandfather O'Hara was an intense Irish patriot, and a friend of Charles Stewart Parnell; among the family possessions was a full-length painting of Parnell, though it stood face to wall in the attic of the Twentieth Street house. I was never one to leave a mystery unexplored, so I sat looking in fascination at that handsome Norman-Irish face and the long slender hands.

"Aunt Constance, is he one of my ancestors?" I asked hopefully, wanting to claim him as my own.

"No, that's Charles Stewart Parnell. Poor Papa, he never got over it. He thought him one of the greatest men alive, but when he heard about Kitty O'Shea he had Jesse bring the picture up here. Papa never mentioned his name again."

I scented a romance, and Aunt Constance, forgetting my tender years, gratified my curiosity.

"Parnell would have brought Home Rule to Ireland, for even Gladstone knew his worth. He was an aristocrat, not this awful American version of an Irishman, brought upon us by the potato-famine Irish and bog-trotters. Peasants with their shillelaghs, their clay pipes, and the pig in the parlor. We, who are a kingly race! No, Parnell towered above Tim Healy and the rabble. That was the trouble. He was the Irish of the Castle, and the priests—though maybe I shouldn't say this—resented that. And then they had him: Parnell climbing in a woman's bedroom window, like a lovesick boy. We Irish don't allow for human frailities, so your grandfather turned against his friend. Parnell would have made us great. But the Irish! Too often is Ireland like the house swept and garnished to which seven worse devils enter in."

In the Seminary Monsignor Drumgoole prepared those famous lectures on the Allied cause that would bring him honors from the Allies and the undying hatred of the Irish-American clergy who still called the English "lobsterbacks" and saw them as the historic despoilers of their religion, homes and children. Monsignor quoted Newman and Bernard, Cardinal Vaughan, and the Church Universal. Cardinal Gibbons from Baltimore advised churchmen to be cautious; and the aging Archbishop Prendergast, with his deathly fear of Rome, said nothing.

In the Rector's room I heard the Hun described in the words of Newman: "They have little hair on their heads, and no beards." But, down the hall, Dr. Heuser, writing his biography of Canon Sheehan of Doneraile, would set me straight.

"The Reformation made one country strong in Europe: England. She solidified the Reformation in its greatest triumph. She gave us the Industrial Revolution—and universal discontent. She feared one thing—the Old Religion. Why has she persecuted Ireland relentlessly through the centuries? The faith—"

"But, Father Heuser," I said, quoting Nana, a passionate Anglophile, "everybody knows a drunken Irish parliament sold us to Queen Elizabeth."

"Such nonsense!" He threw down his pen. "My child, we Americans must keep out of this war. We left Europe. So now we are told we must finish German imperialism. We do that—so Clemenceau of France, a violent anti-clerical, can do worse damage."

Dr. Heuser enlightened me as to Irish history. My ancestral blood stirred in my veins. Cathleen ni Houlihan wove her dark enchantments. He spoke of the sons of Milesius—the four princes of Ulster. The Ireland of the monasteries appeared before my eyes, the land of scholars. I heard Deirdre of the Sorrows weeping.

Dr. Bruehl, the Seminary librarian, challenged Monsignor Drumgoole one afternoon as he was leaving for New York to speak at the Alliance Française: "So you want to make America go to war to save the Morgan loans? You'd finish the Church in Europe for the international bankers. Kill Catholic boys for Morgan's billion dollars. Wilson's pickle—that's all it is."

The rows at the Seminary were splenetic, passions mounted and eminent churchmen sulked like little boys and refused to speak to each other for weeks on end; but they all said their Office, and their Mass, and each in his own way was sure that he served the one true Church. I seem to remember that I was told of a professor who got so excited that he took to sleepwalking, his lanky form sepulchral in a nightshirt, his flowing white hair in wild disarray, and crying in a dreadful voice, "Mary, Mother of the Gael, have mercy on us."

We were as a family completely united, for a wonder, in being pro-Ally; but this state of agreement could not last long. My father became disgusted with Woodrow Wilson who was the idol of Twentieth Street, and declared that Theodore Roosevelt was the only man who could give America back her honor. My father yearned for Theodore Roosevelt to lead an army of American volunteers, of which he would be a member, straight to Paris. "We owe it to Lafayette—to Rochambeau."

"Roosevelt can unite us." My father was passionate about it. "This schoolteacher, this Presbyterian dominie in the White House, makes us the laughingstock of the world."

The chaos of a world did not interrupt the Sisters of Notre Dame de Namur in their main business, which was to preside over what they regarded as a whirlwind of childish savagery, corruption and sin, and somehow educate this unpromising material. Perils grew darker and battles more furious, and no one knew if there would be glory at the end; but there was no lag in the order and discipline and the tremendous pressure of knowledge that certainly was going into our heads.

The unique feature of Catholic education is that its heart and core is based on the sublime truth that all things flow from God not by any fatalistic act of necessity but in accordance with His intelligent purpose and by an act of free creation.

All Catholic educators have an almost fanatic desire to create loyal citizens. We learned civics and American history in the primary department. We rose from our knees slightly groggy from prayer and pledged allegiance to the flag. We were delivered our own newspaper, *Current Events*—an admirable and concise paper dealing with the news of the world—and we were expected to give intelligent comment on what we read.

"Love of God—Love of country," formed the cornerstone on which the Sisters based their whole concept of education. Citizenship in the United States of America was a high privilege demanding service from us, loyalty, obedience to its laws and, because we were young citizens of a democracy, intelligent cooperation and unceasing vigilance.

This was all the more remarkable, because in my youth the majority of the Sisters were foreign-born. The high and holy days of the Church were celebrated with no more temporal splendor than were the anniversaries of George Washington and

Abraham Lincoln. The Constitution of the United States was memorized article by article. We were almost made to feel the drama of Constitution Summer in Philadelphia, the discouragement, the long tedium of the sessions, the rabble shouting curses through the open windows of Independence Hall; and little children were taught to realize the miracle of the Constitution, its identity with the most deeply held of Catholic dogmas—the dignity of man and the worth of the individual human soul.

The main advantage of the Institute of Notre Dame de Namur was that its foundress, Blessed Mère Julie Billiart, had believed in educating her daughters for the world. The startling proposition of females earning their own living was dinned into our ears when we were still infants. Talents were polished like jewels, aptitudes developed, and there never was an iota of nonsense uttered about sitting in the parlor with our embroidery hoops and using our convent accomplishments to catch a solvent husband. It may be a trick of memory, but it seems to me that our teachers assumed we would all grow up to be old maids, our parents would become penniless, and only what the Sisters of Notre Dame could cram in our heads would save us from destitution.

The fact that we could become mothers and wives—certainly the ideal solution for all women—was never impressed upon us. A few of us might be called to religion, but we were made to realize that such a high estate was only for a chosen few. Our vocation was breadwinning, and I regard it as a very great grace that, despite the bourgeois tradition of most of the Sisters, they had such a high regard for the strength of the Catholic faith which they were inculcating in us that they gave us no fears or no limits to the professions we might choose. Concert pianists were trained by Sister Marie des Anges, future actresses by Sister Julie du Saint Edward. The writing of books was a glorious vocation, and if a child could put down one sentence with promise, she was surrounded by mentors to bring the talent to full flower. Little geniuses who could master those awful Dubb's arithmetic books—even their tan and pale green covers and red lettering induced mental biliousness in me—were not taught to be mere bookkeepers, but a career in finance was held before their eyes.

The Sisters of Notre Dame de Namur encouraged ambition and competition. We lived for the blue stars and the gold stars that ornamented our exercise books. That first place at recitation was worth all the effort—just to stand an intellectual leader, and glibly answer the questions, made a child dizzy with power. And pride always came before a fall, for the nuns understood the danger-moment in competition, and slyly phrased a question in an unexpected way, and down a place we went, and if we took it badly the Sister always saw to it that our descent was swift and our humiliation complete.

I remember one afternoon when I was in the third grade Sister Helen Josephine decided that we should write a composition. She was a nervous, pretty young nun who tenderly loved ideal children, and had to deal with real children; her life was one long succession of shocks. She had learned to be afraid of our realism which was sometimes brutal if we were given the choice of subjects, so she read us lovely stories, and we wrote our versions of them. This day she must have been tired of striving to make us into dream children, and we were told to write on subjects of our own choosing.

The little girls groaned; after a few moments of concentration, a few burst into tears. Sister Helen Josephine refused to give aid or comfort. I was as stunned as the others and sat sucking my pen.

Then an idea came to me. I shook with the glory of creation as I endeavored to get every word right. I could see it all in my mind, and it was my awe-inspiring task to make others see it. I forgot everything else. I reached into space for a word—and another—and another. It was beautiful. The universe spread out all ways to make room for this new act of creation. It was finished. The last line had been written. My copybook was a mass of blots, ink dyed my fingers and the front of my dress. Sister Helen Josephine stood beside my desk while the children stared in bewilderment.

I was too spent and too happy to care what happened. Now I knew what to do with my imagination.

Sister Helen Josephine announced, "Constance has written a composition. We will say nothing of the blots and the spelling, for the composition itself has merit."

Sister Helen Josephine herself affixed a gold star on my effort. Her face was flushed with pleasure. My companions looked at me in disgust. Once again I had become a nonconformist; I was a monster who liked to write compositions. Then the instinctive group loyalty of children toward one of their own came to the fore as Sister announced:

"Constance and I are going to Sister Superior. You are on your honor to keep complete silence."

"Sister, she didn't do anything," Anna Pauline Coll pleaded. "You put a gold star on the composition. She only made a few little blots. Her mother won't mind about her dress."

A visit to Sister Superior meant one thing—a crime so unspeakable that even young lady graduates might not survive a trip to her office. It was known that a few who crossed her threshold had appeared in school no more. A child sent alone to Sister Superior was a sinner, but a child accompanied to her office by her teacher was a public criminal.

"Constance is not being punished," said Sister Helen Josephine, carefully holding the composition book open to the place where the gold star gleamed. "She has a Talent."

Sister Superior Adela du Sacré Coeur was so overcome by her reading of this gem that she paced the floor of her office.

"Sister, you are right. This is a Talent. We must guard against pride—but to encourage the dear child to develop this gift is another thing. That we must do."

Sister Helen Josephine went back to her classroom, and I was left alone with Sister Superior who immediately enrolled me as a lady of letters. She read me the parable of the talents; from somewhere she found a little traveling clock and presented it to me with a stern lecture on how much time it was going to take to perfect my gift.

"You are responsible for it even after you are dead," she explained, "because you can do dreadful damage with this gift. Now, you are not nearly pious enough. Non, ma petite, so we have work to do, for Notre Dame, your convent, will be blamed if your religion is not strong enough to protect your talent."

Sister Helen Josephine kept me after school that afternoon to copy my composition in a brand-new exercise book. It was grueling work, and I commenced to see certain inadequacies in my creative effort. I pointed these out to Sister.

"I hope you will never be entirely pleased with anything you write, child," she explained. "That's death to a talent."

I certainly had selected a grim calling.

"Sister," I called from my desk, worn out with this dreadful business of authorship, "I'm going on the stage."

"No, you're not—not after this," she argued. "The Catholic Church in this country needs gifted writers."

I handed her the neatly copied composition to which she put another gold star.

"Sister," I asked, "who writes the plays for the actors?"

"Dramatic authors. There are great ones, of course, like Shakespeare. Why?"

"I'm going to write plays," I informed her gravely.

"Now, Constance, that will be very difficult," she cautioned.

"I could learn how to write them here. I could do the plays for the convent."

"But, dear, the Sisters write those." Sister Helen Josephine was worried.

"Yes, but the ones the Sisters write aren't very good," I reminded her, consumed with earnestness. "I could do much better."

Sister Helen Josephine was smiling at me, and I suddenly realized that under this black veil and demure white coif Sister was a young woman, human and lovable. The Sisters of Notre Dame de Namur had a strict detachment, and they seldom embraced us or encouraged our emotionalism, but Sister was hugging me tight, and like all undemonstrative children I thrilled to affection.

"Darling, I think the plays nuns write are simply awful, but

I'll not let you break your heart trying to be the convent dramatist. The Sisters don't know how bad their plays are—and they'd never give you a chance."

On May 7, 1915, the *Lusitania* was sunk by a German submarine. My father waited for the declaration of war. It did not come. Once I heard him say, "I'll give up my citizenship. I'll swear allegiance to the Crown of Great Britain. A man cannot take this." His cough shook the house. "That letter-writing Wilson. He should be impeached. The United States of America will never recover from this cowardice."

I knew he was trying for a commission in the British Army, this frail patriot with the seeds of death in him. He went to see Cardinal Gibbons in Baltimore, to urge him to make a statement separating Catholics from Wilson's shame; and the Cardinal sat at lunch with the nephew of his old friend Bishop O'Hara and urged patience, and gave him a Jubilee medal to take home to his little girl. The Cardinal was far more interested in the spiritual barricades being built by nuns in quiet Catholic schools than in the world of diplomacy he knew so well.

The Sisters of Notre Dame sensed the uneasiness in their children, and they struggled valiantly to protect us, to plant the faith deep in our hearts. There was the month of May, when every classroom had its altar dedicated to the Blessed Mother, sweet with spring flowers and vigil lights, but most important of all was the May Procession in the garden, with the children all in white, wreaths of flowers on their heads. Each class was followed by its own banner, and to carry a banner meant that you were not only an intellectual giant but a saint. There is no honor in the world comparable to carrying a banner in the May Procession in the garden of the Convent of Notre Dame. I should know, for I carried it just once. The lights spelling out your name over a theatre marquee are dim indeed compared to the luminous glory of the carrying of a banner that proclaims your heroic virtue to the world—the blessed world of the garden of Notre Dame.

The great moment of the procession was delayed till the costume of every child was inspected to see that not one bit of chest showed, that our sleeves covered the wrist, and that stockings were long; if there were any immodesties in our costume the good Sisters covered up the occasions of sin with tissue paper. The adults stood around the garden, and pre-school children were permitted to watch. Around and around we went, singing hymns, pausing for litanies, until the moment came when the young lady graduate who was a model of all virtues, slowly and reverently walked on the anaemic grass toward Our Lady's statue, followed by two small children bearing a pale blue velvet cushion on which reposed a gorgeous wreath. A bench was drawn up beside the statue, and the young lady graduate swept into her curtsy. There was a hush, and then carefully the graduate lifted her floor-length white skirts, and mounted the bench. No one could see so much as an ankle, as she reached up—teetering a bit nervously on her precarious perch—to crown the Blessed Mother, while we sang, "Mu-ther dearest, Mu-ther fairest," right through our noses.

There may have been times when the Sisters made it seem as if Christ died upon that crucifix for respectability, and not Redemption; but the Mother of God they couldn't spoil. She was the Queen of Heaven, with her hands held out for all the faltering, sinning children of the world. There was no prayer she didn't hear, for to say her name was to bring peace to a stormy heart. We saw straight through the humbug of the nuns and all those little niggling rules about modesty, for Mary, the Mother of God, asked us to become her little beggars of grace, pouring our love out toward her in a splendid abundance. We felt that Mary didn't give a hoot for our curtsies and our elegant ways, she wanted to hold us in her arms. We could not quite grasp whose arms were extended wide to us upon a cross of pain, but those arms which held her broken Son, all convent children know them well.

Mary is so close to earth, her robes just out of reach of the hands of a child. Somehow we knew that we were carried with her into the house of Zachary and Elizabeth, and we quickened with Christ, and heard the first "Magnificat." In the month of

May she is present at her processions, amused and loving toward the dear nuns who have rehearsed all the careful ceremony, but fearful that her little ones will be too tired to look into her eyes. She stands there with the bishops and the monsignors looking wistful, till one child sees her, and a Voice speaks:

"You know My Mother, My little one?"

No one hears but a child, for bishops are afraid of voices and apparitions. It means all sorts of Church machinery, and there is such a chance of scandal. The bishops are not the men to understand the miracle of a child and Mary; there are too many administrative problems in the Church Temporal. Mary was used to the Apostles who took themselves seriously, so she has a special and tolerant affection for bishops. But children are indispensable, for she keeps their childhood in her heart to give her Son.

The last week of May we had examinations. We sat at our blue desks with long sheets of foolscap before us, a clean blotter, a new pen, our morning prayers said, and then doom was upon us, for Sister Helen Josephine was handing out the examination questions. Every child was tense with fear, and then a look of relief would come on one young face, while another would sit solemn with sorrow, helpless before failure. Sister would return to her desk, click the signal—and the only sound was the fierce scratching of pens and the heavy breathing of intellectual athletes fighting against time. The birds in the convent garden poured out glorious songs, and the trees in Rittenhouse Square were thick with foliage, the heavy scent of lilacs came in the open windows. . . .

In the afternoon there was another examination. It continued that way for one whole week. On Friday morning, it was mathematics.

I knew the worst when I saw Sister Helen Josephine's stricken face. She had been giving me little secret smiles of approbation all week. There was a council as to whether I could be promoted, but Sister Ignatius Julie felt sure she could teach me long division. There was a slight intimation that as I never failed in any other subject, the right teaching method had not been found.

I was safe, but, as Sister Helen Josephine told me sorrowfully, "This failure in arithmetic pulls down your general average." She had the soundly Catholic idea that a child could climb out beyond its limitations. "Dear, what on earth are we going to do with you?"

## 4

THAT WAS THE JUNE my father and I went to Cape May Point to see Dr. Herman Heuser who was convalescing in a white cottage belonging to the convent across the road. The Sisters were his willing slaves and Father Heuser was going a bit mad with their smothering attentions.

"Peccavi—peccavi," he said as we sat on the porch. "These dear females mistake an aging theologian for St. Aloysius Gonzaga. We are about to be served not a simple luncheon but a Roman banquet. The Catholic sisterhood has always been defective in its understanding of moderation when they feed the clergy."

I sat there looking out to sea. It was a day of wind and scudding clouds and the waves broke with a splendid roar. Great piles of green seaweed had been tossed on the beach by tumultuous surf. The marsh grass waved, and sea gulls flew everywhere; out beyond the breakers a porpoise rose and squirted a geyser of water toward a plumed cloud. There was the hull of an old ship rotting in the boiling waters, ghost of a bygone tragedy. The uncontaminated breezes blew against my face, and I inhaled the Atlantic vapors in a lonely place by the sea—a fatal thing for a Celt to do, for the vapors turn us into mystics, poets and unemployables.

The luncheon was as Dr. Heuser predicted and I enjoyed much more looking out the window where the long, high horizon was unbroken by a sail and tasting this day of light and shade on my palate. Sister stood worrying over me, so I had to eat stewed chicken and dumplings, chocolate cake, and all sorts of sundries.

My father and Dr. Heuser were arguing over medicine and having a splendid time. It was one of those conversations I liked, but Sister stood in the door beckoning to me, and I was taken over to the convent. They made me take off my dress and lie down on Reverend Mother's big comfortable bed. I could see almost to Lewes, Delaware, across the surging waters. The beach at the Point was alive with birds which gave strange eerie cries. It would have been silly to nap with the cool pillows caressing my cheeks, when everywhere I looked there was sea and sky. I could see Dr. Heuser's cottage with the little gold cross on the front door, and the fickle sun made its windows blink like signal fires. I had never been so happy in all my life.

Sister came to waken me. She was a young nun with a soft Irish voice, and she carried over her arm a collection of garments that mystified me. I suddenly realized it was a flannel bathing dress with great full bloomers, a pair of long black stockings, and a straw bonnet.

"Now, you put these on, dear," she said, "and I'll get on my bathing suit, then Sister and you and I will go swimming."

I was engulfed in these garments which flapped around my feet. The two nuns joined me, wearing black flannel suits that covered their ankles and large straw hats tied so that no one could catch a glimpse of their faces. Their eyes were shining.

"Father Heuser wanted us to go in swimming with you; of course we never go bathing while the dear man is staying at the cottage. Reverend Mother wouldn't like it," one of them explained to me.

Sister whispered to her companion, for the stockings were flopping down my legs.

"Constance hasn't any . . . you see, Sister," she said in a distressed tone.

I was rather worried, for it always had seemed to me that physically I was entire. Sister laughed at my anxious face.

"You see, dear, you're too little to wear them."

"Oh, I don't wear stockings when I go swimming," I explained, relieved.

Sister acted as if I had said something not quite nice. She whispered again to the other nun, who left the room and returned with tapes. They yanked up my stockings, wound the cording around my legs, and then Sister made it clear.

"You're too little to wear . . . well, corsets, so you had no garters to hold up your stockings."

My companions were wearing whalebone corsets with all their other garments. I am sure they were so weighted down that they were in mortal danger of sinking without a trace.

"Father's not on the porch, Sister," the young nun called.

They each took one of my hands, and we tore over the beach and out into the ice-cold sea. I gasped and screamed with the shock, but they pushed me into a big breaker and held me there till I tingled. They had eyes as young as my own. Their laughter rang out as they churned up the water with their hands. We could not swim with all our engulfing clothes, but we stood waist-high in the ocean waiting for a breaker to hit us. I forgot, and came charging into shore on one, and my straw bonnet floated out to sea. The Sisters were plainly worried at this loss of community property, but were too polite to complain.

An America which loves youth should discover the cloister, for nuns never grow old. They keep the clear eyes of good little girls all their lives; and, though many of them know great suffering, all is absorbed in simplicity and resignation. They are walled in by ramparts of order and discipline, they may grow impervious to certain levels of human experience, but I remember the goodness and the happiness of those two nuns bathing with me in Cape May—so much God's children that they could keep their innocent gaiety—as one of the most beautiful gifts of Catholicity. With such women it would always be possible to believe in the

Kingdom of Heaven. I laughed into the china-blue eyes of the young Irish nun, and we splashed each other with abandon, and suddenly she lifted me, great leggy child that I was, straight out of the ocean, and tipped me over on the sand.

My father had hired a noisy automobile whose engine made tremendous rocketing explosions as we rode through Cape May. What a beautiful little town it was, with the great elms of Washington Street and hydrangea bushes in the gardens of white wooden houses that were thick with wisteria vines. We stood before the old O'Hara cottage on Jackson Street, and I could feel my grandmother, whom I had never seen, presiding over that tumultuous family with gentle calm. I could almost see my grandfather turning the corner like a dancing master in his white linen suit. My father showed me Lily Langtry's cottage on Stockton Street, and I could understand what it meant to a susceptible boy to see the Jersey Lily pass by, smiling under her ruffled parasol with Kyrle Bellew by her side. The long rambling Congress Hall with its high white pillars was then empty and deserted—an ante-bellum relic—with the rats playing in its long corridors; but it was filled with memories of gay summer evenings. There is some charm to Cape May that eludes the pen, for it is only a sleepy south Jersey town, half colonial, half the weird architecture of President Grant's America; yet once you become accustomed to Cape May it is impossible to get along without it. The Cape weaves a spell, no matter how long you are away—you wonder why you should have bothered to travel when you have this tiny point of land jutting into the Atlantic Ocean as your own.

This was my first day at Cape May. It was as if nothing much else had ever happened to me.

That summer Dr. Heuser persuaded my father to send me out to his sister, Mother Hildegarde, at the Convent of Mercy in Merion. I was a child of the town, and now had my first taste of country. A gentle old cow used to move among the summer boarders complacently, and I accompanied the determined little German lay-sister when she milked it; and the cow would look at her mournfully as she wrung the last drop of milk from its udder with Prussian ferocity. I remember the Sisters of Mercy as being sensible human women with enormous kindness and understanding of children. There was a blind girl among us, and they treated her just like one of us, with no emphasis on her affliction. We children were encouraged to describe things to her; the fields, the flowers, the colors of vestments in the chapel at Mass. I can see her yet—and it makes the tears sting my eyes—playing Blindman's Buff and going around in circles with her good patient face shining with happiness.

The whole environment of the Convent of Mercy was filled with common sense and realism. There was not an iota of false piety or religiosity to stamp out the love of God by formalisms and conventions. The big, clean, white-walled convent was open to the sun and air, and I never saw any tight-lipped nuns. There was a true devotion about it all, and not a trace of melodrama. It had an air of health and sanity and unforced goodness which kept my dramatic imagination subdued, and I slept soundly at night, waking up rested and happy when the convent bell rang.

I came home from the Convent of Mercy that summer grown a few more inches, relaxed and at peace. The Sisters had taught me the humanism of religion. But in the Convent of Notre Dame poor old Sister Perpetua still lit countless vigil lights before the Infant of Prague, with her dark foreign face screwed up in tremendous misery. I was in a new classroom facing the convent garden. Sister Ignatius Julie, in less time than it takes to tell, actually got the principles of long division in my head. She was a comfortable happy nun, whose bushy eyebrows had turned gray, the only way we could guess she was old. I felt like a mental giant when I had grasped long division, and it made Sister Ignatius Julie glow with pride. There had to be an extraordinary ability in anyone who could teach me a mathematical formula; the miracle only happened once in all my schooldays.

This was the year I commenced not to take school too seriously, as I became aware of many other things in the world about me. My mother and I began to be friends. I remember her then as tall and stately with an arrogant tilt to her head, and a straight back. She had quantities of red-gold hair, and greenish gray eyes. She was a perfectionist, with exquisite taste in all material things. The beautiful old pieces of furniture in the Pine Street house were placed to advantage. There were no bad spots or concessions to the current mode in home decorations. She bought like a connoisseur, with a driving brutal skill at acquiring a bargain. She bought nothing quickly and never spent much money—for we never had much money. I have spent whole afternoons with her tracking down a piece of china in an antique shop, or rummaging through remnant bins for some of the fine laces she could spot at a glance.

She loathed anything commonplace, and had a contempt for bourgeois and conventional standards that was years ahead of her time. Intensity and enthusiasm bored her, and her sense of humour is so keen that I have seldom seen her without an ironic smile on her lips. My mother believed in brains, for her taste was so unfalteringly good that she agreed with Montaigne, "Whatever are the benefits of fortune they yet require a palate fit to relish and taste them." She never ceased to have faith that my father and I were equipped with superb mental endowments —and on that account were worth every sacrifice.

"Thank God," she often said, "I'm not married to a dull conventional man, or the mother of a boring normal child." In that respect, at least, I never failed her!

My mother's ambitions for me conflicted with the aims of the Convent of Notre Dame. She heard my catechism with a wry smile that used to make me feel ridiculous. My mother was not a bad Catholic. She simply had a reasonable mind which had never been even remotely exposed to the superb logic of Catholic dogma but only to sentimental platitudes and dreary piety. A formal rejection would have meant scenes, and my mother detested vulgarities. So she became indifferent. She was born to be a lover of Catholic liturgy, her keen mind was created to go below the surface into the rationality of Catholic truth. My father could not help her, because his soul was restored from an interior spring. "All the glory of the King's daughter is within . . ." External beauty of worship meant a great deal to him, but he was serene before the lopped-off horror of Low Mass at St. Patrick's. He knew priests of vast theological learning and infinite social grace; but the hundreds of shambling seculars who sought his ministrations affected his faith not one bit. Some of them were eccentrics, a few drunkards, but to him they were all dispensers of the Sacraments—men who walked a hard and difficult road. He was patient with their old-womanish ailments, their waspish dispositions, and their complete lack of gratitude. A group of them were known as "Dr. O'Hara's Zoo," and these faltering men he loved the best. He could forgive a priest anything but clerical unction, a trait he despised. He called it "the Monsignor's disease." My father was never an alien in any world. He took his whole being with him everywhere.

We were an Irish Catholic family living in the midst of the "charmed circle" in Philadelphia, but not of it. The great names and great fortunes of the city clustered around the Rittenhouse Square section in those days. I was a sensitive child and felt my isolation keenly. It was not that my mother was raising me to be a snob, for she detested the bombast of false superiority, but she did believe that to touch mediocrity was to touch pitch, and that her child must rise above the common herd. In consequence I was very nearly without a friend. The one Catholic child in the neighborhood belonged to a famous family of dressmakers, and she would identify the social position of the children in the Square with such reverence in her voice that I squirmed in irritation.

Philadelphia seems to me a strange unhappy city to grow up in, yet one side of my nature was fiercely attracted to its quiet security. It offered great rewards to the people it accepted as its own. It was never vulgar or blatant; its richest citizens drew up to the Girard Trust Company in ancient wheezing town cars, wearing what they pleased, and that was always far from fashionable. Philadelphia, in my youth, laughed right heartily at Eva Stotesbury, her diamond dog collar and her Rolls-Royce with two men on the box. The Wideners with their mansion at Elkins Park would have been dismissed as utter parvenus, except that Joe Widener had married Albert Pancoast's daughter Ella, which helped. No one ever forgot to mention that the Wideners had been butchers. "A hundred years is but a day in the memory of a Philadelphian," as someone has said.

There was always an air about Philadelphia as if some of its most successful citizens were invited to its council tables, but not its dinner tables. A few of the Irish with their passionate snobbery had tried to crash the citadel, but they spent their money fruitlessly, broke their hearts, and ruined their children's lives. This inner world was not without charm; some of the finest minds in America, the keenest wits were of this circle. It stretched out into every field of human endeavor in the city, dominating the University, the Academy of Fine Arts, accepting new blood and making no crass demands about money. No one could buy his way into this strange American society that was so typically British, and in that respect it was admirable.

It offered a beautiful life and fair rewards, but it demanded conformity. This world was not for me, but it infected me in such a way that I could not turn for human happiness to the Catholic world into which I had been born. Philadelphia taught me to be ashamed of my richest endowment. And yet it was my home! I knew Philadelphia was possibly as Protestant as any American city and that Catholics there never rose to great eminence from the worldly point of view. The knowledge consumed me with anger and rebellion.

The one Catholic who made me feel better about the situation was Miss Agnes Repplier. She *was* Philadelphia—and it was her co-religionists who rejected this witty and wonderful woman, not the inner circle where she was a fêted and sought-after personage. When I was a child she had an apartment with her brother Louis and her sister Mary at Twenty-first and Pine Streets. She was a slight woman with keen gray eyes behind nose-glasses that gave her a Pecksniffian expression and she had then a nervous jerk to her head. Miss Mary tutored me in French, for that was a language my mother insisted on, and each time I went to the Reppliers Miss Mary, who was a dear affectionate old lady, used to bring me in to Louis and Agnes, and after I made my curtsies, tell me how her father John George

Repplier had given my greatuncle Bishop O'Hara his ceremonial robes and his ring. Louis Repplier sat looking at me like a gentle spaniel, Miss Agnes' head jerked in bored annoyance and I writhed in shame.

"Why did your father do that, Miss Mary?" I burst out on the twentieth rendition of this story. "The O'Haras are not deserving poor."

A gleam of delighted amusement came in Agnes Repplier's eyes and she roared with startlingly robust laughter. I had become an individual, and I could have won her friendship then and there, but I was too shy. I heard that Miss Repplier wrote books, and that is how I became a member of the Philadelphia City Institute Library. The librarian looked like Agnes Repplier, and gaunt gentle old men read books beside a pot-bellied coal-burning stove. The librarian was appalled at my choice of books, assuring me I couldn't possibly understand them. I read straight through Miss Repplier's collections of essays; occasionally I was stirred out of my genuine boredom at her pedantry by a jeweled and perfect phrase of such scathing wit that I yearned to tell her how much I liked it.

I owe my rejection of children's books and my introduction to the world's great literature to my curiosity about Miss Agnes Repplier. I discovered Scott and tossed him aside for Dickens; then I found Thackeray and, one magnificent afternoon, Victor Hugo's *Les Misérables.* I studied my lessons superficially, but I commenced to read a book a day. I sneaked books to bed with me, and lit the Welsbach burner when my mother and father had gone to bed; then, when I was caught at that, retired to the bathroom and read for hours. Finally when that was forbidden I took my father's flashlight to bed with me and read beneath the covers. I ruined my eyes and never had quite enough sleep, but that sudden immersion in the world of books, with a new discovery on every page, is a delight no human being should miss.

The Sisters of Notre Dame had no idea I was heading for trouble; on the surface a trick memory enabled me to know my lessons, and the enormous amount of reading I was doing enriched my mind to the extent that I always knew a little more about the subject than was in the lesson book. The Sisters would have been pained to learn that I was bored with convent school and that the innocent and intense faith of my early childhood was being replaced by something ugly and unnatural, for I had commenced to live on a relatively superficial level of consciousness, governed by intellectual appetites and a craving for the ideal material life in which my unfettered ego would rise to power and glory.

I lived alone, apart from my nine- and ten-year-old companions, and was too shrewd to share my impressive dreams with children. They would have been amused indeed to know that I visualized the day when my name would go up in lights over the old South Broad Street Theatre, when proud stiff-necked Philadelphia would be at my feet. I sat impassive and docile in school, seeing the First City Troop galloping around South Penn Square to meet my train at Broad Street Station. I saw stacks of books coming from the printing press, bearing my name, but that was only my second-best dream. The dream that came before all else was a theatre with the footlights lunging at my teeth and hair, as I bowed and bowed to thunderous applause. The good nuns tried to humble my hungry spirit in the dust of history, to exalt the majesty of God. They tried to show me the great lights of the City of God—but I had turned to the artificially lit City of Man.

Every month or so my father and I went to the dark old Jesuit church of St. Joseph, and on the eve of great feast days my mother accompanied us. I duly confessed my sins of temper and disobedience—nice little girl sins—and never thought to reveal the mad fantasies that were slowly and surely destroying my spiritual vitality.

There were other distractions than books, for the old silent movies where my father and I went each Saturday afternoon were places of enchantment to me. In the morning my father's office was filled with nuns, but the afternoon was mine. Saturday was his happiest morning of the week, for the nuns brought their doctor presents, exquisite pieces of hand embroidery, crochet work, bedroom slippers. All the gentleness and sweetness of his nature came out as he dealt with the physical ills of these modest abashed women. In their dear and innocent way they had crushes on their doctor, and every once in a while we would hear one of them chirrup, "Doctor, did you know your name Michael means 'like unto God'?" What mere man could resist being the center of a spiritual harem? Saturday mornings my father was never tired, despite the crowd. He was never shrewd about investments, save this one, for in many convents ancient nuns are praying for his soul to this day, and he knew the priests would forget.

He would go off on his calls, a happy man, and return early in the afternoon with the odor of cloves on his breath. He had stopped at the Ritz for a quick one, or maybe a couple, and announced gaily, "What enters in at the lips cannot sully the soul."

Those afternoons, he and I would stop at the Nineteenth Street Market, eat a plate of raw oysters, and then go on to the old Stanley Theatre at Sixteenth and Market. I cannot remember all the movies we saw. I loved Wallace Reid and Norma Talmadge and Marguerite Clark. Mary Pickford inspired me with unholy contempt. Alla Nazimova was a real favorite, Elsie Ferguson another. As for Marie Doro and Elliot Dexter, they were superlative. Francis X. Bushman and Beverly Bayne annoyed me. I could not share my father's enthusiasm for William S. Hart, though I liked it when the horses went into action and there was shooting. There was a great deal of impassioned lovemaking in the movies which bored me. Everything was about love, and I was sure there were other emotions. Those silent-movie clinches in which the hero panted and the heroine heaved seemed to me absurd. Geraldine Farrar as Joan the Maid was different. It seemed logical and sensible to want to save France, and hear voices, and go to the stake for an ideal. That was theatre and drama as far as I was concerned, but Geraldine Farrar in *Carmen* failed me—for the kissing was excessive.

It was on one of these Saturdays that something happened to me that still fills me with fright, for it is without logical explanation. I was a sheltered child, who lived too much alone and in my own imagination, I was deeply intuitive and I sensed many things that had never been spoken before me. But I had never been exposed to an evil person in all my days.

My father and I were coming through Rittenhouse Square. It must have been close to seven o'clock, for we were hurrying to be on time for dinner. The sky was soft and blue, and I remember how happy my father looked, for he enjoyed our Saturday afternoons at the movies. Then in a split-second, a thought rocketed through my mind, "*There is no God.*" And the sky seemed to turn dun color, and I could not breathe. It was an experience and a perception I can never forget, for though I was only a child, yet I was bowed down with horror and desolation. Without a God there was no reason for even my childish sufferings. My will fought this terrifying mystique, and I found the words of the "Hail Mary" coming to my mind. And I remembered my father's revolver, lying neatly on a pile of handkerchiefs in his chiffonier drawer.

*There is no God. . . .* I prayed desperately, but my mind was shadowed with hideous doubt. I knew that what had happened to me was shocking and fearful and that if I talked about this experience to anyone I would be judged a monster child. I needed tenderness and love and to be taught, in Heraclitus' phrase, "to listen to the essence of things." It was too much for me to bear alone, for I had been shown in a swift unveiling the horror of a world without God, without hope, and in this perilous darkness a loved and cherished child walked without a friend. The world was joyless. The tensions and anxieties of adults began to affect me, and I became imperative and demanding. My happy little-girl talent of mockery became old and evil and spiteful. I learned to hate with intensity.

I knew somehow that Monsignor Drumgoole could help me, but I was too vain to disillusion him. I did not really know how to use the Sacrament of Penance, which is true of innumerable Catholics. I yearned to go into the convent chapel and pray, but then my companions would brand me "pious," a charge that is heinous to a convent child. I was never left alone long enough to go to church by myself, and thrash out my trouble before the Blessed Sacrament.

I got a little help in an unexpected way, for I was promoted to Sister Marion's class. She was a slight, dark-eyed nun whose frail body seemed consumed by intense fires. She had a blazing temper before our stupidities, and on secular subjects was dogmatic and irritable. However, on religion Sister Marion was inspired, for there emerged from behind every dull question and answer in the Baltimore Catechism, from behind all the Old Testament stories in Bible History—the figure of Christ the Lord.

I do not think any of us had ever before been so conscious of the humanity of Jesus Christ, nor how lovable He was. Sister Marion never once struck a false note of silly sentimental piety. She took us to the hillside cave in Bethlehem. We went on the flight into Egypt, sharing Mary's fears. We had that magnificent intimation of the omnipotent God in that strange, almost cruel answer when she found Him in the Temple: "Did you not know that I must be about my Father's business." She took us into the hidden years at Nazareth, and we almost heard Him speak in His Aramaic tongue, loved His quick sensitive nature responsive to every touch of joy or pain. Sister Marion was healing the dreadful wound in my soul, and I never minded when her quick temper mastered her as I stood at the blackboard doing fractions, and she made an example of me with her cutting sarcasms.

Sister Marion made me realize that holiness was essentially the experiencing of divine things. I hung around her desk, to her evident displeasure. She did not welcome childish confidences, and so I was pleased with the eagerness in her eyes when I told her I was going to see Sarah Bernhardt during the Christmas holidays.

In December of 1916 Sarah Bernhardt, who recently had had her leg amputated, was making her farewell appearance—one of those many farewell tours—at the Metropolitan Opera House, Broad and Poplar Streets. The building was known as Oscar Hammerstein's "white elephant," because Philadelphians simply would not go north of Market Street for the arts. I had heard my father tell how he had gone with hundreds of other enthusiasts to meet Bernhardt's train in 1911, and paraded down Broad Street before her carriage. Nana was taking me and she had the best seats; for days before the event I assembled my wardrobe, admiring my red coat with the astrakhan bands, and the black beaver hat with the red bird. I took out my white kid gloves, my ribbed silk stockings to inspect them, as if somehow Bernhardt were going to see me. I yearned for silk underwear as appropriate to the occasion, for the long flannel drawers worn under my cambric panties seemed dreary, respectable, and most un-French.

The great night came, for Nana, the most conventional of women, saw nothing unusual in taking a child to the theatre at night—not for Bernhardt. Nana in her sealskin coat looked every inch the proper Philadelphian as we entered with all the women in their handsome evening gowns and the men in toppers and tail coats. We were right down front and the excitement was unbearable.

"You will remember this all your life," Nana said, and her eyes were misty.

She told me of the great Bernhardt performances she had seen, and described *La Tosca* as the most memorable experience of her life. Now Bernhardt could not walk; old and ill, she had come to us to recoup her fortune.

The lights went down. Bernhardt was doing the death of Cleopatra, speaking half in French, half in English, and all I could see was a woman with heavily made-up eyes, whose voice was old, lying perfectly still, making stilted gestures. Bernhardt was boring me, failing me. I looked at Nana. Her lips were parted, she was transported. I commenced to feel restless, pins and needles stabbing my legs. It seemed to go on forever. Applause rocked the theatre. I could not speak to Nana between the acts, I was so disappointed. The curtain went up again and this time Bernhardt was propped against a tree in a soldier's suit. I was interested, but not enraptured. There was one moment when she whispered, and I felt my spine tingle; but my French was not expert enough to follow her without making translations in my mind.

She had chosen, as her last scene, the death of Camille. I was yawning and irritable when the curtain went up—and then suddenly I understood. This was not an old woman lying on a bed, for I could see Bernhardt's face and it was unlined. The startling eyes drawing me to her were blazing with fever and death—but they were the passionate eyes of youth. She cried, "Armand! Armand!" and there were harps in the air and the golden voice filled the theatre. It was too marvelous and too beautiful to live through; I was dying with Bernhardt on that stage.

It was over, and a staid Philadelphia audience was on its feet. Cheers rang through the house. "La glorieuse blessée," they called. Nana was bravely waving her handkerchief, the tears running down her cheeks, and people smiled at an emotional child, who had forgotten all self-consciousness, shouting: "Vive la Sarah Bernhardt! Vive la France!"

And then we had to go out into the sharp December air of a Philadelphia night, into a world that was practical and filled with the tensions of the commonplace.

"Never forget Sarah Bernhardt," Nana admonished. "That is the only way an actress can live—in your memory. She's older than I am, poor Sarah."

I was indignant, for it seemed to me that such a woman had no age, and I tried to point that out, as the cab drew near Pine Street; but Nana was so delighted that her investment in my culture had been entirely successful, she refused to get into one of our arguments.

"You know," she said, "I thought for a while you weren't interested. Imagine my granddaughter bored at Sarah Bernhardt!"

I remember that Sister Marion questioned me closely about Bernhardt, and in a dramatic mood, for I was a frightful poseur, I said, "What would the world be like without a Bernhardt?"

She was never amused by me, but she had learned tolerance, so I was surprised when she answered with a passion that felled me, "Will you stop saying ridiculous things! You know better. Ask yourself: 'What would the world be like without the Cross of Christ?' "

I can still hear the bitter pain in her voice as she told us, "The

Jews who had the joy of being His chosen people rejected Him. Their sorrow is the most infinite in all history."

That noon at recreation one of my classmates, a stupid, spoiled child with golden curls, asked me with a leering smile, "Did you know Sister Marion was a Jew?"

"You damfool," I replied.

I knew in my heart that what she said was true, and I rejoiced in it. Nevertheless, the word "damfool" was not in general usage at the Academy of Notre Dame, and a gentle sweet Sister was summoned to admonish me. Sister Genevieve Mary misunderstood my rage and informed me with great gentleness that though Sister Marion was a convert from Judaism, she was a most devout Catholic. I tried to make it clear that I loved Sister Marion's Jewishness.

"But, Constance, dear," Sister explained, "he who calls his brother a fool is guilty of Hell's fire."

In some way I made it clear to Sister that my feelings about the human family of Jesus were very intense. I was rather incoherent, but she patted me on the shoulder.

"I see you've been calling people fools for Christ's sake." She laughed at my expression. "You're supposed to be a fool for Christ's sake, that's what Thomas à Kempis recommends. I understand what you mean—but just as a concession to good manners run over and apologize to Miriam."

I apologized to this mindless child with the beautiful Hebrew name of Christ's Mother, who had been informed she had given me a great shock.

"I'm sorry too, Constance," she said. "School will soon be over and next year we won't be taught by a Jew. My mother thinks it's awful."

I wanted to kill her. But the bell rang and side by side we returned to our classroom. Sister Marion was looking at me as if she were seeing me for the first time. Later when school was over for the year I was elected to write the tribute to Sister Marion. I yearned to give her the real reasons why I admired a teacher whom in many ways I disliked heartily; but I could not distinguish between supernatural and natural love, so I wrote the usual childish inanities. Sister Marion with a sad smile on her face tied the foolscap with green ribbons, and put it in her desk —then she gave me a present. It was a handsome toy theatre, on which I was to work out the directions for many of my grown-up plays. I never liked a present so much, and when my mother gave it away without consulting me I felt actual grief.

Holy Week in 1917 is very clear in my mind. Nana took me to the old Jesuit church of St. Joseph on Good Friday, and for the first time my mind and heart were filled with the agony of Christ. The church was crowded and we stood together in the balcony. The black-robed Jesuits, going toward the altar carrying the Cross, were like so many Simons helping Christ on that dreadful journey. The voices in the hymns were rough and broken. All history began and ended on a Cross. The thorns, the wounds, the mocking rabble—for me . . . for me. . . . The sorrow of Christ was all around me, and I was safe, for in this anguish I, who never quite knew where I belonged, belonged to the Christ of sorrows.

Then it was over and Nana and I were walking down Spruce Street on an April afternoon. We met people she knew and we stopped to talk—though Christ had died. What little things we say and how unimportant they are. We stopped to buy hot cross buns at the French bakery. The children were playing in Rittenhouse Square and a few of them called to me. They didn't seem to know that Christ was dead on Calvary. The rabble who shouted and mocked and the soldiers gambling for the seamless garment were somehow more human and understandable than this indifference on the Philadelphia streets. It was more frightening than Golgotha.

My father came home from the Seminary early, and we sat by the window in the front bedroom. Good Friday, 1917 . . . First we heard the iron-throated bell of St. Patrick's, then the air was filled with bells and shrieking factory whistles. The old quiet city of Philadelphia had wakened to clamorous life, as she always did in times of war. For America was again at war. Windows were going up all over Pine Street. "War is declared. War is declared." Woodrow Wilson had read his message to Congress and Jeannette Rankin, the first woman member of Congress, staggered to her feet, gasping, "I want to stand by my country, but I cannot vote for war," and sank down in a state of collapse; a tale of heroism too little known.

Good Friday, 1917 . . . America was at war. The bell of St. Patrick's rang on and on. It was terrifying and it was beautiful. Someone leaned far out a window and blew a bugle. Good American laughter rang up and down the street. That is the way I remember it—and that it was Good Friday.

## 5

THE O'HARAS WERE TOGETHER that first war summer for the last time in the old expansive and highly expensive life. There was a big cottage in Cape May taken to help Uncle Tom over a nervous spell. The vast double bedrooms were stuffed with children and relatives. Lizzie and Robert presided over the kitchen. Uncle Tom attempted to cure his nerves by chanting the Dies Irae, or sitting on the front porch facing the sea, plucking at his eyebrows, and discussing the world's philosophies. I was his chosen companion, and often we would walk straight to Sewell's Point as Uncle Tom tore apart Kant, whom he detested, and offered me Hegel, who, as the strange inspiration of Karl Marx, was to get the world into a lot of trouble. All Uncle Tom's philosophers seemed troublemakers. I liked him best when he recited the Pauline epistles, on which he was something of an authority.

These walks of ours seemed highly cultural, but the truth is I was interested in Uncle Tom, but bitterly ashamed of him; from a man who had been a Beau Brummell addicted to plunges into cold tubs, he had adopted a singularly careless attitude toward his attire and the whole subject of bathing. He insisted on wearing a child's floppy linen hat to protect him from the sun. The women, who regarded him as the most eligible bachelor in town, saw him pass with their eyes lowered in genuine sorrow. In those days he was comparatively moderate; his Benedict Joseph Labre period was ahead. A few of the more intrepid women tried to save him, and I remember these sessions of redemption on a bench in front of the old Cape May Hotel (then a sailors' training base) as singularly revealing of the courage of women confronted by disaster. He had only to speak the word, and they would have assumed the burden. Uncle Tom quoted the Greek dramatists, spoke of doom, and I can hear them say, "Buck up, Tom. That's all nonsense. You're so brilliant."

Later these same loyal women would say, "He couldn't help himself." I know each one felt in her heart she could have made something of him.

The truth is Uncle Tom could have helped himself, for he had a mind of great power and an extraordinary medical ability. He had every gift with which God can endow a man, including startling good looks, and even a touch of genius. He had only himself to blame, for into a heart that was meant for love he poured black bitterness. He hated everything—the world, his relatives, his God.

I remember one day in Cape May, I had had all I could take of Uncle Tom's nerves and I taunted, "Weakling—that's all you are —a weakling."

His deep-set eyes, filled with hurt, looked at me, for in his curious way he loved me, then they looked out to sea.

"You're like me. You're very like me," he said.

He never made a remark more profoundly true. He frightened me. This man was sensitive as I was, a self-dramatizer, an egotist, gentle and sweet when he felt himself loved and needed. I leaned against him and wept, sensing our bitter identity.

The summer went on, and I recited Edgar Allan Poe to my young cousins, with Robert draped in a white sheet ready to appear in the darkened room on the right cue. The children loved to hear me do "The Tell-Tale Heart," and Uncle Tom, not to be outdone by my dramatic ability, read us *The Confessions of an English Opium Eater*, with deep, throbbing organ tones in his voice. Once he recited Oscar Wilde's "*E Tenebris*," and he seemed to share the tragedy of that poor sinner who understood, "The wounded hands, the weary human face." Uncle Tom cried out with Wilde, "Come down, O, Christ, and hear me! reach thy hand. . . ."

We O'Haras in our last summer at Cape May were eccentrics, no doubt about it. Aunt Constance hired bicycles, and we wheeled up and down the beach, while Uncle Frank Matthews and Uncle Tom argued about Huxley and the world's dark imperfections. Once a periscope appeared on the horizon, and Aunt Constance shouted madly for the family to assemble on the boardwalk, as a German submarine was off Cape May. She was quite unaware that a salvo from a gun might end our earthly careers, she simply wanted all the children to witness history being made. I don't remember what happened, but binoculars were trained on the speck, crowds gathered. Navy boats were being launched at Sewell's Point; from somewhere Aunt Constance procured a supply of small American flags, and we waved them bravely, just to show the Germans we weren't afraid. Eventually the periscope disappeared, and at sundown one of our battleships steamed magnificently past with a huge escort. At that point Aunt Constance led us all in "The Star-Spangled Banner."

The bills for feeding all the visiting relatives must have been immense. I imagine Uncle Frank Matthews, who was meticulous about bills, paid them; then stiffened his spine against the fatal charm of the O'Haras, who broke the hearts of all who ever loved them, and moved his family away.

Uncle Tom's nerves were no better, and Lizzie Cheyney, the family cook, commenced to die. She kept on her feet till the last minute, but she heard death coming for her every night. Frances, a good sensible little girl, took her home. At the station the neat old colored woman stood looking for the last time at all of us she had loved and served so faithfully. She had been born in slavery and remembered it well; her freedom had been to slave for us. She looked at us with her dimming eyes to see that we had the appearance of "quality children." Uncle Tom, whose nurse she had been, picked her up in his arms and settled her in the seat of the train.

We heard her say, "Doctah Tom, remembah whose son you is. Please, sah, you remembah old Doctah and Mrs. O'Hara."

The train pulled away and she waved at us feebly. We went home feeling tremendously sad. My mind was thronging with arguments about the injustice of it. Lizzie, going home to die in the ward of a city hospital, receiving this slim reward from our hands, was a bitter commentary not only on our individual failure but on the failure of society. Robert was breaking in the new cook, a pretty, pert mulatto from Whitebro; whatever else happened in 1917, people did not do without cooks. It seemed disloyal and wicked of us to replace Lizzie so quickly.

Those war years went by with the speed of light. I remember standing at the corner of Forty-third and Locust Streets saying goodby to my cousin William Anthony Purcell—Corporal Purcell with the Princeton ambulance unit, resplendent in a Sam Browne belt and glistening puttees—then, later, sitting with Great-aunt Jen as she read over and over the newspaper headline, "Killed in action in Soisson, France, aged twenty-one years." He had been an unhappy, tense, bewildered boy, trying to find a place to fit in the world, sensitive and quick to anger, now he was a gold star in a window, and a Croix de Guerre.

In late February, 1918, Archbishop Prendergast died. I felt the tension of church politics starting, and was repelled. It seemed the Church should be a spiritual institution; these jockeyings for place and power were ugly. In the Seminary it was a foregone conclusion that Bishop McCort would become Metropolitan of Philadelphia; then, as everyone knew, the Right Reverend Monsignor Henry T. Drumgoole would be given a bishopric. Monsignor Drumgoole was then one of the most prominent churchmen in the East. He had joined with Cardinal Gibbons in the war effort and his days were filled with speaking engagements.

My father was not sanguine about the appointment of Bishop McCort, who was a man of immense charm and suavity.

"There are changing times," my father said. "The diocese is in a bad way. Rome will send us a man who will study the needs of all the people."

Rome did—for on April 30, 1918, they appointed Denis Dougherty, Bishop of Buffalo, head of the See of Philadelphia. He had been a professor at the Seminary for thirteen years, and he was not an admirer of ecclesiastical charm. I remembered the man I had met at the Seminary on my first visit and I was furious. Eminent monsignors were closeted with my father for hours. There was no rejoicing in Philadelphia. Everyone begged Monsignor Drumgoole to ask for his exeunt and go to the Archbishop of New York.

Monsignor Drumgoole smiled and said, "I was born in Philadelphia. Here I shall stay all my days, God willing."

Monsignor was not an administrator, neither was his distinguished friend and predecessor Dr. Garvey, so a great deal of paper work was necessary in the Seminary before the installation of the new Archbishop. Peter Drumgoole, his brother, worked day and night trying to bring order out of the books; unopened letters, some of them bills, were found everywhere. Monsignor was appalled, but in those days he was advising statesmen on the present condition of the Church, acting in many cases for the aging Cardinal Gibbons, and all he could do about the paper work was to plunge in after midnight. He broke down and had to have a few weeks at Hot Springs. On the Fourth of July, 1918, he made his most famous speech at Independence Hall, despite warnings that the new Archbishop did not like priests mixing in secular affairs. The evening of July ninth, Bishop Dougherty arrived at the Broad Street Station from Buffalo. Beside him, as distinguished laymen pushed forward to pay their respects, stood the Right Reverend Monsignor Henry T. Drumgoole, looking a trifle baffled and being sparing of those light, graceful gestures of his hands.

The next morning, with Cardinal Gibbons presiding and Monsignor Drumgoole as his chaplain, Denis Dougherty became

Archbishop of Philadelphia. This strange blunt man was to do terrible and amazing things as a scholar and contemplative became a bricklayer for God. There were so many things to be said and written about the Old Cardinal. He hated publicity, but kept on his bedside table in the last year of his life the novel *The Cardinal.* It is no secret that Lawrence, Cardinal Glennon of the book, is given many of his character traits; and the belated arrival in Rome for the election of Pius XI is a true story of Cardinal Dougherty. He said to his niece, "It may well be that writers will besiege you with requests after my death. In a tin box I have assembled all that I wish written about me." In the long week before his funeral she opened it. There were a number of papers neatly written in his handwriting. They were all in Latin. The Cardinal knew that classical scholarship was a lost art among contemporary writers. Who can say he was without humor?

That morning in 1918, standing outside the Cathedral of SS. Peter and Paul, I saw that the few papal knights, with their self-conscious, Celtic faces shining with pride at their rank, were only simple, hardy men who had made some money. The people filing into the Cathedral were not impressive from any worldly point of view. Many of the priests were fat and flabby, and the crowds outside the Cathedral were largely poor and ragged. The old Cardinal Gibbons from Maryland, where Catholicism was more firmly entrenched, lifted the procession for a moment out of its mediocrity. But no matter how it hurt we seemed rather like a Red Indian tribe going through ceremonial dances on our own reservation—primitive, laughable and unwanted. Later I told my father how I felt, and we had one of our infrequent quarrels when it dawned on him that I was ashamed of being a Catholic. He poured out invectives on the vulgarity and ignorance of the whole tribe of snobs. He dipped into history and threw the illustrious pageantry of Catholicism in my foolish young face.

That summer a dress rehearsal of coming horror took place when the Czar was murdered. To Nana the Czar was simply Victoria's grandson, and she denounced the rabble as "scum of the earth." No one understood the Russian revolution very well.

Nana saw only the half-mad Czarina in a cellar with the sickly Czarevitch torn from her arms, and prayed at the Lourdes grotto in St. John's Church that Victoria's family had had a quick and merciful death. My father was against the Russian revolution in the name of the three major virtues of his Catholic creed: Faith, Hope and Charity; but for the same reasons he had been opposed to the Romanoff dynasty. In some indefinable way the fierce intellectual pain of the Russian masses battered against the walls of a snug little house on Pine Street.

The flaming events of those tightly packed summer months in 1918 turned Americans away from Europe, made us yearn to break our ties. It was a summer of rain beating down on the new graves of the war dead, filling the trenches with slime, descending in long gray sheets over France. It was whispered that an apparition of Benedict XV in his white papal robes was seen on the fog-shrouded battlefields, promising peace.

I became physically a woman that summer, and the agony of my young body in this strange rhythm was intense. It seemed ugly and dark and primitive. It was not explained to me entirely, for certain Victorian pruderies still prevailed. I was warned not to talk about it to other children, to whom it might not yet have happened. I could not imagine how anyone would want to discuss anything so revolting. I lay in my bed, frightened and desolate, and wept in agony. I fought with bitter and futile rebellion against a physical law that governs women's lives. I was a prisoner in God's scheme of things—and the loveliness and wonder were out of the world. I felt degraded and violated to the depths of my soul.

Everyone was kind to me, and I clung to my mother with an infantile desperation, even while I read H. G. Well's *Joan and Peter* and thrilled to the advanced views of the intellectual bourgeois world. I shrank away from the companionship of children, envying them their immaturity. Nana went away to the mountains and I stayed home, going to the movies with my father and mother, dining in adult grandeur at the Arcadia Café, tasting the heady delights of after-theatre suppers at the old L'Aiglon, which Nana regarded as "very fast." I watched the soldiers on leave, dancing the foxtrot with the lovely girls, and became more reconciled to what was happening to me. Then, with an elegant new patent-leather suitcase and a floppy leghorn hat, I went to visit my cousins in Hoboken.

I had never been to New York, and I fell wildly in love with this crazy city. She took me in her embrace, and I was a child of Manhattan forever. Marguerite and Frank Gowen expected to entertain a little girl, and had all sorts of educational tours planned for me. They put these plans aside hastily and Frank, impressive in his captain's uniform, called on various young officers to entertain a super-sophisticate. I wanted to see Broadway after nightfall, and, in a Model-T Ford driven by a respectful sergeant who broke out in a snappy salute at the slightest provocation, and was in civilian life a New York millionaire, we rode through the home of the American theatre. I made my cousins take me to old Rector's and I looked up the red velvet stairs and almost wept with sheer joy.

The sergeant, who knew a lover of New York when he saw one, said respectfully, "Sir, might we take the little girl to the Cascades at the Biltmore?"

Frank Gowen was a man of deep understanding, and as a doctor in the French Army he had seen enough of war's horrors and tragedies to respect the transient nature of happiness, so although he couldn't approve my unchildlike tastes, he consented. Maurice and Florence Walton danced, and they knew the sergeant so they came to our table. Marguerite took me to the Plaza and who should walk by—as if to give me a special treat—but my idol, Irene Castle, picturesque in widow's weeds, for Captain Vernon Castle had been killed that winter.

Marguerite got me up to Sunday Mass, and I begrudged the time spent in the Hoboken church and eating the good breakfast we had at a shining, clean German restaurant. I wanted to meet David Belasco, and tell him I was preparing myself at the Convent of Notre Dame in Philadelphia for a stage career, and ask his advice. It seemed to me that some of Frank's Army friends could help me, and he came up with Lieutenant Luther Reed who wrote movie scripts in Hollywood but did not know Belasco. They took me to Coney Island to console me, and I rode the roller coasters with exuberant delight.

On my last night in New York we drove up to the Palisades, and then down Fifth Avenue to Gramercy Park. We parked outside the Players; inside the lighted rooms there were actors, acting like people. The statue of Edwin Booth looked down at the Model-T Ford, and I vowed by his shade that I would return to New York and the theatre. I had only to grow up and meet some people who would give me letters of introduction to the managers. Next morning a train pulled into Broad Street Station, and I was home again in quiet placid Philadelphia that had, as far as I was concerned now, only one thing to redeem it: it was only two hours away from New York. I scoffed at the slumbering Leviathan Philadelphia, with its low, irregular skyline and its long dark nights.

My father had astounding news. He had offered his resignation as doctor of the Seminary to the new Archbishop, as was customary. It had not been accepted, and his salary had been doubled. He had also been told to present bills to the faculty. It was startling indeed for the hierarchy to give any consideration to the economic needs of the laity whose services the Church required. Archbishop Ryan had settled the whole matter of salary by informing my father, "It's the grace of God that comes with the office, dear Doctor." Archbishop Prendergast had made no changes, but the new Archbishop was an innovator; such a lavish tossing around of Church funds had an almost pre-Reformation splendor. He had carefully listened to my father's list of requirements for the Seminary, even to the inadequacy of the plumbing and heating system. Archbishop Ryan would have accused him of Masonic leanings.

"Come to me for anything you want, Doctor—but never let the faculty send you on their errands," the Archbishop told him.

My father pointed out the superb sense of justice of the new Metropolitan, his Latinity. . . . It did not interest me, and I was frankly skeptical about the increase in salary. I was sure my father was being fattened for the slaughter.

"We belong to the old regime," I pointed out, my snobbish young soul in revolt at rule by the plain men.

"It's about time we changed over then, for general conditions in the Church have appalled me. We must raise the living and the educational standards of the people—or we'd better be consistent and abandon the Gospels. Archbishop Dougherty is the man we need for these times."

"Don't expect me to meet this person," I said. "You know as well as I do, this means Monsignor Drumgoole's bishopric."

"Archbishop Dougherty is your father's friend," he told me sternly, "and I don't want to hear any nonsense."

My father suffered during the war because of his inability to put on a uniform. He offered his services to every medical unit that was formed, and returned from the physical examinations, tired and crestfallen. He insisted to the examiners that a double hernia gave him no trouble whatever, and the condition of his lungs was a slight injury of the ribs incurred in the Spanish-American War. He beseiged Washington, used all his political pull, from Senator Boise Penrose to Charles B. Hall, the boss of the Seventh Ward. Everyone tried to be tactful, but my father realized the truth, and the wound went very deep.

The influenza epidemic, however, starting in late September, 1918, and culminating in the tragic weeks of October gave him his opportunity to serve. The Archbishop called him into conference, and the religious walls came crumbling down. The teaching sisterhood were ordered out as nurses into both religious and secular hospitals. The Sisters of Notre Dame were among the first to leave their cloistered convent; and the Archbishop never forgave those who pointed to their rule and remained within their walls. He had a long memory for a grievance. The seminarians went out as orderlies and to dig graves. All parishes were ordered to open emergency hospitals. Soup kitchens were opened and food was taken to stricken homes by children from the parochial schools. The impact of Catholic social action and its genius for organization were felt as never before in quiet Quaker Philadelphia.

My father was in the center of it, working the clock around.

The door of our house stood open, for servants refused to stay, and all the sick who could walk crowded into his office. The disease broke out, though lightly, in the Seminary and Monsignor Drumgoole, soon to leave, nursed the boys as gently as a woman. It broke out in the Convent of the Good Shepherd—the soiled linen from the emergency hospitals was washed in the laundry. In the occasional moments my father could snatch, he leaned over his microscope. He never bothered to think of money, and sternly refused to go to his prosperous patients unless they were really ill. Dr. Morris Lewis put his car at his disposal, and his secretary, an intrepid girl, drove my father through the town at all hours of the night. He refused to experiment with drugs or heart stimulants, and when he got to his patients in time—they lived. My father understood the human element. He had no time for medicine that excluded psychology, and he breathed the will to live, going from hospital to hospital, convent to convent, and in the dead of night to his beloved Seminary.

In those weeks my father was brushed with greatness, for he thought only of doing his work as well as he could. He never thought of himself, or of the danger. I was relegated to the top of the house, but saw him frequently, thin as a blade, standing to drink a cup of coffee, leafing through the telephone engagement pad, for the telephone rang all day and all night.

I could see from the windows the long line of open trucks carrying caskets for mass burial. Sometimes a child's tiny box teetered precariously on top. Soon there were no caskets, and wooden boxes were used.

Then it was over, and my father went about his life quietly, and had no share in the applause or glory. The influenza epidemic cost him a few of his richer patients, and we were financially rather strapped, as the riches he had laid by in Heaven were not negotiable on earth. He was at the end of his strength, and now in the early morning I could hear him moving quietly into the sitting room where he could sit up in the Morris chair and have relief from his hacking cough. He followed the sunshine wistfully and made no complaints.

The false Armistice in 1918 was a magnificent day. School was let out as the whistles blew, but not before Sister Superior Adela du Sacré Coeur had led us all in a Te Deum. Passing soldiers on the streets were beset by women and strewn with confetti and kissed. Horns blew, ticker tape flowed from office windows. Aunt Constance, who had joined the Navy and was now a yeo-woman, led us up Chestnut Street to Independence Hall, for history was being made again, and she always took children to the source. We touched the Liberty Bell and I forgot I was a young New Yorker and snake-danced through Independence Square.

## 6

In the Convent of Notre Dame the nuns knew what President Wilson did not, that in the divided soul of Europe, Catholicism still had deep roots, and only a man who understood this could make peace. Woodrow Wilson saw the Vatican as only a distasteful symbol of a once universal religion. Europe welcomed him with passionate hope, for his ideal was a noble one. Cardinal Gasparri, the Papal Secretary of State, knew that this man with the bony scholar's face to whom millions turned as to a messiah would fail, because to him Catholicism in Europe was only a dead weight of empty forms and superstitions which crushed the human spirit.

Modestly and without fanfare His Holiness Benedict XV, put forward his peace proposals, but Clemenceau with his savage anti-clericalism, aided by the irreligious Welshman Lloyd George, saw to it that Wilson would not even study them. It is no easy thing to be a renegade Catholic for a man is tortured by demons, and cannot know when his sleep will be haunted by the Sanctus bell. Perhaps it was this torment of conscience deep in the mind of Clemenceau that set its stamp on our tragic century. Curiously, Woodrow Wilson who died a martyr's death for the peace he lost, and Benedict XV, who could have won it, both suffered a long agony of failure and misrepresentation.

America, most people supposed, would now go back to normal, back to her elm-shaded little towns, her Puritan ways. "It was all over, over there." Instead, America, with its living war heroes disillusioned, its indifference to political action that had led to widespread corruption, was heading for the mad roaring twenties, the booming good times. The Volstead Act had been passed in an attempt to legislate morals and that strange character, the bootlegger, was much in evidence. Everyone became a little shallow and shrill, and the good Sisters of Notre Dame were about to be confronted with the jazz age and the flapper.

My convent school meant nothing to me but hours of painful boredom. I was reading avidly the strangest hodgepodge of books that ever went down one mental digestive tract. I was at once a young intellectual who contemplated the disintegration of capitalistic society as depicted in Herbert Croly's *New Republic*, or a hedonist and scoffer delighting in Mr. Nathan and Mr. Mencken's *The Smart Set*.

A strange unhappy thing had happened: Monsignor Drumgoole had left the Seminary. The story was a tragic one, for this fastidious man had been given what was then a desperately poor parish, St. Gregory's. The good and devout people, most of whom worked on the Pennsylvania Railroad, were astounded at their new Rector, and soon indignant. Archbishop Dougherty had exposed a congregation of hard-working people to one of the most brilliant men in the Church. They yearned for the comfortable mugginess of the religion they knew and Monsignor Drumgoole, with his assistant Father Edward Hawks, the converted Anglican, made it a dazzling, golden thing. It was perhaps as well that Monsignor Sigourney Fay, another converted Anglican, died the year before Monsignor Drumgoole became Rector of St. Gregory's, for Father Fay was something of an aesthete, a lover of epigrams, and, devoted to Monsignor Drumgoole, would often have been in residence at St. Gregory's. The puritanical

Archbishop would have had something to think about since Monsignor Fay, a close friend of Cardinal Gibbons, was not sparing with the perfume he used. He achieved a brief fame as Father Darcy in Scott Fitzgerald's *This Side of Paradise*, the novel that heralded the arrival of the twenties.

My father and Monsignor Drumgoole had become estranged, though there was no ill feeling between them. It was perhaps a matter of policy, for Monsignor was sensitive and aware and knew my father could not afford to alienate the new Archbishop. My father had too much sweetness and too much intelligence to recognize social distinctions—in that he was a true aristocrat—and I think Monsignor Drumgoole, appearing at all great social functions, going from dinner party to dinner party, from his broken-down parish, rather shocked him. In social matters I have always been like a porcupine yearning to be cuddled, so the new Monsignor Drumgoole, with his immense suavity and irony, made me feel awkward. I did not like the plain men of God who thronged our house, but this worldly priest, who in many ways was my only friend, filled me with unhappiness.

The Lord must have thought I was worth salvaging, and paid me the compliment of sending me another friend. We went into the convent refectory one day and, standing there to supervise the riot and the babble of childish voices and the brief violent quarrels, stood a Sister I vaguely remembered from my infant days. Her folded arms were not tucked neatly into her habit and her eyes were not lowered decorously, for every child was aware of that blue steel. She said grace, and gave full expression to the prayer. The voice itself was light, but it was colored by her moods—and she was not a miser of moods. She was small and thin and moved with the grace of a dancer. She swung up and down the refectory imperiously, surveying us like a general inspecting an army. She clasped her wrist with one hand, and seemed to drum out a lively measure. It was the aliveness of this nun that caught my attention. I stared in open fascination, for this was a virtuoso performance from a woman who could gauge her audience. I spooned up the last of my soup carelessly, intensely absorbed in watching this regal little nun.

"Mademoiselle O'Hara," her voice came like a whiplash, "soup should be taken from you—not toward you."

She had made me conspicuous before the entire refectory, and she knew as well as I that I had been too fascinated by her to bother about etiquette with the last spoonful of that warm water briefly exposed to a chicken, known as soup in the Convent of Notre Dame.

She gave me, this extraordinary nun, a gamin grin, and that is how I met Sister Julie du Saint-Esprit, whose conscience was so good that she restored gaiety to a convent. And if convents are not gay, where else in the name of God may gaiety be found? There was nothing plaintive or restrained about Sister Julie. There is no way to get her quality on paper, for her facile charm was like the flash of quicksilver. She suffered the deep, excruciating loneliness of Christ, and she had learned His forgiveness and compassion. Nothing shocked her—except dull hypocritical piety. Everyone who guessed her quality knew what this radiant and spectacular woman must have suffered in locking herself up in a cloiser with the dull, nagging dispositions of other women, her sisters in Christ; not to mention what these unimaginative women must have endured from Sister Julie. She had fought her bitter wars with pride, and won. In all the years I knew her she was riddled with cancer, her last years must have been an agony, but no one even dreamed she was suffering.

Sister Julie du Saint-Esprit was mistress of the young lady boarders, directress of the Children of Mary, the Christian Mothers, author of *Cresting the Ridge,* and innumerable other books, pale gleams of her best creation, which was her inimitable self. She had no fear of the emotions and I suspect never perfectly learned detachment from creatures. In her cloister she knew more about the world's people and events than most people outside; she knew the exact moment when a worth-while Catholic talent peeped over the horizon, and she reached out her hand to help. (Her critics said, to grab at a bargain price.)

She liked children with dangerous tendencies, for she saw in rebellion the germs of sanctity. I can see her little room yet, its one window facing the garden, her good secretary-desk, and the crucifix so placed that the eye never escaped it. I can see her sitting at the desk writing, and putting her pen aside to talk. And what talk it was! Those blue eyes gleamed with amusement, or were veiled by sorrow, and the wit was as robust as Chesterton's. She made my idol, George Bernard Shaw, seem a verbose Irishman with a shallow mind. Sister Julie demolished the whole tribe of skeptics with laughter. She hadn't the slightest hesitancy in talking about herself, and she could make you see the spoiled, fêted rich girl, born a Morgan, turning to the cloister under the influence of Catholic Europe where she had spent most of her youth. She let her friends understand that she had had masculine admiration and enjoyed it. She gave her Lord no pallid spinsterish emotion; this woman was a romantic.

She would sit at her desk describing with pleasure some party she had gone to when she was young in New York or Washington, when her father was a senator, and suddenly she would say in the midst of a dazzling paragraph:

"Constance, He wants all of you. He said so, just then." And her eyes were on the crucifix.

She was not recruiting a candidate for the convent. Sister Julie du Saint-Esprit thought I should go on the stage till my writing developed. She studied my first sonnets with intensity, as well as my essays. She was not sparing of her criticisms or at all gentle.

"Constance, I will get this streak of fatalism out of you, or God will judge me severely," she warned.

"Renegade Catholics, you see, my dear," she said at another time, "ruin their own lives, and in their desperation wreck others. You hate failure, don't you, Constance? The way to every sort of failure lies in deserting your Church. It makes you a traitor, and even the British who fêted Benedict Arnold despised him a little. It is your path to horror and Hell. You shall not take it, my child. He and I won't let you."

She talked to me of Teresa of Avila, for she was a Teresian. She gave me Francis Thompson's poems to read and Everard Meynell's wonderful biography of Thompson. She handed me Belloc's *Danton*, his *Marie Antoinette*. She taught me mental prayer. She raged against my silly Philadelphia snobberies, and often insulted me publicly when she observed this obnoxious trait in action.

Once she saw me hurt, when Monsignor Drumgoole, presiding over the Christian Mothers retreat, glided by in the corridor with his court in attendance. He gave me a chill smile that had in it something of embarrassment for the tall, lanky adolescent with braces on her teeth that I had become. I felt that his action was quite deliberate, for I did not dream that he was a hurt and wounded man. Sister saw my stricken face out of the corner of her eye as she walked down the corridor with the "best people" who always followed in the train of Monsignor Drumgoole.

It was unquestionably because of a rebuke from Sister Julie that in a few days I received a letter from Monsignor Drumgoole, beginning, "Dear little friend," and continuing in the gay mocking style of the old days. Sister Julie knew how far a temperament like mine could be hurt, and she knew that to be snubbed by someone loved could send an insecure person into arrogance that demanded consolation through insulting the great, into desperate inferiority that would crawl to a kitchen maid for approval.

She was the greatest woman I have ever known, the most human, the wittiest, and the most loving. No one now living who knew her will ever forget that keen ironic wit. No actress ever made such an entrance as Sister Julie, at the Children of Mary meetings, briskly stepping across the stage of the hall, sitting down before the table with its green baize cloth, ringing a little bell, surveying us with those cold, amused eyes, and commencing her instructions.

I can hear her voice saying, "I would much prefer the society of an adulteress to a gossip. Adultery can have in it elements of generosity, gossip nothing but evil; slimy and hateful."

There was another gem we all remembered. "Well, gels, I suppose you will all drink these cocktails. I can't approve, for most of you have Irish blood. I wish I could say to you, 'If you must drink for Gawd's sake take it straight.' "

There was that memorable day at a Christian Mothers conference when she faced the finest representation of "lace-curtain Irish." This is what she said:

"Umph! what a large audience. My, my, the dirty dishes that must be in the sinks this morning."

Her wealthy audience had just recovered from this astounding sally when she said, with that slow smile:

"Women, I have been hearing that quite a few of you have been standing in your alleys leaning on your brooms and gossiping to the neighbors."

A few of those present who understood this masterly sleight-of-hand, this deadly contempt for pretentiousness, said that many of the women were on the verge of apoplexy, but there was more to come.

"Some of my young Children of Mary are rather discouraged about the prospect of getting husbands. I have suggested that they come up and look at the Christian Mothers, for when they see the women men marry, and how generous they are to them, they will get over their hopeless feelings. Now, women, I don't want any of you coming to me complaining that your husbands do not love you. I know what you mean by love. I am not that sheltered. Such nonsense! Do they respect you, Christian Mothers? Do your husbands respect you . . .?"

Despite these brutal assaults on the tender sensibilities of the rich Irish, Sister Julie packed them in, robbing the other convents of their trade. Up the stairs to her little room came all manner of women with all manner of troubles. Simple devout women came with money troubles, a husband that drank, an errant son. . . . Complex worldly women came with other troubles, no less real for being more selfish. Young wives came raging about that third pregnancy in four years of married life. She steadied them all. She loved them all. She must be in Heaven now, and can hear us say, "Help us, Sister Julie."

Those years were happy ones in my convent school. My writing commenced to be published, and I won prizes in contests, right and left. Sister Genevieve Mary, who finally received me into her room, was not only an inspired teacher but the right one for me. She got my sloppy mind tidied up, and set me to work. It was then I was sure I was college material. I was not pious in any conscious sense, but Sister Julie had quieted me down and taught me adoration and praise of the Lord. In those years religious mediocrity, as exemplified in St. Patrick's Church, ceased to bother me, for I had been given what seemed a real insight into the true meaning of Catholicism.

Uncle Frank Matthews had inherited a legacy from Eleanor Donnelly, the poetess, and bought a summer place at the end of Ocean City. It was a primitive wilderness and here I spent the happiest times of my life. The sea was at our front door, at the back green fields recoiled before the brown stretch of the marshland and the bay. We were almost at land's end and the curving beach at Fifty-ninth Street. I would lie there in the sand dunes sheltered by the wild grass and read English poetry. The sea beat against the jutting rocks and life was very good.

I can remember waking up in the cot surrounded by six windows and looking out on a world too beautiful to bear. The noise of the children ascended from the dining room: the firm little boy voice of Frank Matthews, Jr., called Brother; Margaret and Constance feeling out as to which twin would dominate that day; Mary and Louise too interested in everything to waste words. Genevieve protesting because someone was calling the baby "the last of the litter." She always insisted on respect from her brothers and sisters. Frances came in, pink and scrubbed from the bathroom, and together we would rouse Tommy with his beautiful eyelashes sweeping down on his cheeks. Tommy made my heart melt and he was my favorite, as everyone knew. He had no false shame in appreciating the beauty and the tears of things. He was considerably my junior, and yet he would sit for hours hearing me read the poems I loved, his whole body shivering in delight at an exquisite phrase. We liked the same records on the portable victrola; whether or not the rest of the family appreciated Mozart, it was Mozart they heard, and we never compromised our musical taste much below Grieg's Peer Gynt Suite.

Aunt Francie had sweetness and grace, and her lovely nature shone on her pretty face. She stood at the stove fixing great platters of fried tomatoes for breakfast—there never again will be anything that tastes like those fried tomatoes. I sat on Eleanor Donnelly's saratoga trunk in the kitchen discussing philosophy, and even if my cousin Frances put a dish towel in my hands, no one minded too much that my conversational talents were more impressive than my ability at chores.

We lived in the water like human fish. Brother and I sometimes went crabbing from the old railroad trestle. At night we walked to the rocks, and sat there with the moon casting its reflection on the sea like a pavement of pearl. We loved clear days, but we thrilled to the wild nor'easters and walking in the stinging rain with the wind beating down on us. All of us read books incessantly; Aunt Francie even read in the early morning on the side porch. Many afternoons the hammocks, the swings, all the beds were occupied by recumbent figures reading. On Saturday we girls put on dresses which seemed awkward and unfamiliar, and the two boys white knickerbockers and shoes which made them walk mincingly like Chinese girls, and met Uncle Frank at the station, trying to appear civilized. On Sundays we piled in the big Buick car and drove into Ocean City, which seemed an urbane and overeffete community, to attend Mass at St. Augustine's Church. I didn't have a pin-point of skin without a freckle, my reddish hair had turned almost straw color. My mother's stylish daughter had "gone native," and I was completely content without a social pretension to my name.

It seems almost impossible that we will never be young any more, and turn up the road to the old place that Eleanor Donnelly's legacy bought. She never wrote a poem that touched that scene, and her brother, Ignatius Donnelly, who tried to prove that Bacon wrote Shakespeare's plays, never expounded a theory as wild as those we children, drunk with the miracle of words and our own expanding minds, shouted over the booming of the surf on summer nights long ago.

It was in a sense the Catholic heritage that made it rich in beauty, for we loved and enjoyed each other so much that no distrust was possible. There was no piety or preaching but a deep inborn sense of God. This was the home Aunt Francie created from a heart that had created goodness to surround us all. It was an ecstatic adventure in holiness, and yet she never uttered a prayer aloud, never preached, never scolded. We never yearned for material things, silly recreations, we were never bored. I knew Catholic joy once—what life should be like—and I grow sick with yearning to find it again.

It was strange and oppressive to go home to the loneliness of being an only child, to have my mother feverishly working on my freckled skin with bleaches, my dry scalp with oil till my hair shone again. My anxious father used ointments on my mosquito bites. Nana almost fainted when I read her passages from St. Augustine's *Confessions*, and felt sure it was dangerous heresy. I got tired of all this fussing over one individual, and retired grumpily to my bedroom to read H. G. Wells's *Tono-Bungay*, when I wasn't trying on my new school clothes. I went to see *Treasure Island* at the Stanley Theatre, wrote an essay about it, and received a check for fifteen dollars. It was the first money I had ever earned, and the shock was too much for me. I sneaked downtown alone and went to Binder's and had a Castle-bob frothing with curls. I gave dollar tips to everyone who served me and departed in a flurry of bows, feeling like a millionaire. I bought a lipstick, a pale blue leather-bound edition of *Thus Spake Zarathustra*, because the title appealed to me, and returned home in triumph without a dime.

My father closed his eyes and said, "You look like Zulu Zingarra, the snake-charmer."

Nana was eloquent in her demands that Binder's be sued, for after all I was a minor. Mother said I looked "common," and Aunt Caroline said I would not be received at the Newport Apartments until my hair had grown in. I felt myself a tremendous rebel, a worthy representative of what would soon be called "flaming youth," and secretly smoked a Melachrino cigarette, which together with Nietzsche and a Castle-bob, not to mention the lipstick, made me sure I was the only one in the whole house, from my father on down, who knew anything about real life.

It was time to go back to Notre Dame school, where my companions were duly impressed with the Castle-bob. My excellent scholastic record sent me to Sister Catherine Patricia first in my class; and nothing so wonderful ever happened to me as when my companions made me class president. I needed the sense of belonging to make up for my nagging insecurity, and this approbation from my contemporaries made me a "big person" in my own eyes. My future college career seemed secure.

I was determined to make a success, and Sister Genevieve Mary and Sister Julie du Saint-Esprit were perfectly sure that Notre Dame had triumphed; from now on I would be all right. Sister Catherine Patricia was easily the most popular nun in school. She was American to her backbone, a college graduate, a modernist, who liked her girls to confide in her about their social invitations and what they were going to wear. She was the basketball coach, and thought nothing of picking up her habit and running fleetly with the ball. I had often seen her walking in the garden with girls at each side of her, girls with linked arms walking backward to face her, and envied them this laughing, happy nun. She was filled with energy, directness, enthusiasm, and intelligence. In a few weeks I was her sworn enemy and my scholastic career was in ruins.

Sister Catherine Patricia had delegated me to write the class song, which was to be a splendid rousing thing to be chanted at basketball meets. I was incapable of any enthusiasm for this sort of effort and my effusion, which was as obscure as T. S. Eliot, whom I was reading at that time, was rejected. It hurt my pride, and I was rather supercilious toward the "Rah Rah Notre Dame '24' " which was selected. She ordered me out for basketball and I felt a perfect fool running up and down the cloakroom which served for a gymnasium, getting sweaty and uncomfortable in black cloth bloomers. I got my father to write me a letter excusing me from this childish nonsense, on the grounds of a weak appendix. She learned, at about that time, the type of books I was reading and was sure they were all on the Index, or should be. She sent for my mother, who sent my father, as she always did, to confer on these matters. Sister suggested supervised reading, and pointed out the fearful spiritual condition of his only and beloved child. He was not too worried, but was polite with this concerned young nun.

One incident led to another, and soon in study period I was reading Oscar Wilde's *Picture of Dorian Gray*, with a brazen disregard of discipline. I nicknamed her "Cat-ty Pat," which she heard about; it did nothing to improve our relations. English was my best subject, but I had started literary attitudinizing, so that many of my compositions sounded like Louisa May Alcott trying to be Havelock Ellis. Scornfully she read aloud one of these effusions, uttered a terse, "superficial and flowery," and I hated her with blind ferocity.

My companions, not guessing my hurt and misery, decided I had the most impenetrable egotism they had ever encountered. I made futile gestures of defiance. Sister Genevieve Mary had had my mind under a state of cultivation, Sister Julie had reached my soul, now both sank back into heavy underbrush. I suspect that they pleaded for me and that Sister Catherine Patricia, resenting this, struggled with stubborn courage to save my soul in her own way—which God knows was the wrong way for me—by means of simple, wholesome pleasures, regulated reading, and school spirit.

Class elections were held again at midyear. By this time I was an anti-social being and my companions were against me. Someone else was made president, and I was relegated to a desk in the back of the room. I was at that stage of adolescence when youth fluctuates between one world and another. My unpopularity and failure at school, which had never happened to me before, filled me with bitterness and shame. I ceased even trying to pray. Raging with misery, I left in my desk a letter written on lined paper, placing it on top of my schoolbooks. I knew Sister Catherine Patricia inspected our desks each afternoon when school was dismissed and would surely find it. I hoped to be expelled, but I trembled in anticipation of Sister's reaction and shock.

The writing of this letter was a tremendous relief to my feelings of resentment and inferiority. Had I torn it up my whole life might have been different. It began:

> To Sister Catherine Patricia,
> O! woman with your devil's
> heart—your serpent's tongue . . .

About eight hundred words of it ran on in similar vein. This effusion deeply hurt Sister Catherine Patricia, as well it might. When Sister confronted me at the noon recreation the next day with the first of my awful letters—there was to be quite a series in my life—I saw with astonishment that her lovely blue eyes were red-rimmed and that her voice trembled with real pain. My sorrow for the hurt I had given stretched right down to the soles of my shoes, but I tried to carry it off with bravado. It is painfully easy to slip over the line and become the type of person you're pretending to be, but my "pose" was so transparent as I expressed disgust at the narrowness and tyranny of convent school life that Sister should have seen through it.

There is nothing more amusing, and tragic too, than a self-conscious adolescent who has become a pseudo-intellectual. However, Sister Catherine Patricia was wrong in assuming that my character was deeply flawed and that I was filled with secret wickedness. I had read every sort of book, but I was completely innocent of the literal meaning of the facts of life. I assumed they were splendidly romantic, but there was a fierce young purity in me that prevented me from even speculating on such subjects with my friends. Sister lashed through my intellectual pretensions, informed me I was mentally rather dull, and not the genius I imagined myself to be; as for my talents, she could not find one that was in any way exceptional.

I did not survive this estimate of myself, though I struggled to keep my equilibrium for the next few weeks. I longed for a chance at a secular school like Miss Agnes Irwin's, and vowed I'd win a scholarship to Bryn Mawr. I tried desperately to win good marks, and never achieved them. I commenced to accept Sister Catherine Patricia's view of my mental mediocrity, I read

Thomas Hardy's marvelous *Jude the Obscure* and thought of suicide. I did not resent being regarded as a great sinner, for that had a certain dramatic notoriety, but to be accused of possessing only a fair intellect condemned me to obscurity. And what could be more unpleasant? I prepared showy recitations, but was cut short in my attempts to prove I knew more than the books. No one at home took very seriously my stories of persecution; indeed, I was dramatizing the situation. I died before the chill scorn of Sister's smile as I recited in class. My remarks to my young companions, made to bolster up my vanity, were creating life-long enmities. I crashed into a nervous breakdown.

Dramatic fancy worked spells on an overwrought mind, and in those brief weeks of intense suffering, I was spiritually wrecked. My father took me to specialists who tried to patch up my nervous system. I lived in a nightmare, till my phone rang one night and it was Sister Julie.

"I am on my way to chapel to pray for you and you are to believe you will be better. I am going to ask Saint Teresa to care for you because, my own dear child, in your way you are very like her and she will intercede for you."

I giggled at the absurdity of resembling a saint, and before I knew it Sister Julie had reached down in my sick and defeated will, revived my Irish spunk, given me the strength of knowing I had a friend, and soon I was ascending out of the gloom and the fear.

The next summer I went to Aunt Francie's, thin as a long drink of water, with all my schoolbooks because in the fall I was going to make up examinations which I had missed because of my illness that spring, and in due course I was going to Bryn Mawr. The family had to watch me being impressively scholarly in horn-rimmed glasses, pacing the floor conjugating Latin verbs, and in grim despair working algebraic formulas. I only stopped long enough to pound out a short story on my typewriter called "The Quintessence of Modernism" which I sent off to *Snappy Stories.*

I received a letter, in which appeared the sentence:

> This gay rigmarole has flashes of cleverness, but it isn't for our audience.

It would have taken the most heroic humility for a fourteen-year-old girl not to be dazzled by such recognition.

I passed my examinations at Notre Dame without distinction, but to pass them at all was a tremendous advance in self-discipline. I settled down with Sister Margaret who had brilliance and insight, and was not the hundred-percent American-girl type. Then trouble struck again—and through Sister Julie, who had the senior French class. She believed in a stern Christ so as we entered her room she noticed my insolent withdrawal from a girl I didn't care to sit with for no better reason than that she wasn't attractive from a worldly point of view. In short, she was poor and dowdy and stupid enough to admire me. My eyes were being treated at the time and I wore black glasses. I pointed to them as Sister called on me, as the reason why I hadn't studied.

"Gels who do not know their lesson in my class go to the baby room."

I lowered my dark glasses in astonishment, half-blinded by sparks coming from those blue eyes. My classmates giggled at my discomfiture, but I understood the source of her rage. The girl I had snubbed was looking at me wistfully, and I burned with shame at the honest liking on her face. The whole thing was too much for me; I rose grandly and proceeded to the baby room. Sister Mary Immaculata was horrified and the dear little first-graders regarded me as the Lilliputians did Gulliver. My knees touched my chin when I sat down on a Lilliputian blue chair. I continued this remarkable performance for one week, to the consternation of poor Sister Immaculata. It was the talk of the school. Sister Julie appeared at the door; a woman who could have ruled an empire had been forced to go on a ridiculous errand to fetch a ridiculous school girl. I shook before the blazing scorn in her eyes. She cut my pretensions in little pieces, and was in a mood to toss me to the crocodiles. I was as nothing before this righteous rage, while one part of me was admiring Sister Julie intensely and admitting that she was entirely just.

Unfortunately I buried the latter realization under tons of indignation when I reported the incident at home. All they could see was that I had been unjustly censured for not doing my lessons and accepting the penance given me. I knew better, but I was withdrawn from school, and lay on Nana's couch reading Scott Fitzgerald's *This Side of Paradise*, thrilling to the brave new world in which I was a citizen, while my elders debated what to do with me. My mother could get me the proper social sponsors for Miss Irwin's, where I would be prepared for Bryn Mawr. It seemed the only sensible thing to do, for in convent school I was not making the right contacts. We were either very prosperous—or very imprudent. My father said with gentle firmness that I would go to a Catholic school. The battle raged on, while I read Anatole France, sulked at my father, and went with Mother to the South Broad to see Frances Starr in the revival of her greatest Belasco success, *The Easiest Way*.

That play which, at the outset of the roaring twenties, was curiously dated in its point of view, brought me the greatest single sustained influence in my life—the friendship of Frances Starr. Her portrayal of Laura Murdock's efforts to lead a good life in the midst of temptations, and that curtain line when she was licked, "I'm going to Rector's—and to Hell with the rest," seemed to me unbearably poignant. I didn't know that demimondaines were going out of fashion, and that the age of the flapper was removing love nests into the back seat of automobiles.

I was swamped by the art of Miss Frances Starr and wrote her an impressive letter, together with a prose gem which I called, "A Pen Portrait." She came into my life, and remained there, the best and most gracious friend any woman ever won. She is still in my life.

There is no more intelligent actress in our theatre; Frances is an artist without extravagances of temperament and her feelings toward life are essentially religious. It is no accident that she will be remembered in the history of the American theatre for her Marie Odile, that exquisite role of a young nun. Prince

Pierre Troubetskoy caught the quality of that performance in his haunting portrait, while her first husband, Haskell Coffin, intensified the beauty and sensitivity of the young actress in his more famous picture.

I carried her first letter around till it was frayed and torn, reading it to anyone who would listen. It was from a world-famous actress, after all.

*The Seelbach,*
*Louisville, Ky.*

DEAR MISS O'HARA:

Thank you for your letter and the very flattering "pen picture." Good taste forbids me to say it is an excellent likeness—but it doesn't prevent my liking to think that you think so! Many many thanks and every good wish.

Sincerely
FRANCES STARR

Tuesday

Forgive this wretched paper—but it is the last sheet and I *must thank* you now!

The letter was overwhelming, but the postscript seemed to me a touch of intimacy that left me limp with glory. I didn't protest too much when Miss Irwin's was finally vetoed and my mother compromised on the Convent of the Sacred Heart. Mother gave her views on the education of girls to Mother Helen Lucas in the dark parlor of the Arch Street convent, Reverend Mother Grace Dammon was sent for and I was enrolled at once. Mother Dammon had no misgivings when she informed my mother that I was the type of young girl just meant for the Convent of the Sacred Heart. Mother Helen Lucas, a woman of great charm and sweetness, put her arm around me. "She's such a gentle refined girl that she'll be much happier at the Sacred Heart."

Mother Lucas was either an incurable optimist or a poor judge of character.

The next morning I appeared at the convent, for the Mothers had decided I needn't wait for my uniforms to be made. I was filled with good intentions and made up my mind to conform exactly to the requirements of my new school. The dramatic intensity of my performance made me stand out as an odd and unusual person, which was not the impression I intended to convey. It was the essence of the Sacred Heart manner to be considerate and gentle in all things and never to appear to take anything too seriously. It was faintly diluted with hypocrisy. We were to be prepared for an upper-class world and Protestant associations, which we were to uplift by spirituality and unobtrusive virtue.

I tried my best in those early days, and in an effort to impress the Mothers visited the school library and asked for *The Education of Henry Adams*. Mother Carpenter was overcome by delight, and I enjoyed the aristocratic and wistful cadences of Adams' prose. Mother Saul was an excellent teacher of English, and as I was really serious in my determination to succeed I accepted her blue penciling and brutal criticisms without resentment. I was having a strange craze for Algernon Charles Swinburne, and had fallen in love with words.

"Cellar door is the most beautiful combination of sounds in the English language," said Mother Saul. "Just write it over and over when this word-madness comes upon you."

Mother Saul was the only robust individualist I encountered at the Sacred Heart, for truth to tell in this atmosphere of gentleness and sweetness I was going mad. The discipline was relaxed and after years of the iron of Notre Dame I commenced to judge the Mothers as spineless for what they endured from "the little brats." I had a vague liking for Reverend Mother Grace Dammon who had extraordinary qualities, but I got the impression she had a provincial type of worldliness. The Monday ceremony of Prime, a Sacred Heart function in use to this day, in which we were awarded medals for our virtues and excellencies bored me. No child played the piano, or recited a piece, we just walked up and down the aisle getting silly ribbons. Changing schools is hard on an adolescent, particularly if the new one is so different from the old. It seemed to me they weren't even teaching the same religion. I knew that the Mothers believed in mortal and venial sins as did the Sisters of Notre Dame, but there wasn't so much emphasis put on sins; perhaps they thought the well-bred avoided excesses. Strangely, I recognized the snobbery, which was akin to my own, and it horrified me. I demanded of religious people that they should not share my faults, and as I daily detected the same worldliness that I possessed I developed reservations about the sincerity of the Mothers of the Sacred Heart.

In the midst of my miseries I made an enemy—a formidable enemy, aged fourteen. Regina was a beautiful child with an excellent mind. I realized that while my intellect would never be as well-rounded, I had a force and drive in one direction that she could not eclipse. She sensed it, too; and she had ruled the roost intellectually for too many years to tolerate any competition. In the rapidly developing tension she learned a way of saying biting things, with a slow, sweet smile, never losing her temper but giving me every provocation to lose mine. She led me into show-off statements at dinner, and then when she had me blind with fury at my own absurdities would remind me that I had a long way to go before I became a Sacred Heart girl.

Mother Saul tried to help me, for she realized, as I did not, that Regina was a remarkable child, who suffered torture at being a poor girl in a rich girls' school. Mother Saul taught me a profound truth for, as she interested me in my first enemy, I commenced to understand that every vice, and every virtue, contains its opposite. The strength of my hatred had in it a capacity to love the child Regina. I could rise above my fierce dislike when Regina effortlessly translated pages of Latin and once I saw her looking at me with unconcealed admiration in English class. We stood together one day at Recreation and discovered we both shared the same sadness—delicate fathers. She had read things I hadn't and made me yearn to get the books.

"We're both going to be somebody," she said, and turned away.

Then my theatre craze struck again, and all was lost. Sacred Heart let out early, and I went to B. F. Keith's where Irene Castle was starred. Irene Castle didn't dance, she drifted on a stage; all the beauty of the world was an echo of this graceful woman. She was Debussy's "Afternoon of a Faun," she was a poem by Sappho. . . . I stood outside the green stage-door and waited for her in the immemorial tradition of stage-struck girls.

It was perhaps unfortunate that the shy convent girl attracted her attention and that she singled me out of the throng of noisy flappers. We walked back to the Ritz and she laughed in her throaty voice; consumed as I was with shyness and awe, I was an original. She invited me to come back the next afternoon.

Mother was amused and understanding and saw no harm in it, so I returned. Outside the theatre stood her Hispano-Suiza with a pale gray body by Fisher. She decided to walk, and her splendid car trailed us, while her quaint little Belgian griffons trotted at our heels. We went to the Academy of Music to meet Isadora Duncan. I remember her square bare feet, and the flabby fat on her body veiled in chiffon. She was drunk to the point of incoherence, but with a noble generosity she greeted, as she said, "her lesser sister in the art of the dance."

She looked at me with haunted bloodshot eyes, and I became aware that this woman had had greatness.

"The child has a soul," she hiccupped.

I stepped away from her embrace, terrified. Isadora began talking about a festival of the dance. She was erecting a Parthenon. Nothing much was left of the fires of Duncan except the evocative spark of a lost genius.

To put it mildly, such experiences were not usual at the Convent of the Sacred Heart. The Mothers were horrified as I plunged into this new friendship, which had the fierce ardor of love. Like a young Sara Teasdale writing sonnets to Duse, I wrote a notebook full of poems, which I entitled "Pale Enchantments," to Irene Castle. She commenced to write me letters and deluged me with pictures. She decided I was brilliant and showed my "juvenilia" to Elizabeth Marbury who, as a devout Catholic convert, became interested in the young girl at the Convent of the Sacred Heart in Philadelphia.

There was no harm in it, for I was only in the grip of a "crush," and my intense nature demanded I give it my all. Regina took to insulting me about it in her gentle nasal voice and with that exasperating smile, but there was no zest in it, for I wasn't even annoyed. I had ceased to be conscious of school, for Elizabeth Marbury was sending me lists of plays to read, and my extracurricular activities were completely absorbing me. My compositions were tame and dull, all my energies being given to writing letters to Irene Castle, for which I stole liberally from Somerset Maugham and Oscar Wilde.

In the storms and confusions of adolescence my heart was ready to explode; and I suddenly realized I wasn't enjoying my torments at all. I met a buck-toothed Princeton freshman, with a hound-toothed check jacket from Brooks Brothers, against which he pulled me for a most inexpert kiss. I confess I enjoyed the experience, though he did look silly with his mouth hanging open and all those big teeth gleaming. My devotion to Irene Castle burned itself out then and there.

My father was again very ill. I realized once and for all I was not a favored child of fortune. By this time I loathed the Convent of the Sacred Heart and I saw the understanding in his eyes when I assured him that I would not return. I wanted to talk to Sister Julie du Saint-Esprit, but Notre Dame had not recovered from their resentment that I had been removed from the school to which my family had gone for three generations. I had been trained in reticence, and all the social inhibitions which had been drilled into me made it impossible to admit we couldn't afford things. I also had had it drilled into me since my baby days that people with our background never accepted favors—we gave them.

It was a miserable, confusing time and I grew very angry at God for complicating my life with such problems. I talked to no one and made a decision alone that started me on adult living intellectually ill-equipped.

Thus I was at sixteen the true modern, priding myself on complexity and allowing my complexity to get the best of me. In the twenties youth never despaired, for the best thing in that mad decade was the glittering assumption that anybody could do anything.

# 7

THAT WAS AN UGLY PERIOD in which to be young. We were going to be honest about everything, and as the old moral values were based on hypocrisy we would dispense with them. A God who was our loving Father would never have let us get into such a mess, therefore, God was a name for a mysterious force that had nothing to do with our survival in the welter of defeat and hope called civilization. We were about to debunk the old heroes of America, to laugh at George Washington, to find that our government of laws had always been a mass of corruption. It was stupid to be concerned with the social question; just get as much pleasure from money and our senses as possible before it all ended in the final defeat of death. The New Testament had ceased to matter and nobody any more knew the words to "The Star-Spangled Banner."

I was at this time in rebellion against faith and decided I would only give lip service to the Church, for the sake of my father. I felt quite noble about not hurting him, and admired my deception for years. Actually I deprived him of the chance to protect and defend the richest heritage he had to leave me–*faith*.

In this tawdry era my family became householders on a grand scale. I think my mother, with the realities of life swamping her, returned to the precepts of her ancestors–a belief in bricks and mortar. We bought a vast house on Baltimore Avenue, its front windows flooded with sunshine, its back rooms dark and damp. It faced Clark Park which seemed like the wilds of the country. The oak paneling was solid and magnificent, as my mother pointed out; the furnaces consumed tons of coal and we were never warm. Over this uneasy home was suspended a mortgage bearing a staggering interest rate. This move had been made to conserve our assets, in recognition of the fact that my father was a delicate man.

The good paintings were hung on the walls. The mahogany bookcases gleamed like satin, and the bound volumes had an opulent look. "Benjamin Franklin at the Court of France" hung in the dining room, and every mantelpiece had the ornaments from the old family homes. My mother was holding on to tradition, to an age of vanished securities. Sometimes she looked haunted with the effort, and my father shivered before the gas logs in the cold of winter, or sought the sunshine on the front porch when summer came. Nana's health was breaking, but she loved this house and firmly announced she would move from it only in her casket. We were all worried and tense with the strain of it, and I was thankful to escape from its walls, to pursue my unique ideas of what constituted an education.

I had enrolled for a two-year evening course in playwriting at Temple University. In the daytime I took a business course at the Pierce School, and suffered the torments of the damned while doing so, once pouring out my heart in a poem I submitted to the *New Republic*, commencing, "Gnarled tortured fingers of immature senility," which was my salute to the secretarial profession. I entered the University of Pennsylvania to take French, in the late afternoon and at summer school. Somehow I was also studying speech techniques at the Emilie Krider Norris dramatic school. I exploded the time theory and studied the dance with Mrs. Littlefield, and fencing with a brutal Irishman. Each Friday afternoon I joined the queue outside the Academy of Music, and after an hour's wait I climbed the endless stairs to the amphitheatre. Suspended in this perilous spot, a trifle dizzy, I listened to the Philadelphia Orchestra led by Stokowski, and staggered out of the Academy drunk with glory.

In those days I read a play a day. I started to write mannered but sound criticisms for the Philadelphia papers. I was paid nothing, but I was acquiring a reputation which was a bit difficult to live up to, for I had only turned seventeen. I lived intensely alone, for the Catholic world of my youth had ceased to have any meaning for me and I was too shy to make new friends. I was not an unattractive girl so I had a small court of earnest and complicated young men who talked about the Russian experiment, and won scholarships to Harvard, and were filled with social generosity and political idealism, which made them take sides in the Sacco-Vanzetti case. They were on the side of art, revolution and, a bit later, psychoanalysis. They read Stephen Vincent Benét's *The Beginning of Wisdom*, and Floyd Bell's *Moon-Calf*, and John Dos Passos had settled the business of war with *Three Soldiers*. These youths held no great interest for me, but I sat with them on the steps of the University Library and read Scott Nearing. I made fun of blue-nosed respectability, but these associations remained embarrassingly platonic, though we all talked endlessly about sex.

The theatre in the early twenties had a splendor, a questing that satisfied my hungry spirit. I remember Duse in *Ghosts* and *Thy Will Be Done*. It is impossible to recover a young ecstasy, but while with Sarah Bernhardt the proscenium arch had always been present in your consciousness and the awareness that this was theatre and acting, Duse came to you with the intimacy of the printed page. The Mrs. Alving of her *Ghosts* was universal woman, aware of sin and doom and unseen forces as Oswald cries for the sun. The peasant woman of *Thy Will Be Done*, offering her sacrifice of love for the life of her doomed child, was in its deepest sense Catholic theatre with its awareness of human values and its deep sense of the divine.

I stood outside the Academy one morning for I had been told Duse was rehearsing. I was alone, save for a few cynical stagehands. She came out wrapped in veils, her eyes dark with actual physical pain. She looked at me, and she was sullen and old and I was an intruder. She passed hurriedly to her waiting car, and I croaked, "Ave atque vale." I had been reading George Moore and I could not help being ridiculous. I was filled with desolation at my own gaucherie and absurdity and slunk away. I felt a pair of hands almost electrical in their strength on my shoulders. I turned around to face Duse. The dark velvet eyes were still tragic, but her smile was tender and amused by the agonies and the self-consciousness of youth. She held me at arm's length, kissed me lightly as she finished this inspection and then as if warmth and youth were flowing in her veins she cried out, "Ave! Ave! Ave!" She was gone and I do not know what saved me from pitching in front of her car, to be destroyed at the height of this splendid moment. I walked through the streets of Philadelphia for hours, hearing that triumphant Ave. I was intense. I was pathetic. I was seventeen.

It was about this time that I met Eva Le Gallienne, co-starred with Joseph Schildkraut in the Theatre Guild's production of Molnar's *Liliom.* She was then in her early twenties, a slight, stoop-shouldered girl, whose remarkable pallor emphasized the tragic beauty of her gray-blue eyes. She was Russian and Danish on her mother's side, French and English on her father's–Richard Le Gallienne, one of the famous romantic poets of the Yellow Book era. She had in her something of those doomed young men, Aubrey Beardsley, Ernest Dowson, and all the sad and gifted men of letters who sat in the Café Royal listening to Oscar Wilde. She had also the fierce honest integrity of the Danes, and the mysticism of the Russians. In the theatre sense she had no glamor, for she wore rusty black suits winter and summer, surmounted, though the warm spring had descended on Philadelphia, by a Persian lamb cossack hat. She was intense and unhappy and spoke of "the tragic sense of life." Her sensitive nature was jarred by many emotional currents that would have destroyed a lesser woman.

I interested her, and we used to walk through the streets of Philadelphia, discussing what the theatre should be, for she had grown up in Europe and knew the repertory theatres that kept the great classics alive. She talked of subsidies such as art museums were given in this country, and popular prices that would bring the theatre within reach of the masses. She spoke to me gravely of the destructive things that could happen to me in the theatre.

"It's not the judgment of people you mind," she said, "it's living with your own conscience."

She introduced me to Russian literature, in particular the novels of Dostoevsky. She called herself "a free thinker," but one day in her thrilling husky voice she read me sections of "The Hound of Heaven," which her intimate friend Father Will Whelan had brought to her attention. She pored over the Bible which she carried with her, and no nun in a convent has ever been more aware of the meaning of St. Paul's First Epistle to the Corinthians; in fact, the character of St. Paul fascinated her, as did Jesus, the Man of Sorrows. She had read Marx and Lenin, but the Communist Revolution did not stir her, for she had an individualist's worship of man as a person, not a unit in society.

Eva Le Gallienne was a hero-worshiper, and in that we met on common ground. She was not a great actress, and the Ibsen heroines she loved to play limited her range. She was then, and is now, essentially a theatre person who understood every phase of this complex art form, bringing to it a mind of much power and a lover's sympathy. I knew her at the beginning of a career that in a few short years would make her one of the most astounding women of her time, for she did the impossible; she opened a repertory theatre and on the stage of the old Fourteenth Street Theatre which had once echoed to the voices of Booth, Barrett, Modjeska and Janauschek, gave America some of its best theatre —the tender *Cradle Song*, *Peter Pan*, *The Master Builder*, *The Cherry Orchard*.

In the days of *Liliom* she was a young girl, with her dreams and visions consuming her, who reached out to a younger girl who also was living in her own mind. She gave me the demanding journal of Marie Bashkirtseff, made fun of my love of grandeur, my ambitions for wealth and fame. She was content with her little apartment on a corner of lower Fifth Avenue and dreamed of a cottage in the country. She scoffed at worldly pleasures with the contempt of a young nun; indeed every great theatre woman I have ever known has in her make-up the qualities of a contemplative nun. She gave me glimpses of a tragically sensitive mind and a wounded young heart, but she had great reticence. I was too gay, too worldly, for her to have a profound influence on me. She did give me, however, a respect for the theatre, its traditions and its people that would never leave me. She also turned my mind back to religious influences that were in essence deeply Catholic—notably Dostoevsky. I felt the impact, but religion as I found it in the Catholic Church in those days was made up of Celtic puritanism and a cult of respectability. In turn I think I crammed Shakespeare down her throat, for to my horror she detested most of the plays, and when I quoted the sonnets she told me to read John Donne—and once more turned my mind back toward its natural Catholic bent.

I could chatter with her a mile a minute, for though she was a personage with her name in lights over the theatre, I was thoroughly at ease with her, and my shyness only overcame me when I tried to make her see world theatre, from the *Oedipus Rex* to the latest musical comedy, as spectacle. She would become all Danish moralist and insist that "Not just for entertainment" was the goal of the theatre. She was so earnest, so much the reformer, that she embarrassed me, and brought the classroom into the theatre, which I resented. She had genuine humility and sweetness of character, or she would not have tolerated me. I owe her a great debt, for she was aware of the tensions that lack of faith was breeding in me, and turned me back more than once in those years to the source of being.

"You're more than ever a Catholic, my girl," she used to say with her odd half-smile, "when you're most heretical."

I was involved in an incredible series of interests, flirtations, literary strivings, conflicting philosophies, family squabbles, and money worries, all of which minor troubles I lived through in major key till the air around me vibrated with the orchestration of my presence on earth. I must have been a great trial to my family. I had a consuming, conscious drive to be an overwhelming success. I was eighteen when I sat down to write my first full-length play.

It was all about Dr. Gordon Halliday, a famous physician, who through a series of misfortunes has become a general practitioner. His wife, a brilliant woman, yearns to see him rise again, and when a crippled young man becomes enamored of their only daughter, Dr. Halliday is persuaded to do a bone-grafting on this unfortunate youth, his hand shakes, the knife slips, and the last state of the young man is worse than the first. Mrs. Halliday has to see her daughter—who, of course, is a genius—give up everything to marry a helpless cripple.

My father suppressed his smiles, supplied me with the medical information, and with Strindberg and Ibsen as my literary models, I turned out a technically competent but unconsciously very funny play. My professor at Temple, Dr. Arthur Burton Cleveland, had to find somebody on whom to bestow a prize; therefore I appeared at a luncheon at the Bellevue and news photographers took my picture. I was famous in my own mind for the play selected as the prize winner was to be produced at Hedgerow Theatre. Jasper Deeter, horrified by the script, tossed it back at me without even an explanation. I forgot my glory, wept like a baby in my mother's arms, my father paced the floor at my first failure, and Nana crept around as if someone had died. I had a long way to go before I learned that the writing of the plays is the most demanding and complex of all art forms.

I still went to Sunday Mass with my father, often to the ornate Church of St. Francis de Sales where Bishop Michael Crane met us at the door, saying in a booming cheerful voice that maddened me:

"It's time you got a nice Irish Catholic boy to marry that one. I've just the lad in mind. I'll send him over tonight."

Unfortunately, he sometimes did and Joe or Aloysius proved hearty boys inarticulate about ideas or scornful about discussing them with girls. The Jesuits were usually educating these youths, and teaching them just who was the ruling sex. They were simple, good young men. I confused them and they bored me.

At about that time I discovered Frazer's *Golden Bough*, and that settled everything. I do not know why the musings of an anthropologist should have excited me so much, save that as I was mentally undisciplined, sensuality of the mind took the place of reasoned thought processes. Had any theologian dared to make so many wild guesses as Frazer I would have chortled in amusement. I should have recognized it as a study in the God-craving nature of man—but to me it was emancipation from God. My father, now thoroughly alarmed at my spiritual state, called in

Father Fortier, the Jesuit, and I was enrolled in a special afternoon class at St. Joseph's College in scholastic philosophy.

I couldn't penetrate the solid reasoning of Aquinas, and slipped around on the edges of his thought. Father Fortier had a Jesuit's scorn of bluestocking women, and tried to put my feminine mind in its place, to the delight of the loutish youths who were making up conditions. I insisted that Aquinas' conception of the universe was stern and unlovely, making no allowance for the frailties of human nature, and to bolster up my argument quoted the greatest of modern skeptics, David Hume. Father Fortier paled but tried to show me the delights of reason; he was tolerant as I floundered hopelessly in the profundities of the Angel of the Schools. Yet despite that, some of his clarity penetrated my brain and I understood, however dimly, the comprehensiveness of Catholic thought. I was able to understand everything I read a little better, I learned to extract the kernel of truth from all my favorite heretics. I even recognized Voltaire's fierce passion for justice as Thomistic. I commenced to see the Catholic point of view, and that awareness never quite left me.

It was that year, 1925, that Thérèse of the Infant Jesus was canonized. The little French Carmelite with her pretty face and her shower of roses struck me as the most doll-like and insipid of characters. I was ashamed that my father, an intelligent man, was carried away by these events. Someone gave him a first-class relic of the Little Flower, and I never saw him so pleased. He carried it in his wallet with a pressed rose from the garden of the Carmel at Lisieux. I teased him for liking a pretty little girl saint, and said, God forgive me, that she was canonized so that celibate priests could have something feminine and young to pay homage to.

My father sat talking about Thérèse and his haggard face was illumined with sweetness. He spoke of her Little Way, the difficult road of obscurity. He spoke of those nights when this tubercular girl was tortured for lack of sleep and tormented by doubts. He looked at me searchingly as he described that dying girl being deprived of the consolation of believing in eternity. My father described the strange sadistic Carmelite prioress, and

Thérèse with her little acts of kindness and love loomed as a figure of heroic proportions. I understood that my father took great comfort in the friendship of this saint. He did it without self-consciousness or ever seeming to be pious, for he laughed at the pious prigs and the fuzzy sentimentalists who were joining in the cultus of the Little Flower.

In those days I did not see much of his family. I was secretly aware of the disorder that lack of faith was breeding in my soul and I avoided Catholics whose minds I had the grace to realize were infinitely superior to my own, yet who refused to face with me that the Church was in a state of collapse. In that year I was fond of the phrase, "the great free men of the Reformation," and enjoyed involved arguments on how thought had at last freed itself from the dominance of theology. I laughed scornfully at the Chesterton-Belloc school as exemplified by the O'Hara family. But I did love the family and miss them, so occasionally I took my emancipated self to visit.

Aunt Constance had turned Grandfather's old home into a boardinghouse, and I seem to remember another mortgage was draped around it. In the usual order of things boarders keep the people from whom they rent rooms, but Aunt Constance reversed this and kept her boarders. She had acquired an artist who, in her middle forties after sacrificing her entire youth to her family, had come to Philadelphia to study at the Academy of Fine Arts. Her funds were giving out when she discovered Aunt Constance, and she painted all our portraits, including Jack, the Scottie dog, in payment. She was worth the trust, for she became quite famous, winning scholarships to Europe and having one-man shows at all the big art galleries. There were future opera stars in residence, who were studying at Curtis. Uncle Tom, with a crimson face, once helped one of them assemble her costume for *Thais*, even to hammering breast plates. There was J. Joseph Murphy, oldest member of the Philadelphia bar, and Katherine Crosby, his wife, who wrote poetry. J. Joseph was a splendid old gallant who put humanity in jurisprudence, and nearly went to the Supreme Court. They had, in that most dramatic phrase, "spent money like water," and now they were star-boarders at Aunt

Constance's. The servants were still with her, Robert and Mary, as well as various other colored people who gave a certain deceptive air of grandeur to this unique establishment.

Aunt Constance devoted her life to making everyone feel successful, and she saw with her keen eyes the awful hurts that strugglers for fame and fortune go through, the pathetic blows to pride when money is gone and old age has descended. The best and sweetest qualities in her nature came out in this experiment with "Papa's old home"; but the virtues cannot be used at banks. Aunt Constance with her boarders around her seemed like a character from a Chekhov play rewritten by Sean O'Casey.

The canonization of the Little Flower stimulated all the dwellers on Twentieth Street.

"France," Aunt Constance pronounced, "since the days of Clovis has always been the favorite child of the Church."

The artist wanted to do a picture of the Little Flower with all the sentimentalism removed, but Aunt Constance was against it.

"Now, Myra, don't pander to the intellectuals," she ordered. "Thérèse was a bourgeoise, and let her have all the trappings of bad taste. She'll reach the mightiest minds on earth, just as she is. It's the paradox of sanctity. Am I right, Doctor Tom?"

I had to cut in and remind them that the saints were only canonized as money-making schemes for the Church.

"Constance is certainly a smart girl," Uncle Tom contributed. "My niece is almost as brainy as Calvin Coolidge."

In the shrieks of laughter that greeted this sally Kate Murphy, who was a convert, was diverted from her purpose of annihilating me. My father's family refused to argue with me. They left books by Chesterton and Belloc lying around helpfully, even on the bathroom window sill, when I was visiting. Their method in treating a lapsed Catholic in the family circle was: say nothing, *pray*, make the sinner welcome. It is a good system.

I continued to be disdainful of the Little Flower, though I was kind enough to forgive Teresa of Avila her canonization, because she had genius.

"Better start learning to pray for yourself, daughter," my father said one day.

I looked at him closely, and I saw how thin he was, and how he shuffled his feet as he walked. His exhaustion was bone-deep, and I realized, without putting it in words, that the end was coming. In that final year we were very close. He thought it dreadful for a woman to be alone on the streets at night, and he used to pace the porch nervously peering out in the darkness as I crossed Clark Park. His thin face was flooded with relief as I came up the steps. We sat at the dining room table drinking buttermilk and smoking Camel cigarettes, while I explained to him out of my immense sources of wisdom the real meaning of life. He would dig out of his past some dramatic memory, and we would debate whether or not there was a play in it. Sometimes we took the trolley car and went down to a Bohemian restaurant on Camac Street. He hated growing old, and liked being taken as a gay blade escorting a young girl. At times, though not often, when money was burning a hole in his pocket, we dressed in evening clothes and went to the South Broad Street Theatre. We saw *They Knew What They Wanted*, Sidney Howard's first success, and Marjorie Rambeau in *Antonia*.

The best and most perfect relationship a young woman can have is a friendship with her own father. It prepares her for all others, though she must be reconciled that no other man will give her such poignant affection or regard her with such idolatrous pride. Any father knows that a young girl (even in the naughty nineteen twenties) has an innocence that tears at the heart, that this radiance must soon go to another man, and the thought of that unknown man is painful to all fathers. My father was terrified by my admiration for the handsome-actor type and by my court of earnest young iconoclasts.

At last my father's illness became so pronounced that our little excursions were impossible, though he kept on his feet. I tried to spend most of my evenings at home; sometimes we sat in his office not even talking, or walked down to the drugstore on the corner. At night I listened for that pathetic cough, for that I could still hear it gave me comfort—he was still in the house. I was reliving the emotions I had felt as a small child during his illness, for my love for him was the most profound thing in my life. We never used endearments or caresses, but every time he looked at me in that year it was a farewell.

It was not his lot to live those last months without worries. He could no longer keep up with the demands of a strenuous medical practice, so, one by one, he turned his patients over to other doctors, keeping only those who were able to come to his office. Finally it was almost too much to attend to his beloved Seminary, yet he could not bear to relinquish it. The Church in its temporal works is no more sentimental than any other institution, so the pressures started for the appointment of a new doctor. One of the deans was blatant about it, and my father was deeply hurt. Whatever love or respect I had left for the Church belonged to Father Philip Donahue, for his kindness, his tact, as he protected this broken, ill man.

"Tell the Doctor to come out this afternoon," his splendid voice would say to me on the telephone.

Father and I both knew that this meant an interloper was due to appear, and so my father would get in a taxi and go to the Seminary. One day I came into the office and found him weeping, his haggard face gray with despair.

"I'm not able to keep the Seminary," he said.

It was difficult to understand that, quite apart from the salary, my father loved the Seminary. The number of vocations he salvaged is known only to God, but he understood the exact moment a boy should be sent home for a little breathing space. He knew how to coddle the seminarians, and how to recognize a misfit at a glance.

"My son, you have a vocation," I'd often hear him say in the office. And then the long, pleading session, when a boy was hurt and sure he was unfit for the priesthood, would commence.

But I've heard others beg him for "just another chance, Doctor," and been amazed at the cold decisiveness of his refusal.

And now they couldn't wait for him to die. The Cardinal knew nothing about it, for the moment in the crisis had not yet been reached when he could be approached. The situation grew each week more painful and Father Philip Donahue must have said a great many prayers.

It was the spring of 1926 and everyone said, "Doc's bronchitis has never been worse." Nana even begged him to take Brown's Mixture regularly. One rainy Friday at the Seminary he caught a cold, but still he came down to breakfast each morning, saw his few patients. He even tried to work in the little garden back of the house. My mother with her Spartan qualities guided us all through these difficult days. She pretended not to notice my intensity. She acted with my father as if he were perfectly well, and it cheered him. I couldn't concentrate on any of my manifold activities until one day the telephone rang.

"Constance," said the well-remembered voice, "this is Sister Julie. Could you stop in at the convent today, dear? I need your help."

Once again I walked up the steps of the Convent of Notre Dame, down the long corridor past the refectory, up the stairs by the bridge to Sister Julie's little room. She looked at me, and a shocked expression came on her face. I was abnormally thin, my eyes were deeply circled, but she was looking into a mind that was in the first stages of the spiritual apathy which was to afflict my generation. She rallied from her realization of my bitterness and despair and, with her mocking smile, informed me that the graduating class had to give a play on Alumnae Day which was three weeks away and I was to help them. She handed me one of those amateur plays, all about a jury trial. She looked at me as I leafed through it.

"Sister," I said, with an interest I hadn't felt in weeks, "this is terrible."

"Oh, child, it's just a play for amateurs."

"May I do one of my own, Sister?" I questioned.

"But of course you may." A quickly suppressed smile played on her lips. "Very few of my gels would do this on such short notice. Constance, child, I could always rely on you."

Suddenly I wanted to do this play for the alumnae more than anything in the world. It would make my father happy, and for a brief handful of hours I would escape his tragic face. It made me feel alive again just to be with Sister Julie. I could not deceive her, so I told her the truth, quickly.

"Sister, I go to Mass because I don't want to make my father unhappy—but I don't believe in it. I haven't been to Communion for two years."

She took it without flinching.

"Dear child, Gawd said to me, 'Julie, you have a flinty heart. I want Constance.' And He's going to have you back." She raised one imperious little hand. "Wait. What you believe, or do not believe, does not alter the fact that *this is your convent.* We love you and make you welcome. I will not discuss it with you until you wish me to—but remember *your faith is as important to me as my own.*"

I was on my knees, my head in her lap. She said not a word. She never touched me. She let me sob out my desperate young heart. I went away to wash my raddled face, and came back.

"I'm sorry, Sister. I didn't mean to do that. I never cry, you know *that.*"

"Aren't you strong-minded?" Her smile was sly. "I've wept every day of my life. I had red swollen eyes all through my novitiate." Then that robust laugh rang out. "My dear young atheist, He and I have won the first round. Tears are the gift of the Holy Ghost. Scared?"

I was so glad to be back that I'd have succumbed to any suggestion. Sister Julie had too much understanding to prey on weakness.

"Don't put on your make-up without a pocket mirror," she ordered. "Don't put your rouge so high on your cheekbones. It broadens your face. Here. Here, child."

Sister Julie finished my make-up expertly, drawing the lipstick a little longer than my petulant mouth.

"Constance," she said, knowing that she was flattering me outrageously, "Ethel Barrymore and you are my favorite gels."

That night I sat before my typewriter pounding out an original one-act play, for nine characters, all female. It was a workmanlike comedy, well plotted, with amusing dialogue. It was called *Exit the Grand Duchess,* and somewhere it is probably still being played at a girls' school. I read it to my father the next morning at breakfast, and he looked at me in astonishment.

"Dear Lord," he exclaimed, "it's a play. It's a damn good play. I'm going to call Herbie Carpenter."

Dr. Herbert Carpenter had a brother, Edward Childs Carpenter, who wrote professional plays, so my father could pay me no higher compliment. He spoke too of getting in touch with Langdon Mitchell who had written *The New York Idea* and lived on Delancy Place in Philadelphia.

I drilled my company like a martinet. I flattered and cajoled, I stormed and raged. The play took life and form. It is true my young amateurs could not stand up to my demands, and a few of them tossed their parts in my face, while others less spirited stayed away from rehearsals. I made replacements. One of the nuns had once had a small part in Maude Adams' *Peter Pan*, and enlisted as my electrician. Her lighting effects were splendid. Ethel Barrymore Colt provided most of the stage-setting, including a large photograph of her mother. I studied professional make-up and the alumnae provided funds to buy a kit of grease paint and a rabbit's foot and eye shadow and a spirit lamp to melt mascara.

I took the leading role as my star, worn-out by rehearsals, had gone to the hospital three days before the opening. There was a hum of voices and then the curtain went up with that lovely sound of creaking pulleys. The play went well. The alumnae shrieked with laughter as smart, worldly dialogue floated over the convent footlights, but one laugh soared over the rest—Sister Julie's, from the dais with the other nuns. I entered as Countess Maritza Ivanova, grasping the high cane contributed by Ethel Barrymore. I knew the exact moment the audience forgot who I was. My timing was professional. The punch at the final curtain was good. I heard the screams of amazement. The curtain was down, and then the applause roared through the hall. . . . We were on for the bows . . . the curtain calls came thick and fast. . . . I was pushed on the stage alone. . . . It was a good moment.

Sister Julie was embracing me. "B. F. Keith's never had any

thing as good as this. My child, you belong in the theatre. And I'm going to help you get there."

Aunt Caroline and Nana were transported with pride. There no longer seemed any doubt as to my career. It had not only been good theatre, it was box-office. I came home from dinner at the Union League flushed with triumph. It was late May, 1926.

I mailed the MS of my play to a publisher, and received a letter suggesting that while they had grave doubts as to its commercial value, they would buy all rights for fifteen dollars. It was a reputable publisher, I was quite inexperienced, and I signed the copyright release of a play that is still being produced.

The sixth of June was the Sunday within the Octave of Corpus Christi. My father stood waiting for me at the door to go to Mass.

"Daddy, I'm not going with you." I said. "I don't believe in any of it any more."

He went out the door, his shoulders bowed. My father's convictions were concerned not so much with what he was against as what he was for, and that excluded a lot of things automatically. He had no room in his mind for negative doctrines.

I endured my conscience for ten minutes, and then I was beside him at church.

"Look, Dad, I'm sorry," I said as we walked home at a snail's pace. "I don't mean all I say."

"Well now, daughter," he drawled, "if God could forgive doubting Thomas, I'm sure he'll forgive one foolish little girl."

In that one remark my father packed the breadth, the tolerance and compassion of Catholicity. He made me feel foolish, but most of all he made me feel protected. We sat on the porch together smoking, which shocked the passing Catholics. Some of them spoke to us with pursed-up lips, and he rose each time and bowed, which antagonized these worthy souls even more. We sat there talking theatre and it was peaceful and good. I never went to church with my father again for it was his last Sunday on earth.

On the morning of June ninth I received the munificent check for the play, and feeling well launched on my professional career with plenty more where that came from I debated how to spend it. My father was late coming down to breakfast, and he could just manage a smile as I showed him my fortune. Where did that day go? Little events still stick in my mind. We sat in the second-story front room, and he took Conrad's *Suspense* from the bookcase.

"Daughter, why don't you try to write a novel?" he questioned. "I think you could write a good book."

The sun was shining all day, a good warm sun. He sat on the porch. Great-aunt Jen sent him roses, because he'd looked so ill when she passed the house on her way to visit the grounds of the Sesquicentennial. He stood there looking at the crimson roses with a gentle smile on his face.

"Jen should have sent these to St. John's Avenue," he said.

St. John's Avenue—the Old Cathedral Cemetery! He looked at my horrified face and I saw the death longing in his eyes. I managed a jaunty smile, and he cocked his eyebrow as he returned to the porch and his book.

Where did that day go?

He came in with one of the boys up for examination in the Seminary.

"That's all right, son," he said, "you needn't wait for my regular office hour. It crowds up then. The Cardinal has a number of recruits this year. Best bunch of boys we've ever had."

He said that every year. The front door closed after a while, and he was coming up the stairs. Then it wasn't a day like any other. Time stopped crawling in its familiar way. It went by so fast that the minutes are blurred. He was lying on the backroom bed. My mother was telephoning doctors. . . . Dr. Brown rushed up the stairs. I heard his gasp.

"This man is dead."

My feet had wings. I was running, running—up Baltimore Avenue, up Springfield, to the church and the priests. No one had told me to, but I kept remembering, "The soul doesn't leave the body till fifteen minutes after death." I was in the rectory.

I who didn't believe in anything was standing with Bishop Crane's great arm around me.

"Father McCarthy's gone for the Viaticum just in case. We used to say in the Seminary he was cracked on the Last Rites. And now . . ." Bishop Michael Crane could be as kind as a woman. "He didn't need them—not the Doctor. Stop shaking, girl, stop shaking." His face was working pitifully. . . .

Father McCarthy was standing by my father's bed and I was on my knees. My father looked so pathetic and lonely lying there with his thin beautiful hands so still.

It was death. Everyone has been through it, this always violent and mysterious disruption of life, this wound to intellectual pride. The Church had finished anointing her faithful son. I was alone with my father. His jaw muscles had not yet gone slack—and I watched it happen. This worn sad face became young. A look of beauty came on it as if he looked on the source of all happiness. And there beside my father, as I would never know it again, I recognized the presence and reality of God. I vowed I'd go back to confession. Emotional, unstable, yes of course . . . but I know now as I knew that June evening, that as surely as Ignatius Loyola experienced the beatific vision by the river at Manresa so did my father in his first minutes of death.

There was much to be done, and when Saturday afternoon came there was no time to go to the Jesuits at St. Joseph's. I went to the Church of St. Francis de Sales and with burning contrition in my heart took my place in line.

It was my turn. I was in the box. I had lived for two years without the Sacraments, and without grace. And now a priest was talking to me, and he was saying cruel things.

"You're not a Catholic girl at all. You're a disgrace. Think you're better than other people, do you?" I gasped out that my father was dead. He snapped, "I know your father's dead, but don't come in my confessional box indulging your self-pity. I shouldn't give you absolution."

I leaped up in the middle of his tirade and walked out. I am not blameless, for my love of my father was not sufficient for me to rise above my wicked pride, but had that priest given me the kindness of Christ my will and my soul might have been put in order to face the years ahead. I say *might*—because perhaps it was emotionalism that sent me into that confessional box, but I think it was more.

It was my father's last night among us. I put next to his heart the relic of the Little Flower, and the rose from the Carmel at Lisieux. I gave him a daughter to care for him, for the daughter who had deserted him. I know that she was kind to him.

He wasn't a saint, far from it, for he, too, had tortured nerves. Life had brought him crushing disappointments. His fine mind had not been rewarded with fame or fortune. Many times he had been weak where he should have been strong. But he never failed to do a kindness. He had carried through life a transcendent faith in God and a beautiful tolerance for his fellow man.

The next morning they carried him through the door. The ostentatious lilies on his casket seemed inappropriate to this gentle, unassuming man. I heard him say many times, "I want all the honors of my Church." He had them. Bishop Michael Crane celebrated the Solemn Pontifical Requiem Mass. The Seminary Choir sang gloriously. The monsignors and the priests were there, even his beloved "Zoo," looked sacerdotal and impressive. The nuns from his convents filled the pews. There was a slight stir, and there stepped forward to preach the eulogy his friend the Right Reverend Monsignor Henry T. Drumgoole.

The text . . . "Honor thy physician for the need thou hast of him; for the Most High has created him. For all healing is from God, and he shall receive gifts of the king. The skill of the physician shall lift up his head, and in the sight of great men he shall be praised."

# BOOK THREE

## 1

IT WAS RAW AND RAINING steadily the week Aunt Caroline and I went ahead of the family to the cottage she had taken in Ventnor, a deceptively simple white colonial house with a quaint picket fence around its neat garden. Roses grew in trellises on the side wall and over the garage, but everything was disciplined to the demands of a certain standard of living. One positive enjoyment I did have from that summer—the owner of the cottage had an enormous dramatic library, and I read plays and biographies when I was not being courteous to the suave and worldly people who came to play bridge.

It was understood that this summer would help my mother pull herself together, and I would do something about the future. Girls of the best families were no longer content to sit at home, but earned their own money in the interval before marriage. It was admitted that I had unusual talents, but then we didn't come from theatre or literary people, who were after all, in the main, dissolute Bohemians.

When we returned from Ventnor the walls of the house on

Baltimore Avenue seemed to breathe: "*Money*, *Money*, *Money*." We were certainly not starving or in debt, but fear and worry were never out of our minds. The house wasn't worth the struggle, for it was eating into vital reserves. Nana had a strong character and she fought for what she wanted.

"You will marry and go away," she pointed out. "Then where will your mother and I be without the house?"

I sat down to write a letter to Eva Le Gallienne who that fall had opened the Civic Repertory Theatre. I knew she was fond of me and theoretically I had an enormous knowledge of my subject, from omnivorous reading. I knew also that in a whole lifetime I could never learn all I wanted to know about the theatre. My letter was, for me, strangely humble and sincere. It was not sent, for the family erupted into violent life. They were concerned with the moral aspects of a young impressionable girl thrown into the maelstrom of the New York theatre; but they were also concerned with my selfish desertion of my mother, my self-sacrificing grandmother. I was a monster of selfishness. Our family did things in a certain way, and that way did not include going off "free as you please," to New York.

My mother, torn between her sympathy and ambitions for me and her fears as to my youth and inexperience, joined the enemy camp. Various cousins of my mother's came to visit and add to the uproar. They loved great noisy family parties filled with backbiting and contention, and when they had a victim who was filled with "crazy notions" their zest for the fray was twice as keen. I could not fight them, and I sat, cold with contempt, before their vast complacency.

I sold a few little pieces to "arty" magazines and another one-act play, but I was certainly no economic asset. It was in a mood of desperation that I went to see Monsignor Drumgoole. The maid led me up to his study on the second floor where Monsignor greeted me with delightful urbanity, but no real warmth.

He sat at the desk toying with his many handsome ornaments, every inch what he was in those days—the socialite priest of Philadelphia. He seemed remote and rather annoyed. I tried to tell my story without emotion, and with a decent reticence. I could see as I talked the cold indifferent eyes of city editors refusing me, the competent women at personnel desks and their impersonal dismissals.

He was looking away from me wearily, and I realized he understood my fierce pride and shame before my failure. He would turn toward me in a moment with a charming gracious bit of consolation, to which would be added a fillip of classical scholarship. He would arise, and I hoped I could hold my head high as we said goodby. . . .

I looked up and a pair of heaven-blue eyes were looking into mine, and the whole face was softened by kindness. He put that gentle hand over mine.

"My dear lone Bandit. I shall join you on your career of crime. We shall point our guns straight under the noses of these cold-hearted wretches who will not give up their wealth to us. Jobs? Horrid word! We want something much grander than that—fame, fortune." He was moving toward the cellarette where he kept his wines. "Is it the occasion for dry sherry or burgundy? I think burgundy is more full-bodied—a bolder drink."

I laughed aloud, for my friend was back. This impressive prelate who could dazzle an embassy ball had taken on the task of getting me started in the world.

"I must teach you about the wines," he said worriedly, as I refused to join him. "And now, child, Father Drumgoole and you will make a plan. We will not be timid in our demands. We will deal realistically with your talents. What a beautiful voice you have, cultivated, elegant—an asset, my child. These fearful voices of our co-religionists!" He shuddered in mock horror. "You've got a quality of aliveness, excitement. That shyness is attractive, but it can be overdone. My dear, we're going to do very well—"

The plan took quite a few weeks, and included many visits to the study at St. Gregory's, for I was preparing a lecture: "The Theatre and Its Relation to the Church." Monsignor by this time knew the story of my loss of faith, and he sympathized with my disgust at the dreary side of Irish Catholic life. He meant to fix that up as soon as he could give me enough worldly gloss to introduce me to a Catholicism that was wealthy and cultivated but secure in the faith. It would not be long, for I was an apt pupil in worldly ways, before I could be taken to the Lesleys', to the Reppliers', to the Arnolds' in New York.

Monsignor Drumgoole's scholarship was sound, and I had the ability to create a dramatic sequence, as well as a talent for spoken English. "The Theatre and Its Relation to the Church" was therefore quite a striking lecture.

Agnes Repplier arrived one afternoon when we were at work. The attention Monsignor was giving to a young girl depressed her. She regarded me as a rather stupid character and refused to participate in my emergence as a brilliant Catholic intellect. She was in one of her mannish moods and sat sulking at the front window. Actually Agnes Repplier was being intensely feminine, for I was poaching on her preserves.

Monsignor and she had been friends since the day when, as a young curate at St. James's, assistant to the fiery Dr. Garvey, he mounted the pulpit, faced the congregation, froze, the crimson blushes coming and going on his agonized face, stammered an apology, and left the pulpit. . . .

Dr. Garvey had not been gentle with his young assistant. How expect that from the irrepressible priest who once began a funeral eulogy, with the remains of the deceased in the casket before him and the mourning family in the front pews, with this startling tribute: "If I had depended on this laddie-buck in the casket here to support St. James's I'd have been begging pennies on Chestnut Street Bridge."

It was no wonder that the young Father Drumgoole who had forgotten his carefully prepared sermon lay face down on his bed, terrified and broken. The news that Miss Agnes Repplier was waiting to see him in the parlor was scarcely cheering. He had had to call on this bluestocking lady during the Block Collection, and he'd been frightened out of his wits. He entered the parlor to confront the erect birdlike spinster. She wasted no time on preliminaries.

"Father Drumgoole," she said in her clear, precise voice, "as you are obviously the type of priest who only visits his parishioners on collections, I had to come call on you. I was in the church this morning."

"Miss Repplier"—his face was crimson—"I—I can't preach. I—I can't stand up before people. And I can't visit, for you see I have no social graces. I belong in a country parish, where people will understand that I'm a very simple priest."

"Hush, Father Drumgoole, you are nothing of the kind." She looked long no doubt at this handsome blond curate. "Now, never as long as you live memorize another sermon. Make a few notes on a piece of paper—think about them—tear them up. Augustus Thomas told me the whole secret of oratory. It is: 'Look after your consonants, and your vowels will look after themselves.' " She rose, an elegant little figure. "Father Drumgoole, I am going to Doctor Horace Howard Furness' reading at the University and to a tea in his honor afterward. Will you escort a lone spinster?"

"Miss Repplier, you can't know what you're asking. Why, I'd be ridiculous in such company."

"You will charm them. I make no mistakes. I will expect you at a quarter of four." At the door she made her prediction. "Father, I will live to hear you one of the greatest pulpit orators in America."

The friendship between this unpredictable lady of letters and Monsignor Drumgoole had been famous through all my life. She had the finer mind, had guided his reading, saw to it that he met the right people. He had battled the whole Catholic world, who were not too fond of the tart little lady, for honor and recognition of her talents. He accompanied her everywhere, to the Acorn Club, to the Cosmopolitan in New York. And now she sat sulking by the window as he guided the faltering footsteps of a rival lady of letters. Agnes had bossed him unmercifully, but I was more pliant—and we were both Celts who laughed at the same things. He worked with me a little longer, asking her questions, which she refused to answer.

"I am not dramatic, you know that," she snapped.

He pulled my chair to the center of the room. Agnes lit a small black cigar with a splendid defiance, glaring at me, expecting that I would be goggle-eyed. I looked at her with polite expectancy. Monsignor was proud of me. He gave her brandy in a huge balloon glass and took his place at the other uncurtained window, warming his brandy with his hands. Agnes was puffing away at her cigar, as he looked down on the empty street.

"Ah me! Think of the scandal we may give a stray passer-by—some good and worthy soul." That silvery giggle floated out. "Is it perverse of me to enjoy throwing the parochial mind into confusion?"

His blue eyes looked wickedly at the photograph of Denis, Cardinal Dougherty, on the mantelshelf between Cardinal Gibbons and Cardinal Mercier. I always felt the position of that picture was by design, for the Cardinal, glaring at the camera, was not impressive between the two ascetic but carefully posed Princes of the Church.

The air was filled with electric currents. Steel met steel and sparks flashed. Agnes Repplier's sword of wit was cruel and brilliant. Monsignor's swordplay was light, delicate, infinitely graceful, and the point sank in slowly, as if there were no malice in the murderous blade. I was dazzled.

"Constance," said Agnes Repplier, "do you know Anatole France?"

I was not eloquent, but I proved to be intelligent.

"*At the Sign of the Reine Pedauque*," she repeated. "How curious! Distinctly a minor novel—yes; yet it is delightful. Monsignor, that is the most implicitly Catholic of his novels. Interesting she should like that. Short stories? 'The Procurator of Judaea'! The child has the artistic temperament—sloppy—but she has the religious sense of life. Your girl has possibilities, Monsignor. The lyrics of Sappho, Constance? No. Well then, you must read them."

Agnes Repplier was at Monsignor's bookcase. She rooted around rapidly and came back with a translation.

"Here you are, child."

She kept the book in her hand, reading to herself, murmuring, "Lovely. Lovely."

"When you have read these, Constance," she said, handing them to me, "and I think it may well be a perfect experience for you, Monsignor will bring you to tea. We'll make you a Clinton Street regular. Then you may tell me which are your treasures. But don't pose or we will see through you, and cast you down—down. . . . Monsignor and I will declare you anathema, if you are ever a poseur."

The lecture was finished and I was packed off to New York by Monsignor Drumgoole to make engagements for the next winter. Nana, not without a few protests, had turned over the savings account she had kept for me since my birth, and which was to be for my trousseau. I was a well-dressed young girl, with the air of assurance that Monsignor's friendship had given me, when I presented my first letters in New York.

I did not know that his illustrious friends had also been provided with a complete dossier and instructions on how to treat a sensitive girl who had lost her father. He advocated, that dear man, though I did not know it till many years later, a touch of deference. I realized as I went from fabulous house to fabulous house in New York, that Catholicism had many facets. Some of the nuns I met in their East Side convents, in their Fifth Avenue mansions, were twice as worldly in their manner of approach as any actress. A few were remarkable writers and scholars. The Jesuit priests at St. Ignatius Loyola were like my romantic conception of the diplomatic corps. They were suave and distinguished men; but, for all their gracious manners, remote in the vastness of their strong, sure acceptance of God, the Lord and Redeemer of all. I met the Dominican Fathers at St. Vincent Ferrer, who preside over the most beautiful church in America. I talked to Reverend Mother Grace Dammon again, who was now at the Sacred Heart Convent on Fifth Avenue. This time I liked her completely, and she was pleased with me for I was doing my best to live up to Monsignor Drumgoole's dictum: "You must be a thorough woman of the world before you can even claim to be a good Catholic."

It was in a mood of subdued triumph that I finally presented my letter of introduction to the Right Reverend Monsignor Joseph McMahon, a colorful churchman, at the rectory of Our Lady of Lourdes. I had called to ascertain what time would be convenient for the Monsignor, so I was faintly amazed when his housekeeper waved me down on a hall bench at the front of the dark stairs. I heard a deep rumbling voice, plainly annoyed, coming from the upper regions where he was being informed of my presence.

"You're to wait there," she snapped crossly on her return.

It was most uncomfortable, and the cooking odors assailed my nostrils as I waited and waited. I was getting furious, for I had been well spoiled during this visit to New York. I was on my feet going out the door, when a deep voice said, "You've a temper, haven't you? Well, so have I. I'm the most impolitic priest in the United States."

I turned and looked into a pair of ironic blue eyes belonging to a tall old gentleman in a watered-silk dressing gown. His house slippers were notable for their wide silver buckles. In fact, the Right Reverend Monsignor Joseph McMahon was an eighteenth century figure, with all the fierce independence of mind, the love of freedom, that characterized the famous men of that century. He waved me back onto the hall bench, sat beside me—and led me on to make a young idiot of myself. I gravely informed him that the Church was not progressing as fast as she should in this marvelous twentieth century of enlightenment. I informed him she made too much ado over dogmas, which anyone knew were merely past generalizations declared eternal truths by some council or other. He was much entertained, and in his mighty voice called out, "Miss O'Hara will be dining with us."

He was a fascinating host, looking at me over his rows of wine glasses, beaming impartially on his curates who remained gravely silent. His wit was violent and blunt. Somewhere he had met my grandfather and found him a man of his own kidney.

"Now mind," he said, "there was your grandfather coming up the steps of the Cathedral in full papal regalia, but the knee pants he wouldn't wear. Right ahead of him was Martin Meloney, satin breeches and all. Your grandfather said, 'Martin, if you had a tail, an organ grinder could use you for a monkey.'" Monsignor laughed heartily and wiped the tears from his eyes. "Martin for all his dignity was an Irishman, and out came his sword, right there on the Cathedral steps. Your grandfather backed away and whipped out his own sword. It was a sight to see. Well, sir, they pulled themselves together, and there was no murder. Not a Meloney has ever forgiven your grandfather for that–and they'll have it in for you."

Monsignor McMahon gave me spectacular help in the next days, and coerced all the best convents into promising to pay much more for my lecture than it was worth. He spearheaded his attack through the Sisters of the Holy Child, for he had decided I was not the "Yes Sister-no Sister," type; I would get myself in trouble at the Mothers of the Cenacle whose New York convent, St. Regis Priory, was in his parish. Mother Margaret Bolton was safe enough but more the type for converts who are inclined to be in awe of religious regalia.

"There's no awe in you, lassie." He smiled. "You're filled with dangerous tendencies."

He arranged an appointment with Cardinal Hayes, and I knelt in the episcopal residence, kissing his ring. He had a face of surpassing sweetness, and his soul could transcend every private bitterness. He was gracious to me, and never betrayed that he realized a stormy petrel was being sent out of Cardinal Dougherty's jurisdiction. . . .

Dr. James Walsh knew my grandfather and had been an intimate of Twentieth Street; in fact, he had been something of a protégé of Bishop O'Hara's. He was the only one who was at all curt with me, and did nothing whatever, except to advise me to learn to cook. It was sound advice, but at the time I was indignant. Dr. Walsh found me artificial and theatrical and wondered where the family had got me, for he regarded them as the highest type of Catholic intellectual; and though he didn't say it, he strongly intimated that Monsignor Drumgoole was turning me into that most incredible of creatures, "a Catholic snob."

In between my visits to the Catholic great I went down to the Civic Repertory on Fourteenth Street, where Eva Le Gallienne was doing magnificent things. I learned not to scream when patriarchal rats with impressive whiskers jumped out at us from the dark corners of that old theatre. I talked convents so much that I think I may have persuaded her into doing Sierra's *Cradle Song*, one of her greatest triumphs.

I was a happy and joyous girl when I returned to Philadelphia with an impressive list of dates for lectures the next season. I plunged into work, for one lecture was not going to be enough. I wrote some character sketches and haunted Ruth Draper, the most gifted diseuse of her generation or any other. I had some Presbyterian friends and I tried my art out on their church gatherings at $5 an engagement. I did so well that the Lutherans grabbed me for $7.50, but not before a Presbyterian young man had written me a poem of sorts beginning, "Cynic, well mayhap you are one," and ending, "Exquisite piece of modernness."

I was twenty years old and the world lay at my feet. On Sundays I went to St. Gregory's to Monsignor Drumgoole's late Mass, though I had not returned to the Sacraments. His wealthy friends had helped him renovate that undistinguished church, and it was starkly simple and beautiful. It was known as the Mass of the Cardinal's malcontents. Many distinguished Catholics came to it, and the shabby street was lined with handsome, glistening town cars. The organist, a friend of Monsignor's, was almost Anglican in her correctness. Then Monsignor, in his red robes with the duchesse lace on his sleeves and his beautiful white hair gleaming in the subdued light, would step to the altar rail and preach. Who could resist the charm of the man? Monsignor was *not* a pulpit orator, but his voice haunted you; his irony was enchanting, but there was an undertone of pity and tenderness for all of us who had forgotten Who died for us.

I had gone back to the Children of Mary at Notre Dame and my friendship with Sister Julie. There was that nasty business of confession to be got through, but I meant to stop sometime when I was in New York at St. Jean Baptiste, which I had heard of through my cousin, Mother Mary Agatha Scott of the Georgetown Visitation, who had been editor of the Eucharistic magazine *The Sentinel* and translator of the life of the founder of the Blessed Sacrament Fathers, Père Eymard. Mother Mary Agatha Scott, who had been interested in my literary career, was a romantically satisfying figure to me for she had run away from a Philadelphia ball to take an early train for Baltimore to be a nun, in defiance of her mother, but with the permission of Archbishop Wood. My own great-grandmother McCunney, her aunt, had taken this beautiful Fanny Scott of the flashing wit to the Visitation Convent in Baltimore, where in the sixty-five years of her profession she had become among other things literary assistant to Cardinal Gibbons, and a famous translator. But I could almost see her dancing that last dance in a Philadelphia dawn in the year 1860, and turning to my then-young grandmother O'Hara: "Little Fan—little Fan, kiss me goodby, and remember Fanny Scott this way." I could trust a woman like that and be sure her Blessed Sacrament Fathers would make it easy for me to put things right with God. Once I sat in St. Jean's through an entire afternoon, but could not get up the courage to go to confession.

The renegade Catholic who has been fifty years out of the Church and the renegade of a few years are both equally out of the Church; the only way to return is sacramental confession. The longing of the Catholic to return is the deepest thing in his nature, both when it is an active torment and when it recedes to the back of his mind. It sounds almost too simple to say that the fear of confession is the root of the trouble; nevertheless, desertion of the Church is based on fear. The will is locked in a paralysis and only the power of prayer or a crisis, will make possible the return through the confessional. "All you have to do is to go to confession," but that *all* is a tremendous thing.

In the autumn I set off to New York, with an evening dress that barely covered my knees and the manuscript of my lectures.

My first stop was to be the school of the Holy Child in Suffern, New York, one of Mr. Thomas Fortune Ryan's contributions to the Church, for he had given part of his estate at Suffern to the Sisters of the Holy Child to conduct a school for "the poor little daughters of the very rich." The country was beautiful, and I was pleased with the splendid car and liveried chauffeur that drove me up through the Ramapo Hills. Reverend Mother Mary del Carmen was a marvelous person, and if she felt betrayed by Monsignor Drumgoole when she beheld the youthful lecturer, she did not make me feel it. We dined at small tables in a pleasant dining room, and I sat at the faculty table discussing Molière with the French teacher. "The poor little daughters of the very rich" gathered to hear my lecture which was way over their heads and the main thing they got out of it was my flossy pronunciation of "sacrifice," taught me by Elsie Ferguson, that radiantly lovely actress. My youthful audience frightened me to death by releasing white mice on satin ribbon leads from their uniform pockets. They came perilously close to the lectern, as I led the theatre from the St. Nicholas Day tropes straight up to Eugene O'Neill. The mice seemed more intelligent than the children.

I seemed always that year to be in convents, and discussing theatre in the parlor with one interesting Reverend Mother after the other. In common with all Catholics they understood the crying need for a theatre and that it was a maternal duty to reclaim our own child reborn in the Mass. Instead we turned it over to secularism, protested its morals, and never supported one worth-while Catholic theatre movement. I daresay to this day Reverend Mothers are discussing drama with some young lecturer, but a theatre craving spiritual rejuvenation gets nothing of all this wasted enthusiasm. In any event, I went about my assignments with joy, prayed in convent chapels and grew to love New York state, its miles of wilderness and the gleam of the Hudson River.

I began to realize that what was making me so happy that year was the Catholic atmosphere, the beautiful security of convents. I understood, however dimly, in these quiet cloisters with black-robed figures moving noiselessly around, what mental, spiritual and material security really meant. The convent bell came to mean the only rational guardian of time on this sorry earth. Out of these convents through the ages had come gifts to civilization. Hilda of Whitby in her Benedictine convent welcoming Caedmon and his song, and giving birth to English poetry. The Abbess Hrosvitha writing the first plays of modern drama in the tenth century in a Benedictine convent. (And what naughty plays they were—for hers was a robust spirit.) Sister Mary Madeleva in our own day writing stirring poems from a western college. Sister Miriam in her mountain-bound convent in Pennsylvania giving us the most haunting poetry of our literature. Sister Julie du Saint-Esprit in a convent in Philadelphia, bound in by order and form and discipline, whose soul adventured to the high heavens. I came to the conclusion that the only people who have any emotions worth mentioning are those who do not fritter them away on sensation, but enclose the fire in the mind and heart.

My sponsors, Monsignor McMahon and Monsignor Drumgoole, became aware of the tenor of my thoughts and, delighted with my radiance, they put their heads together and hatched a plan. They decided I didn't have the temperament to face a competitive world. I was sensitive, idealistic and a scholar. The religious rebellion that kept me away from the sacraments was a phase; and in some way they'd break down that resistance without frightening me. They decided I was going in the convent, and as my big lecture of the season was scheduled for the College of St. Elizabeth at Convent Station my mind must be skillfully prepared to select as my order the Sisters of Charity. My great-grandaunt had been one of Mother Seton's nuns and beloved by Mother Seton, therefore tradition would make up for my modest dowry. I would have a happy life, teaching and writing, growing in sanctity and wisdom, and not getting myself in trouble in this abominable world. I was too intellectual to attract the right man; and on the other hand too stupid about emotional matters to recognize the wrong one. Left to my own devices, my childishness and romanticism might get me into a serious disturbance of the senses.

Monsignor Drumgoole sat in his study at St. Gregory's drawing a gruesome picture of modern life for a sensitive woman. He spoke of the agonies of financial insecurity, pointed out that in the battle of life the awards and victories do not go to the brave. He spoke of failure. . . . He spoke of people who would be cruel, selfish, intolerably unkind. He pointed out that the twentieth century was divided into two camps—the tough- and the tender-minded; as I was in the latter grouping I had no protection against the hurts that would inevitably befall me. And then he departed from the heat of the battle, and opened the cloister door.

My imagination took fire; I saw myself a young novice in some dimly lit chapel, consecrated, apart. I was professed, and I sat in a great library and wrote, with no thought of money, literature that would be enduring. I saw myself middle-aged, a Reverend Mother in some shining convent, celebrating my feast day with my daughters all around me. I was Teresa of Avila, a saint, the beloved Madre. St. John of the Cross was coming toward me, and my voice said, and it did sound like Ethel Barrymore's, "Ave, Maria Purissima." I was being laid to rest in Mother Seton's graveyard, quite near the sainted foundress, her grandson Archbishop Seton, and her nephew Archbishop James Roosevelt Bayley, with all the great dignitaries of the Church standing there beside my open grave. I yearned for convent life and the repose of all passions. Monsignor had planted a seed, and I had a vocation in half an hour.

"Do you want to make your confession now, dear child?" he queried.

That was too simple a solution, for I was wicked, and I wanted some strange ascetic monk with burning dark eyes to absolve me. I saw myself rise at midnight and don the silicio—yes, I needed a hair shirt—my hand reaching for the whip as I flogged myself till the blood came. I would do great and tremendous penance.

There was, too, in justice to myself, a hard core of common sense that warred against my capitulation. My nature is not a spiritual one, I am more dependent than most on the love of creatures. I missed my father poignantly, and I knew I could only recapture his essence in the Church. I realized that his Catholicism was more profound than these glittering surfaces, filled with compromises with the world. I loved the atmosphere—but I judged it.

However, I left for Convent Station with a full-fledged vocation. Monsignor Drumgoole and Monsignor McMahon had prepared Mother Alexandrine that I was ready to renounce the world. I barely saw the luxurious limousines at Convent Station. I was through with all that, protected by the vow of Holy Poverty. The impressive gray stone College of St. Elizabeth was before me. I mounted the high steps joyously. I was commencing my climb to sanctity. I rang the bell and stood there. Nothing happened. I rang and I rang—and there was silence deep and profound. I was getting a bit nervous, for the winter sky was darkening and it was bitterly cold. Desperately I descended the stairs, walked along the side of the building—a door opened and a nun dragged me inside. She shook me vigorously.

"So I've got you, Jane Smith. Sneaking off to New York without permission. You thought you wouldn't be caught."

Under this rude treatment my teeth rattled like castanets. I explained, "I'm Constance O'Hara. I'm here to lecture."

I spoke to the wind. The wickedness of Jane Smith was too awful. I saw that this Sister of Charity was very old, even her eyes behind their steel-rimmed glasses were encased in wrinkles. She was shrieking *Jane Smith* and I was howling *Constance O'Hara*, as I tried to pull myself out of the clutches of her bony hands without toppling her backwards, when two nuns appeared at a brisk run. Behind them walked a stately Sister of Charity.

"Mother Alexandrine," said the aged nun, still holding me firmly, "I've caught Jane Smith."

"I'm Constance O'Hara!" By this time I couldn't stop yelling. "I'm here to lecture."

One of the Sisters rescued me, explaining soothingly, "Poor Sister is quite deaf and almost blind, she made a mistake."

Mother Alexandrine was laughing in great shuddering gasps and couldn't stop.

"Mother," said the nun, reaching for me, "are you going to let her off again? Racing to New York without permission!"

The other Sisters led her away soothingly, patting her back, treating her like a naughty and beloved child.

My hat was jammed down on my head from the pummeling I had had, my face was beet-red, and my voice still cracked nervously. Mother Alexandrine pulled herself together, and came toward me.

"Child, child, dear, you look all of sixteen. Monsignor McMahon has spoken so glowingly of you, that I have invited quite a few outsiders. Mr. Theodore Maynard will be here. . . ." Laughter overcame her again. "I don't believe you can really lecture. You're only a baby."

I didn't know what to do or to say. I was still shattered; for the first time I was filled with doubts as to my abilities.

Mother Alexandrine led me upstairs, a lay-sister trailing us with my bag. "You must forgive Sister. She helps us with the freshmen. Jane Smith, by the way, is a homesick freshman, who every now and then kicks over the traces, and goes home to New York to see her mother. She's our youngest, not quite sixteen."

On the door of the room we were standing before was an impressive sign: *Cardinal Hayes Suite*. We passed through the reception room and into a bedroom where my eyes fell on an enormous bed canopied in crimson damask. All the chairs were in the same impressive hue. Through the open door to the reception room I could see a high-backed chair pulled before a single place set for dinner; on the chairback was the Cardinal's coat of arms. Long windows to the floor overlooked the countryside which was grim and eerie with snow flurries. I was filled with the pathetic gaucheries of youth; moreover, I was scared to death. I wanted to turn and run.

Mother Alexandrine felt put upon, and she was doing her best to maintain her composure.

"Your dinner will be served here," she said. "I will come for you a few minutes before eight."

Alone, I tried to remind myself that I was a woman of the world. I sat in my dressing gown, smoking a cigarette, trying to be courageous. Mother Alexandrine had not selected my familiar "The Theatre and Its Relation to the Church," but the "Comedies of Shakespeare," in which discussion I would give readings from *As You Like It* and *Much Ado About Nothing.* I was cold with terror. I had never done public readings before, and even though I had discussed the techniques with Minnie Maddern Fiske I knew with an awful certainty that I was going to be a failure. This Shakespearean lecture in my list was one of those I had never expected to be taken up on by the Catholic trade. Mrs. Fiske, whom I had met at the old South Broad Street Theatre, had talked about the boy-girl motif of Shakespeare's Rosiland and Beatrice, the witty surfaces that disguised a fierce romanticism more demanding than Juliet's or Cleopatra's. . . . I tried my black mask for the provocative Beatrice, and looked like a child at a Halloween party. I walked with Rosilind's graceful lope—and I was downright silly. In desperation I went in to take a bath. Isadora Duncan always took baths at life's great crises, and I was certainly facing one.

I felt a little better as the hot water laved my tense muscles. I reached for the faucet to make it a trifle warmer . . . Steam poured from it and a burning agony hit my legs. It was an enormous tub, and I could not get out easily. I pulled to the rear, I got one leg up, and fell over the side to the wooden floor. The bathroom was filled with steam. I managed to turn off the faucet but not to reach the plug. My hip was agony; I limped bone-naked into the next room, clutching a bathtowel. In the reception room a lay-sister, laden with a heavy tray, walked by my open door. She did not drop the tray, though it shook perilously, her eyes lowered, and her face turned scarlet. I squirmed into my dressing gown, resentful that she looked so stricken; after all we were made the same. She made a hasty retreat, and I slammed the bathroom door from which steam was still pouring.

I walked with a limp—well, Mrs. Fiske had played Beatrice with arthritis. In the steam bath every twist of curl had come out of my hair. I managed to swallow two or three bites of dinner, and drank a cup of tea in quick, nervous gulps. I put on my evening dress, which was one of my mother's exquisite creations with the fashionable short skirt and long waist-line. I had always felt secure in that beautiful pale blue panne velvet with the gleaming silver grapes at the belt and shoulder. Tonight with my straight reddish hair hanging dankly around my broad childish face, my appearance gave me no pleasure whatever, for I looked a gawky overgrown fourteen. I could find no comfort anywhere as Mother Alexandrine conducted me to the Assembly Hall.

I stood backstage and gasped in horror. The hall seemed to be the size of the Academy of Music in Philadelphia and every seat was filled. The college girls in their impressive caps and gowns were terrifying enough, but, since obviously there wasn't much to do on winter evenings in Convent Station, the townspeople also were there in full force. Mr. Theodore Maynard sat in the third row and his intellectual countenance was not reassuring. I heard the last words of my introduction.

I parted the curtains and faced that audience with the worst case of stage fright I ever had in my life. I was grateful for the exquisite torture of my hip. I opened my mouth with my many plagiarisms from Georg Brandes. Mr. Maynard, recognizing them, frowned. I was interspersing my lecture with my readings from the plays. I tried to move around the stage, and I winced with pain. Then it was time for the masked-ball scene and those delightful lines of Beatrice. Giggles broke out in the college section. Never once was that audience mine, for I moved around in a fog of pain and bewilderment, my voice echoing hollowly in that tremendous hall and coming back to me light and childlike. Finally it was over, and Mother Alexandrine was merciful. I had that condemned-to-death feeling of a bad performance, the most desolate and abandoned sensation in life. She led me offstage, remarking:

"Child, you're too young to go through the strain of a reception. You did the best you could. I should have let you choose your own subject."

She opened a door and I plunged through it; I hung in space; I fell into blackness. A concrete surface hit my chin. There were stars, my breath was gone. I had pitched down a dozen steps to the path below. I lay there speechless, while Mother Alexandrine and a college senior—the president of her class and head of student dramatics, as I later learned—leaned over me anxiously. Silver grapes lay all around me, hundreds of imitation pearls, links of my prized blue enamel bracelet; and both my knees were bleeding. Teresa of Avila, remembering her trouble with the one-eyed Princess of Eboli, obviously had decided that no more misfits would get in cloisters. I got to my feet. I managed to smile. Finally I was alone in the Cardinal Hayes suite, after refusing first aid. My chin was bruised, my arms; by now my hip was blistered. I crept into bed after I had managed to stop the bleeding of my knees. I slept. I woke. The snow was falling. The quiet was driving me mad. I woke up suddenly. It was just before dawn, and a bell was ringing. I heard footsteps, many footsteps. I opened the door of the Cardinal Hayes suite; nuns were coming down the stairway opposite, a window at the head of the stairwell silhouetting their black-clad forms. Their long square faces were white and melancholy, the rattle of their rosary beads was the most depressing sound I'd ever heard in my life. These women were walking corpses. I threw the remains of my finery in my bag, I dressed; I had to get out of this convent alive. I was weak with hunger. On the bureau I saw an envelope; Mother Alexandrine had paid me. I felt dishonest to accept it, but it was money, and in the world, the thrilling world outside, you needed money. I sat there for what seemed hours, shivering, for convents are cold on winter mornings.

The lay-sister brought me breakfast, looking at me, fully clothed, with definite relief. "Mother Alexandrine will see you at eleven. Meanwhile you are to meet our young ladies."

I wolfed the breakfast. I was in hat and coat, firmly clutching my bag when the senior class president arrived. She was only a little older than I was and we understood each other perfectly. In ten minutes there was a train, and I could go by tube or ferry to New York. I shook her hand. I admitted I had given a rotten performance.

"No," she said, "it was interesting. You have a quality. It's not that carefully proficient Catholic thing. It's modern. I liked it."

I hope she has had a wonderful life and that she may go to Heaven!

It was that winter I went to a Catholic luncheon at the Bellevue, and a priest who moved with the grace of a matador rose to speak. His subject was "The Divine Sense of Humor," and he pulled out all the stops. His voice was shaded with tenderness, it throbbed with passion, and taut like a dancer he came to the ending, hands outstretched with infinite grace, his voice down to a mere thrilling whisper, he breathed, "His smile." The Bellevue ballroom rocked with applause. My program read the Reverend Fulton J. Sheen, Catholic University of America.

Someone led him up to me, and I was shocked by the smallness of his stature, for he had seemed ten feet tall. His blue eyes were amazing, they changed color and the dark pupil seemed to spread with his mood. I fought off his charm. I resisted him with all my might. There was some fire along my nerves that day that said if this man ordered me I would go to confession to him openly in the main corridor of the Bellevue Stratford Hotel. I felt resentment too, for he was so dramatic that my own dramatic nature was engulfed by his.

That winter was also memorable because Frances Starr and I became really intimate friends. I had been writing to her since *The Easiest Way*, grave, erudite letters about the drama. She answered, not guessing my tender years, respectful of my knowledge. She came to Philadelphia in a play called *Immoral Isabella* —the title will place its quality. Lawton Campbell, who was an advertising man, wrote it in imitation of Robert Sherwood's highly successful and delightful *Road to Rome*. I went to see Frances, and there she was in her dressing room in the Walnut Street Theatre, attired in the beautiful sky-blue robes of Isabella, her Most Catholic Majesty of Spain. She had been up to all sorts of pranks with Christopher Columbus, because in 1928 it was the fashion to think the worst of history and treat the mighty dead with irreverence.

Frances looked enchanting, which was the only redeeming thing about that miserable piece of bad taste, and when her erudite correspondent walked in, not yet twenty-one years old, she flushed in momentary resentment—then held out her arms.

"My baby! It's too wonderful. So you're my intellectual correspondent? Thank God, you don't look as bright as you are. What a fate that would be! And now, darling, you know everything—so find me a copy of Sardou's *Diplomacy*—because I'm closing in this Saturday night and starting rehearsals for an all-star production of *Diplomacy* on Monday."

I found her a copy of *Diplomacy*, and in no time at all she was opening at the Garrick with Margaret Anglin, Helen Gahagan, William Faversham, Rollo Peters, and that wonderful actor and human being Jacob Ben-Ami. I started then on one of my subordinate careers—attending Frances Starr during the period of gestation prior to a New York opening. All that company understood the theatre in a special and miraculous way, with complete realism but devotion. It was a rewarding experience to be with them. The theatre is only good when a company gives it that special quality of monastic life—discipline before its rules, and an awareness that it is worth the tremendous sacrifices it demands, for it draws forth the most profound things in human nature.

One night, Philadelphia was blanketed in a blizzard. The snow had been falling since six o'clock in white sheets that blew in a tremendous wind. I was a headliner on the radio that night, but Mother tried to convince me that no one would be expected to keep an engagement in the midst of such a storm. She could not understand the unbreakable rule of "the show must go on," and she was furious when I insisted on keeping my engagement. She wouldn't let me go alone, so we stamped through the heavy snow to the corner streetcar. There was not a vehicle in sight in the white wilderness. We were the only passengers on the subway surface car that crawled through the night. There was a long wait on the platform at Thirteenth Street for the El and Mother was shaking with nerves as we went past the guard who checked us into the radio station. She identified herself somewhat startlingly.

"I'm Miss Horan, and this is my daughter."

It gave me an illegitimate feeling as I entered the old station WFI with its pie-plate microphones. The engineer and the pianist were on duty and startled to see me. Everyone who had a radio was before it that night. In 1928 network broadcasting was in its infancy, so I had no out-of-town competition; as that night I was one of the few local artists who kept their appointments I was heard in Philadelphia, up into Pennsylvania, in New Jersey, Delaware, and parts of New England. The station phone rang incessantly. Letters, telegrams, poured in, and I was acclaimed not only as a performer but the writer of my own material. I only had to stay at home and wait for offers, which came thick and fast.

The storm had given me a brand-new career!

## 2

AND NOW I STEPPED INTO the world of materialism—the heart of America's "thing worship." I advertised products, stirred up acquisitiveness, speaking on the radio each morning to make foolish women desire every sort of possession but self-possession.

I almost believed my own idiocies. I did not say, because I hadn't given it much thought, that in an age of rising prosperity, the national income for the working classes was going steadily down instead of up. Charlie Weir in the control room on the roof had been wounded at the Battle of Belleau Wood and had certainly earned the right to pull a switch that would shut my ridiculous voice from the air-waves, but he thought I was wonderful. In sugary tones I wished my audience "a happy day," and was off the air.

Then in my office, with my own name on the door, I interviewed buyers, who are the most warlike and neurotic of moderns, fighting like wolves for advertising space. In the main they were lonely and defeated people, but their voices were loud and dissonant and I learned to be wary lest the endless sheets of blue paper they handed me contained a "dud" which would threaten my own job.

I was twenty-one and money was burning a hole in my pocket, so I appeared in Lucille Paray dresses or English tweeds with Knox hats. I knew them all—Herman Tappe, Sophie Gimbel. . . . I lunched, when it was a matter of policy, with the stylists. They hated me, for despite my tinted hair I was authentically young; and their carefully massaged faces hinted at deep lines soon to appear. They wore black dresses, and careful hard hats over cold eyes.

In the midst of this tawdry world the Smith-Hoover campaign of 1928 recalled me to my origins; although by this time I was too intellectually bogus to admit the source of my loyalty to Al Smith. The division of the Catholic heritage from the dominant strain of American democracy was never so clear. The conciliating voice of Cardinal Gibbons was stilled and the sense of our own rejection was an agony to all of us. We plunged into the crusade with an intensity that cannot be recaptured, for the wounds of that time went very deep in the Catholic consciousness.

To me "Al" with the brassy voice had that quality of *New Republic* liberalism which had formed my social thinking. He was a defender of civil liberties, the hero of the social legislation brought about by the Triangle Fire tragedy. I spoke before mill-workers in Kensington, and they were impassive under my spell-binding, till I dragged in the religious issue, when they cheered. A small boy hurled a rock that narrowly missed me, and I felt like Joan of Arc. I drove through town in the motor cavalcade that accompanied Al Smith from the Delaware River Bridge.

He wore his brown derby and chewed on his cigar, driving past the stern and empty façade of the Union League with its banners proclaiming allegiance to Hoover.

On the night of the election we wept a little; it was Katie Smith's birthday and Al Smith said, in the midst of heartbreaking failure, "Come on, Katie, let's go home and cut the cake." As a speech to concede an election that is still the most gallant I have ever heard.

In September, 1929, there was a sharp unexpected break in the stock market, which upset the advertising department of Gimbels—but then the market rose again, sank a few more times. On October twenty-ninth the whole flimsy structure of paper profits collapsed, and the catastrophe was upon us. Mr. Hoover assured us that, "under the guidance of Divine Providence, we will have a greater and more wholesome prosperity than we have ever known." Despite this encouraging statement a number of millionaires jumped out of windows and a number of people lost their jobs.

Ellis Gimbel decided to sponsor a series of dramatizations that would highlight our national origins. We would once again live with the lofty ideals of our Founding Fathers; and our programs, to be known as "The Quaker City Plays," would be centered in Philadelphia, "the cradle of our greatness." Ellis Gimbel did not demand copybook maxims from me and I had enormous satisfaction from this work.

Tensions grew and mounted—and I went on producing, writing and directing plays about our national origins. I engaged for my leading actor in these broadcasts a friend of Monsignor Drumgoole's, a lawyer, William Ashton Lapetina. Part English, part Italian, he was a many-faceted human being. A lawyer with the most astounding record in his class at the University, he tossed it up to found a theatre in honor of Duse whose tomb at Asoli he visited yearly. William Lapetina had little histrionic ability and could be embarrassingly bad, yet he had given all of a fine mind to the theatre. His English and Latin ancestors made him completely an individualist, and his life was spent in a pleasant dream of the arts, with long leisurely summers in Europe.

He had the imperial head of a Caesar, bald pate and all, resting on a rather frail body, and hands of exquisite beauty. He was a bachelor in his forties when I met him, with prudent ways. He was the first intellectual lay-Catholic I had ever known; and it was a unique experience to encounter Italian Catholicism with its currents of opposition toward the Church Temporal. After the Ghibelline movement in the Middle Ages, the Risorgimento in the nineteenth century kept alive the anti-clerical tradition. It was startling to me to hear Ashton Lapetina make anti-clerical remarks of great pungency, and to realize that he was a man of intense religious feeling that had in it no trace of superficial piety. I once had him give Pirandello's *Henry IV*—the best of his plays—in the Gimbel auditorium. The Catholic schools attended, with delight, on the strength of my name. After the first act, however, indignant Sisters rose in a body and withdrew their charges from exposure to a Catholic mind studying madness and delusion in a profoundly Catholic way. Many Catholic educators still have the naïve belief that our art and literature dealing with sinful man must ignore the sins. The progressive educators present stayed with their student bodies, and complicated young men from Cambridge and Oxford, teaching in Quaker institutions in Philadelphia, overwhelmed Ashton Lapetina with accolades. He cursed the Irish-American Catholic mind with ferocity; then tore away from his well-wishers in time to make confession at St. Joseph's.

He became more than my leading actor, for he was my escort throughout that season. I lacked Ashton Lapetina's perceptions, his culture, and his undoubted brilliance. We were both inexperienced, both playing a role: and underneath there was a genuine pathos for he had won spiritual security, an oasis of beauty and peace, and I insisted on replacing it with a Hollywood version of a man of culture. My feminine love of transforming made me nag him about his abandonment of the law. I went to work on his good, old-fashioned clothes, made fun of him for not having a car. I wanted to see him in a Hispano-Suiza. (A year or so later he was killed driving over the Kentucky mountains.) I bloomed under my cold dynamism—and he grew shrill.

He introduced me to garlic—and I prodded him into conformity. I saw in my mind's eye, apart from an established position in Philadelphia, an apartment in Rome in an ancient palazzo, with Princes of the Church at small exclusive dinners. I saw an extension of my own ego—and forgot that in the theatre the curtain always goes down and the puppets take off their grease paint, but in marriage the curtain does not go down and in that relationship even the most imperious woman does not rule.

My friends supposed I was leading a very fast life. It was fast in the mad pace I was going from interest to interest. Even I could not have stirred up enough energy for a grand passion, and beneath my sophisticated veneer I was as green as the endive salads Lapetina and I ate in dimly lit restaurants. I was living on cigarettes and nerves.

The depression was widening and deepening and reaching people in all walks of life. I could no longer remain oblivious of the suffering around me. Mr. Andrew Mellon said, "There is no reason for pessimism," but that did not seem to help a frail old lady with shaking hands removed from her job, or a fresh-faced youngster on her own in the big city. It seemed to me stupid that the people who could least afford it did most of the suffering, but I didn't have much in the way of a social philosophy to offer. I was filled with sympathy, but the only conclusion I came to was that something should be done. I did not like the frustration and agony that I saw all around me, but I wasn't suffering and my spurts of generosity were dramatic and useless; although my own selfishness was not abated I could no longer endure discussions about Proust, and readings from Pater's *Marius the Epicurean.* There was something indecent about such preoccupations in those days.

Aunt Constance had, quite as a matter of course, opened a soup kitchen. Grandfather's house was gone by then to the mortgage holders, and she had removed her boarders to Delancey Place. Twice a day one of the colored people rang a little bell, and around the corner came a line of men. Aunt Constance was completely without self-consciousness or a feeling of virtue, most of all she was unaware of the tremors on Delancey Place as she filled the pails with thick soup, gave out the rolls. She rose before dawn each morning to get her supplies on Second Street. Every market house knew her, every baker, every grocer. On her travels for supplies for her soup kitchen she learned of every job opportunity in town—and grabbed them for her friends. She put the spunk back in a desperate man, a broken girl. She hauled sacks of potatoes and bags of coal to her poor. At night, not having the faintest idea how she herself would fare economically the next day, she sat saying my father's Dominican rosary. The statesmen muddled along, but Aunt Constance took constructive action. A philanthropist was not to her the one who had money and gave it away; she believed that everyone should be doing something about these desperate times. Giving was living as far as she was concerned. The beatific vision was the Christ she saw in her neighbor's face. He was crucified anew every time a child wept with hunger or a human being felt forsaken. I know *one* Constance O'Hara who will go to Heaven!

Now Ellis Gimbel decided that one of the luxuries of merchandising would have to go—the radio station. Entertainment was coming increasingly from New York and was rigidly standardized. Benedict Gimbel, Jr., took over the station, which was to become the Philadelphia outlet of the Mutual chain. Local broadcasting would still fill selected spots, but sponsors had to be obtained to bear the cost.

I took my chance of going with the new station and attracting sponsors. I had an offer to go with National Broadcasting in New York, but by this time I had become used to the inertia of Philadelphia and assured myself that I could not leave in the middle of my grandmother's illness, for Nana had broken her hip that winter and had become a complete invalid. I had nothing to do but watch expenses going up, thus reversing the downward trend of the price spiral. I sat in the midst of confusion while the new station was being built around me, all in light woods and low, soft, upholstered furniture. It is amusing enough in retrospect, but it had its fearful side. Sponsors were not only attracted by the legitimate pressures of advertising agencies, but by the party-route. These parties started in hotel rooms, usually the home of one of the women. The men and women lounged on the bed, sat around the floor. A sullen bellboy came in and out with ice and bottled water. The party roared on, with smoking-room stories the usual opening gambit; and theatre gossip the next best bet. To me it was rather like Teresa of Avila's vision of Hell. . . .

One day I sat in the pale pink and chrome office of the program director, with a book I had picked up at Leary's bookstore. The loud-speaker blasted its noise which was never turned off in the offices. Announcers came in and out, and stopped to chat. They were as vain as peacocks and loved to show off articles of attire. "Isn't that sharp?" they'd question. Another favorite description they had for their enthusiasms was "sincere." "The thing is so sincere," they'd say of a program. Newspapermen lounged around the walls; they had lost their jobs and craved a broadcast spot. The program director was worrying about the problem of sexual frigidity which was, she said, alarmingly on the increase.

She broke off with a little scream as she read the title of my book: *The Irish Nuns at Ypres*. I had ceased to hear the musings of my companion. I was back in the silence and peace of the Convent of Notre Dame. It seemed like centuries since I had seen Sister Julie. A play was forming in my mind—a convent play. The diary of the Irish Benedictines was the nucleus of my idea; an enclosed convent caught in the path of war.

I was by now twenty-three years old and I had seen all of life I could stand. Still clutching the book I said goodby to Benedict Gimbel, Jr.

"It's been slack, I know. Take a rest and if anything comes up I'll send for you. Next season we'll be ready to go."

"I'm just not coming back any more," I assured him.

I went upstairs to the third story front on Baltimore Avenue, and started to write. Nana was by this time sitting up in an invalid chair, and my typewriter overhead was to her "the sweet music of achievement." Her granddaughter was writing a play! I appeared for meals too tired to mind the chatter of the nurse, an elderly Irishwoman who had worked with the best families and was filled with scandalous information. Lucy, our friendly colored girl, kept filling my coffee cup. Mother looked at me, vaguely worried, for my O'Hara genes were in complete control.

The sun poured in the windows of my room, and the tall trees in Clark Park had never seemed so beautiful. I could see each action of the play forming in my mind. It was unnecessary to make a note. I wrote without hurry, without fret. I preempted all the sections of the diary of the Irish Dames I needed, but my characters were drawn exactly from the Sisters of Notre Dame. Dame Patrick was Sister Julie du Saint-Esprit. Dame Walburga, Sister Mary Immaculata. Mother Prioress Maura, Sister Genevieve Mary. Dame Josephine, Sister Helen Josephine. Old Edmund was straight from Rittenhouse Square; and Dame Perpetua with her vigil lights had never been in the Benedictine convent at Ypres. Sustained throughout was a note of quiet exaltation. In the ordinary sense of the word there was no drama in this portrayal of cloistered women, yet when in three weeks it was finished I knew I had done something enduring. I was to read John Gassner calling it "the most beautiful religious play ever written." Sir Barry Jackson was to come on a stage in England and declare it, "the most beautiful play I have ever produced."

I did not know as I tenderly put my play, *The Years of the Locusts*, away, for I had no idea it would ever be produced, that I had written a profoundly Catholic play from a faith that was real but hidden. In what is extreme youth for a playwright I had written a play of maturity and insight.

I rested a while, and started another play which I meant for production. This was called "Opportunity Knocks Twice," and was a comedy of the depression. It was too flip and not deep enough, but it had observation and point. I selected a producer with a name like a character in a George Meredith novel. I received this letter:

April 15—1932

Dear Miss O'Hara:

Don't let anyone tell you you can't write plays in spite of the fact that this one does not meet my production needs.

It is brilliant—it is technically competent. Best of all the wit and humor is genuine.

Do something more and don't forget to send it to me.

Sincerely,
BROCK PEMBERTON

It was such a nice letter that I saved it. I took the play to Jimmy Potter, a Philadelphian who was by way of being a producer. Jimmy said it was brilliant and tried to get backers. I learned the length of time between completion of a play and production.

I took my comedy away from Jimmy Potter and went by appointment to meet Jasper Deeter. He was a product of Greenwich Village and the Provincetown Players. He had known Jack Reed and Eugene O'Neill. He had been part of that eruption of thought before the first World War that had brought, among others, Edna St. Vincent Millay to the Village from Vassar with the glory of her young poem *Renascence* giving her a halo that wasn't tinsel. Everyone was reaching for something new and untried; in rooms overlooking Washington Square, from cellar restaurants, a ferment of ideas and attitudes commenced to brew that would change the face of America. Jasper Deeter had been part of it, then he had slipped away to the life of a tramp; starving, he had been taken in by the Christian Brothers in Chicago. Fed at last, his jangling nerves at rest, after two years, he had come back to the Pennsylvania countryside of his Quaker forebears, and in an old mill in Rose Valley started Hedgerow Theatre.

We sat in his house near the theatre on a golden October day which filled me with energy, and talked about my comedy. Jasper Deeter could get past his attitudes and create a vision of theatre that had as its heart pure mysticism. There was an integrity about him that set him apart. He had shattered every moral concept, talked a heady materialistic philosophy that was a sort of wedding of Marx and Freud, but he had a contempt for theatre as some sort of sensible pleasure, or to stir up a transitory thrill. He knew the theatre was to induce a kind of contemplation, that it involved the action of the highest faculties of man.

There was a tranquility about this little man who somehow resembled Percy MacKaye's Scarecrow but, in a curious way, was a Francis of Assisi. He talked about my comedy with interest while young men in odd garments wandered through the room, and hefty maidens who looked as if they needed a good bath went upstairs with a great deal of unnecessary clumping. I was not the Hedgerow type, and young John Beal, waiting for his future wife, the amazing actress Helen Craig, scowled at me horribly.

I said goodby to Jasper Deeter on the porch of the house in Rose Valley, with the autumn air as sharp as knives and the country one splendid riot of color.

"Do you have another play?" he asked.

I told him briefly I did, but he wouldn't be interested as it was a religious play.

"I thought as much." His smile was cryptic. "Mail it to me at once."

I went home and sent him *The Years of the Locusts*, and I heard nothing for weeks and weeks.

The winter passed quickly. I had a new beau now—a Serbian studying medicine at Jefferson. I was obviously making an attempt to learn modern European history at the source in my romantic life. I learned that the Slavic temperament and the Latin are quite different. This was an immense young man, with a face that was at once tragic and handsome, and he had no feminine streak. He was reaching for a philosophy of life and medicine that would give him something more than comfort and ease and human respect. He was baffled and amused by the exclusive Philadelphia society that was embracing him, for his story, which he made no attempt to disguise, was one of those extraordinary American sagas that gave a certain glowing fairy-tale quality to a nation that was then fearful and fretful in a depression. His father had been almost a slave in Serbia, a bond-boy, and had come to Pennsylvania at fourteen to work in the mines. In some way, in a few years, he was running cheap boardinghouses for immigrant labor. Now he was in Pittsburgh, with a chain of hotels, and here was his youngest son, a product of the University of Virginia, who had traveled all over Europe, and would shortly be a doctor.

We went to little cafés where they played gypsy music. We went to the Philadelphia Orchestra, and he came alive with Rimsky-Korsakoff and you could feel him living beside you when Tchaikovsky's *Pathétique* was played. I was in love, but not enough to be of much benefit to my soul. I was being intensely feminine, without indulging in the female caprices that would have sent us off into storms of sensuality. I was proud of his enormous shoulders, his towering height, and his sleek dark head. We went dancing together, but the shrill and ugly music of jazz bands was not meant for his easy grace.

Jasper Deeter called me to announce that he was doing *The Years of the Locusts* in March, and would like me to play Dame Patrick. Here it was—my first production, one in which I would participate! I should have been stimulated, but oddly, though I was doing no great amount of work, I had begun to feel ill. I dreaded the rehearsals at Hedgerow. Even the country-wide interest in Franklin D. Roosevelt left me apathetic. I had always had a tremendous vitality, and I fought off these queer spells of sickness and dizziness accompanied by violent pains in my stomach.

One Sunday night the pains became too much for me. I crawled in bed early, shivering with illness. I had to come downstairs to talk to Jasper Deeter on the telephone, and each step was agony. I assured him I would be there Tuesday morning for the start of rehearsals.

Monday night they carried me out on a stretcher to the Misericordia Hospital for an emergency operation. I remember pain, a priest bending over me, my rejection of him, his stubborn insistence, I remember sinking into oceans of pain, drowning in it, rising—sinking—sinking. . . . I was wheeled out of the room. The priest was talking to one of the white-robed Sisters. She walked with me to the operating room her face stern, horrified; just before I went under the ether she held a crucifix before my eyes, to my lips.

I had peritonitis, and a few other things besides.

I came to in a vast peaceful room with an umbrella-like arrangement over my head, bristling with tubes. The rest of the night, and most of the day, went by as I lay there weak as a baby. Then through my door came a simple, humble priest, with his silver-white head bowed. He came toward me gently, and I looked into the eyes of Monsignor Drumgoole. I had avoided him since my radio days, and I was startled by the ivory whiteness of his face, which somehow had shrunken, so that I could see the cords in his neck. His broadcloth suit was faintly shabby, and his worldly aura was gone. His blue eyes were infinitely sad, and never once did he rear his head imperiously. "*Never bow your head to anyone but God*," he had told me long ago. He just stood beside my bed not saying much, but enfolding me in holiness. The witty, dashing prelate was gone; this was a priest who loved only his God. He sat down beside me, and as he crossed his leg I noticed that the leather of one of his shoes, made for him by a famous bootmaker in London, had cracked.

He commenced to talk to me of the depression. Monsignor Drumgoole had become indeed the pastor of St. Gregory's, for the agony of his parishioners weighed heavy on his soul. The good pastor now knew his sheep!

"Your play about the convent?" he asked. "Will it make one person love God more? The life of the Church is at stake in these times and we must keep her alive by our collective kindness as Catholics, our vision of the love of God."

I had heard him speak of the Royal Christ of the Renaissance. I had watched him in his purple robes, a proud man speaking to the proud. I had loved his wit—but always there was something lacking. Now abashed at his sanctity, I crept nearer to his heart. I asked him about his old friends, priests we had known. He shrugged a little sadly; answered that he had small time to see friends these days, even admitting he had lost most of them. He spoke of the coming term of Franklin Roosevelt with hope. His face grew stern as he spoke of the apathy and indifference of wealthy Catholics.

"Ah, yes," he said, "the more I see of these Catholics the less I like them."

The familiar ironic smile was on his tired face. He never once reached for his snuff-box. He had, in fact, long since given up all luxuries. The daylight faded, and he sat quietly with me, urging me to sleep. His presence was like a benediction. The last thing I saw was the crack in Monsignor Drumgoole's custom-made English shoes.

## 3

CONVALESCENCE WAS A JOY. I lay in the Misericordia Hospital surrounded by kindness and solicitude in the midst of a stricken world. On the morning of March fourth, through the open door, I heard a golden voice saying, "This is a day of national consecration. . . ." The white-robed Sister, standing like a sentinel, touched the crucifix on her rosary.

That triumphant voice sounded in the hospital corridor. "The only thing we have to fear is fear itself." It was as if the burdens of men were lightened, now that government was no longer cold and impersonal. The glorious voice became gentle, for this was not a politician claiming God as a constituent, but a man of faith. "In this dedication of a nation we humbly ask the blessing of God."

"The dear, dear man," said the Sister at my door, "we'll all pray for him."

Monsignor Drumgoole came often to the hospital, for this time he meant to see I did not escape. That tired, patient man sat as if he didn't have a thing in the world to do but restore a selfish, vain young woman to God. He brought me papers and books and he discussed the world. . . . A renegade Catholic, Adolf Hitler, was rising to power in Germany, for he too had won an election in March, 1933.

Monsignor begged, "This is not the time to desert," and he

drew out his purple stole. I said those awful words, "In a little while, but not yet, Monsignor."

There were other things in the papers besides unemployment and crisis and Russia. I was in the papers, the young Philadelphia woman whose play was being given its world première at a theatre in Rose Valley. I had been interviewed before my appendix had burst, and I seemed to have behaved with restraint and intelligence; for I was being quoted as possessing a certain amount of humor and a sense of balance.

The limousine purred luxuriously with a faint note of contempt as we rode through the silent country still locked in winter for the first night of *The Years of the Locusts*. The little theatre was crammed. The curtain went up, and Jasper Deeter had given me one of the miracles of my life—a production of a play perfectly realized. He had gone beneath the surface, and each moment came to life, glowed, and the action flowed on effortlessly. There was not a single note of religiosity, no Burne-Jones stained-glass prettiness. I lived the happiest moments of my creative life out there in Rose Valley. Mother Prioress spoke the curtain-line: "God of all pity, have compassion on the world." It was over, and the lights came up.

No matter what happened now, I was content, for Jasper Deeter's best had met the best I had to give. There was no deafening applause. The audience seemed quiet, rather as if they had shared an intimacy with the unfamiliar. It made no difference to me. I saw the faces of a few friends from my convent days. They were amazed—almost embarrassed. No one said much of anything. I went down a flight of stairs and met Jasper Deeter. I didn't have to say a word. His hair was wild and his shirt was torn and he had needed a shave for days, but I loved him with that emotion only a playwright knows when all the divergent elements of humanity and mechanics have come together in the hands of a great director.

I went home both depressed and exalted. Mother was proud and fearful, for there was no compromise in *The Years of the Locusts*. The first review I read the next morning was bad. The critic had been bored and he had a blind spot about convents.

He damned the writing, the direction, and the acting. And then the other papers came, and I began to love critics.

Nana carefully cut all the clippings from the papers and put them in envelopes. The small grandchild she had taken to the theatre, the schoolgirl who had gone with her to see Bernhardt, who had sat beside her for George Arliss, Sothern and Marlowe, and Henry Miller, now belonged to the profession Nana loved. The Sunday papers carried an article on "The Distaff Side." Rose Franken's *Another Language* was playing Philadelphia that week, and Rachel Crothers' *When Ladies Meet.* I was elevated above these talented writers, above Miss Crothers' years of successful writing, "as the most aspiring, the most soul-searching of the trio, and the greatest dramatist." Nana, at that, was ready to leave Baltimore Avenue and go to New York. She sat reading the apartment house vacancies in the New York *Times.*

That summer I often went out to Hedgerow and sat on the porch in the Rose Valley house with Jasper Deeter. He understood, as I did not, that I might never write another play that would touch the excellence of my first. He knew it was assumed after its production that my apprentice period was over, and that I would go to the robust world of Broadway, meeting the demands of box-office. He understood that when I wrote it I was in headlong flight from the uproar of twentieth century America and found my solutions in the Catholic atmosphere of my youth. He found my agnosticism superficial; in his phrase, a "damn lie." He understood more profoundly than I did the depths of my roots in the Catholic world. He knew I would fail as an artist when I left the material that had meaning for me. It was peaceful out there in the quiet country; the sheep came up on the porch and nuzzled against me, and we drank homemade root beer with silver balls to cool it.

We walked through the woods and he looked up at a great tree and quoted, of all people, Sidney Lanier:

> "Ye spread and span like the Catholic man,
> Who hath mightily won God out of knowledge,
> Good out of infinite pain, sight out of blindness and
> Purity out of a stain."

The Christian Brothers in Chicago had given Jasper Deeter one fundamental Catholic principle, the sympathy and understanding to neutralize the great sin of hypocrisy. He abhorred smug assurance, and the spilling out of emotion. He was confident that I was essentially a Catholic writer and he saw no point in destroying my powers. He was a little vexed that the Catholics were not flocking out to his theatre. Catholics did not want to see the familiar in the theatre, nor read about it in novels. Philip Barry's shimmering talent was to be crippled as he reached out for what he loved in *White Wings*, *The Joyous Season*, *Hotel Universe*, and met immediate failure. Two Catholic Bishops were expressing more than a superficial preference when on being informed they were to be entertained at Eugene O'Neill's religious play *Days without End*, they asked that the tickets be changed for the *Follies*. The Catholics were quick to protest an offense, but slow to support any defense.

Sister Julie du Saint-Esprit sent the Convent of Notre Dame out to Hedgerow, and they proved what Jasper Deeter had suspected—the play came to flaming life when its audience was composed of those to whom every line, every situation, was a tug to memory. Other Catholic organizations ignored me. A few priests roamed into the theatre, and wondered what all the fuss was about. A besetting sin in the contemporary Church is lack of clerical imagination, so when their Anglican brethren commenced to heap praise upon me they decided there must be heresy in the play. In fact, there were a few protests that the doctor didn't go to Mass, yet the nuns prayed for him instead of condemning him. When has judgment of another been a Catholic dogma? Then there was the scene when the young priest, enraged at the agonies the Germans were inflicting on his country, discovers he has hate and the lust to kill in his heart. Up against the central reality of Christianity—to love one's enemies—he says, "A priest must—a man cannot." The decision was made: I hadn't written a Catholic play.

I accepted the clerical verdict immediately. It eased my own bewilderment that I, who called myself a heretic, had written a play of faith. It was now understandable to me. I was a brave, free soul, who had written a play of humanity with agnostic overtones. Eighteen years later it was decided I had authored a play of profound spiritual content; and the Church, rather late for me, decided I had been a Catholic playwright after all.

That fall Nana broke her other hip and after three agonizing weeks died on a Sunday afternoon in October. She suffered dreadfully, and in her delirium relived the past. She said the names of children she had known and loved. . . . She was going to her music lesson—to dancing school. . . . She was eighty-three years old. It was a death with meaning and point and beauty.

We left her in Old Cathedral Cemetery, the Marble Park of my childhood, and into that grave with her went my most innocent days. It was Nana who had formed my taste with the splendor of English literature—who had given me the theatre. I had adventured in the realms of greatness with this reticent, clear-eyed woman. I had walked the tree-shaded streets of Philadelphia beside her; and she had nurtured in my heart the charmed associations of Victorian security. Monsignor Drumgoole stood at her grave. And then it was over, and we came away.

We closed the house against the impending winter, and took a little apartment in town, close to the Pine Street house of my childhood days. I went to New York to settle with an agent and commence my theatre career. I learned very quickly that despite the impressive reviews, Broadway was not interested in a play of convent life.

I was in my middle twenties. I had talent. I didn't know what to do with it. I had no philosophy to help me. The thing that was gnawing me alive was that I was not at peace with my God. Monsignor Drumgoole followed me patiently, never losing touch with me. One Sunday I went into his church for the last Mass. There were no town cars outside now, but the church was crowded, though the congregation was different. There were innumerable young men and women of my own age, with serious, intent faces. The pews were jammed with his own parishioners—decent, tidy men and women, gaunt after years of depression. Monsignor stepped to the altar rail and preached. His subject was

Fear. This priest of God was offering me all that any twentieth century citizen needed, or for that matter any other—the directions to Heaven.

He spoke of fear, the companion of pride and lust. He showed modern man afraid of his health, afraid of poverty and insecurity, afraid of death, afraid to trust, in the grip of a thousand little fears, hiding what he would not admit, fearing a God he was too cowardly to love. He spoke of a Catholic Church riding out the storms of man's terrors, like a splendid ship. He spoke of the men coming toward it, and salvation; and the men turning away from it to illusive lights on the far horizon, lights they would never reach.

I went into the rectory of St. Gregory's. He was alone, for Monsignor now followed a Christ who was on the side of the poor and forsaken, who had preached a humble gospel based on the words, "Learn of me, for I am meek and humble of heart." This doctrine was as uncomfortable for wealthy Catholics as for any other affluent citizens: more terrifying than Marx's "Proletarians of the world, unite." Monsignor was losing his wealthy friends; even the conservatism of Agnes Repplier was affronted by his uncompromising Catholicism.

She had come recently to take him to a dinner at the Acorn Club, and insisted that he wear his ceremonial robes. Monsignor stood at the door of his study, a glittering figure in his red-purple sash, moiré soutane left over from the old days, and his biretta, saying:

"O God! I am so silly."

Agnes turned to him sternly. "I cannot stand this modern carelessness with the Lord's name. I am shocked you would be guilty of such bad taste."

Monsignor, a little sadly, waved toward the crucifix on the wall, "I was addressing a comment on my appearance to my naked and bleeding God on the Cross."

I sat there with him while he told me this and other stories. His face was white with exhaustion and his mind was thronged with worries. The parish finances after years of depression among a poor congregation were in a dreadful state. He was using his own money to help the poor and distressed—and lecture fees were decreasing. Newer men were coming to the fore. The triumphant star of Father Fulton J. Sheen, of Washington, had risen. Nevertheless, to be with Monsignor was happiness.

The only people who are really exciting are holy people, for the dissonance of human pettiness is gone, the ugly distortions of sin. They have a radiance—a love for all living—that makes being with them an adventure, unmarred by emotional and intellectual thrusts; and yet what they are must be apprehended by the emotions and the intellect.

Monsignor reached me, as he always had, by stories and comments on life, by wicked little parries at the Church Temporal. He spoke of a Catholic gangster, recently dead, and observed, with a twinkle in his eyes, that he was sorry he had been denied burial from a church and a blessed grave.

"You see, child, he was open and frank about his misdeeds. He stole. He murdered. There is this difference, he wasn't a Catholic politician taking bribes or passing corrupt laws that will murder the souls and probably the bodies of helpless working people. Now if he'd been a politician and not a gangster . . . he'd probably have died a Knight of St. Gregory." His blue eyes gleamed. "Ah! think of all the priests at that funeral. Now I would rather have been at the gangster's. I have this old-fashioned, almost Protestant feeling, about honor." The echo of his giggle floated in the room. "The Irish Church has ruined the Roman Church, you know!"

I laughed—and then he pleaded with me. What difference did any of these superficial things make—tiresome priests—small-minded Catholics? One thing mattered, and he quoted: "There was no beauty in him nor comeliness . . . despised, and the most abject of men, a man of sorrows, and acquainted with infirmity."

I wanted to come home. I wanted nothing else. But because I was filled with pride I could not put my hand in his, as I had as a little child, and bow my head till I saw only his purple stole, and get rid of my shadowy burden of sin and delusions. I had my chance of years of grace.

And Monsignor said to me, "Goodby, child. Will you pray for me?"

There are many finalities in life—so many that it seems as if there is nothing constant but endings.

I never saw Monsignor Drumgoole again.

I saw no other life possible but the theatre, and I had nothing to give it but my own confusion. I needed, as did every other writer of my and every other era, something to believe in. Anatole France has written truly, "It is sweet to believe—even in Hell." I determined to discipline my questing spirit into creating plays that would make people laugh, and cater to their preference for sex. I would acquire riches and then I could lead a brave, free life in all the capitals of Europe, and the little islands of the Pacific. I would always be part of the splendid world of New York. . . . If I could only get away from Philadelphia which walled my spirit in like a prison, then I would have the life I wanted, the only life possible, riches, fame. I was absolutely self-centered and miserably unhappy.

I received this letter just after I persuaded my mother to burn our bridges behind us, and depart for New York—an adventure she would finance.

*THE PHILADELPHIA EVENING BULLETIN*

Dear Madam: Your "Jibes and Judgments" struck a responsive chord or something like that, in my mind, and I am using an installment on the editorial page of *The Bulletin* on Wednesday of this week. I should be pleased if you would come into the office Thursday or Friday afternoon sometime about four o'clock, if that would suit your convenience, and talk over your idea with me a little.

Sincerely yours,
Fred Fuller Shedd
*Editor, Philadelphia Evening Bulletin*

I had become a newspaper columnist without conscious volition on my part. At dinner a few evenings before Mother had rebuked my rugged individualism, and my insistence that no one needed influential connections to get any sort of writing job. I had come to maturity in the nineteen twenties, and despite the prophets of doom I still had lingering faith in Horatio Alger—or perhaps I just had enormous conceit. I had no thought of becoming a columnist, my bet had simply included the sweeping statement that all I had to do was mail a contribution to the editors of the leading newspapers, and I would receive a reply from all of them.

It amazes me now to think I won that bet, for the letters came, but Fred Fuller Shedd published my feature before I had a chance to decline.

I achieved a minor celebrity for being a woman on the editorial page which meant, they said insultingly, that I had a man's mind. The star columnist was William Lyon Phelps, whose cheer spilled beyond the confines of the space he occupied. T. A. Daly, the poet, was another featured writer, and the combined sweetness of these gentlemen soured my disposition and introduced a petulant note into my column. There was a minister on the staff, Dr. Samuel Purvis, and another distinguished gentleman, Leigh Mitchell Hodges. They peered at me kindly from under their green eye-shades, as I swept through the office, quoting Oswald Spengler or reminding them that the vote in the Saar meant the end of civilization. I raved over Sean O'Casey's play *Within the Gates*. I was for the new music, the new world. . . .

Eventually I learned a trick. All you had to do to get a pithy and revolutionary thought past the copy desk was to express it with brevity. The column attracted attention and began to be quoted in out-of-town papers. It was the last straw, and out of their cubbyholes, leaving their roll-top desks without guardians, so great was their agitation of mind, came the old gentlemen to protest to Fred Fuller Shedd. The upshot of all this was that I stormed down to the office and resigned my job.

Shedd, who looked like a cheerful Santa Claus, but had the spartan spirit of a Puritan Father hidden under a patient and tolerant manner, leaned back in his swivel chair and gave me the names of the syndicates who wanted my services. He told me what I was losing by my lack of faith in God and mankind, and how my skepticism was ruining my copy. He challenged me by saying if I had any character I'd stay with the *Bulletin* and conquer the opposition. But I found it pleasant to stand before him, free.

I did not do much brooding, but promptly went to New York and met my Serbian at "21." He was finishing his internship at Welfare Island, and he had never looked so handsome. The women at adjoining tables had alert and interested eyes. This day he refused to play the role I had assigned him, which was to be European and devilish in his conversation. He was, poor man, tired of conversation. He was enmeshed in his love of medicine, his compassion for the people he saw at Welfare Island, and his own desire for the good life according to the best American standards. He was restless, rootless; he talked of going to Spain which was in the throes of revolution—unless he was given a good reason to stay in America.

I didn't want to be "a good reason." I found myself walking with him down a street in Manhattan near the New York Hospital where he had been offered a residency. A doctor he knew had recently married and taken an apartment in one of these nondescript buildings.

"It's not so far from Park Avenue," he assured me.

The doctor and his wife were cordial young people. She had been a nurse, and was now in the last stages of pregnancy. She had black circles under her eyes, and the thought of cooking a dinner in that stuffy kitchenette would have been a torture to me. She seemed outrageously happy. The windows looked out on the teeming East Side street, where dark foreign children, who looked like my Serbian, played with noisy abandon. Great trucks rolled by. Finally a constraint fell on all of us. The doctor's wife with the keen perceptions of women was rejecting me. She sensed that her condition of which she was, with the health and mental wisdom of a woman fulfilling her destiny, inordinately proud, inspired no envy in me; that, in fact, it depressed me.

I was glad to get out of that apartment with its installment-house furniture and the steady, honest disgust in the eyes of a woman who realized that love was unselfishness and struggle, and not a lot of impossible demands on life. The Serbian was angry.

We walked to the Plaza Hotel, and outside, at the entrance, began an argument which got nowhere and was filled with the subtle cruelties of a selfish young woman. It was a bad business. I jumped on a Fifth Avenue bus, and just as it started he made a spring and landed on the platform, kissing me with Hollywood abandon. The end had a theatrical flourish, for he jumped off the bus, now threading its way through the traffic, with a catlike grace; and, led by the conductor, the amused occupants burst into song. The woman has not been born who would not delight in such a situation.

On Sunday October 18, 1936, Monsignor Drumgoole died.

I knew he'd wanted to see me, but because I dreaded the emotion of visiting him, because of the hurt I'd heard in his voice when he had telephoned me, I had put it off. Now it was too late.

The day of his funeral came and I turned my face into the pillows. I could hear in my mind the bell tolling at St. Gregory's. I could see that regal figure in the monsignor's purple lying there; but like all pagans I was now afraid of death. I could not even learn, for I did not have the courage, who came to mourn him. The other day I read the yellowed paper for the first time. They were all there: Bishop Leech of Harrisburg, Bishop Fitz-Maurice of Wilmington, the long line of monsignors, the priests who had been his foster-sons at the Seminary. The Cardinal presided. . . .

Sister Julie sent for me in a few weeks. This time I went. She came to the point at once. I was to make a radio broadcast for the Clinic of Notre Dame des Malades; it would be a good opportunity to pay a tribute to the last great work of my friend Monsignor Drumgoole.

I did not want to do it but Sister would hear of no refusal. It took courage for her to force my acceptance in the face of Catholic opposition. I said, "Yes."

I am grateful that I never made a better speech. It was simple and sincere. It wove my instinctive reverence for my father's profession into my account of the clinic. It tied it up with what Monsignor represented as a priest. I could see him as I spoke;

and my words, which were from my heart, were profoundly Catholic. The green walls of the broadcasting studio faded. My friend Monsignor Drumgoole was leaning forward to listen to me.

There was praise from Monsignor's friends. And then protests started.

"A renegade Catholic . . . A Judas speaking on a Catholic program . . . A disgrace to her father's memory . . ."

I consoled myself by deciding I'd always loathed Catholics anyway. And then I entered that worst of all the phases of lapsed Catholicism—indifference. The memory of Monsignor Drumgoole receded very fast. I found that my father seldom came to my mind. It is an obscure despair in which nothing seems worthwhile and no one important enough to love. It is a loss of belief so absolute that it can only be known by someone who has broken from a tremendous belief. All faith seems worthless; everything and everyone that represent beauty and meaning go. Emotional energy and mental integrity commence to dissolve. It is the beginning of the end of the creative life of an artist. It is the Devil's device to claim his own. It seems to happen quickly. There is the aching conscience, the grief over someone loved, and then there is nothing but apathy, and a fading memory. It is a modern mind's anticipation of Hell.

My surfaces, however, were pleasantly bright and gilded with wit and still youthful charm, and I now had quite a taste for wealthy and sophisticated society. This led me away from my contemporaries into a group of much older people with years of distinction behind them. Frances Starr, on her second marriage to Golden Donaldson, a Washington lawyer and banker, had taken root in such a world, but refused to be taken in by it. I visited them in their vast apartment in Wardman Park for the second inauguration of Franklin D. Roosevelt. I was lapped in the warm felicity of luxury and superb taste. Frances trailed negligently through the great rooms with their handsome paintings as if through the setting of a Belasco play. Goldie Donaldson seemed rather more like Sir James Barrie than a banker.

He sat waiting to show me his Lincoln collection in the pine-paneled library, while Frances and I braved the winds and rain of that horrible week. A few of the Republicans who believed in omens were immensely cheered by the black clouds and the sheets of rain. Frances had just closed in *The Two Mrs. Carrolls,* many years later one of Bergner's great hits, where she had been a murderess; being a superb actress, she was not quite out of her role, and viewed the political scene with a combined look of tragedy and remorse that made it rather sinister.

We went to a dinner party given by Mrs. Harry Wardman, and there I met my first authentic Fascist, Juan Francesco de Cárdenas, who had been and was again to be Spanish Ambassador. When someone questioned him about Jacinto Benavente, one of the world's greatest Catholic dramatists, he shrugged. "They say he is a Jew." With his green Spanish complexion he was by all odds the most fascinating man I had ever met and I did worse than accord his views polite attention, I drowned in champagne and made the most of being a young and reasonably attractive woman.

He was suave, he was insinuating, and he was dangerous. This man was a representative of a true Catholic culture, but he had the mediocre mind of all totalitarians whether of the right or the left. The Church was a necessary instrument, but definitely the Church was subordinate in his mind to the new nationalism. Spain was not to be a tidy corner of Europe run by a benevolent dictator, not a Portugal with a Salazar; once again it was to sweep the world. They were all dreaming dreams, these little men, and finding the disgruntled in America to press their claims in the halls of Congress.

The champagne made me talkative and apparently more ingenuous than I was, and he told me with great displeasure of a Spanish cardinal who had formed an underground of priests who were slipping by the enemy lines, as waiters, or laborers, and the cardinal's refusal to have them serve as spies for Franco. Their purpose was only to minister to souls.

"The Church! The Church!" he said, clenching his hands in disgust.

Juan Francesco de Cárdenas was doing more than flattering me vith his attentions; he was giving me the subject of a play. A ittle later Frances decided I was much less experienced than I retended to be, and someone had better see what he was saying o me, with his head almost on my shoulder. Mrs. Wardman, vho was certainly the handsomest woman in Washington that ight, approached tactfully, and her highball glass nearly fell rom her hand. The Spanish Ambassador and I were discussing vith wistful longing our First Holy Communion.

"I had a little satin suit and a candle in my hand. We walked ıp the hill to the Cathedral. . . ."

It was a long way from a world of Juan March and Franco ınd the Duke of Alba.

The Spanish Ambassador kissed my hand, his eyes amused and ıdmiring. It was the high gloss of civilization, and you couldn't hink as you went out into the Washington night that he could e responsible for a bomb dropped on a little Spanish town or hat his eyes as he drove through the deserted streets were alert nd watchful, for Communist agents had threatened his life many imes.

Washington had a glamor and a falsity that I liked; I missed he aura of wealth when I got home to Philadelphia. Mother nd I by now were free of the Baltimore Avenue house, and had big rambling apartment at the Netherlands. I had my own tudy where I could sit at a typewriter and work all day long. Iarry Wardman had interested me in George Eliot and George ewes, and I wrote one of those plays that everyone said was excellent." All it needed for production was a celebrated star o want to play the role.

A producer named George C. Tyler had written me. I conıected his name with the all-star tours in which Frances Starr ıad been involved as well as with the Abbey Players of Dublin, Ielen Hayes, George Kaufman. His letter informed me that *The Years of the Locusts* was a glorious play and did I have anything else"? I sent him "Honourable Estate," the George Eliot play. I found myself well involved, for I went to see him.

George Tyler was seated at a roll-top desk in a second-story office in the Ziegfeld Building, overlooking Forty-second Street with its flea circuses, second-run moving picture houses, orangeade stands. Men with sandwich boards on their back advertising sales of "two pant suits" milled around in the throngs. Loudspeakers blared jazz music from tin-pan alley. Tyler was a short, stocky old man with a heartbroken face and a lonely smile. His world of glory had crashed around him in the Klaw and Erlanger failure; he had been worth millions and now he had nothing but a crumbling old house in the Nineties where he lived, and an office with walls papered with autographed pictures lavishly inscribed by the theatrical great and playbills of his productions. Over his head there hung a picture of Christ crowned with thorns, and in the frame in large lettering there was this caption: "*WHY DID I DO IT?*" It was the ultimate in pessimism, and yet George Tyler had sweetness and compassion warring with the bitterness in his heart. Agents no longer even bothered to send him play scripts, yet he had been a great producer. The blue eyes looking at me were filled with the anguish of the little hurts that keep piling up on the agony of failure.

He dressed in the late afternoon in his good London clothes that hadn't worn out, and visited his friends. There was Eleanor Robson Belmont, who had been his star and the love of his life. There was Helen Hayes who had been his star, and in his heart was his daughter. There was Maude Adams at her New York retreat, the Convent of the Cenacle on Riverside Drive. There were William Brady and Grace George, and at the Gotham there was kind Pauline Lord. At the New Weston Jane Cowl welcomed him. His old friends sent him tickets to their plays; and he sat before them fretfully—for this was not his theatre.

All he needed was to discover a new talent. I was—God help me—that talent. I knew better, but this sad old man had so much splendor that we became friends. The dominant disposition that had ruled generations of stars with a rod of iron came back in all its strength. He would not only establish me in the theatre, but he would re-establish himself. I would rewrite "Honourable Estate" and with his name and mine in lights and Helen Hayes as the star, we'd show this impoverished contemporary theatre what the American public would do before an unusual play.

I had been taught to believe in miracles at the Convent of Notre Dame, so I rewrote the play. George Tyler began to wear all his best English cravats. His derby went on at a jaunty angle. He was a showman once more. He bragged about my fiery temperament to Bill Brady and Grace George. He consulted Eleanor Belmont, "The Lady Eleanor," about my manners; for he was worried I mightn't be sufficiently dazzled with "Queen Helen," which was his name for Helen Hayes.

"She's an arrogant Irish snip," he said of me fondly, and swung a crook-headed cane on his arm, in anticipation of his return to Broadway. He was sure he could handle me.

He'd sit with me in that old office and tell his memories. He'd dreamed for years of a play about "a good little priest." He'd tried to make Chesterton write it, put his Father Brown in a play.

"He was the laziest of men," Tyler complained, thumbing through his letters from Chesterton, angry that he had dared to die before he wrote that play.

"Just a simple, holy, human man," Tyler said, "a priest. The world hasn't changed. A play like that would make a fortune."

It is real tragedy to be an old showman who has outlived his time.

It was during this period that I was invited to address the opening meeting of the National Conference of Christians and Jews, on the subject of tolerance. That permitted a broad scope for philosophic meanderings, and high sounding platitudes on the subject of human brotherhood. I was vague, impressive and dramatic. The large audience burst into vigorous applause. Two priests slunk out the door of the Bellevue ballroom on their way to assure His Eminence I had said nothing heretical; in fact, they may have told His Eminence I said nothing.

Afterward I was one of the guests of honor at a luncheon. There was a Rothschild on my right who spoke Oxford English and was interested in Indian mysticism and mediaeval MSS. He also knew the theatre.

"Sir Barry Jackson should see your plays," he told me firmly.

That night I wrote a letter to Sir Barry Jackson enclosing the published copy of *The Years of the Locusts.* In about three weeks I received a cable from Sir Barry asking to present my play as part of his Silver Jubilee Festival at the Birmingham Repertory Theatre. We arranged everything by correspondence, for I would not go to England till the autumn opening in London.

This production stirred up a little dust of wrath in Broadway circles. Who was I, after all, to defy the laws of production in this manner—sit down at a desk, write a letter and put a play in an envelope? The most famous dramatists in America had not interested Sir Barry. In any event Sir Barry Jackson and I happily wrote letters to each other across the Atlantic. He sent me genial and flattering messages from G. B. S., who looked forward to meeting me, so Sir Barry wrote. What greater glory could happen to a comparatively young playwright than that a skinny old Anglo-Irish dramatist, named George Bernard Shaw, should recognize my mere existence?

In March, 1938, when *The Years of the Locusts* was produced in England, Mother was lying in the Misericordia Hospital critically ill. There was a curious thing about this play; in every one of its major productions some catastrophe came into my personal life. The doctors said to me, "Don't leave. It will all be over in a few hours."

Then the tide turned. The battle was won.

Mother was sitting up in bed when I read her the English reviews, which were exceptionally good. Sir Barry Jackson had come on the stage to say, "*The Years of the Locusts* is the most beautiful—and most satisfying play I have ever produced." He wrote that at the dress rehearsal the company came to the end with "tears streaming down their faces."

The Germans in 1938, as the Birmingham Repertory Theatre traveled from Station Street to Manchester to Belfast, were storming up the Brenner Pass, and Catholic Austria had been extinguished by "the showman Hitler." The English weather was glorious; everyone was playing cricket and not paying much attention to a play by an American woman. Sir Barry believed the Malvern Festival would be another story; and planned to open in October at the Shaftesbury Avenue Theatre in London. His agent would shortly arrive in America to attend to the details of the London production.

Mother threw Philadelphia prudence to the winds and made up her mind to "take principal" and go to New York. This meant I was a playwright!

## 4

IT WAS LATE AT NIGHT and the taxi sped up Park Avenue—for with a prodigality typical of me, I was conquering New York from a Park Avenue hotel. The stars were in the sky: but who looks at the stars when the lights blaze in the hard, clear buildings.

It was the long, warm autumn of 1938, an autumn of New England hurricanes and world crisis. I woke up each morning and called Room Service. Coffee, toast, and orange juice tasted completely different smothered in white damask, served on gleaming silver dishes, by a bowing Austrian waiter. There was nothing to do after breakfast but read the papers. That autumn Brock Pemberton was producing a play called *Kiss the Boys Goodbye*, by one Clare Boothe Luce. I had to write one of those smart, glib comedies at once. . . .

I walked in Central Park with my Boston bull terrier. I rode down in the elevator with Sir Cedric Hardwicke. Once on the avenue Elsie de Wolfe looked at me closely, and I forgot I didn't know her and smiled in delighted recognition.

"Don't you let New York take away that smile," she said.

It made me feel happy all over, and there was no reason why anyone shouldn't be happy in this dream-world in which I was living. I needed a suit, so I bought one that fitted like a poem and fortunately, which redeemed my extravagance somewhat, lasted a dozen years. I bought a green hat with long quills that threatened the eyesight of whoever came near me. I bought a brown hat with a swirl of coque feathers, a mouth-watering hat that stood alone in the window of one of those artful Park Avenue shops. I bought and I bought. . . . I bought nothing cheap. I found just the woman to do my hair, and Ilka Chase in the next booth, who didn't know me from Adam, invited me to a cocktail party.

Frances Starr was rehearsing in a play called *The Good* and was close by at the Fairfax. Sometimes, late at night, we sat in the Lombardy and I learned the smooth taste of Scotch; liquor started at lunchtime in New York, and the clean electrical air of Manhattan blew the fumes of dry martinis from the brain, just in time for champagne cocktails at dinner. It was an idiotic performance, but the whole world was washed in wonder, and I swept into paganism and materialism like an eager child.

George Tyler sat in his office and growled at me throatily. "Buy your clothes at Orbach's, move to the West Side, and write another play," he ordered.

Everyone was going back to work, or tramping the canyons off Broadway to casting, or an agent's. To be "at liberty" in late September meant there would be a long stretch before the first salary check. Even I realized playtime was over.

And now over the great noisy city there fell a hush. The Germans had occupied Czechoslovakia and war was about to begin. Everybody hated war, but everybody was an individual —and individuals didn't count. The contradictions of the society in which I lived were getting ready to explode in my face. With the fate of millions hanging on the considerations of a few, I worried over the fate of my play in England. War would mean the end of a London production.

And then Chamberlain stumbled out of a plane at Croydon Field in England, announcing "Peace in our time."

It had a good sound, such a good sound that I went to church at St. Patrick's Cathedral. The ritual of Mass still had the power to stir me, and I had to bow my head against that shattering second when the Host is lifted aloft for the adoring eyes of men. The words, "My Lord and my God," formed on my lips. I chiefly remember the sermon because, though the world had whirled in anguish, the young priest spoke on the Blessed Mother. He had so much simplicity and holiness in him, preaching his stumbling little sermon filled with humility and love, that the home longing stirred in me.

I came out of the Cathedral, which was still draped in mourning for Cardinal Hayes. The pigeons whirled and came to rest, and the blazing sunshine with no tang of autumn in it felt good.

A woman with a brassy-dyed head turned to her companion. "Imagine such a sermon at late Mass in the Cathedral! Why don't they send priests like that to the Bronx?"

The little flicker of grace died down. I turned my back on my peace and survival as a human being and walked toward Park Avenue, in the hot American September. Why did I do this cruel thing to myself? The truth about me, and about every other lapsed Catholic, is that we have no reasons whatever—we have created them. We have woven a whole spiderweb of reasons, beautiful and intricate. We go on from pattern to pattern, till our mind is strewn with cobwebs, and the light of truth shines ever dimmer.

The next morning at breakfast I was amazed to find a letter from Sister Julie du Saint-Esprit, who had taken the trouble to find out where I was living. It was a gay and pleasant letter on the surface, filled with pride at my English production, which she had heard of from the Notre Dame convent in Liverpool. She assured me of her prayers, and in a flash I saw the convent chapel and the ancient statue of Blessed Mère Julie Billiart with that awful artificial simper. The silence of my convent, and a longing for peace, swept over my heart. I answered at once, and I said none of these things to my dear friend, but expressed amazement that she would notice "the convent black sheep."

In two days an answer was back, an answer that I never forgot, that would one day help me to start the difficult climb from the depths of despair.

> Now, Constance, do not dramatize yourself: you are not a black sheep; merely an unattractive, dirty gray.

Sir Barry Jackson wrote that the crisis of Munich meant he would not dare produce a play about the last war. He was filled with sadness and appalled at the world, as he wrote from a mountain retreat in Switzerland.

I was spending too much of my mother's money and not getting down to work. There was still my George Eliot play, and I went to the Hotel Fourteen to see Laurette Taylor and discuss whether it had a chance of production. The first taste of fall was in the air, as I turned the corner leading to one of those off-the-avenue residential hotels, where aristocratic old ladies are always walking toward the desk to see "if there's any mail"; or giving well-bred orders about their telephone calls. It was a strange retreat for the extraordinary Laurette Taylor, whose dramatic imagination must have kept the elderly room clerks in a ferment.

Laurette Taylor in 1938 was becoming very stout. She met me at the open door, wearing a clean white silk slip whose seams were straining with her bulk. Her neck and shoulders were beautifully firm and white. She had on a black off-the-face hat with stiff little feathers, rising from the brim. She made endearing noises over me, as if I were a young smart child. She smelt of soap and excellent Bourbon, and gave me a somewhat rambling account of people who had invited her for lunch.

"The nice kind, you know, dear and sweet and good. Used to the best in life and the arts. Intelligent, but they've no idea what it takes to create the best. The heartache and the pain of getting to be 'the best'! . . . But is there anything more hideous than niceness? Oh, you're not nice—not with that name. That's one charge they can't bring against the Irish: niceness. Now about your play—"

And she began a masterly analysis of my biographical play. She knew every excellence and every hidden flaw.

"It's one of those plays, my dear, that everyone will praise, and no one will do anything about; and yet it's an audience play. You've more than a talent, you're ready. All there is to do, is meet the right people. George Tyler is a lovely fellow, isn't he? He's a has-been, you know that, and you've got to take the bit in your teeth and push him out. It'll break his heart, but no matter, in the days of his glory he broke hearts himself; and you can't have a dotty old man gumming up the works." She rose and pulled off her hat, reaching for my script on the bureau. "And now, child, this is the way George Eliot should be played."

She turned with the script in her hand, a lock of brown hair fell blowsily over her face, she shook it back impatiently—and spoke. I was looking into the stern face of a long-nosed Englishwoman with tragic eyes; the pink and white creased face of Laurette Taylor, with a round little button nose, was before me but I couldn't see it, for this superb actress *was* George Eliot, a poorly-paid, ugly, spinster journalist wearing a bright bonnet for Herbert Spencer, and being rejected. She breathed deeply and turned to another scene, in which George Eliot lay sobbing on a bed in a Berlin boardinghouse, demanding that Lewes, who could not gratify her flesh, sacrifice his genius to hers. Laurette Taylor was standing at the bureau all the time; but we were in George Eliot's London home that winter night when she was at the height of her powers and Lewes gave the reception to which only a few distinguished men came. She led up to the woman's hysterical outburst with a delicate precision that left you limp....

She was without a doubt the greatest actress I had ever seen in my life.

Frances Starr and I said goodby in the Lombardy bar, for she was going home to Washington, then off to do some stock, and I was moving to the Gramercy Park Hotel to write a play, as it was obvious I had no script that would sell immediately.

The Gramercy Park Hotel was pleasant in the extreme. Our fourth-floor rooms faced Lexington Avenue and the little enclosed park. Around the corner was the Eighteenth Street apartment of Clayton and Gay Hamilton. Clayton had been a playwright, a teacher of drama at Columbia, the author of innumerable books on his subject. Gay was a wonderful humanist who understood her great white-haired husband and her two sons, who were both writers. It was one of those lovely old-fashioned apartments with loads of room, always pleasant with soft chairs and good lights and books strewn around. It had no formalities. Clayton would sit in the big chair that Eugene Meyers had sent him and, calling himself a Presbyterian pagan, would pontificate on "the parlous condition of the modern theatre." He thought me a dramatist, and was lending me all his energies and contacts. The Walter Hampdens dropped in for Sunday supper. Ida Tarbell, then past eighty, lived in a fourth-floor walkup apartment near the park. The famous muckraker who had denounced John D. Rockefeller wore long, black, flowing skirts, and a net guimpe edged in black velvet. Only the keen eyes behind her nose-glasses betrayed the quality of this fiery woman. Rosamond Gilder, Richard Watson Gilder's daughter, lived at 17 Gramercy Park South, and was one of the greatest theatre enthusiasts in New York. She fought for the survival of *The Years of the Locusts* in America, and had it endorsed by the National Theatre Conference. Arthur Train was close by; and Katherine Hepburn was always visiting in the vicinity.

The febrile excitements of midtown New York were over, and I settled down to work. I had to find a play idea among the many that were chasing around in my brain. I sought for a subject that would incorporate what I believed was my humanistic appreciation of priests and nuns. Finally, I decided to write a play of religion set in the Spanish Revolution. I bought the books of André Malraux. In *Man's Hope* I expected to find a synthesis on which to project my vague idea. Malraux represents a great intellectual experience in my life. André Malraux had accepted Marxism not as glorious or a cause—but fate. In a way he demanded of Christ's Church—Christ; and in the vacuity of Marxism, remained a noble human being. His books were filled with the most dangerous fatalism, but the soul of Malraux shone from his pages like a crystal in a glass of muddy water, and he gave me some of the living water of faith. He prepared my mind for Maritain, and I owe him a great debt.

The play formed itself easily. The half-forgotten story told me by Juan de Cárdenas of the Spanish Cardinal who sent priests into Madrid in the guise of laborers, was my basic plot. It was a great and dangerous theme. I rose early in the winter mornings on Gramercy Park, and started my writing day. I worked with discipline and intensity. I was doing almost no drinking, and it was good to be free of a world that was so taxing it demanded stimulus. The theatre that winter was splendid, and sometimes I went to see such plays as *Our Town*, or the fascinating *Oscar Wilde* with the brilliant portrayal by Robert Morley. More often than not Mother and I sat together with WQXR playing us a concert; not later than eleven I walked the dog around the park, and went to bed. It was one of the good winters of my life.

Christmas did not stop my work. Gramercy Park recovered much of the English spirit with carollers, shining lights, and the gleam of Christmas trees in every window of the apartments and houses. I went uptown on the eve of Christmas, just at dusk. All the stridencies and noise of the commercial preparation for Christmas were over. A few of the smaller shops on Madison Avenue were still open, but there was something wistful and humble about their invitations to buy that last-minute gift. The clean smell of pine trees and evergreens filled the air. The stars straggled out in the pale sky, then deepened till the heavens were blazing. The Cathedral was white and silver in the light of the Christmas moon smiling over its spires.

Mother and I were alone that Christmas, but there was no loneliness about it. The hotel dining room with its quaint wallpaper looked like a nice Victorian home. Gertrude Atherton was dining with a friend. I think her granddaughter had just entered the Convent of the Sacred Heart, where another of Gertrude's granddaughters had long been a professed religious. I am sure that Gertrude Atherton was close to eighty that Christmas night, but her face was as young as a girl's with white, unlined skin, and her pale blond hair was impressively natural.

The crowds thinned out, and Gertrude Atherton began to tell stories that were richly funny, and always a trifle wicked. The Walter Hampdens had introduced me to her a few weeks before at the National Arts Club, and seeing the delight in my eyes she included me in her conversation. She was telling of a visit to Alice Meynell, that most exquisite Catholic poet, at her London house. I could hear those wonderful lines ringing in my ears:

> But when sleep comes to close each difficult day . . .
> I run, I run, I am gathered to thy heart.

I remembered Francis Thompson's tribute to Alice Meynell:

> How should I gauge what beauty is her dole,
> Who cannot see her countenance for her soul?

Now Gertrude Atherton sipped her old-fashioned reflectively. "This little cockney maid took me up to Alice Meynell's study. She was sitting there with a hat on her head—two birds perched on the top. She gave me a languishing look, and a boneless handshake. She talked to me . . . all very high-minded. A wisp of a man like a beggar with broken shoe-laces came in and sat in the corner. It was Francis Thompson. Then the children started to come in; the little girls with dirty panty frills hanging below their dresses, and the boys with uncombed hair. But what was so funny, every child had a cold in its head and not *one* handkerchief between them. Mrs. Meynell kissed them and fondled them and let their noses run. The sound of snuffles was all over the room. . . ."

She told stories of Aubrey Beardsley and Oscar Wilde; of queer fantastic little Ernest Dowson, drifting past her in Brompton Oratory with a heavy sweater hanging under his coat, and no collar and tie. She had the air of a woman who has lived always in the midst of Catholic culture; her mind, her imagination, and her senses were deeply rooted in the Spanish Catholicism of early California. She was a strong yet supple person, with a disciplined mind; and was outrageously frank because she had such reticences, such depths, known only to herself and God.

Piety was as ridiculous to her as it is to all people who understand prayer. Those blue eyes were inscrutable, they read your secrets but did not reveal her own.

"Your daughter likes you," she said to mother, "you interest her. Much better than love or duty."

I went on with the play, and His Holiness Pius XI died; and then on a day of false spring there was a new Pope, Pius XII, and none of this interested me very much. George Tyler and Clayton Hamilton were against the play, and I did not agree with any of their reasons. I wrote to Philip Merivale.

He answered from Toronto, where he was trying out a play of Sinclair Lewis', saying he would be delighted to read the script.

He telephoned quite formally. I made an appointment for the next day. In the narrow little sitting room of our suite sat the Earl of Bothwell, straight from Max Anderson's *Mary of Scotland*, a marvelous, dark and vivid Celt. There was not a single cheap element in his theatre judgment. He liked the play, and gave me an extraordinary contribution from an actor—the sense of scene that eliminated the overwriting with a few minor changes. He'd promised his wife, Gladys Cooper, that if he could find a play they'd co-star; and here was a play he liked with the heroine a seventeen-year-old Carmelite novice.

Philip would beg me to get the play ready, and then he would go over to the Players five minutes after leaving me and compose a wonderful tempestuous letter. Indeed life swept him in such gusts and storms of feeling that it was difficult to take him seriously. He had spent his early life in India, his young manhood in England, and the days of his fame in New York. His mind was beset by the contradictions that divide us today. He flashed like a comet through the peace of Gramercy Park, torn between his desire to play the Cardinal, and the knowledge that when I fixed the play we would run into one of those religious controversies which terrify theatrical managers, the least religious of men. He would sit with a tea-cup neatly balanced on his creased trousers, brooding over me like Ignatius Loyola, an old soldier turned ascetic.

Then Mother became quite ill, and I decided to be sensible and pound out a formula play. I wrote night and day, turning out one of those smart glib comedies, naughty and romantic. I copied it neatly and sent it to my friends, among them George Tyler. He stood waiting for me like an angry turkeycock. His face was flaming.

"Plain dirt, all slicked up with lovely writing. You get on the train and get yourself back to Philadelphia. The next thing you'll meet Brock Pemberton and start in with the society crowd. Glamor! There's people who'd put on this truck. You're a dramatist, you hear me—not a cheap little wisecracker. *NOW DON'T LOSE YOUR TEMPER—*"

That is just what I did, and I said unforgivable things, but human things, in the rage of ambitious youth against conservative old age. A new day had swept upon George Tyler, and he wasn't prepared to accept it. He fought me with the fierce possessiveness of a man who had broken the most flaming temperaments in the theatre.

"You'll not disgrace the theatre," he stormed, "with this rot. I've got friends—try it, and I'll break you. I've given my life to the theatre."

His muscles were standing out on his neck as he tried to tear the script through. Someone came in quickly, a nice gentle little man, who took it from him.

"Now, now, George. You're just mad."

"She looks at me with her beautiful eyes like the Lady Eleanor's," he was sobbing like a baby, "and says heartless things, and puts her lovely mind to writing this trash. *YOU GO HOME TO PHILADELPHIA!*"

The man's face was concerned as he took me to the door. "Poor old fellew. You're not to blame. And you can't say you're sorry yet—because you've got to get away from him."

It developed into a feud. Jane Cowl was outraged. Laurette Taylor stormed at me in furious letters. Pauline Lord telephoned, Grace George and Bill Brady took sides. Helen Hayes was horrified. The battle raged for several weeks with all the intensity that theatre people love. Frances Starr poured oil on the troubled waters, though she agreed with George Tyler about the play.

After an operation, Mother had to lie immobile in bed. I wanted to go home to Philadelphia. The money would not hold out with the expense of an illness. Aunt Caroline and Uncle Frank read the play, decided there was a fortune in it, and I had to remain in New York. It was now the end of May. I sent the play to Clayton Hamilton, almost sure he'd side with George Tyler. I received this letter.

*The Players*
*16 Gramercy Park*

Friday evening
May 26th 1939

DEAR CONSTANCE:

Your new play is a brilliant achievement reeking with ability of the rarest kind. It will be produced by a first class management—it will in fact be grabbed; and if properly cast and appropriately directed, I would be willing to wager that it will earn a *cool million* for you.

I must have a practical talk with you at once, before I leave town—in order to make sure the 'ms' shall be shown to the best people, Gilbert Miller, George Kaufman, Brock Pemberton.

I am speaking at the Seville [Scoville] school tomorrow, but if I don't get hold of you later tomorrow night, please assume that we will expect you some time on Sunday.

Ever yours faithfully,
CLAYTON HAMILTON

On Sunday afternoon I was at Clayton's apartment. The sunshine and the river breezes made me feel happy and confident. Clayton laughed at the battering I'd had from George Tyler. He seemed to think I had given all the old people in the theatre an unusually stimulating two weeks.

"Where shall we take the play first?"

I should not have made a choice, but there was that name I'd always loved, and he had praised my long-ago play in a gracious letter. I said:

"Brock Pemberton."

"No," Gay called. "Gilbert Miller."

"Gilbert has a kink in his back from sleeping on my trunk when he was a young boy just come to New York. His father, old Henry Miller, used to disown his sons periodically—turned the boys into geniuses. Gilbert will do anything for me," Clayton explained.

"Dad," Donald broke in, "the Clare Luce play, *Kiss the Boys Goodbye*, is petering out. It never did too well at the box-office. Constance will get on with Tony Perry."

"I'll write Brock at once," Clayton promised. "Tell you what, I'll write about the play and introduce you. Then he'll make an appointment with you and you take it there yourself."

It was the beginning of June when I first turned down Forty-fourth Street. I knew next to nothing about Brock Pemberton, but I wore a white flower on my navy blue dress, an extravagant camellia, and my heart pounded as I stood before the sign OFFICE OF BROCK PEMBERTON, and turned up the theatre alley where there was one naked bulb over the green-door. Inside I stopped at the self-service elevator and had all sorts of grim visions of being stuck between floors. I walked four flights, three of them in Stygian gloom as the Little Theatre was then untenanted. I heard rustling noises. I thought a gray furry body was just ahead of me on the stairs. I heard a squeak. I ran toward the feeble daylight. I collapsed on the chair beside Grace Riley's switchboard.

My breath was still coming in gasps when I stood before Brock Pemberton in the inner office. A bald head, with the clean brilliance of a billiard ball, raised itself from a play script, and a pair of amazing blue eyes looked in mine. They betrayed bewilderment as I continued to gasp. He knew his charms were fabulous, but I doubt if he had ever seen a woman knocked breathless on such short acquaintance. A voice, flat as the Kansas prairies, drawled at me:

"What's the matter?"

I told him of my fear of self-service elevators, and his curiously mirthless chuckle sounded for the first time. He was homely, yet in an odd way he was the most attractive man I had ever seen. Those eyes were always arguing with his sensuous mouth.

"You know," he said, "there's one chance in a million I'll buy your play. You couldn't be as good as Clayton Hamilton says you are."

"Mr. Pemberton," I replied with genuine feeling, "I'd drop dead if you bought my play."

"You'll live a long time," he snapped.

I noticed the curious glaze over his eyes—a bitter delight in dampening my enthusiasm. I sensed that this Mr. Pemberton was torn by all sorts of conflicts.

He rose when I did and with an amused smile not only took me to the elevator, but ran it down to the street level. He looked at me closely, fingered my camellia.

"I used to work in Philadelphia—went to college there for a term. Philadelphia women! I keep seeing them on a spring afternoon passing by the Bellevue, in navy blue. Best-looking women in the world."

The smile and the gleaming blue eyes there in the darkened theatre alley were most potent. His shoulders were broad, and he was splendidly tall. He walked with me, and he had a graceful spring that was sinuous, and yet he was intensely male—a tomcat quality, a sleekness, a grace. And then he turned mild, fatherly.

"I know what it's like to come to the big town to make good. Did it myself. I never go up and down Forty-fourth Street, I don't pinch myself to see if this really could be Brock Pemberton—Robert Brock Pemberton of Emporia, Kansas—Brock Pemberton that got kicked off the *Bulletin* in Philadelphia. I'll send you a line when I'm ready to talk to you. . . ."

Brock Pemberton did not immediately grab at my play about young people. In fact, he kept me waiting a good long time to hear from him. I worried and fretted and then on August fifteenth I received a letter requesting me to come to Brock Pemberton's office at noon. It had a peremptory note, as if there were no doubt I would be sitting in New York in the midst of August ready and available to dash up to Mr. Pemberton's office. The New York *Herald-Tribune* and the *Times* announced that

Mr. Brock Pemberton's first production of the season would be a play about young people, written by a Philadelphia newspaper-woman.

The lightning had struck in eleven months. Mother nearly tossed the breakfast tray on the floor. Elizabeth, the German chambermaid, clapped her hands in joy. I dressed to kill, and arrived in midtown, hours too early. I went to St. Patrick's for Mass, remembering it was the Feast of the Assumption, and sat on the Sacred Heart altar side, feeling rather foolish. I sneaked up to the altar of St. Louis and St. Michael, because of my father's name, and lit a candle, as if I were doing something wrong and might be caught at it and then, still furtive, I ducked into the Lady Chapel and said a "Salve Regina." I had involved Heaven in a very bad business. . . .

This time the whole atmosphere of the suite of offices atop the Little Theatre building was humming with activity. Grace Riley—my dear friend Grace Riley—looked up from her switchboard to greet me. Mr. Brooks, who did their publicity at that time and looked like a professor in a Quaker college, shook my hand; standing in the long hall waiting for me was Brock Pemberton.

"Here she is. Here's my playwright."

A stout blond woman was smiling at me. She had violet eyes and a peaches and cream complexion. She had the most beautiful voice I had ever heard in my life.

"I'm Tony Perry," she said. "Brock, how *do* you attract them? She's young—she's lovely—she writes like a streak."

We sat for a few moments in Brock's office while Tony Perry flattered me outrageously. But when my interest veered toward Brock she pulled it back into her own orbit.

"Your play is good," he said. "It's the most brilliant writing I've seen for a long time. It needs a little work."

I smiled at him blissfully, for I did not realize what his definition of a "little work" was to mean. Tony assured me that Brock laughed aloud—and wept, which was the sign. She promised to let me in on the secret of the Perry-Pemberton formula which would save any play. She made it sound slightly Rosicrucian.

And then we were lunching at Brock and Tony's table at

Sardi's. It was the equivalent of being bidden to Buckingham Palace to meet the King and Queen. Sardi's is as intimate as a drugstore on Main Street. It utterly lacks concealment and is frankly curious. I was on the Broadway grapevine, and these actresses knew more about me than I will ever know about myself. I commenced to feel different, I was a celebrity to be gaped at, and it made me demanding and important.

Antoinette Perry was one of the most extraordinary and baffling women in the theatre. She was born with riches. She married greater riches—the sort that include private homes on Fifth Avenue, castles in England and Scotland, yachts, dresses from Worth—but she had no consciousness of money. She was utterly without arrogance. In the old-fashioned sense of the term she was a very great lady. She had been a great beauty. She had no vanity. Years before, when increasing flesh commenced to obscure this beauty, she had given up fashion and its demands. She had deep inner resources—and yet she was destructive.

I was now in a unique part of the theatre world where the wealth and fashion of America converged, and all the amusing people. No one in this world knew the pinch of poverty or any pang of frustration. Producers put off productions to go shooting after big game in Africa. Cole Porter, the composer, even held up a production because he couldn't miss the season at Cap d'Antibes. Everyone went away for long week-ends.

Work on my play started after my social potential had been explored. Margaret Pemberton, Brock's wife, was in South America, so I only had to cope with Tony. I was always tripping over a piece of spiderweb.

I was more and more aware that when Brock and I worked alone he was keen and alert. He was an intelligent and perceptive showman who, like a good editor, could spot what must be eliminated, what must be substituted. Tony and he, instead of complementing each other, in a subtle, dreadful way were wrong for each other. She warred against his taste and judgment, he battled against the intensity and creativeness of what might have become a superb theatre gift. There was always unfulfilled greatness in Tony Perry, and without recognizing what was happening she struck out at Brock's excellent disciplined taste, his comedy sense. It was she who cheapened it, and filled him with uncertainties. They made each other so miserable with their jealousies and conflicts that they thoroughly enjoyed each other's society.

It was the last of August, and we worked, and had dinner. We worked some more in Tony's little office with Brock Pemberton lying prone on the hard wicker couch. Tony and I left our work and went into Tallulah Bankhead's dressing room after her last curtain in *The Little Foxes.* The portable Victrola was going full blast, Tallulah, expansive and wonderful, was shouting through the din; a midget arrived with his manager and sat on her lap. Glenn Anders came in from *Skylark* and talked of a real world: German troops were on the borders of Poland.

The next morning the Germans bombed Warsaw and war had begun.

The play conferences continued and Brock spoke of a November opening in Philadelphia. Tony's daughter Maggie, looking like a sea nymph, returned from Hollywood and with her two ex-husbands, Winsor French and Burgess Meredith, as escorts made the gossip columns. This brought our work to a halt, for Tony Perry went conservative and spent hours weeping to her best friends.

There was another lull while Tony rehearsed the road company of *Kiss the Boys Goodbye;* while she was in Boston I persuaded Mr. P. to let me read Clare Luce's original script. There was a haunting quality under the glittering surfaces, of an idealist gone bitter in a lunatic society. The play in manuscript was excellent. The revisions made under the supervision of Brock Pemberton betrayed just what I was feeling, confusion.

I felt that my skepticism had a foundation and I pressed for a contract.

"I'm not interested in working with playwrights who want piffling sums," Mr. P. drawled, his blue eyes shrewd and cold.

Tony cautioned me: "He takes it from Clare. She comes dashing in and asks for five hundred dollars, and, of course, it is cute. Why, she doesn't know how much she makes from her plays. She just puts the money into her gardens at the plantation."

Clare Luce didn't have to make explanations to a practical family in Philadelphia who saw only one thing: I had no contract, therefore I must exaggerate Brock Pemberton's interest in my play. Clare Luce could get five hundred dollars to plant flowers while I had to worry over a few measly dollars.

My worries propelled me into the office of Audrey Wood, then a young redhead with a sturdy handshake and kind blue eyes. She listened to my story, read the play, my version, and the amended Pemberton script. She didn't want to take it away from the great man, for his system of brooding, driving an author to a nervous breakdown and at the last, hopeless minute rushing into rehearsal and emerging with a smash-hit, was too well known to discount. Instead Audrey reached for the telephone and got me a job. That is how I became a reader at Paramount Pictures.

I took to going to Vespers at St. George's Episcopal Church in Stuyvesant Square. It was picturesque to see the ebony face of Harry Burleigh in his cardinal-red choir robe, and to hear that rich magnificent voice. The minister was a gentlemanly old man who preached a quiet sermon. The vestrymen took up the collection on velvet-lined plates which didn't make money sound so crass in church. It aroused by Irish Catholic risibilities.

I cannot now remember how I found the shabby little convent church on East Twenty-eighth street. I entered and instantly knew it was a Catholic church. Children were soliciting money for chances, selling Bingo tickets. It had the earthy realism of Catholicism. I liked it. A high grille separated the nave and the altar from the congregation. I was curious; then through the door on the Epistle side there entered nuns in habits of white with heaven-blue scapulars and long white veils over their faces, two by two they approached the sanctuary, prostrated themselves and drifted to the stalls. A bare-foot Carmelite friar read the lessons and then it came, that wonderful chant with the awe of Heaven in it. It broke through the hurt in my stubborn heart: "O, Mary conceived without sin, pray for us who have recourse to thee."

My happiest Sundays were now spent at the little church of the Convent of Mary Reparatrix. I could feel Our Lady's consolations all around me. I asked her help with that awful trashy play. I made extravagant promises to her if she would just see that it was produced and I became rich and famous. Our Lady knows children are greedy and foolish and though she yearned over my wasted years that denied me the real sorrows and joys of womanhood, I could feel her pity. How on earth does any woman get on without Mary?

Finally Pemberton decided there had been enough revisions. He asked for the week-end to make up his mind. He sat there in Tony's office late Friday afternoon as I delivered a few minor changes he wanted, admiring his flat-as-a-wafer watch designed by Paul Flato. Tony implored:

"Brock, tell Constance we're going to do her play! We're going to open after New Year's. What's the point in letting her worry?"

"I will give her a definite answer on Monday morning," he said.

Tony, who could weep at the drop of a hat, burst into tears. Brock was unmoved.

That Sunday afternoon I was again in Mary Reparatrix. An emotion swept through me that was more than an emotion, for it was a keen, cold flash of insight that made everything clear and bright. The knowledge came to me that what I really wanted was here in this church. The chant of the blue-and-white-robed Sisters reached my inmost depths, and I was in a state of prayer that had nothing to do with my hungry little petitions.

Brock summoned me by telephone Monday morning for a two o'clock appointment. He had to hang on to his uncertainties and prolong my tortured suspense as long as he could. I arrived at the office through bleak November rain in anything but a happy frame of mind. He sat at his desk looking irritable, cursing cocktail parties, especially the one he had been to Sunday afternoon.

"About your play. It's good. I know it's good. There's something wrong with it. One of these days my mind will hit on the solution."

"Brock," panic had me by the throat, "either you are or are

not going to produce my play. If you are–I want a contract."

"Look here," he shouted, "that's the trouble with all you kids who come to New York. You get swelled heads. Here you have a chance of working with the biggest management in America, but you scream about options. I'm not interested in piffling sums, I told you that."

I had started to slide into debt, not through extravagance but because of unforeseen expenses.

"I love piffling sums." I pounded the desk. "They can be the difference between life and death, success and failure. My play is either worth a contract, or it's worthless."

Brock Pemberton looked at this unwonted show of spirit with interest, then suddenly he roared with laughter. I did not know that the peaked crown of my hat had in my splendid outburst suddenly burst a stitch and shot upward like a Jack-in-the-box. Brock Pemberton was daring to laugh at me and a hundred generations, or whatever the requisite number is, of haughty Celts. I demanded my script.

It was my first experience of absolute failure and while Tony Perry kept one of my manuscripts, assuring me she would work on it and turn it into "a million dollar hit," I knew my toehold in the Broadway theatre was tenuous.

I was sent to George Kaufman who sat studying me, his long legs curling around a chair.

"My God, lady, you certainly can write," he said. "This play isn't it. Brock has mauled it. Send me anything else you do. I'll shove you over the top."

He resembled a good-natured workhorse with his shaggy mane and big yellow teeth. He rose, cracking his bony hands like Ichabod Crane, and let me out the door with a wonderful grin.

"The school you're in now is where you get plays. Worry–heartache. I dare you to fall in love."

There was Gilbert Miller to assure me that I could write plays, but this one was not what he wanted. There was Alfred de Liagre, Jr. There were many producers, and Jed Harris. I had no lurid experiences to put any of my virtues, save patience, to the test. Maxie Gordon advised me to drink milk because I looked too thin. My memory of Broadway producers is a group of benign fatherly gentlemen. It may have been that I was neither producible nor seducible.

I went after a variety of jobs. I had interviews with career guidance experts. One looked like Anna Held and assured me I had a big future in the industrial world making statements for Alfred Sloan or the Fords.

That winter everyone said the phony war would go on forever without a shot being fired. 1940 came in bleakly. In Philadelphia Great-aunt Cad died just after New Year's; Great-aunt Jen died the month following. I did not go home to their funerals. The impending Pemberton production of my play had been well discussed by the family. Now they shrouded my shame in silence. I did not want to face them. They did not understand failure. Perhaps they had too little imagination.

My phone was always silent. It is uncanny how Broadway friends desert, like lemmings swimming out to sea. The truth was I had not made one real friend. These successful men and women who had found me amusing a few months ago knew exactly how to dispose of me. They assumed I knew the rules of the game. I did not stop to realize that there is a grace God gives talented people which allows them to meet the right people at the right time for their development. Those who are indulging in self-destruction, thwarting the essential thing in their own natures, reach out to destructive people.

In this mood Tony Perry and I quarreled. She is dead now and it is pointless to revive the reason for that ancient grievance. We are punished more for our imprudence than our meanness, so my imprudent rage did me far more harm than Tony's action.

And meanwhile debts, of which my mother knew nothing, crept up. I had a polite reminder from the hotel. I was terrified. . . .

Then Belgium fell, and the Notre Dame convent in Namur went up in flames. English boys died in Dunkirk in that bitter summer. Hitler forced an armistice from the French. The Luftwaffe rained bombs on London. Death was everywhere. And I sat in a New York hotel room brooding over my worst enemy: myself.

Frances Starr came to New York definitely worried about me. The story came tumbling out as we sat at dinner in one of those wonderful little places in the East Fifties that used to be speak-easies.

"Frances," I said, "I won't fail. I tell you I won't. . . ."

"O, dear Lord! Somebody has to be nobody. Whatever difference does it make? If you can't take care of yourself, drink too much, and go all nerves and bitterness—then you're too damned weak for the theatre."

"*Somebody has to be nobody.*"

I went to Philadelphia. The doctor had warned me that Mother had better be near her family and friends. I didn't try to see any of the family. I didn't want to see anyone. Philadelphia was stifling in the stale, late August heat, but rents were about one half the New York rate. I found an apartment in West Philadelphia on the second floor of a tall building set in acres of pleasant green gardens. Mother was pleased with the floor plan I brought back to New York, and we wired acceptance at once.

The tenth of September, a clear bright day filled with expectancy, was my last day in New York. I dressed, taking pains with my hair, my make-up; my eyes now were always a little bloodshot. I walked the splendid streets. The Waldorf Towers loomed in the sky. That was where Clare Boothe Luce lived. A few short months ago they had called me her successor. I walked by the Cathedral. I had no inclination to stop. God didn't exist for me.

Was it only two years ago that *The Years of the Locusts* had been running in England? In Manchester, Coventry, Birmingham . . . I had dinner, and went to see Lynn Fontanne and Alfred Lunt in *There Shall Be No Night*, and then came home and wrote them a letter filled with my passionate love of the theatre, and my sorrow at having to leave it defeated. I mailed it. I undressed, took out the vial of sleeping pills, and came back to the sitting room. The lights went out one by one around Gramercy Park. A harvest moon shone over the waterstack on Rosamond Gilder's house. I saw clearly the green pattern on the upholstered furniture. The design remained in my mind forever. What were my thoughts? I had no real thoughts. I was afraid. I wanted someone to help me. I wanted love and protection. Perhaps there was an Eternity, a Hell where the clocks would tick forever and forever. I heard Mother's gentle breathing in the next room. I had asked the chambermaid to come in at seven-thirty. She wouldn't be alone. . . .

I couldn't face life any longer. I put the tablets in my hand. I swallowed them and gulped down a drink of water. I rose quickly and flushed the vial down the water closet. Mother murmured in her sleep.

I lay looking at the moon. It happened very quickly, and suddenly fear caught me. I fought against oblivion. I could feel the drowsiness creeping up. I tried to scream. Blackness smothered me. There was a dreadful second of consciousness in which a black round funnel engulfed me. Nuns in sky-blue habits behind an iron grating in the Chapel of Mary Reparatrix. . . . I could no longer fight. Hell was everywhere, except in the fading blue of the nuns' robes. . . .

## 5

THE SUN STREAMED IN the windows of the bedroom in the Gramercy Park Hotel. The chambermaid was shaking me vigorously. I could feel the agony in my head, the slow heavy beating of my heart. I got in the shower somehow. The cold water was torture; now my heart was beating terribly fast. I wanted to sleep. I dressed, swallowed two cups of scalding black coffee. The trunks stood by the door. There were things to be done. Mother sat there, every inch a lady of Philadelphia, protected by its securities, by the caste into which she had been born. She was sad and disappointed, but she had control of her emotions. I made my arrangements with the hotel manager. He made no threats, he was even kind, but I felt degraded.

It was a commonplace story; it happens every day among theatre people.

My heart was skidding and my eyes didn't focus normally. I was living on time I had forfeited by my own act. The train stopped at Trenton; there followed the long drab miles of Philadelphia. . . . Soon we would be "home."

Finally, the old familiar furniture had been put in place, Mother's cherished china stood in the glass cabinets, my books spilled off their shelves as they always had; it was a pleasant, normal homecoming quite in the family tradition. I was well-dressed, there was the aura of theatre about me. A society reporter announced we had returned from the Gramercy Park Hotel to spend the winter in Philadelphia. One of the papers called for an appointment for their photographer. The little stores where we had dealt begged for our custom and would present monthly bills.

And then I was told I was to get a small legacy left me by Great-aunt Cad. I could send that to New York; it would almost cover the debt Mother knew nothing about. I sat in the gardens with the little dog in that September of 1940, and the golden sun streamed down on my wretchedness and vanity. The skies over England flamed with death, and hearts broke for real reasons. People who live by the world are hurt by the world.

The long days faded into one another. Tomorrow—that hope of humanity! Well, the damned day was waiting for me, and it was just like any other day. I was free of the nagging terror of debt, and I ceased to have any desires. I slept, I ate, I could afford to do nothing else.

There was one thing that kept me sane: seeing Aunt Francie. She knew without being told that I was swamped in my own crazy nature, and she smiled with welcome—that gracious welcome of the heart—each Sunday afternoon when I entered her house. I never knew how much she guessed till one day, a year later, she suddenly cried out, "Stop asking her things, that New York look is back in her eyes."

Uncle Frank Matthews sat at the dining table discussing the conditions of the world, and he forced me to think. His son Tommy, lately become a lawyer like his father, battled with my creative inertia. I became aware of what a remarkable human being my cousin Margaret had developed into and, though I found her Catholicism irrational, I avoided religious arguments, but gave vent to outbursts of shallow wit at which Aunt Francie, in her infinite wisdom, led the laughter.

Occasionally I'd go into a tirade about the Fascist mind of the Church, its love of money, its opposition to every step of man's enlightenment through the ages. I'd rage about Franco, one of the favorite bogey-men of the lapsed Catholic; or Cardinal Innitzer sounding the church bells in Austria as Hitler came in as conqueror. I'd find myself with a volume of Maritain in my hand, or one of Pius XI's encyclicals. I'd brandish the volume, saying dramatically. "Fair words! Where are the Church's fair deeds?"

I drifted in with strangers, and I learned about idle women in apartment-hotels. Most of them were the veterans of one divorce, few of them had any children. They were rootless; their husbands had usually come from out of town to accept positions as executives in one of the large companies in Philadelphia. They had plenty of money, their brains had atrophied, and they sought the stimulus of liquor to keep going. Afternoon after afternoon they gathered in each others' apartments, the cocktail shaker rattling like their vapid laughter. At night they swarmed into the hotel bar.

A group of much older women sat around the lobby or the Blue Salon, or the gardens, being scandalized and interested in the wild young set. They were filled with sly malice and hypocrisy but most of all they were old and empty. Diamonds blazed on their fingers, correct hats were on their carefully coiffured heads. They always looked as if they were going somewhere, and sometimes they did—they slid into death.

In that environment I heard the news of Pearl Harbor. Fear was a sound the ear could hear, a gray shape the eye could see. I walked through the streets the first day of America's war on two continents, and they were deserted. Terror had gripped every heart; a snub-nosed plane barely skirting the roofs of the houses sailed over the city. It was going slowly, the still air heavy with the noise of its throbbing engines.

There was one thing I made up my mind to do, and I did not connect my resolve with my Catholic background as I tried to enlist for every dirty unglamorous job open to a female volunteer. I asked of it only that I could hate it. In that way I could identify myself with the young men going to war. I who hated mathematics, who loathed and feared all transactions with money, dealt with millions of dollars. Each night I checked out the war bond saleswomen, counted the money, entered it in the books, dolefully rechecked on an adding machine, and sobbed with nerves. I who hated exactitude spent my days making bandages. It was, of course, my Irish streak of Jansenism and not virtue; but I think my agonies before these dreary tasks may have been of use to my soul.

It is impossible to recover the tempo of those years, for we all worked so hard that there was no time to think. It was during these crowded years that my cousin Margaret announced she was going to be a nun. She was entering the novitiate of the Convent of the Cenacle at Ronkonkoma. My reaction to this news was panic. I was sure she was suffering from a frustration that we could not understand, but Margaret was radiantly happy, waving from the train platform at an unearthly hour of the morning.

In a few months Margaret came home from the convent. All the bright youth was gone from her eyes, but they were filled with quiet courage. The story was simple; her health had not been good, and I suspect the Mistress of Novices, Mother Mary Judge, had come up against that strong will. What astonished me was her lack of bitterness; failure to me was the ultimate horror—that is, not to be glorious before the world. Margaret had met a defeat in its way as crushing as mine, but she had drawn together the bleeding wound with fortitude. The whole thing amazed me, and I became very fond of Margaret.

I was working hard at a variety of interests, meeting dozens of new people, trying to help the war effort in any way I could. I should have felt happy and useful, but I felt only emptiness and futility. I disguised my wretchedness in wild high spirits, exuberant bursts of humor which made me quite popular. There was no peace in me and so I was never quiet.

Eva Le Gallienne in those years stood looking at me. "Take it off," she said. "You know what I mean. Take off your mask. It's wonderful, all these wisecracks, but it isn't you. Give up these compensatory illusions. Go back to your convent and your nuns. You're dying inside. Constance, I mean it. Why run away from your Church? It's *you*."

I was humiliated that my posturing was seen through and that this suffering and intensely sensitive woman knew I was a mass of wretchedness inside. Like the child in *The Insect Comedy*, I wanted something. I didn't know what I wanted. I wanted it. Eva Le Gallienne had dared to put it in words; and even as expert as I had become at self-deception, I could still recognize a truth.

And now my beloved cousin Tommy was called into service. He had no mock-heroics, no love of the soldier's calling, for he was deeply in love with his beautiful young wife who was about to have her first child. We all decided to go back to the old cottage at Ocean City for a rousing farewell party. Henry Van Riiswyck was staying at the cottage having a brief vacation; someone was always staying at the cottage.

The clean sea air came through the windows of one of those rickety old coach trains the railroads used for shore travel during the war years. The wild grasses blew on the Fifty-ninth Street beach, around the bend we could see the weather-beaten shingles of the green cottage that had housed our youth. The smell of the sea permeated everything.

It was a good week-end, for the ghosts of the children we had been accompanied us everywhere. Frances, this carefully corseted matron, wasn't Frances, mother of two sons. Frances was an apple-cheeked little girl walking primly down the beach with her book under her arm. Tommy wasn't the husband of Eleanor, a man going off to war; he was swimming like an eel, a ten-year-old boy, trying to breast the tricky currents around the rocks. I—I wasn't this woman who mixed the cocktails, I was fourteen years old and I was going down the beach with Walt Whitman's poems in my hands, making for the sand dunes where I would lie and read with the sea gulls whirling and diving over my head. Brother was the lucky one, for Brother had been killed when he was eleven. Somehow you could see him come through the dining room door asking, "Remember me?" And then we'd reminisce, "Will you ever forget the time Brother made the radio and strung the aerial on the bed-springs?" It was a glorious week-end, though when night came we pulled down the black-out curtains and if we stood on the porch we could see the coast guards patrolling the beach-front and the gaunt shape of the great dogs that walked with them.

I got up at daybreak, the sun just peeping up out of the ocean, and went to early Mass with the family. We had all been so happy I didn't want tensions and tacit disapprovals, I reasoned to myself, excusing my peculiar conduct. I sat in the back of the church where the open doors gave on a balcony that seemed to jut out over the sea. There weren't many people, as this was the first Mass. It was said by a gentle, stooping old priest with a crown of soft white hair. He turned from the Latin gospel, and walked down to the altar rail and preached a sermon of tremendous kindness and simplicity and godliness. I was moved by it. Impelled by some urgency I did not understand, I left the chapel before the Sanctus and sat on a wooden bench overlooking the sea. I could hear the bells ringing; from where I sat I could see the family kneeling at Communion. I was given no vivid flashes of remorse, but a calm deep contentment to be near these mysteries.

We had breakfast at one of those clean, old-fashioned dairies, and terrible news came over the radio. A battleship had gone down; the Germans were sweeping across Russia. In a sense that Mass at the chapel of the Christian Brothers had made the war recede. I had a feeling it had been reduced in scope. I did not realize I had been close to the primary cause, that wars and all the bungling cruelty of mankind are secondary. The important thing was our and the world's insignificance in the face of Eternity. We were only in a new crisis, and what I had felt as I sat there leafing through Henry's vast missal was the force of God's love reaching out toward me—toward the tortured of the world—reaching out in His Church, in His Real Presence. I did not know why it should be so, but this morning was the first time for years I had known what it meant to feel happiness.

Tommy went off to war, and in due time he came back from a camp in Texas for a brief furlough, and his son was born. I tried to make his last evening one of splendid gaiety, and we saw him off in a train filled with soldiers. A young corporal kissed his mother goodby with jaunty casualness, and burst into tears. I wonder if he came home alive?

I recaptured integrity occasionally with my cousins, but the germs of bitterness were still breeding in my mind. I had now a sort of compulsion to cynicism, a belief in the second-rate. I had a sense always of watching my own disintegration. The years had thrust their sword in the uncertain crevice between my vanity and my pride, the pride was damaged, therefore the vanity smarted unbearably. I felt myself a failure, moving in an atmosphere of failure. I had made no serious attempt at writing for years. My basic insincerity in my relations with my fellow man did not disturb me; I merely sought out their insincerities, and fed their vanity. Everyone said I was such "a good sport"—much easier to be that, than a good writer. The fearful tempo of the war years freed me from thinking too much of what I was doing to my life, what would become of this or that responsibility. I needed to find the prose for God, which alone can save a woman as she starts the middle years. A brief and charming incident happened to me at this time that brought back my belief in my own value as a person, rescued me from my desperate feeling of mediocrity.

I opened a door into the past, and through it came my Uncle Si's boyhood friend General Malin Craig, former Chief-of-Staff of the Army, then Chief of Personnel. I asked General Craig a favor. Not only did he grant it, but he gave me an insight into a first-rate human being. Somehow he was glad to be reminded of the old days at Georgetown Prep, and his long-dead friend Simon Horan. In a way this kind, busy old soldier stopped in the midst of a brutal modern war to recapture the essence of other days, to reminisce of the time when his class at West Point had been graduated to serve in the Spanish-American war. The discipline of Old Army was deep in his soul, given him by his father, a cavalryman, Captain Craig. General Malin Craig was an old man of the golden age, and he brought back something to me that I valued, tradition. Our correspondence enabled me to throw off my sense of defeat. His humor was delightful, and he urged me to write a play about "snobs on the General-staff." I yearned instead to write a tribute to a splendid soldier who could laugh at himself. I read his military biography, all that list of decorations from every government in the world, and impressed as I was, knew that General Craig saw them for exactly what they were, and had no extravagant sense of their importance. It was like the quiet dignity in the man, to elect to have private funeral services at Walter Reed Hospital, where he spent the last year of his life near his old chief "Black Jack" Pershing. A Low Requiem Mass was celebrated for him in the early hours of a gray day by a Jesuit from Georgetown. It was like the start of a soldier's day at Fort Sam Houston, or at Bragg, a little cold with smoke drifting in the air. The Army going on, an old soldier going out, with the wind whipping a four-star general's flag. . . .

My friendship with the General had put me on my mettle, and I determined to rehabilitate my talents, to cease my drifting with the second-rate. My first cousin Lieutenant John Balderston O'Hara, a pilot on a B-17, was killed in action over Norway on September 9, 1944, aged twenty-one years. He was a handsome giant of a boy, Uncle Thé's only son. I kept seeing him at his father's grave, a bewildered big child. He had turned when he was fifteen or sixteen to the Protestant religion of his mother, and in the midst of the family uproar drifted away from us. I saw then, and I see no reason now, for this attitude of mind. If a Catholic makes a mixed marriage, how in the tensions of modern life can he expect children of divided loyalties to remain steadfast? His memorial services in the Protestant church caused eddies of agitation; the word "apostate" was used; and in the row I severed my ties with my father's family, and the last of my Catholic influences. Family quarrels are bitter things. They're not aches or wounds to heal, but amputations for all to see.

I thought deeply of young John O'Hara, who had accepted the responsibilities forced on him by the relentless press of history. All those young men were so much more worthy of life than we who were left with it, and dared to misuse it. I determined to force my way back to creative writing. It was not easy. The most frightening thing was that I had no belief in anything, except a few frayed rags of liberalism. I had this vast contempt for people, and without love and pity a writer is impotent.

The subject of the new play was big enough, for my central figure was a columnist spreading fear and dissension through a war-torn land. I depicted him as a shoddy character who believed himself a great crusader. Many of the popular columnists at that time were shrill and hysterical demagogues who had developed extraordinary techniques for the use of the lie that would skirt around the law of libel. My plot was simple: my columnist discovered that a prominent member of the State Department had had his only son draft-deferred. His reasons were legitimate, but when the public learned of a figure close to the President keeping his own son from a war in which theirs were suffering and dying, his usefulness to the nation was at an end.

I called the play *The Magnificent Heel.* It was disciplined work; a picture of the general disintegration of inherited illusions about morality, honor, justice. Nearly everyone in my play was an opportunist of one sort or another. The audience had no one to root for—but it was interesting. The one chance it had for successful production was the Theatre Guild.

I had lost my theatre contacts. I did know one person who might guide me to the Theatre Guild, and as his own current play was one of the smash-hits of the season, there would be no danger that he might take a personal interest in *The Magnificent Heel.* I might flatter him into calling it to the Guild's attention, for the directors were his close personal friends.

I wrote a breezy note to which I received a short, amused reply asking for my script. I put it in a manila envelope and sent it to him in the middle of February, 1945. I hoped for the best—but expected the worst.

A telegram came, making an appointment for the next day, just before I turned on the radio to hear President Roosevelt address Congress after his return from Yalta. Did that mean my play was good? I fretted about it, and then I heard a sad, tired voice come on the air. Catholic Poland had been severed by the demands of the Soviet Union; again the President of a democracy was baffled by the currents of Catholicism in Europe.

The next day, the third of March, I went to keep my noon appointment at the Thirtieth Street Station. The Washington train was in. I saw a tall man with a light dancing step coming toward me, and the gleam of blue eyes.

"Constance, it's a magnificent play. My God, how you've grown. Wait . . . wait . . . you'll have an immediate contract. The play is ready for rehearsals, which will start at once. There are no seasons any more. I open in late April in Washington. We'll start casting today."

We started toward the station restaurant and I could feel those blue eyes looking at me. The recent disciplines I had put myself through made it seem as if the years had been kind to me.

"Tony's sick," the voice drawled. "It's going to be you and I, Constance. You and I. We'll show 'em. Two hits in a year. *Harvey* and *The Magnificent Heel.*"

Brock Pemberton and I sat at lunch together. I stifled my misgivings. Things were different now. I suggested Orson Welles as the Heel, Ina Claire as Susan, his wife, Philip Merivale as Denis

Reardon, my beloved Celtic philosopher. Brock agreed, wrote on the menu. I wanted an agent, I wanted the great Harold Freedman. Brock said he'd make an immediate appointment. Margaret Pemberton wanted me for lunch in New York. She liked my play. . . .

I had won the first round. My head was light with victory. I'd win all the rounds. I'd learned how to live—how to be ruthless. I'd learned how to handle men. In less than five years I had come back to Brock Pemberton, victorious.

## 6

BROCK STOOD WAITING at Sardi's door. Donald Cook craned his neck. John Golden waved. He led me to their table on the aisle. Harold Freedman stood up looking like a timid bank clerk, only his alert eyes betrayed his quality. A little old woman, snuggled in a faded pink sweater with a floppy velvet hat shading her face, sat with her back to me. Who on earth was it? A pair of eyes looked up at me, and I gasped. Those eyes had once been so beautiful; they were the eyes of death. This was a dying woman; this was Tony Perry.

"Darling," the voice was still exquisite, filled with cradle notes. "Constance, they said you had changed. You haven't, dear. Kiss me."

I leaned over and those tortured eyes were coming toward me.

"Forgive me, Constance?" She was smiling in a pathetic attempt at gaiety, but there was more to that smile. She knew I was still vulnerable.

I couldn't think of anything to say and the ghost of the old quarrel, the quarrel that seemed so dreadful now with this pathetic face across from me, haunted both of us. I watched her little stubby hands moving among the glasses.

Tony at Sardi's after months away was a sensation. Everyone wanted to talk to her and get a close-up view of the new female author. Harold Freedman was interested that it bored me. I was amazed at my own annoyance. Was I, at last, showing signs of maturity?

"Constance," said Tony with her heartbreaking little cough, which was sometimes genuine, sometimes faked, for this tremendously strong woman knew the strength of weakness, "your wife in the play walks out on the heel. Women will never forgive you for that. Nice women never desert heels." Again that sidewise, arch look at Brock.

Tony threw down the gauntlet when we returned to the office. "Constance, I think you should write this as a novel."

Brock compared me to Behrman and she smiled gently with a roguish childlike quality. I saw the doubt coming in his eyes.

"Tenacity. Capacity. Courage," she said, patting my hand. At that moment genuine pain clutched her. I held on to her while the paroxysm lasted. The mussy little organdy bow on the front of her dress was moving in time to the rapid beating of her heart.

"We haven't taken away her kindness, Brock," she said as the pain ended.

Tony was back. That was plain from her dramatic return that April day. The second company of *Harvey* had been delayed to wait for her recovery. *The Magnificent Heel* would remain in the wings till she gave the nod. She was too ill to endure the work of a new script; but she had no intention of putting down the reins. It was a let-down after the terrific stimulus of acceptance. I went back to Philadelphia cautious and dispirited.

On April 12, 1945, a voice over the radio said an unbelievable thing to which you listened, but the mind could not encompass it: "President Roosevelt died in Warm Springs, Georgia, of a massive cerebral hemorrhage."

I returned to the concerns of the play.

Though Brock claimed to be entirely satisfied, I learned that a play about a heel is hard to cast. *The Magnificent Heel* aroused the ire of every leading actor; moreover, they were afraid of stirring the wrath of the columnists. Mr. Orson Welles wired his regrets. Mr. Glenn Anders left Brock's office in a rage after reading the script. Mr. Brian Aherne was mortally wounded when the role of the columnist was offered to him. Mr. Louis Calhern refused to read the play, because he might like it; it would be dangerous for him to play the heel. Brock assured me he was going to direct *The Magnificent Heel*, though in deference to Tony's condition no announcement would be made. I now decided on George Coulouris as the columnist, Sidney Greenstreet as my Irish philosopher, and Edna Best as the columnist's wife. Brock agreed with me, over Tony's opposition; assured me he had the Erlanger Theatre in Buffalo for a split week before Washington—but there was nothing positive being done about casting, and we were now at the beginning of summer.

I was fretful, so Brock, who liked his fun, offered the leading role to Walter Winchell, and we were in for a deluge of nationwide publicity. I opened my closets gingerly for fear a skeleton would fall out.

The war's end brought black panic to Broadway. Nearly all the plays had war backgrounds. The central theme of my play concerned draft evasion—and here was peace! The draft was a dead issue, or so we thought in late summer of 1945.

Brock, Tony and I met at Sardi's. He was starting one of his liver attacks and his face was saffron yellow. Tony was almost chipper, still wearing her black velvet picture hat, the little pink sweater over her shoulders, and the black dress with its limp organdy bow. A lesser woman would have been a freak—Tony was still a personage.

It was an uneasy luncheon. Brock fled back to the office before we had finished. Tony dawdled, talked to actors; she couldn't conceive of a life away from the theatre and New York. She would have liked to live in a theatre. The tired heat of the last day of August assailed us as we turned in the alley of the Little

Theatre. Tony held onto the wall breathing deeply, and we managed somehow to make the fourth floor. Brock Pemberton lay on the hard rattan couch in her office, limp with nausea and pain.

He had explained at Sardi's that as we had a box-office idea, all we had to do was change the plot, paraphrase the dialogue, and everything was set.

Tony sat bolt upright at her desk, still wearing her floppy hat. She reached for my script and a freshly sharpened pencil which she held in her odd, little hand. Instinctively I thought of a surgeon's hand holding a scalpel. She said with deceptive gentleness:

"Now tell us the story of your play?"

The basic situation in a play should be stated in twenty-five words; and from that conflict the story line must stem—or the chances are you haven't got a play. I floundered badly. Tony sighed.

"Essential weakness disguised with brilliant writing," explained Tony.

"The story is too complex." Brock was frightened. "I was afraid of that."

"You know," said Tony, without a vestige of malice and quite urbanely, "I find myself terribly bored with this play."

And then and there commenced the longest, hottest, most exhausting interview of my life. A meeting that was to determine how best to get the draft-dodging angle out of my play became a dissection. I lost all sense of reality. My play was without point, and without joints. The wreckage was strewn all over the floor of my mind. There was no doubt about it, this woman had with uncanny accuracy torn apart a play; but in my bewilderment I began to see that the destructive method could be used on almost any play in dramatic literature.

"By Heaven!" Brock kicked up his heels in glee. "The boomerang. She always does that. Now I haven't a drop of faith left in the play."

"Brock," I said, all sweetness, "you've made a fortune with unconventional plays, plays that nobody else wanted because you pay no attention to formulas. There's *Personal Appearance*—

you worked on that alone with Larry Riley, when Tony was in Denver."

The thrust had gone home. He looked pleased. Tony's head under her velvet hat was raised, and her enormous eyes were looking at me speculatively.

"Tony usually keeps these bombshells for rehearsal. She likes you. We're going in with a tight script."

"You mean you're going to produce this play?" I gasped.

"Sure—" a spasm of pain sent him rolling back and forth on the couch. "You can fix it. Get out the draft-dodging. Now let's see if we can find a plot. I can't bear a play that pertains to the past, recent or otherwise. There's Russia." He went into a trance. "There's the State Department. Take over from there."

My play *The Magnificent Heel*, which on production dealt with a plea for Russo-American friendship, was dubbed Communistic. My leanings that way were gravely studied. That staunch conservative Brock Pemberton germinated the wicked idea during a liver spell. I was called "a tainted liberal," and an "undercover Marxist." These are the facts of how I got mixed up with Karl Marx on the last day of August in 1945.

"We've got to kick Russia under the play," moaned Mr. P.

Tony ignored us, wrote on the margin of the script, suddenly burst into tears. "I despise generalized staging. Another one-set play. I can't do it. I won't. A davenport again . . ."

Mr. P., suffering from the ebb and flow of his gastric juices, offered, "The atomic bomb! Forget Russia. The way things are happening these days an unpleasant fact will send your play to the junk-pile. The secret of the bomb. Russia and us. Keep that wonderful dialogue. Don't be afraid of melodrama."

I stood up weary, defeated. . . . In two weeks the option would terminate.

"Don't you panic," said Brock putting me in a cab. "I'll expect the play in a month. I'll make another tentative date with the National in Washington."

In three weeks of concentrated frenzy I laid under my play the entire Union of Soviet Socialist Republics. I cannot think of any suggestion left out of the script except the atomic bomb. The critics were to remedy that lack a year later. Brock renewed the option.

Brock had a "father complex," or in simple language he had no children, and his paternal instincts, which were quite well developed, found an outlet only with his playwrights. He bossed them unmercifully, and felt he had the right freely to criticize the conduct of their lives.

I saw this amusing aspect of his character when one day we hailed a taxi in front of Tony's after a play-session. There was a neatly rolled tabloid on the back-seat, and nothing delighted Brock so much as a free newspaper. He opened it, and slapped it down in rage.

"Look at this," he said.

It was a picture of Clare Boothe Luce emerging from St. Matthew's Church in Washington after her reception into the Catholic Church.

"You wrote me last summer she was thinking like a Catholic and you bet she'd come in. Well, she has," Brock's Methodist blood had come to a boil. "Understand me, I've nothing against Catholics who are born that way—but this—"

And then Brock and I were snarling at each other. I was defending Clare Luce, of whom I had never spoken a good word. I pointed out that she had known unendurable sorrow, but, even apart from the death of her only child, no one with a mind or heart could face the world in our time without a co-ordinating philosophy.

"I was devout as a boy," Brock explained, suitably impressed by my impassioned argument. "But I haven't given a thought to these things in years. It's too big for me. And then religious people are such damned hypocrites. Clare Luce a Catholic! Going to church with the maids. . . . It's that priest," Brock added airily, "that Sheen fellow. He gets around 'em."

I remembered that slim young man with the startling eyes talking on the Divine Sense of Humor at that long-ago luncheon in Philadelphia.

The hot June had commenced and we were preparing the producing script at Tony's apartment. These had not been happy sessions at "510." Tony and Brock were in their wealthy amateur mood. The impulse to destroy which is at the root of hedonism was clearly before me. I was not only suffering from a barely suppressed Celtic temper, but my Irish Catholic sense of sin was commencing to stir at this airy ignoring of all the hopes and fears and grim realities tied up in the production of a play.

This Sunday when I arrived at Tony's I sensed something different about her. There was a half-ironic cadence in her voice as if she guessed my thoughts and judgments. She decided we'd change the title of the play. She telephoned people. I suggested John Donne as a fashionable source of titles. She found the Sonnets. We read John Donne. Her face was beautiful and peaceful as I read the familiar lines:

> "Death, be not proud, though some have called thee
> Mighty and dreadful, for thou art not so:
> For those whom thou think'st thou dost overthrow
> Die not, poor Death; nor yet canst thou kill me."

She pulled the book away from me, and her voice was exquisite:

> "One short sleep past, we wake eternally,
> And Death shall be no more: Death, thou shalt die!"

I was reading the Divine Poems—the lovely *On the Sacrament*, as an indignant Brock Pemberton stepped through the door.

"Is this a poetry session?" he demanded. "You going to have poetry in the play? Do you realize we open in September in Buffalo?"

Brock irritated me for, in some undefined way, the good and natural sacramental life had been a presence in the stuffy foyer where we always worked. The lines,

> And what the Word did make it,
> I do believe and take it.

spoke to me with tremendous peacefulness. It was like water welling up from a spring. The image of that clear water had such reality that I asked, "Tony, who is the saint that always speaks of water?"

"Are you two crazy?" The Pemberton countenance was puffy and irritable. "Is this Gertrude Stein or something—"

"We were hunting for a title, Brock," I said placatingly.

"So it's a religious play?" he asked sternly. "Tony and you going to have saints in it and fountains—?"

"Ernest Hemingway got his title from Donne: *For Whom the Bell Tolls*," I explained.

"And if you ask me," Brock was angry, "it's a helluva title."

"For whom the bell tolls." Tony's inscrutable eyes looked at Brock. "It tolls for thee."

The quarrel between them was swift, intense. He leaped from his chair and left. The power and the simplicity of John Donne had vanished; there was only a woman crying convulsively.

I reached over and touched her hand. She was burning with fever. I was conscious of nothing but her eyes.

"Constance, there's something I've always wanted since I was a child. Will it happen to me, dear? It's all misty—and maybe it can't happen. It's all I want. What does your religion tell you about it? Oh, you haven't got any religion . . . I forgot—"

I realized that Tony Perry was mortally ill. I wondered if her daughter Elaine was home.

"Constance," her eyes were imploring me, "will I see God?"

All the hates and vain strivings of the world seemed to turn to dust. This hour was given to me, in which a soul asked for my help, asked me to heal her with the tremendous wellsprings of Catholic faith and knowledge. And I failed.

"I want to see the face of God." She was weeping quietly. "I am afraid, dear, but if I could be sure of that—"

I mumbled some nonsense about forgiveness.

"Oh, Constance, of course He forgives if we love—of course. What else do you know?"

"I know that every pain you've borne with courage is His grace. I'm—I'm sure of that, Tony."

"You think I will see God then?" It was like a child being promised a treat, and having faith in the word.

I went down the long hall to see if I could find someone in the apartment. It was silent and still. I stood in Maggie Perry's bedroom and I could feel my knees shaking. "Constance, will I see God?"

Finally, I pulled myself together as best I could, and went back to Tony. She was sitting bolt upright, her tears dried. She waved me back to my place, and with pencil in hand commenced the third act. She spoke with authority and sureness of touch. There was terrific power in the inspiration that moved her. Tony Perry was giving me the last work of her life, and in that I failed her too, for I could not fit it together. She gasped for breath, and stopped.

I stood at the door; as long as I live I will feel those great tragic eyes looking at me, filled with tenderness and affection. It was a promise and a portent. It said: "God brought us together for me to ask you, 'Constance, will I see God?' He brought us together so you would never forget my question, and one day would kneel and pray for me."

Tuesday night in Philadelphia my phone rang. I could barely hear her voice; she was telling me of Brock going to buy her gingerale. She was telling me she was in bed and though she never used the word "ill," I knew from her voice how bad it was.

"Constance," she said, "my mother sent me a little picture of St. Elizabeth. Do you love St. Elizabeth? No, I mean the mother of John the Baptist. I love her so much. I've been crying over her picture. You know Mary has come to her to tell her of Christ, and Elizabeth feels her unborn baby kick in the womb. Dear, that's the first worship of God—dark and hidden in Elizabeth's womb, John the Baptist stirs as he feels the unborn Christ. That's what prayer is—dark and hidden—and then we feel God's presence, and it brings life." I could hear her weeping quietly. "Darling, don't you share it with me? Don't you know what I mean?"

The words came from a long-dead memory of convent days, " 'My soul doth magnify the Lord—' "

"The Magnificat!" Her little laugh was heartbreaking. "That's a formal prayer; but it's not sweet and trustful like John's. Mary says that to Elizabeth, but those unborn babies Christ and John are so hidden—so loving—"

There was a long silence, and the voice was a mere thread. "It's going to be all right about your play, dear. It's going to go on. Don't worry. But Constance, I wanted you to love St. Elizabeth."

I went to an old book of my father's. I found Teresa of Avila's "Rain from Heaven," that exquisite intimation of the Beatific Vision. I tore it out, put it in an envelope with a special delivery stamp.

Thursday morning they found Tony Perry lying beside her bed. She was dead and clutched in her hand was the prayer of Teresa of Avila stained with blood, for she had cut her head as she fell.

*"Constance, will I see God?"*

If I had had a strong and ardent Catholic faith I could have brought peace to a tortured modern heart; but with what was left I did my best.

## 7

ON AN AUGUST AFTERNOON Brock Pemberton and I walked on the stage of the Henry Miller Theatre in New York, where in a matter of minutes, *The Magnificent Heel* was to go into rehearsal under his direction. The actors were on their feet; flashlight bulbs went off. In the front rows of the theatre I saw the experts lounging, splendidly independent of reverence, cigarettes hanging from their mouths, dilapidated hats casting gray shadows over their sallow faces. They lived surrounded by "phonies" and had utter contempt for them. In the midst of the rebellious and scrambled emotions of the theatre they could spot the genuine and fight for its survival. The rest of the audience were hangers-on of Broadway glories, bored Park Avenue blondes, female journalists, a few crackpots, dazzled backers who had to have all sorts of influence just for the privilege of investing in Mr. P.'s new play. The columnists had scouts on my trail. *Life* magazine was going to give us a two-page spread. I was at the peak of my professional life, and I no longer had one consecutive sensible thought about the play.

"It is always," said Mr. P., now launched into one of his witty and gracious speeches, "a pleasure to start one of my plays at the Henry Miller Theatre. Miss Perry and I—" a catch came in his voice. He straightened his shoulders—"have always had good fortune here. *Personal Appearance. Kiss the Boys Goodbye* . . ."

Six weeks before, the day after Tony Perry's funeral, I had gone to Brock's office. During those sad and difficult days he had assured me that my play was going on, that Tony wanted it that way. I knew with every instinct that my play was not right, that this provided me with a gracious exit. He sat there bewildered and saddened, surrounded by pages of revisions, and blueprints of John Root's design, and listened to me.

"You don't trust me to do your play?" he questioned. "You think I can't—without Tony? Someone has been after you. I didn't think you were like the rest."

It was a frightening moment. Though neither he nor I realized it, I had never altogether lost the sanely Catholic way of looking at things, and now I gave Brock Pemberton a gift from my Catholic past: disinterested affection and trust.

"I would rather have you produce my play than anyone in America, Brock," I said.

His face flushed with pleasure. I accepted the inevitable. Mistakes made in generosity are less horrifying than mistakes made for ambition. Although sardonic in humor, intolerant, an implacable enemy, he was capable of the most tender solicitude for his friends. I do not regret our friendship.

Friendship was to be the rewarding experience of *The Magnificent Heel.* Brock led me forward on the stage of Miller's to greet Peggy Wood who had flown in from California that morning. She had been my choice for the role; I had known her when I was a stage-struck girl in Philadelphia and hadn't seen her since.

We were both highly conscious of this association, but she was not old enough, and I was not young enough, to make a point of it.

Peggy like all actresses hurls her vivid dramatic imagination against the drab colors of reality, and a weary playwright was sometimes sucked into the vortex of moods. I never minded because she never lost the intense sincerity of a kind, real and simple human being. We almost never said a mean word—about each other. I have a great regard for the gifted Peggy Wood, who has that highest gift, the art of being a loyal friend.

There is no way to convey to the lay mind the history of a play that fails. *The Magnificent Heel* was one of the notorious failures of 1946. It offers an opportunity for an orgy of self-justification. There are stories of company feuds, uproars and ineptitude that can give me an old age of lurid memories. But most of all what I remember is the naked electric light in its wire cage casting eerie lights on the stage. That bulb gave it a mystic air and did keynote the best part of the profession—that you live apart from the world in a fierce discipline, and no matter how dreadful the period of rehearsal may be, you are drawn away from participation in life, and live intensely in something outside yourself—the play. The bulb, which I found pleasing, an almost religious note, a twilight atmosphere of devotion, is there to save an electrician's wages. It is one more absurdity of a wildly uneconomic profession.

And then somehow the madness of a disjointed play and a disorganized company were on the Empire Express bound for our first stop, Buffalo.

The road! Unfinished meals lying on tables piled high with manuscript. Smoke-filled rooms. Exhaustion dragging you down to the weak self-indulgence of sleep. You dare not give in. There're lines to be changed, scenes to be sharpened. Try coffee and benzedrine tablets. You sleep—come to with a start. Where are you? Out of town for the try-out of your play. You're crossing a strange street in a new place. Those people gathering in a theatre lobby are coming to the first night of your new play out of town. Those nice, unsuspecting people. . . .

The next thing I knew we were in Washington blanketed in a September hot spell. It was a full-dress glamor audience. I saw General Omar Bradley pass. I stood beside Brock and Harold Freedman like an interested observer of something in which I did not have the slightest concern. *The Magnificent Heel* on that night fell heir to every theatrical disaster. Next morning the press lashed Brock Pemberton and myself in merciless words, that now I must admit were models of gentle kindliness compared to the reality.

*The Magnificent Heel* was so frightful that even a normally sensitive dramatist would shrink away from all human contact, and be inclined to ask no greater understanding of a dearest friend than an affirmative answer to: "Will you be free for lunch on Judgment Day?"

Brock and I went together to the National Theatre to announce the closing. The actors sat around in a semi-circle, Peggy Wood knitting busily. It reminded me of the French Revolution and the women knitting at the guillotine. I was the chosen victim. It was almost interesting. Then Brock did a generous thing, an act of kindness that took away the sting of failure. He rose to face the company and made a gracious speech, assuming the blame for the failure of *The Magnificent Heel*, from its first revisions to production. It is difficult to judge the point at which a showman remembers that he is a human being capable of compassion, or is an artist making an effect on his public. I prefer to believe that Brock Pemberton forgot everything but his compunction and did not stop to remember that the worst of human circumstances cannot wreck a good play. His tired face, looking at me, watching anxiously for my reactions, remains a good memory of *The Magnificent Heel.*

I said the words I will never have to take back: "Thank you, Mr. Pemberton."

As I remained in Washington with the company I was mercifully unaware that the publicity stories appearing daily in the press announcing that Brock was applying to Actors' Equity for use of the six-weeks clause and planned to reopen *The Heel*, were entirely serious. The Monday after we returned I sat in his office, somewhat spent from a day in Philadelphia, trying to explain failure, not having the courage to refuse Pemberton's offer because it had in it a certain exoneration. I agreed to rewrite the play in the six weeks' time allowance. Wanton stupidity is a fearful thing!

And for a few weeks I sat at home hammering out a play that had in it pieces of every hit Brock had produced. The seduction scene from *Strictly Dishonorable;* the dialogue from *Kiss the Boys Goodbye;* the characters from *Personal Appearance.* This multiple plagiarism finally brought on violent pains in my face. I dosed with aspirin, and then the agony overwhelmed me, and I decided it must be toothache. The dentist hammered at my jaw, teeth were extracted, and then it would break out again.

"You'd better see a neurologist," the dentist advised.

So it was just my nerves! The thing for sensible people to do was rise above nerves. I rose, therefore, even through torments that sent me into paroxysms of sobbing, which I concealed behind closed doors, trying every patent medicine on the market. Finally a small hard lump appeared on my neck, and wonder of wonders, the attacks stopped. A queer thing happened—I started to choke on pieces of food. I thought this rather amusing, for to be free of the pain I would have given up food without regret. We decided I had swollen tonsils. No one is more skeptical about medical advice, nor more scandalously indifferent to their health than the families of doctors.

"Your tonsils should have been taken out years ago," Mother observed, worried, returning to her place at dinner after madly pounding my back during a choking spell.

The play was finished, the intolerable, the silly play, and I sat in Brock's office. My presence in New York was a secret from the actors who were waiting the rehearsal call. Sanity had returned to Mr. P., and he didn't know how on earth to break it to me.

"Connie, I don't know how you did it. The dialogue's wonderful, technically there's nothing to be desired—"

"Except, Mr. P.," I observed, "it just isn't a play. They'll laugh this one straight off the boards. The monster had moments and scenes, it even had an idea."

He breathed a long sigh of relief and relaxed. I had never bothered him with lamentations or tantrums. Too bad he had ever got himself involved with "this dish." You could see the thoughts forming in his mind. But what was it made me tick, stand up to these experiences? Damn it, he thought, this isn't fair. She can write. She loves the theatre. He said those were his thoughts.

"Connie," his face was gentle, "what do you want me to do for you?"

"Send me to Hollywood, Brock. I need the backlog of a writing job."

"You're not going to Hollywood," he said. "A sensitive woman like you would be finished out there. All you need is a little peace and security. That's not a helluva lot to want. You like to read those crazy poetry books. Tony and you and the poetry!"

Something made us both stop and listen, waiting to hear that exquisite voice.

"Come on," he said. "We'll go to Sardi's and talk. We're not giving up. There's a play in you, Connie. A great play."

Genuine kindness led him to persuade me to rewrite *The Magnificent Heel;* a refusal to face realities led me to agree. He was to subsidize me while I finished the play and he really meant to.

"Take your time, Connie," Brock advised. "Think it out. We'll talk over every detail."

Murdock Pemberton, Brock's younger brother, had come with him. It would be interesting to know what might have happened if those two had become a producing team. They had the same sharp wit. Murdock stubbornly remained a newspaperman, laughing at his famous brother's suavity, but he had the richer mind. In those last months of 1946 there was an air of masculine intelligence about the Little Theatre that gave me confidence.

Brock went away to Hobe Sound happy about the play, for I had two sound acts and if I could pull out a third it might be possible to go into rehearsal in the late spring. I didn't mind the

February thaws or the interminable train rides between Philadelphia and New York. I was completing the third act at home when my telephone rang.

"Constance," said one of those convent school voices unshattered by life, "Sister Julie died yesterday."

There had been a call from the convent some weeks ago. A message had been left that Sister wanted to see me. It was easy enough to pretend I had never received it. Someone had told me she was seriously ill. Naturally she knew I was out of the Church. It worried her, of course; which made it pointless for me to visit a poor, sick old nun, for I would never return—of that I was sure.

"Constance, I know she would want me to call you," the prim little voice went on. "You were one of her favorites." I thought I detected a note of reproach. "She's being laid out in the chapel and the Children of Mary are invited to her funeral."

I saw the long hall leading to the front door of the Convent of Notre Dame. Sister Julie was walking along with me, surrounded by her girls, several of the nuns in the background. She knew how to dwarf lesser lights by the sheer impact of her personality. The portress was opening the front door; I could see her peering at the well-dressed man standing there, not quite knowing what to do with him. Sister Julie stepped up briskly, and led him graciously toward the parlor. She heard, as I did, the whispered comment of one of the nuns, "Sister Julie is so masculine she always likes to go to the parlor with the gentlemen."

"Sister dear," Sister Julie du Saint-Esprit's head tilted provocatively, "wouldn't you say that's the survival of my feminine instincts?" She flashed that gamin grin at me, the girl who liked her best when she was being outrageous. "And I assure you they'll last till the twentieth, no the twenty-fifth, spadeful of earth goes in my grave."

The gentleman was, needless to say, enchanted—of which fact Sister was most aware. I hadn't seen her since that day—why, that was nineteen years ago—and now she was lying in state in the convent chapel, the Sisters of Notre Dame praying for the respose of her soul. Blessed Mère Julie's statue keeping guard over this unpredictable daughter.

"I'm sorry," I said, a tight band around my heart, "I'm going to New York, besides I never go to funerals."

"You'll pray for Sister Julie, Constance?" The voice was sad. "She prayed for you."

I slammed down the phone; sanctimonious idiots deserved that sort of treatment. I stood in Rittenhouse Square in the shelter of the Park guard's house, where no one could see me, the afternoon before the funeral and watched the Children of Mary mounting the high brown steps of the Convent of Notre Dame. The schoolchildren were coming out the little gate from the garden. I knew I was being sentimental, having one of my attacks of nostalgia. It was foolish and morbid of me to stand here thinking about an old nun, I scolded myself. She believed in Heaven, and that was a consolation I didn't begrudge her, dying in agony of cancer. The myth called Heaven certainly wasn't enough for me, or anybody else as far as I knew. A wave of melancholy descended on me. I kept remembering Sister Julie, little things she'd say. I couldn't get that sentence out of my head:

> Now, Constance, do not dramatize yourself: you are not a black sheep; merely an unattractive, dirty gray.

Mr. Pemberton returned from Hobe Sound and professed delight with the completed script. It was difficult for him to concentrate on anything as serious as play production for any consecutive stretch of time. He was at the peak of his profession and was enjoying all the rewards that go with it; but he had a keen intelligence and in those last years seemed to realize that he was only the head of a somewhat unattractive and degraded profession. Some of his pranks went deeper than clowns' tricks, they had a bitterness that seemed to proclaim he realized he was over sixty and at the back of his mind wondered why he was alive at all.

The groundwork of our association had been built by the press into a beautiful thing made up of a great and generous producer's faith in a playwright who had failed. Brock loved a legend like that; and my remaining under his banner had become an imperative.

I suffered tortures of uncertainty about the script, writing, endless rewriting, waiting, endless waiting.

Once I sat in the Drake bar with Peggy Wood.

"Constance," she begged, "give up. You can't work on this play any more. It's masochism."

I couldn't explain what I had done to my life, by following the will-o'-the-wisp, stage gold. There was a decent reticence about these matters, not to be imposed on people who had been brilliantly successful.

"Constance," she was looking away, embarrassed, "I put a great deal of money in plays. I've been lucky. Could I put a little money in a playwright to take a rest?"

I felt a hot flush coming to my face and then I looked at Peggy. She was worried that she might have hurt me. My pride only seeped a few drops of blood. She squeezed my hand.

"Can't do it, Peggy Wood. I never have. I'd come all to pieces if I did. Besides there isn't anything left of me as a playwright. It's gone. I've got to find something to believe in before I can write again."

There were more weeks of inactivity, fits and starts of interest. I would sit before a typewriter in Philadelphia, and the keys wrote shimmering dialogue and I wept inside: "Long, long ago I had something to say, there was something in me, and now that thing is gone. What is so dreadful, I don't seem to care."

The new version of *The Heel* was finally scheduled for production. Tommy sent the notices to the papers. Rehearsals would start the first week in February, with an early spring opening in Philadelphia. Glenn Anders was to play the columnist. Vivian Vance and Phil Ober joined us nearly always at lunch in Sardi's. Shirley Booth, it was almost sure, would play the columnist's wife. The backers' copies were out. I interviewed actors by the score. In the excitement I forgot how wretchedly ill I felt. Time enough to attend to my offending tonsils when the play was on.

I was in Philadelphia packing my bags when a letter came, a

special delivery letter from Brock. It squirmed around, but it was definite. Brock was not going to do the play. He made excuses such as the new *Harvey* company, the replacement of Frank Fay with Jimmy Stewart. Everything he wrote was complete nonsense. I was numb; too numb to despair; too tired to fight.

I was summoned to New York. Brock Pemberton was aching all over from what he'd done. It made him difficult. We sat at Sardi's, Brock, Murdock, Maggie Perry, Jack Pulaski of *Variety*. It was a familiar group. We all tried to look excessively friendly. A look easy to summon, but difficult to preserve. I ate scrambled eggs so I wouldn't choke in public, and three years of my life ended.

I had to plan what to do with the future. About that time a letter came from the Authors' League. A priest in Philadelphia named Father Joseph Collins had gone in bookstores with police warrants to protest indecent literature. I was asked to join in the protest. The Catholics were at their tiresome tricks again. My liberal conscience was affronted. I sat down and wrote a flaming letter expressing my rage at the whole tribe of book-burners from Savonarola right on down to Father Joseph Collins of Philadelphia.

Then because I couldn't put it off any longer and to silence mother who was vehement about the whole thing, I went to see a doctor. My father's old medical friends were dead, and I selected a neighborhood physician. The office was crowded and I was consumed with impatience. Then I was looking into the doctor's appraising eyes, describing my symptoms which I called tonsillitis.

"I think you'd better go to the hospital at once," he said. "I'm on the staff of the Misericordia and St. Mary's."

I didn't want Catholic hospitals. I hadn't thought about the doctor's religion. I now realized his name was Polish.

"I think I'd better see a nose and throat man, Doctor, before I make a decision. I'm sure it's my tonsils. I had bad ones as a child."

"It isn't tonsils," he said. "We can't delay. I'll have a blood count made tomorrow." He wrote on a card and handed it to me. "Go there the first thing in the morning, please." He hesitated. "You know this may be Hodgkin's disease."

"What on earth is that?" I was annoyed. "Is it going to mean an operation?"

He was a blunt honest doctor, used to dealing with people whom life forced to be realistic. I could sense in my bones that he was a good doctor. He toyed with an instrument, then made his decision: "Hodgkin's disease is cancer of the glands."

Cancer! I had no resources to prepare me for this. I walked home, to my mother, stiffly, rigidly, holding myself together. In that terrible way of mothers, my life had become hers, and now I was bringing myself back to her with cancer. It was a dirty trick of the fates! There was one thing: I'd not go to a Catholic hospital with their pious gibberish about offering up pain. I would have the most cold-blooded, advanced science. I wouldn't suffer. . . . Perhaps modern doctors did help cancer victims to mercy deaths.

In this moment of need, a family that didn't understand Broadway plays rallied around. Jefferson Hospital was selected. My surgeon was one of the most famous in America, Dr. Thomas A. Shallow.

Then it was my last night at home. In the morning I would have the hospital to face, doctors, endless examinations. Mother was tremendous, but in her eyes I saw that bewildered pain of the old who see the young taken from them.

We did the familiar things. I sat writing letters, and a pattern started to assert itself in my consciousness. We call it coincidence, but we know that is not the right word. In my heart was that bewildered loneliness of the woman who had not married or dedicated her life. I thought of my Serbian of long ago, the children we might have had. Then my telephone rang and he was speaking to me. Where had he been in all those twelve years since he jumped off a Fifth Avenue bus?

"I'm at your Aunt Constance's," he said. "She's in the telephone book, and you're not. I can't hear you," he kept repeating to my explanations; finally he understood. "You're going to the hospital tomorrow. Wait. I'm coming right over."

I met him in the lobby. Mother could be spared the intrusion of my ex-romances. It was ten o'clock at night. He was a giant of a man now, foreign and remote. He stared at me blankly as I questioned him. I realized he was deaf. I led him to the bar. His sad, dark eyes kept looking at me.

I always see the great solemn dignity of that Serbian telling me of the years between our meetings. He had been in England when war came, and then as a medical officer in the Army had been sent to Belgrade. The war over, he'd gone to Detroit to work in tubercular surgery. And here he was.

A juke-box played a discordant tune in the dimly lit bar. A man who had been young and danced with a girl in an American Beauty dress at a County Medical ball to the music of "Smoke Gets in Your Eyes" now looked at a woman with a gray face and a mass of lumps on her neck. A girl who had been in love with herself, who wanted a career, and had sat at the Academy of Music beside a young man with an intense Slavic face while Eugene Ormandy conducted the *Pathétique*, now looked at a heavy-jowled stranger whose ears had been deafened in a bomb blast in London.

"I heard the bomb coming down; everything falling, crashing. . . . And then the silence was queer. I knew that little girl must be roaring at the top of her lungs. She was hurt. I didn't hear a sound."

He ran his doctor's hands down my neck. He was worried. It was dreadful somehow; the past held us there till everyone had left the bar and the waiters were washing glasses with a defiant racket. Why did we sit there so long with our ghosts?

We went out on the dark, tree-lined streets, and suddenly we made love to each other like a sailor and his girl; as if all our capacities for affection had been starved and this bitter hunger in the face of death and ruin must be appeased. I sought light and heat and, being what I was, some intensity of meaning. He sought the caress of someone who had been a red-headed girl, mad as a hatter. "Don't be a damned fool, Constance," I told myself. "Don't be a damned fool." There was an immensity of loneliness as we stood there together.

"Why did you come back?" I said to those sad, foreign eyes.

"I remembered you. I kept remembering you. I think you were curious. Yes, you were so curious." He smiled. "I don't mean that to be rude. It made you kind."

He went away and that scene in the darkened Philadelphia streets moved off into inconceivable distance. I often doubt if it took place at all. It was too dramatic to be altogether real, but it haunts the "troubled midnight."

The next day I sat in a room in Jefferson Hospital whose windows faced stone walls. Someone had sent an orchid! An orchid! There were letters. One praised me for my splendid, courageous words denouncing Father Joseph Collins, and asked permission to quote them in publicity releases. It was quiet in my room. A nurse had taken my temperature and blood pressure and left me alone. I found that I missed the nuns in Catholic hospitals, the feeling of safety and discipline. The days following were filled with tests, conferences with doctors. At day's end I'd hear the sound of many footsteps, and Dr. Thomas Shallow would march in my room like a general with his staff. There was Dr. Wagner, his first assistant, smiling at me, his second and third assistants standing straight and grave, the young doctors on his service lined up in formation. It was a magnificent spectacle! Dr. Shallow gave me one look from his extraordinary eyes, but not one moment to ask him questions. Out the door they'd go, leaving me too breathless to bemoan my fate. All sorts of things were happening like an accumulation of fate's fury. Mother came one day and her face was white with strain. She'd had a fall. I saw she was about to faint and rang for a nurse who took her away in a wheelchair. They notified me from Accident that her arm was broken and she was being taken to Aunt Caroline's at the Barclay.

I wrote a series of orders about my funeral. I was to be cremated, and there were to be no religious services of any kind. I was sure I was being nonsensical, I wasn't going to die, of course. I heard a floor nurse outside my door arguing with an interne on a scheduled blood transfusion:

"What's the good of wasting blood on a woman in that condition, just because she can pay for it?"

I hadn't been play-acting after all.

A fitful sunshine burst through the clouds on Sunday afternoon. I dressed and went up to the roof solarium. The sick people were all around me. I looked outside at the railing. It was quite low, you could leap over it, and in a second it would be all over. I would frighten the sick people badly, of course. . . .

I heard loud laughter. An old woman was seated in an invalid-chair surrounded by a big, jolly family. Why was it that common people had to be so common? A priest was coming toward me, a young priest, but he crossed over to the old woman. Odd that I should feel let down. They greeted him as "our Joe." They "fathered" him all over the place. The oils of ordination still lingered on him, but it was obvious he was the source of all wisdom. Father had an opinion on this: Father had an opinion on that. Father dripped parochialism from every pore. He held his black homburg impressively and he condescended to tell them a joke. Screams rolled over the roof; the old woman stopped it finally, tears of mirth streaming down her face.

"Father's a card," she explained. "Now, Joe–"

Father looked at me directly. Father wasn't a card. He was a Catholic priest and his eyes were fine and good. His look claimed me, drew me back to the boundaries of my childhood's faith.

Then my cousin Margaret stood beside me, with a worried look on her face, and a little round hat on her head.

"Margaret," I said, "go get me a priest."

She was calm but her frown vanished and while she didn't run or leap she moved quickly away. "I'll go to St. John's and then I'll be back. We can sit here a while." I noticed that she walked very fast as the elevator came into view. The big, noisy family quieted down, amazed at the sudden appearance and disappearance of my visitor. The young priest looked worried till Margaret came back.

We didn't mention her errand. Instead, she told me all about Dorothy Day of whom I had never heard. I was not enthusiastic. She spoke of the Baroness de Hueck. I was about to ask her about this ignoramus Father Joseph Collins who was burning the books, but I decided against it. She might defend him, and we'd argue. The young priest stood beside us, smiling: "Goodby, now. Good luck to you."

I was startled but not angry. I loved this priest's good apple-pie face. Perhaps he'd heard my name and assumed I was "one of our own." I didn't mind. I needed desperately to belong somewhere.

"There'll be a priest from St. John's here in the morning," Margaret told me when she said goodby.

The hours went by, the long, bleak hours, and my mood started to change. I realized I was a coward trying to immerse myself in the mysteries and hocus-pocus of the Church. The night was silent in the hospital corridors. Death and the Church, that's all it was! I wanted the world. Gaiety, laughter, wealth, an extension of my own ego. The scenes of a Diaghilev ballet seemed to form in my mind. I had a sense of luxurious decay, of disgust. Friends? They were good things to have. Frances Starr came close to my hospital bed, a half-sad, half-ironic smile on her face. She vanished as if she understood friends were useless at a time like this. Art? I couldn't recall a masterpiece. A picture postcard of the Mona Lisa came into my mind. It was not consoling.

The night went on. I was so lonely—if only someone would speak to me. I couldn't ring for a nurse. They were busy and besides they were hard, abrupt little girls. I thought of nuns in white habits walking down hospital corridors at night, looking in at doors. I was turning to the Church to stop thinking, to seek protection and safety. It was idiotic. I was unhappy because I'd missed out on fame, fortune. I knew people who'd had all that and were still wretched. Someone was sitting in the big chair in the shadow. I looked into Tony Perry's tragic eyes.

"Constance, will I see God?"

I switched on the light. That was better; she was gone. I

knew people always felt like this the night before a major operation. I'd calm myself. It was fear of the unknown, of the punishment for sin. Of that fear I had never freed myself. What was the difference between mortal and venial sins? "I haven't said my prayers. I haven't been to Mass." The priest would ask, "How many times?" "Father," I said to this imaginary priest, "I have practically no moral sense. I gave up believing in anything and my moral stiffening came out, and I'm all limp." I was being a fool, I admonished myself, and turned off the light. The room was filled with the white-and-blue-clad Sisters of Mary Reparatrix. . . . I'd have to tell the priest about that night at the Gramercy Park Hotel. My mother lying in the next room ill, unsuspecting, and I taking those pills. If I didn't tell it, I'd commit sacrilege. I switched on the light. I'd ring for the nurse and tell her I didn't want to see the priest in the morning. It wasn't long before she looked in the door.

"Could I have a sleeping pill?" I asked.

She came back with a yellow pellet. I choked on it and she patted my back till it went down and then held the water glass for me. She must notice the traces of tears—a middle-aged woman behaving like a sniveling child.

"No more liquids," she said and took away the water pitcher.

I slept and in what seemed like a moment I was awake. The morning had come swiftly. In a little while they'd wheel me up to Surgery. I saw the waiting ward-carriage by my open door. A priest was looking in at me. He was short and dark-haired and wore glasses with shiny steel rims. When he stood by my bed I saw that his eyes were filled with good compassion. He knew all about these hospital nights and poor sinners lying in the dark.

"I'm Father Joseph Collins," he said, "from St. John's."

Father Joseph Collins! This was the book-burner in person. He touched my hand soothingly. I didn't mind that he was Father Collins. I only thought about St. John's Church and Nana praying at the Lourdes grotto, and the stories of Uncle Francis, the martyr-Bishop of Savannah, who had been pastor there. I was without faith in any conscious sense, but there had come into this dreary hospital room a strength outside Father Collins and myself. . . . He lowered his head, and I saw his purple stole.

I was making my confession. I was making excuses for myself, leading up to . . . There, it was out. It was over. What horrid sins they are, these modern sins; not even healthy sins of passion. I hated them. And then they were gone. I couldn't remember the Act of Contrition. I repeated words and phrases of it, and I heard the words of absolution. There wasn't time to reflect on how relieved I felt. Father Collins was kneeling. The Host was on the table. I knew I couldn't swallow it. For weeks I hadn't been able to swallow without choking. He stood there with a spoonful of water and I consumed it. I waited to choke, but I didn't. The Host that was Body and Blood—that was Christ. I closed my eyes and said the "Salve Regina." The words stabbed through me, "And after this our exile, show unto us the blessed fruit of thy womb, Jesus." The Blessed Mother through the fogs of my own mind was coming back to me.

Father Collins was talking to me gently. This was the book-burner. He towered over everyone I'd met in all those desolate years in the world. I had no faith and did not claim it. I had great longing and I sensed the sacramental powers and revered them. I was forgiven. I had a new beginning. The fear was gone.

And then Father Collins made me ready for a journey. My eyes, my ears, the holy oils anointed my senses and I heard the beautiful solemn prayers of Extreme Unction, prayers for the dying. But it was Resurrection. I, who had been dead, lived.

## 8

THE BACKWASH HAD caught me in a treacherous current and I was being swept against the rocks. I could feel their jagged edges catch my shoulder, as the breakers smashed and crashed against me. Now a pair of human hands clutched me. I was being pulled up—up. . . . My body was broken, torn and my shoulder was caught. I tried to get it free. I opened my eyes on white walls. There were nurses working over me with brisk competence. The middle one looked amused. I was in a mold of pain and I couldn't move. My neck and shoulder were in a plaster cast. I couldn't turn my head. I saw them wheeling the transfusion apparatus toward me. Flowers were coming in the door. They looked like funeral flowers, the messenger staggering under their weight. The nurses exclaimed, carried them over to the bedside table, one came toward me with the card. She read:

"Brock Pemberton."

The air crackled with awe and speculation. A little man in black detached himself from the shadows in the back of the room: it was Father Collins.

"How very thoughtful of Mr. Pemberton," he said.

He had a big, beautiful smile and his whole face was lit by goodness. It was the loveliest thing I'd seen in years and years, the holy, humble little man's reaction to these opulent flowers. I remembered I had come back to the Church and my heart felt light and free. Why had I ever left, when all I'd wanted was the radiant goodness in Father Joseph Collins' face?

"Hello, Father Collins," I said. My throat felt as if I'd swallowed liquid fire and damnation.

"Miss Detweiller, she knows me," he exclaimed to the nurse.

Detweiller? Where had I heard that name? Oh, yes, the bakery on Pine Street when I was a child. My father and I used to stop there Saturday nights and buy Dutch cake for Sunday supper. There was a fly-specked plate-glass window with a wedding cake in the center, a mahogany counter with a marble top.

Through the door came Dr. Thomas Shallow, immense and jovial. "God likes you, my dear," he informed me. "It was a completely successful operation. I think I've got all the danger spots. Chart, nurse?"

All his doctors were standing around him. He was on his toes with delight. He gave crisp orders. He marched out of the room. Dr. Wagner stuck his head back in the door. He was grinning.

"I never saw such a piece of surgery in my life." He made a fist of triumph.

"Doctor Shallow forgets we put God on our side, doesn't he, Constance?" questioned Father Joseph Collins.

Pain and accompanying nausea blotted everything out, and in the sick confusion Father Collins left me.

Soon I learned that the operation was not final, it would take eight days to study the diseased lymphatic glands and tissues that had been removed, and if they were cancerous there would be further operations and explorations. It was not a comforting thought. I did not pray about it because I had, literally, forgotten how to pray. Every morning Father Collins came. He brought me Holy Communion and I said the "Salve Regina," and slowly I commenced to remember Mary, the Mother of God, emotionally. I did not realize what Cardinal Newman reminded us of in a famous sermon: "The glories of Mary are for the sake of her Son." Nor would I have understood Blessed Grignion de Montfort's explanation that "Mary is the relation to God," because my thoughts were as simple as a child's—and a not very bright child. I merely remembered from my convent days words of her litanies, the Angelus with its piercing, "The Word was made flesh. And dwelt amongst us." I did not ask the Blessed

Virgin Mary to raise my heart to God—which was just as well, for at that time I would have tacked on another petition to be raised also to a higher income bracket.

The thing that really impressed me was Father Joseph Collins. In my corridor there were six rooms, and I was the only Catholic; yet each morning six suffering human beings waited like children to see a priest from St. John's, whose action against immoral literature was soon to be disapproved in a thunderous liberal opinion from Judge Curtis Bok. In the next room to mine was a nerve case; Father Collins seemed to think her trouble was love. Each morning he came to see her, and listened while she talked about her husband's desertion.

"Now we'll put it up to St. Joseph," he said. "He's the patron of the married."

In a little while I'd hear her laugh. Then Father Collins went into the room of a grandmother who somehow had taken to drink. Her daughters said it was disgusting, but Father Collins seemed to think it was loneliness.

"Now, Mother, have you ever thought how lonely Our Blessed Lord is, waiting for us, just as you're lonely and took that wee nip too much? He understands. Maybe now when you go home you could find some children and help them with their lessons in the afternoon. I'll put my mind to it."

A great voice sounded across the corridor. That was a brilliant irascible Jew with stomach cancer; when the pain hit he cursed horribly.

"I'm waiting to ask you why, Father, the Pope did nothing when Catholic boys were mowed down in Prague by Hitler, or said nothing when decent Austrian Socialists were shot down in cold blood? Give me a reason for the illiteracy and mass poverty in Catholic countries?"

"Give me a chance, man," said the little priest. "I've brought you some books to read. You're a fellow I'd like to have on our side."

Then I'd hear his step going into the room opposite mine. Joey was over there, a nineteen-year-old pre-medical student with rheumatic fever. He never complained, though it was doubtful he'd ever leave his bed. His mother was a nurse who always came to bathe him before she went on duty. She looked so tired. His bureau was filled with flowers, for he had scores of friends. Joey was a saint, but he said he was an agnostic; he wanted to be gentle about it and not hurt people.

"I've got a joke to tell you, Joey," said Father Collins. "And if you let me I'll pin another medal on your pajama coat. This one may do the trick. Give us a little faith, boy."

The last room was always quiet and dark, and the door was seldom open. There was a young man in there with cancer of the lungs. He hadn't long to live—and there were four children home in upstate Pennsylvania. His wife was thin and worried-looking. Once she stood talking outside my door about expenses, and it seemed indecent that the muddy anxieties of life had to harass her in this desperate time. Father Collins' voice could never be heard from that room, but he stayed a long time.

Once he was late, and the wife stopped at my door. "The priest—your priest—isn't he coming?" She was relieved when I told her he was only delayed. "My husband always has such a peaceful sleep after he's gone. We're Protestants, b-but we never bothered much about these things. At a time like this—" Her face started to work. "Your priest is so good."

And that's the way it was on a fifth floor corridor in Jefferson Hospital every morning. These five hungry people waiting for a Catholic priest were the by-products of that single act of mine. But here was a priest condemned by the liberal conscience, who fought Communists violently, and thought they were traitors even when they wore two-hundred-dollar suits and knew the Secretary of State; a priest who seized immoral literature, and hurled himself against articulate and impassioned intellectuals, and yet the measure of the man was in his reaching out to a whole segment of modern society, to whom he was restoring Christ. During my first week back in the Church my intellectual pride suffered a stinging rebuke. Some of my fellow Catholics were up in arms about Father Joseph Collins, they said he was making an exhibition of the Church, they said he was stirring up bigotry and making us a laughingstock. I saw part of the exhibit in Jefferson Hospital. It was magnificent.

I lay there through the April days and the long nights waiting for the verdict. I hoped and I was filled with despair, and I was too blind and deaf and dumb spiritually to comprehend there is no hope more creative and transforming than that of the despairing. I was too passive to fear death, and not even intellectually alert enough to say with Renan, "I am quite willing to die; only I should like to know whether death will be of any use to me." I was not aware of the strength of the sacramental powers in me, but they had given me courage for I kept my terror under control.

Then one day my door burst open. Dr. Lowell Erf stood there and his face resembled the genial sun at noonday.

"It isn't cancer. You're out of the woods. You're all right."

There's nothing to say at a moment like that—nothing. You reach out for a simple, humble, easy word to express glory and gratitude, and from your heart comes all anyone can ever say: "Thank God." And you lie there and nothing else matters but this miracle of escape, and you forget that you're selfish and conceited and narrow-minded, forget the scramble of making money, and impressing people with your worth. Then you think of the others in the hospital who are not so fortunate, and you forget yourself in pity. There are whole minutes in which you sense the intricate, the infinite relatedness of human beings in triumph and trouble—and you, who have done not one worthy thing in your life, have been given back health and they have been denied it.

The thin-faced wife stands in the doorway. She says, "I know what you're feeling. I'm so happy for you."

And you lie there humble and ashamed. What had I done to have this second chance handed to me? I looked up and I felt, though I could not realize it then, the presence of Christ moving in His children, for this woman, who had every right to rebel at my good fortune and her own agony, was honestly glad. In that instant humility—absolute humility—was mine. I owe that woman whose name I have forgotten, if I ever knew it, a most profound debt—for that moment of utter humility was the most beautiful thing that ever happened to me. I was too burdened by my sweet and terrible debt to have words, and I watched through tear-dimmed eyes as she went away from my door. And I prayed God that He might use me in some way to help that burdened woman. It was not a particularly good prayer, or a deep prayer, but it was the best I could do, and this strong feeling burned though all the contradictions in me—a whole world of contradictions in one shallow mind. It was marvelous, for I understood so many things, and I who had been set free from suffering was linked with all suffering, knowing I was unworthy of my escape. I did not burn in shame, for that is false humility, but my spirit bent under its weight of compassion and love.

Then my room filled with doctors and nurses, laughing and chattering. I felt as if the planet had heaved just because I did not have cancer. And I commenced to take up the threads of life, selfish material life, and draft telegrams to friends and call people on the telephone. . . . Father Collins came later that day. He never talked to me about religion, and he never commented on the appalling books on my bedside table. He was always tolerant with me. I had fallen very low indeed, but he knew from that vantage point I had an excellent view of the heights. He put my mind on the heights, and didn't talk about Catholic Action, or plans, or spiritual reading. Now he said:

"We have both prayed. We've had the answer. I am going to say goodby to you now, because I'm going away for a while. I'm going to ask you for a little promise. Will you start going regularly to Mass on Sundays? And say your morning and night prayers? Should you ever want to talk to me, or need me, please send for me."

I never saw him again. I never wrote to him. It was not selfishness, because I didn't want him to see my hurts, my bruises, to know what a terrible mess of things I made, who had been welcomed back by his wisdom and tenderness. Father Joseph Collins is a Christian, and that is the state of being Christ. I will revere my dear book-burner forever, and though it is not fair to quote Santayana in connection with him, I never think of that good little priest without remembering the Spanish renegade's,

> To trust the soul's invincible surmise,
> Was all his science and his only art.

I made up my mind I would keep my promise. There was another week of the hospital—the fourth. And I was so tired of it. I couldn't wait to try and conquer the world again, for "it was all to do over." I had a great grace in those days. My tremendous relief had washed away the sting of my failure with the play, and I had no bitterness toward Brock or any of the people in New York. In a sense I had spiritual health at that time. The past was over and done with; and then too I had never had deep enough trust in anyone on Broadway whom I called friend to be much hurt by defections. I knew the Broadway people's limitations with a shrewd and cynical awareness. I remembered I was restless, roaming the hospital corridors, going up to the roof solarium, talking to Peggy Wood on the phone, or greeting Edith Meiser who came over from New York to see me. Brock and the *Harvey* company were in town, and I was not lonely. Everyone had been very careful not to come near me until I had the good news. Modern pagans avoid trouble; they do not know how to deal with it.

I remember a young Irish Catholic doctor, who had left the Church, came to take out the drainage tubes in my neck, and fit me into a smaller plaster collar. While he worked with his scissors and various probes, I saw in the mirror that I had a crimson scar from the tip of my ear to my shoulder blade. It was horrible, and I closed my eyes while this poor boy spoke violently of the class struggle and of poverty. He was filled with awful scorn for the money-mad Church of Rome. In a way the one thing in the Church of which I was positively convinced was the existence of simony. That had more reality in my mind than the Trinity. This boy and myself were of a piece and yet I did have some sort of idea of the Christian ethic. I gave him my view of it, and he said scornfully, "O.K. O.K. But you're not a typical Catholic."

I laughed and went to pack my bag for I was going home in the morning. I thought of my scar under its plaster covering, and decided my cut throat would be a reminder that I had been a complete fool about the play. I must never again be afraid of insecurity, or put so much of myself into anything. I did a good job of rationalization, considering what I was.

Mother and I were home—she with a cast on her arm, and I with a plaster-bound neck and shoulder. Between us we couldn't open a can, and we couldn't have been poorer, but we were filled with happiness and I spawned plans for writing and jobs. Life was good—good, and I didn't want anything bad and pretentious and silly ever again. Sunday morning came, and Mother had the New York *Times* on my bed when I woke, and I could smell bacon cooking. She stood in the door and was amazed to see me dressing. She didn't say anything about my new spiritual allegiance; she seemed embarrassed and fearful for me. It was as if I were taking up a cross and mightn't find a Christ to follow. She didn't put it in words, but she was right, for an imposed faith without vitality, and so without the possibility of growth, is for the timid and conventional. I think she held her breath before what might happen.

I walked down South Forty-seventh Street on a May Sunday morning, acutely conscious of the plaster collar on my throat, which showed despite my scarf. I had in the conscious sense even less faith than the philosopher William James, who had the emotional will to believe. I began to accuse myself of weak sentimentalism for keeping my promise to Father Joseph Collins. Everybody would say I'd been scared to death and was returning to the Church because I was a coward. I concentrated on all the mean things people would say of me, and cringed. The spoken criticisms of Catholics had never deterred me from doing just what I wanted, but the thought of what they would say because I had returned to the fold gave me enormous concern. They'd say it was middle age. I had change of life—and I'd turned to religion. They'd say I'd made a hash of things on Broadway. . . .

The church stood before me, the great ugly gray pile of it. I hadn't entered its doors since Nana's funeral fifteen years before—I was going to turn around and go home right now. They'd say I had cancer. They'd say—they'd say . . . I climbed the steps. My heart was beating so fast it suffocated me. I decided my stomach felt a little squeamish and perhaps I had better not risk church. The press of bodies against me impelled me through the door. I stood in the center aisle, sure that people were looking at me. I ducked into the last pew. I sat down and, crimson in the face, I knelt. There was a pygmy up there on the altar in green vestments. He was bowing and twisting. He was mounting the altar steps. He stood at the left. He went center. I hadn't the vaguest recollection of what it was all about. The "Kyrie Eleison" came from the choir. More people crowded into the rear pew. I felt like a sardine packed in a can. I had never been more bored or uncomfortable in my life. There was a priest in the pulpit. I made up my mind if he made one remark of an anti-Semitic or Fascist nature, I'd walk out and never come back again. He preached an excellent little sermon which every now and then interested me. It was time for the collection. I noticed with cynical amusement that I had left the Church when it was a silver religion, now it had become a greenback affair. The miracle of Transubstantiation did nothing whatever for me. I felt nothing. I beat my breast emphatically; that was what everyone else was doing.

The Last Gospel came and I made for the front door and freedom; if I waited maybe some of the Catholics would know me and speak to me, say something I'd resent. I could tolerate them only by not speaking to them. That was how I responded to the sublime Mystery of the Mass, my restoration to life as a cell in the Mystical Body of Christ. I do not see how anyone could make a more frightful beginning. A priest on the steps spoke to me pleasantly, and looked at me closely. I bolted around the corner. I was a wreck, exhausted by spending one hour with the Lord.

I continued to keep my promise to Father Collins every Sunday, and the only emotion I felt was relief when High Mass at eleven was supplanted by Low Mass at the beginning of June. I never took a prayer book with me. I had no idea where my convent missal was, but I was taking Catholicism at random which is the principle of liberty. I was not being coerced. I felt filled with virtue for keeping my promise, and strangely I hadn't been so happy in years. Mother was selling her last little property, so that I could keep my pride till I found just the right thing. Everyone felt I should start another play, and Mother was completely in agreement. I felt wonderfully well. I looked years younger, and commenced to think religion was a combination of psychoanalysis and general high spirits.

In this frame of mind I went to New York where a series of "back to life" parties were being given for me.

I was almost childish in my reaction to New York. I told the taxi driver all about being in Jefferson Hospital and being afraid I'd die without seeing the towers of Manhattan again; and he rejoiced in me, being a real New Yorker, which means a lover. There is something good in a city that engenders this enthusiasm.

The next morning which was Sunday I went to Mass at St. Vincent Ferrer's, and the Dominican ritual was beautiful and stately and brought me just a little closer to the meaning and purpose of Mass. I do not know how I could have remained so insensitive, so unvisited by memory. Apart from the Elevation I had no idea what each part signified. The "Orate Fratres" was merely a pleasant break in the long monotony. The wonderful prayers before the Consecration with the exaltation of the command "Sursum corda" meant nothing. There was an excellent sermon that Sunday on the East, in which the priest stressed the need of Japan and Korea for mission priests, and said the strange thing, "that the destiny of faith was in the East." He said quite literally, this magnificent Dominican with strange dark eyes who somehow made me give him the description of Eagle of God, that Western Europe was in crisis torn by secularism and revolution and her civilization would die, save for the torch she would pass to the East—Christianity. He placed America with her eyes turned from the Atlantic toward the Pacific.

The memory of that sermon was still with me when I sat in

Brock Pemberton's office the next day, our grievances forgotten, and discussed the new play I would write. Somehow his words came from an immense distance, and I forgot to be self-conscious that I was not going to work with him again, and I was not being tricky when I didn't inform him of it. In a curious way all of it had ceased to mean anything. I was thinking of that eloquent priest and my concerns seemed childish and unimportant. Brock worked out of me the reason for my indifference, and looked worried.

"Connie, if it's this Catholic stuff took you through all this, I'm not against it for you, because you were born one. But it does bad things to writers. Take Clare Luce. There's a brilliant woman, and all she does is run around proselytizing people, like an evangelist. It worries me."

I laughed at his awful solemnity, and felt detached amusement for Clare Luce's convert zeal. These newcomers who go around giving coverage to the glad tidings which have already been announced by the angelic choir!

In any event when I came back from New York I went again to confession. I wanted to believe, I was determined to give religion a trial. I hoped that it would satisfy my reason and my emotions but apart from desire there was nothing whatever stirring in my soul. I went to St. Francis de Sales to a secular confessor, carefully avoiding the box where the priest had slaughtered me so many years before. I had memorized the Act of Contrition, and that chore was about the only element of contrition in my heart. I neatly parceled up an impressive total of venial sins, paying no attention to the condition of my mind and the mountains of pride that encrusted me and bore me down. The confessor was a kind, tactful man; I could see his profile through the screen and wondered if, after all, the confessional seal was inviolate. The next morning I approached the altar. I desired God to be present in the Eucharist with such intensity that at the moment of reception doubt assailed me.

In a way God had claimed me and He gave me a special grace. He freed me in the beginning from the slightest intellectual curiosity. I did not seek the word and glut myself with philosophies, or retire under the trees to read Pascal's *Pensées*. That was a miraculous thing, for after the spiritual mangle I had been through I would have killed the seed of faith by study and speculation. In a special way I was a child again, and each insight I received came from some response to the dimly remembered. I experienced "the thrill of recognition," and I grew a little stronger, without realizing it. It was a thoroughly Catholic approach, for it came from my heart, and not the word.

One of the deepest passages in the Bible is in St. John's Gospel, about the woman taken in adultery and brought to Our Lord by the Scribes and Pharisees to test Him. St. John writes, "But Jesus, stooping down, wrote with his finger on the ground." And then when they continued with their arraignment of the woman He said, " 'Let him who is without sin among you be the first to cast a stone at her.' And again stooping down, He began to write on the ground." The letters in sand were swept away by the wind. The Reformation which erected the primacy of the word destroyed the Eucharist; people read, but did not understand. I did not have the will to comprehend—I had the will to believe. I who had read myself into confusion and destruction, continued to read, not justification for the faith I was striving to attain but what I had always read, and, beside the faith that was commencing to push upward from the darkness, most of it seemed utter nonsense.

One stifling summer Sunday I went into Mass a few moments late and the back of the church was crowded with standees. I turned around to leave when Bishop Lamb, that wise and saintly shepherd of souls, who was standing near, turned to me with his grave courtesy. "Go up to the choir loft, there's a seat up there, I'm sure." I thanked him, and several people started to follow me up the stairs. He stopped them, "There's only room for one more." He knew of my long defection from the Church, my recent serious illness, and he was not trying to give me a special privilege, only to assure that I would fulfill my obligation about Mass.

On the street waiting for me was a stout, determined woman whom I knew slightly. She looked at me with little, ferret eyes.

She walked along with me, putting her feet solidly down on the ground. The ribbons on her white straw hat quivered with her sense of outrage.

"It seems," she said, "that it's the thing to stay out of the Church for twenty years, and then when you come back the Bishop has no care for people who have been devout all their lives, but he worries whether your kind have a place to put their backside at Mass."

The Tristram Shandy robustness of her description was less startling than the fact that, apart from my family, she was the first lay Catholic who had addressed me. These encounters become monotonously familiar to renegade Catholics; a few weeks before and my snobbish soul would have been in such revolt that I would not have returned to the Church. It happened when I could be amused by it. This attitude is expressed more subtly, and perhaps more fiendishly, by a higher type of Catholic; but it is a careful protection nonetheless that we receive no premiums for delinquency. We are in the eyes of the clergy and the devout laity "those people." It is hard, for we have savage pride, a pride so absolute that we have become traitors for long years. It is not helpful to say we must bear our punishment, and we can't expect to go scot-free.

The ghost of the old play on which I had worked for three dreadful years haunted me. Brock had unwittingly cursed me with his own indecision. I kept on writing, and nothing was right. I was going away from the Land of Egypt, and I could not write of my familiar material with the same disenchanted spirit. I was almost, but not quite, the same person I had been. I was reaching out to a positive, but that had put me as a writer in a state of flux. My lack of success began to frighten me.

The autumn came and the nights fell quickly, and I knew I had to get to work. I still thought of myself as a big person, not meant for any of the little chores of the work-a-day world. This new play with a political angle was the right thing, everyone said. I tried to soak myself in the political atmosphere for the play, and got a volunteer job on the Dewey-Warren committee, which Robert Johnson was heading, and it was fun. But the sweeping victory for Harry S. Truman neither depressed nor elated me. The next Sunday I was at the last Mass, and decided this was a dreary and meaningless routine. Catholicism was not the answer for me. This would be the end of it. I could barely move my arms in the cramped-up pew. The stiffly-patterned Palestrina "Kyrie" soared from the choir, somebody beside me sneezed resoundingly, and I averted my head, terrified I'd catch cold.

At home, I sat drinking more coffee when my eye fell on an item in the paper, "Clare Boothe Luce to lecture tonight at the Sacred Heart Convent, Overbrook, on 'The Playwright in the Pews.' " I telephoned the convent to ask if the general public were admitted to the lecture.

"We expect great quantities of the general public," said an amused voice, "to hear and see Mrs. Luce, and if you want to see her you'd better be here early."

I did not know any Catholics, literally not one, apart from my own cousins and felt sure none of the family would care to accompany me to a Catholic lecture at which I had every expectation of falling in the aisle with amusement. (Brock was sailing on the *Queen Mary* that afternoon for Europe and the London *Harvey*. One of the best parts of Brock's friendship was the short witty letters he always sent his friends, and out of this lecture in a convent by his former playwright Clare Luce I would surely glean something with which to entertain him in return.)

But my cousin Frances accepted, to my amazement, and we drove up to the Sacred Heart Convent at precisely seven-thirty. A carnival atmosphere prevailed, cars were parked as far as the eye could reach, women were storming through the doors, the happy ticket-sellers were scooping up dollar bills. There wasn't a single seat left, but I reckoned without my cousin Frances, normally the most retiring of women. She marched down the aisle, saw coats piled over two vacant seats, stood with a determined expression on her face.

"I am sorry," she said, "but there are no reserved seats."

The coats were lifted and we all glared for an instant at one another.

I couldn't get over Frances, for she wasn't acting in character. She was waving to people. She was exuding sociability. I was sure she had never done such a thing in her life, and with each wave she'd point at me with delight and then sit back wreathed in smiles. At first I didn't know what to make of it. Then it dawned upon me, for whispers were reaching my ears: "Frances and Constance! Look . . ." It took me back at least thirty-five years when she had taken the lead on all social occasions and bossed me unmercifully. The whole thing was clear; Frances was taking this means of announcing my return to the fold. I had served my probationary period, and this was my debut.

The heat poured down in torrid waves. Fire laws were scandalously disregarded, for every exit and entrance was packed with people. The overflow was in the corridors and in other rooms where loud-speakers had been installed. The front rows of the auditorium revealed a solid black-clad phalanx of diocesan clergy. The doors leading to the stage occasionally opened to reveal dozens more priests, obviously luminaries, plus one bearded Capuchin straight out of James Joyce. It was an overpowering tribute to showcase Catholicism. The carnival atmosphere grew more intense by the minute. All we needed was a barker to hawk photographs of Mrs. Luce, and a snack-bar.

There was a ripple of greeting back-stage and awe and expectancy settled on the audience. Several Mothers of the Sacred Heart like agile mice made one last fierce foray, and the curtains parted. There stood Regina, that long-ago enemy from my convent days! She had become a spectacularly handsome woman who could part her hair in the middle and draw it down in a bun at her neck—her features were that good—and look like a Della Robbia madonna.

She introduced Mrs. Luce in a string of impressive adjectives. "In every generation," said Regina, "there is born a valiant woman."

I collapsed in silent mirth and Frances shook me briskly. "Now if you came to make fun we're getting right straight out of here." Her voice was identical with the small-girl bossiness with which she used to subdue me. I could almost hear her plead, "Constance, puh-lease don't be different."

Clare Boothe Luce stood on the stage in a little dark blue dress too good to have ever had a price-tag. A tremulous smile played on her lips, as though this applause were most unexpected.

"Good entrance," I said, into the teeth of Frances' outrage.

My eyes strayed over the audience happily laughing, for Clare Luce had just conceded the Presidency to Harry Truman, it being the Sunday after his election. A brittle blonde with a thousand-voltage charm, was my mental judgment. Why on earth had she turned Catholic?

Frances was smiling maternally; then I realized "The Playwright in the Pews," was to be a talk on the Mass. This really was the limit—standing up before birthright Catholics and discussing the Mass! I heard her say:

"And at the Confiteor in my parish church in Ridgefield the little altar boy turns in his bows and perhaps he has a hole in his sneaker and tries to tuck his foot under his cassock."

There was no necessity for a woman of her sophistication to attempt to be cute, I reflected. She was giving all this with appropriate gestures, and gentle little Oh's and Ah's were sounding from different parts of the hall. . . . I saw my father's face. I seemed to be looking up at it, a little girl in a blue, dotted-swiss dress and leghorn hat with black velvet streamers, in Our Lady Star of the Sea Church in Chelsea. . . . Queer the tricks the mind plays. The altar boy had a hole in his sneaker and was working it under his gown. The priest was bending now for the Confiteor. He was mounting the steps, kissing the altar, going to the Epistle side for the—the Introit. I'd just remembered the word. The picture faded out. I was in the Sacred Heart Convent in Overbrook listening to someone whom I had regarded as a spiritual dilettante describe her emotions at Mass. What on earth had made me think of my father?

I turned a pair of opera glasses on Clare Luce. It was an exquisite face and the eyes were sad. . . . She was talking about the Missal. Where was my enormous convent missal? I had made Nana buy me one just like that of a postulant in a convent. It had been jammed with holy cards. We'd always been trading holy pictures in my convent days.

"I'll give you my Annunciation for your Assumption," I was whispering at the chapel door, a ten-year-old driving a shrewd bargain. "I know your Assumption is a colored picture but my Annunciation's got Sister Angelina's writing on it."

There we were in the chapel of the Convent of Notre Dame in our black veils, Mass about to begin. How we could flip those missals from the special Introit of the day, to the Collects, the Offertory prayer, and the Secrets. . . . The names were coming back, the actions of the Mass.

"And the only sound that ever breaks the stillness is the cry of a child," Clare Luce said.

The priest was bending over the altar. In a moment as a bell rang he would genuflect. I felt the miracle of Transubstantiation. My vision seemed to clear. This was the moment, the fleeting instant when everything was God, and we could adore and our follies be extinguished in sublimity.

I came to, with self-disgust in my heart. I must be a charlatan, allowing Clare Luce to make such an impression on me.

"The only loss the Church recognizes is the loss of love."

"She got that straight from Monsignor Sheen," I observed to Frances.

"Shhh!" she warned me, but her heart wasn't in it. I saw she was bored.

"The loss of love." What was this anguish in the marrow of our bones? This need to be loved? But everyone had lost love somewhere in the wastes of the twentieth century. "Love God!" they told us in convent school. A child pointed out the impossibility of it and was told, "Love is in the will." That made it dry and academic. Catholic children were always being put off without answers. "The loss of love"—there was some deep meaning in the sentence that I was sure eluded the speaker. Everyone I knew was sick with this loss; but we cried out not for health but a pain-killer.

There, Clare Luce had missed the implications of the Pater

Noster, that moment of intimacy in the Mass when we talk to Him in the words He taught us. My sense of superiority was restored. Sister Julie used to tell us, "We can be separated from anything else in life but once we have the Holy Mass, it's part of us." A few words touching chords in memory and all the elaborate defenses I had erected against the power of the Mass were broken down. I felt like one of Professor Pavlov's little dogs whose conditioned reflexes had just gone to pieces. I was also deeply shamed that Clare Boothe Luce, of all people, had done this to me. I hoped she would say something to make me once more her antagonist. It was as if she read my mind.

"The Mass is over," she said, returning to her role as the playwright in the pews, "and I always have the feeling that one thing is lacking, applause. I want to hear the crash of cymbals."

There, that did it, and I was delighted. I saw a vast cathedral, probably St. Patrick's, with thousands standing as the priest left the altar after the last prayer, all banging cymbals. She must have been thinking of the opera *Thais*. I smiled wickedly at Frances.

"Just don't say anything, Constance," she whispered. "I don't want to know what you're thinking."

The audience were on their feet applauding wildly as Regina led Clare Luce through the packed auditorium. It was a triumphant moment, for not only had she inveigled "the most discussed convert since Chesterton," which was the Luce billing in certain circles, to the Sacred Heart Convent, but the lady was going to receive that whole vast audience in the parlor. The laity and clergy in a splendid mass surged forward to shake her hand. Frances had entered into the spirit of the thing and we bobbed up and down in the sea of humanity, fighting for place and air.

"I don't want to meet that woman," I said.

Frances would have been astounded to learn that some secret place in my heart had been deeply stirred by this lecture and I was fighting against it. We were surrounded by old friends and I felt myself being pulled back into the Catholic world, and one part of me rebelled. Catholicism is not an ethical system that excludes psychology, but in the next few minutes enough piercing whispers as to my religious status reached my ears to infuriate the most placid soul, which I am not.

"One more person asks you if I've returned to the Church," I snapped at Frances, "and I will say I'm a devout and convinced Mormon."

"Oh, Constance, they're not being curious or mean, they're happy about it," she explained.

The remark came. It hung in the air. Frances turned white with anger.

"She's never been anything but a silly snob. Did you see that scar? Cancer, of course. She's had her come-uppance now."

My scar! It took all my courage to appear before people. I had learned to say lightly, "The only survivor of a Pemberton-cut throat." To be grateful for the consoling "In a little while you can have plastic surgery, darling," of theatre friends. I herded this whole assemblage together in a scornful "Catholics!"

I walked toward the parlor where Clare Luce was receiving; Frances, all her pleasure in the gala event gone, trailing me, crest-fallen.

"I should have met her while she was a Protestant. It would have been much simpler," I observed, stirring up an eddy of resentment as I entered.

In the center of a group of women I saw Clare Luce. This was, after all one of the most famous women in the world. There were black bruises of exhaustion under her eyes, the hand that she extended looked frail enough to be broken. Well-nourished prep-school boys asked for her autograph and she complied with maternal tolerance. Old ladies were rooting through their bags to give her St. Anthony medals to protect her apartment at the Waldorf Towers against jewel robbers; the recent Luce robbery had been well publicized. The voice that answered them was soft and gentle, the face turned to them was unexpectedly sweet. I was interested in the scene and had forgotten my dislike. I had a queer sense, "I have been this woman." There is no great distance between the illusion of success and the illusion of failure.

It was my turn.

"Mrs. Luce, *this* is Constance O'Hara," Regina murmured.

A look that was steel and flame bored into me. Clare Luce seemed before my eyes to take on stature. This woman was capable of unleashed power and fury. I tried to stare her down, interested in what I had aroused. I sauntered from the room, feeling that stare going through to my spine.

Destiny is always jumbling up our lives like the patterns of a kaleidoscope. Life is one long round of confusion. This experience may be happy; that one have in it the seeds of destruction. I sat in the New York train the next afternoon en route to Frances Starr's opening in *The Young and Fair*, and I still saw Mrs. Luce moving gracefully on the convent stage. I saw the gentleness and consideration of her manner to those boring throngs, then felt that arrogant stare bite into me. Curious! Had I been her adversary in someway I did not understand? But mostly I thought of how she had interested me in the Mass; that did embarrass me.

When I got off the train I stopped in the dark Franciscan church and for five cents bought a green-covered book by a Carmelite, "Enjoy the Mass." At the Algonquin I thriftily steamed my evening dress on the shower rod, then sat down to read. The Mass as sacrifice and prayer entered a deeper level of consciousness. The commemoration of the Saints in the Canon of the Mass for some reason stirred me; from that time on the Mass became an absorbing experience, took its place as the central fact of Catholicism. I looked out my window. It was still daylight, too early to dress for dinner despite the eight o'clock curtain of an opening night. I sat down and wrote to Brock who was at the Dorchester in London. The green pamphlet, "Enjoy the Mass," lay in front of me on the desk as I wrote a jaded showman theatre gossip. I devoted a paragraph to his playwright Clare Luce's lecture on the Mass at the Sacred Heart Convent, giving her a very good notice indeed; remembering our conversation of the early summer and his pessimistic description of her mental state, I wrote:

"And I can assure you, Brock, that the woman is perfectly sane."

# 9

THE PLAY WOULD NOT come right though it was being publicized as a possible starring vehicle for Katharine Hepburn and Spencer Tracy. The wanton destructiveness of the Pemberton years was now making itself felt, for I was manipulating puppets, not creating character. I did not realize how embittered I had become and I struck out blindly that winter at the people who mattered most to me. I still had the confused and pathetic vision of earning great sums of money and spending it in civilized places among interesting, well-to-do people.

My agitations and unrest were not eased by my knowledge that I had become a hanger-on of immensely wealthy, successful people. Something had ended for me at Jefferson Hospital and a new thing had begun. Philadelphia was my home, my roots were there; but I ignored it, as a place where many things ended and nothing began. My friends, my true friends, were part of the New York theatre world, but within me I realized that gay and exciting as they all were, much as our special qualities appealed to each other, the real corrosion of failure lay in refusing to admit that I no longer belonged with them. I risked staying till I was no longer wanted.

In New York in February, 1949, for Maggie Perry's first opening night as a producer, I begged Brock again to send me to Hollywood.

"I tell you what, Connie, send me a copy of that religious play that got all the rave notices. It's had an English production, after all, and I'll see what I can do."

I knew even as I wrote to the publishers for a copy of *The Years of the Locusts* that I had asked Brock for the impossible.

I was seeking something that Hollywood couldn't give me, but if I found it Hollywood couldn't take it away from me. In this mood I started to go to daily Mass. A confessor had urged me, "Go to Communion at least every fortnight." I did these things and also started to make the Stations of the Cross daily. I was not capable of mental prayer so I used the meditations of St. Alfonso de' Ligouri and missed the implications of the Redemption in these archaic, guilt-ridden prayers. My mental state resembled Swinburne's lines, that the end of evil will only come when "this old earth will be a slag and a cinder revolving around the sun without its crew of fools." But despite my pessimism, I was taking my first steps toward Adoration.

It did not occur to me to try to integrate the scattered impulses toward good into a strong Catholicism by talking to a priest. I thought they were too busy to bother about a middle-aged woman nagged by a sense of failure; besides I had a definitely anti-clerical bias. Father Collins had given me his best, but my mind was too clouded by all the intellectual errors of my time to accept the fact that great personal holiness can exist in a man's soul while there is fanaticism in his mind.

Theodore Johnson sent me two copies of *Locusts* and I put one in an envelope for Brock.

"Send the other one to Clare Luce," suggested Mother.

I would not have acknowledged how much I had been interested in Clare Luce since that night at the Sacred Heart Convent. Mentally I had pitted myself against this woman who had everything I had ever wanted, and made her a rival. Mother on the other hand admired her intensely and begrudged her nothing.

I greeted Mother's suggestion about the play with a contemptuous, "Waste this good copy on that woman? I have to pay for it."

"It's a convent play," said my mother, "and Mrs. Luce might have it put on somewhere and you'd get some royalties."

There was no doubt about it, we needed the royalties.

"I have some sort of feeling," said Mother, a witty pragmatist not given to psychic twinges. "I can't explain it, but send her that play."

I nipped the copy in a matching envelope and laid it beside Brock's.

"You're not going to send it without a letter?" Mother expostulated.

"It's rude to write to strangers," I retorted.

We both laughed, for my habit of dropping off letters to the great and indulging in long correspondences was too well known to bear repetition. My tongue was in my cheek as I wrote a brief letter.

That was early in March and things commenced to happen so quickly I was breathless. It seemed that my letter had hardly been mailed before I found in my Servidor a handsome piece of stationery with very bad typing on the envelope. I opened it to find that Clare Luce was answering my letter without benefit of secretary.

A book was on its way; a book I must return because it was a first edition and five hundred years from now that would be a matter of some concern. Francis Thompson was quoted liberally; and I was invited to breakfast in Philadelphia the following Thursday since the night before she would be lecturing at the Philadelphia *Bulletin* Forum. She promised there would be no other guests. I dashed off an amused acceptance.

The next day *Seeds of Contemplation* by Thomas Merton arrived. I was unaware that Thomas Merton was a Trappist monk. I don't know what I expected. The effect was much like being in an automobile when it goes out of control. I wanted nothing to do with this book. Thomas Merton, whoever he was, had kicked me in a most unspiritual style in the usual place up a summit until I gibbered in terror. There was a line that made my heart contract with agony: "Prayer and love are learned in the hour when prayer has become impossible and your heart has turned to stone."

In the morning I sent the book back and canceled my acceptance of the breakfast invitation. Mother was seriously disturbed. "An insult to one of the best known women in the country. At least tell her you're called out of town. You sound like someone having a fit at a Methodist revival. Either stay in the Church or get out, but don't torture people with these indecisions. Converts take people like you seriously."

I had a dread and fear of meeting Clare Luce that was almost a warning. I did have compunctions as to what I had done and wrote to Brock explaining that I had refused to meet his famous friend only because I might disturb the ardent faith of a convert. I really meant this incredible nonsense. I had a great sense of relief that the threat of meeting Mrs. Luce was not hanging over my head; and cheerfully went to luncheon with a television producer where I talked with much common sense about a series of programs that were to feature famous Philadelphians.

My phone rang the next day and a voice filled with all sorts of cadences spoke to me. I listened unbelieving; Clare Luce was offering me a job. A writing job that paid real money, in fact, excellent money, fifteen hundred whole dollars, with five hundred paid in advance. The shock was almost too much. I was to dramatize the catechism, and though it seemed far easier to use dramatic invention on the phone book than on those dull questions and answers in the little green-backed catechism of my convent days, I was perfectly willing to promise that the catechism in my hands would have a potency that might necessitate a new Council of Trent. The job had been offered to Clare Luce, but she hadn't time. If I would accept, a representative of the Vincentian Fathers from Brooklyn would call me. The amazing thing apart from the fact that I most certainly needed this job was that Clare Luce was offering me a "first." No one in all my life had ever offered me anything and I boasted I never asked friends for anything.

I accepted it, calling her in my mind, a "convert angel," and of course I said I'd come to breakfast.

I walked in the door of her suite at the Warwick Hotel at precisely nine o'clock. She stood there in a nunlike gray dress, with a smile on her lovely face; but I looked somehow at her jaw. It was like a bar of iron on which rested an exquisite pale pink rose.

We sat at breakfast, and I was amused and antagonistic. She was a woman of the world attempting to put me at my ease.

Alas, for the cursed shrewdness of a Celtic heritage which makes us so aware that we are always socially uneasy! It has been said that acting represents Clare's only failure, but that was because in Shaw's *Candida* she was playing a role outside herself; she acts the role of Clare Luce with brilliance and verve. It is art of such high degree that you forget you are witnessing something rather tragic, a self-conscious woman's refusal to integrate the one existence she possesses into the many in which she has cast it.

"Constance O'Hara, you've made a mess of the last twenty years. What are you going to do with the next?" Even she was abashed by my look of outrage. "I know what you're going to do. You're coming with me to Sheed and Ward. I'm a Catholic publisher now."

I veiled my eyes lest she see how interested I was in her suggestion. It would certainly be an ideal solution; interest and security—blessed security!—with freedom to reach out to real achievement. I wondered if she meant it?

She took up another topic, the dramatized catechism. She admitted that the dramatized story for audio-visual education was a technique she did not understand, but a Father Michael Mullen whom I was to meet in New York the next day would explain it all to me.

"He's a wee bit hard to get to the point, but he's awfully nice —and so young. Be careful to say nothing to shock him, nothing broad I mean."

I can't think when we commenced to be really interested in each other. Breakfast over, she pushed me down in a big red chair by the fireplace, and curled up opposite like a college girl. The telephone shrilled. Bellboys knocked and handed in telegrams and letters. Flowers came. She glanced briefly at the cards, the floral tributes. I loved the symbols of success so intensely that my Achilles heel was throbbing; and there is no cure for that type of Achilles heel. It just gets more and more vulnerable.

She pushed me down in the chair each time I attempted to leave. We talked about many things, of dramatizing Bernanos'

*Joy* together; of her book *Europe in the Spring*, which she defended against my jeers.

"Don't make fun of that book. It's as sound as the day I wrote it."

It was obvious that Clare Luce as a Catholic had been given no time to learn how to be still and love the Lord. Lecture engagements, even to audiences of priests, meetings with Church dignitaries, commitments to Catholic editors, filled her every hour; all before her faith had even coalesced. "Look at her, rich, famous, beautiful, with everything a heart could desire," these appearances of this glamorous woman before Catholic audiences seemed to proclaim, "and *she* came after what you've always had: *The Faith*." I doubted if anyone benefited by this exploitation, certainly not the Church, ancient and splendid and holy—least of all, Clare Luce.

Then the mask was off and for a while, unveiled and lovely, I saw a woman without falsity, who had risen over the calumnies of the world; I realized the power and, yes, the strength of the spirit behind those exquisite eyes, that tremulous mouth. There was loyalty, there was moral courage in this woman; she had known bitterness, and then sorrow had come which made her realize that bitterness is based on *nothing*: sorrow on *something*. That "something" was the essence of Clare Luce. I knew, and nothing has changed my opinion, that she has integrity. Time passed and still she kept me there; it was a quarter of one when I left the room I had entered at nine.

I still remember the strange experience of feeling less lonely, of making a gift of friendship that was more personal in its essence than any I had ever given.

The next day I sat in a religious art goods store on Barclay Street with a sullen, handsome Italian, a woman artist, and Father Michael Mullen, C. M., who was a tall, slender young priest with a reserved manner and a sudden ingenuous smile. In the glassed shelves pink and simpering statues, and plastic crucifixes in pastel tints which were somehow horrifying, looked down on us. Nuns walked in and out of the store buying First Communion veils, rosaries, and religious statues. Our Lady of Fatima was omnipresent, for there are modes of devotion, I soon learned, and Fatima has eclipsed Lourdes in sales value. An interesting device which attracted attention was a rosary aid that recorded each Ave on a dial with a click.

The Italian proprietor rose from our conference to display to a group of nuns a large, pale pink plastic crucifix which he assured them would not break. They studied it doubtfully and with a sudden gesture he hurled it down savagely on the floor. I gasped.

"Not even a chip, you see." He lifted it up and laid it on a show case. The nuns leaned over, intensely interested, and agreed that no harm had been done.

I was feeling rather like a self-conscious Calvinist set down in the midst of a Roman Catholic country. Clare Luce had said, "Once you're in a Catholic atmosphere you'll be all right." I wondered, as contumacious priests arrived to purchase supplies for novenas, and drove hard bargains. Mother Seton's church, St. Peter's, perhaps casts a benign shadow over Barclay Street and its commercial traffic in aids-to-holiness.

I didn't make up my mind quickly about accepting the catechism, for I saw they were not ready to start work, that it was all a nebulous, splendid dream—save for the five hundred dollars which was ready and waiting whenever I accepted. The dream did have some capital stock. Father Mullen, crestfallen that I had not given them a definite answer, stood at the bus-stop with me, and revealed, I can't remember how, that he had said his first Mass at the Convent of Notre Dame, West Rittenhouse Square, and his first blessing had been imparted to Sister Julie du Saint-Esprit. This convinced me that Heaven was in the whole affair and I agreed then and there to come to New York for one month. Father Mullen flashed me a radiant smile; that smile made me forget, then and always, that the good Father on theology was like a parade taking ninety minutes to pass a given point.

One year to the day after Father Joseph Collins walked in my room in Jefferson Hospital I was on the New York train. Going back . . . going back . . . Perhaps the play idea would come to life under the impetus of stimulating people. Perhaps there'd be a chance at Hollywood. In the Land of Egypt anything can happen. The zany quality of my new adventure delighted my theatre friends. Who knew what might happen? Clare Luce might . . . Maybe I was going away forever and forever. . . . I remembered how my mind had churned that magic phrase when I'd first gone to New York. I picked up the Baltimore Catechism on my lap. How long since I'd seen one? Probably I had forgotten everything in it.

"Who made you?"

I was hurrying up the wide stairs of the Convent of Notre Dame, a plaid schoolbag strapped on my back. . . . Mustn't run. . . . It's against the rules. . . . Genuflect at the chapel door. "Don't let the bell ring, dear Lord." . . . Safe at the door of the baby room. Stand on tiptoe to reach the holy water font. Bless yourself. Curtsy, four to get down, four to come up, saying to Sister Mary Immaculata, "Bonjour, ma Soeur." . . . The great brazen clatter of opening bell sounds, as I scurry to my little blue desk. The crimson-faced culprits straggle in during morning prayers. I just escaped their fate. After prayers, we sing Mère Julie's song, "Ah, qu'il est bon, qu'il est bon, le bon Dieu." Now catechism. . . . I laugh, on a train bound for New York, as I hear a piping voice. Why, it's mine:

" 'God made me.' "

" 'Why did God make you?' "

What's this indeed? They've changed the catechism. I feel a sense of outrage. The answer–not the abbreviation in a new-style catechism–is part of me:

> God made me to know Him, to love Him, to serve Him in this world, and be happy with Him forever in the next.

That tells the whole story. What a cadence there is in that sentence. The baby grade whirls and dissolves. . .. " 'To know Him, to love Him, to serve Him . . .' "

It's the third grade now. Sister Helen Josephine is teaching us about the angels. Here's the very chapter. Sister must have heard the whir of wings, felt our Guardian Angels were only behind a gossamer veil as she looked at our morning faces. She doesn't see Carol O'Leary has a row of hard, paper pellets doused in ink on her desk, and a rubber-band. The whir of wings, Sister? We were little devils, always spoiling your visions of ideal children with our stains of original sin. I wonder if you're still alive, Sister Helen Josephine?

I turn the pages. I know every line in this catechism. Perhaps we were little parrots learning without speculation. But now the formulas I stored up in my young memory are emerging with sudden, vivid flashes. It's uncanny. Here's the lesson on the Trinity. Sister Marion's dark intense eyes glow through the mists of memory. "The second person of the Blessed Trinity is God the Son, Our Lord and Saviour Jesus Christ," she adds. She always puts in the name of Jesus, Saviour, son of the Blessed Virgin Mary, foster son of Joseph. Her voice came down the years to a woman on a train bound for New York, "Saviour–Saviour."

Words and faces keep coming back as I sit with a little catechism in my hand. This is the lesson on Sanctifying Grace. Sister Clare, who died when we were in the sixth grade, tried to get it in our heads. A big subject–sanctifying grace! How solemn it was as we came in the chapel for her Funeral Mass, little girls in our serge dresses and black veils. Death hadn't touched many of us then. Sister Clare had gone from our classroom only a week ago and now. . . . It was "scarey" to see that casket and the tall candles. Then it was glorious. "A place of refreshment, light, and peace," we read in our missals. I'd hurt a girl's feelings the day Sister was so ill. I stood beside Sister Clare's desk as she tried to tell me that Our Lord wanted us to love each other. She was burning with fever, I knew; and she held on to her side when she coughed. That was before noon recess. She'd never come back again. "Forgive me, Sister Clare," I prayed at her Funeral Mass. "For the repose of your soul I'll offer up being kind to all the people I don't like forever." I certainly hadn't kept that vow. On a train bound for New York I prayed for the soul of Sister Clare who died of pneumonia when I was in the sixth grade. This was the Communion of Saints in the Creed. "Rest well, little Sister Clare. . . ."

Get this convent business out of your mind. It's morbid. You didn't really like it. Remember your sheer delight in the splendor of New York when you first lived there? That long warm autumn of 1938. Your enthusiasm crackled in the still air. Phil Barry's going into the Algonquin. He waves to you. Remember when he said, "Your dialogue's like mine." "Sometimes it *is* yours, Mr. Barry," I responded. They loved you then, the brilliant, successful people. Remember the tang of dry martinis? What Tallulah said . . . Everybody talked about "your future." "It's a talent–a big talent." They did say it. . . . The World's Fair was over on the Flushing Meadows, that was the summer of 1939; and Brock Pemberton was going to produce your play. That's what you liked. The world, a great, big, luscious slice of world. . . .

# BOOK FOUR

## 1

MY ROOM AT THE New Weston was as narrow as a nun's cell; from one window I could look up at the haughty towers of Manhattan. I have never liked a room so much in my life, felt such a passionate identification with a place. I liked the narrow couch-bed in the corner, and the desk that would soon be piled with books. I was where I wanted to be—my New York. My phone kept ringing and I talked to all the people I liked best: Brock, Edith Meiser, Maggie Perry, Peggy Wood. . . . Sam Zolotow from the *Times* was on the wire to learn if my projected play, *The Human Element*, had brought me to town. The dramatized catechism was even more newsworthy, and Tommy Kilpatrick, Brock's press agent, blew it up like a balloon.

That night I picked up the New Testament I had borrowed from Margaret and read the Gospel of John at one sitting. . . . "I believe in God the Father Almighty. . . ." I felt as if the book had turned into white-hot bones that seared my fingers; here was the essence of the questions in the opening of the catechism: "Who made me?" "Why did God make me?" No wonder John was called the Beloved Disciple. He did not have to shout, or prove anything, he did not have to speak above a whisper. He could write of himself, "Now one of his disciples, he whom Jesus loved, was reclining at Jesus' bosom. . . ." All the tenderness of the Godhead was, for me, in that one sublime line. I saw dimly that St. John was "the child of God," his was the essence of spiritual childhood. The Apostle who heard the heartbeat of Christ! This was a mind so exquisite in its tenderness, so sensitive, that it was a miracle it could reach to me.

The meaning of the catechism took me by the throat, suffocated me with its splendor. The catechism had to be Christ—and I did not know Christ. So like the children I was to teach, I had to learn Christ. Father Mullen had spoken of an American Christ—a Christ on the baseball diamond. As an educator, Father Mullen wanted to teach children profound truths, universal truths, in the language they understood, according to the contemporary world in which they found themselves.

It was a theme to haunt the mind of Bernanos and Claudel—yet I was a woman with a Celtic imagination, and perhaps I could find the simplicity of a child, and the truth in a child. Here I was in the New Weston Hotel with one of the greatest opportunities ever offered a writer. I forgot all the compromises I had been forced to make in the past, I forgot it was Father Mullen's brain child and not mine and I had only one month to devise a writing technique that would solve the mechanical difficulties of working with still-film.

At midnight my phone rang. It was the lady who had been responsible for all this, Clare Boothe Luce. The author of *The Women* and the author of *The Magnificent Heel* talked about the Council of Trent, about St. John, about Jacinto Benavente that neglected and marvelous Spanish Catholic dramatist from whom all the world's playwrights steal ideas and plots.

That was the first of our Conversations at Midnight. . . .

The next morning I met her for Mass and Communion and we went to breakfast. It is possible to walk the streets of New York with famous people yet attract nothing more than a few turned heads, but I knew this association was different when I felt the stares from the handful of quiet worshipers at early morning Mass in St. Patrick's devouring Clare Luce, who knelt beside me quietly reading the Mass prayers through her bifocals. I felt sorry for her that the Catholics, at least, were not displaying more restraint; after all, rain or shine, she was in church every morning of her life—they should have got used to her by now. Then I commenced to feel sorry for myself, for like a vagrant breeze in these first few days the words, "Mrs. Luce's friend," seemed to drift from place to place.

I was bored and amused at her convert zeal which she referred to as "apostolic." I remembered Louis Rosenthal's remark one Sunday in Baltimore, "I love Jesus, but I never could abide the Apostles." It all seemed to cry aloud for that most misunderstood and forgotten basis of true spirituality: the wholesome rule of minding one's own business.

I realized that Clare Luce's personality was dominant, dwarfing those around her. As a companion she was fascinating and exhausting. There was no peace with her, no quiet moment. And yet there was that sweetness in her nature that made it easy to become excessive, even to worship a little. I was honestly glad when her own uncertainties at being involved in what could be another unhappy friendship took her into the Waldorf Towers, leaving me a memory of startling rudeness. I was glad, but I did have to admit that out of her sight you missed her; granted that she was disturbing and possessive and impossible, you looked toward the silent telephone and wanted to hear that voice.

Father Mullen came with the artist to confer on my projected plan for the catechism and we all went down to the long room off the New Weston bar. Ours was no doubt the most startling conversation ever heard in that restrained atmosphere, for Father Mullen did not mention God in a ministerially polite undertone with vague apologies to the scientific-minded. He did not tie in God with the world's wonders or lecture about God and the atom. He spoke loudly of God as the Father, the Alpha and Omega; he spoke of Him with impassioned friendship. He was marvelously and frankly Catholic. His unruly lock of hair tumbled down, his nice blue eyes shone with enthusiasm. He frisked around Creation unaware of cool Episcopalian stares, or the timid Deists trying to close their ears to the strange, throbbing symphony of the Church of Rome. I tried to keep Father Mullen to Lesson One in the Baltimore Catechism, but he wanted to talk about the Trinity, Lesson Three, which he did.

"Now, some authorities simplify it," he said at the top of his lungs, "and yet it remains a Mystery. I've no time for the school who say, 'God the Father generated God the Son, and God the Father and God the Son spirated the Holy Ghost–' "

Father Michael Mullen, C. M., had his mouth wide open for the next word, unaware of the thud at his feet, where precisely in line with his black oxfords lay an old lady prone on her stomach, save for her face which she raised a few inches from the floor. One lens was gone from her nose-glasses, her gray toque with its trim of flowers rested on her pompadour exactly where she had placed it, but her expression was wonderful to see, for with amazement, consternation and unbelief she was looking up at Father Mullen and speculating on the Trinity, no doubt. He jumped up, raised her to her feet. She hobbled off, petrified, without a backward glance, and he resumed his place.

"She just sort of skidded. She acted like she was stunned. Now, as I was saying, I have no time for such simplified statements on the Trinity–"

I worked out a script incorporating such fancy touches of my own as a scene in which children from all over the world say the first line of the Apostles' Creed in their own language, ending with a view of St. Peter's and a great triumphant "Credo in unum Deum." (In actual production it came out not as a mighty surge of sound, but a shrill squeak.) Father Mullen got Alfredo Antonini, head of the musical department of Columbia Broadcasting and faculty member of St. John's University, Brooklyn, to supervise the music. I read Teresa of Avila's autobiography for the first time, and Teresa got into the catechism, and some of Thomas Merton. The synchronization of words and pictures to fit an exact time limit was a technical problem which the old master, Brock Pemberton, took over with alacrity.

He not only proved that he had learned his catechism backwards and forwards in the Methodist Sunday school in Emporia, Kansas, but he had ideas which exactly coincided with Father Mullen's.

"The first point is, Connie," said Mr. P., "have the little children in a home where the mamma and papa love each other. God is love. You believe in Him and thank Him if everything's peaceful and happy in the home. Have the mamma and papa nice to each other."

Equipped with a stopwatch, he beat exact time on the seventeen-second schedule in which the pictures would change, and so must the dialogue. He became quite enamored of the catechism children who are represented on a picnic with their mother and father. He grew wistful over this happy family out in the green fields under the blue sky by a silver stream. He shook his head in longing.

"The little girl looks up at the sky, Connie," he said, "and all around her on earth. She's a cute little girl and everywhere she looks is God. That's the way my mother taught it to us."

Broadway's first gentleman, the discreet Casanova, couldn't have been sweeter and nicer in his absorption in the catechism, and from his musings, emerged the line: "No matter how far you look you can't see outside of God."

Father Mullen ordered the line out because it was pantheism. It nearly broke my heart, and I never told B. P., till the day he died that he hadn't been responsible for his proudest boast, "the best line in the Catholic catechism."

On Palm Sunday I went to the Cardinal's Mass at the Cathedral. It was a pleasant day. I kept a dinner engagement and returned to soak myself in Mother Margaret Bolton's books, for no one has touched or equalled this Mother of the Cenacle in a realistic approach to children and a refusal to compromise with vulgar taste. She reduced to the most exquisite simplicity St. Thomas Aquinas' mighty profundities and all her work had a lilting gaiety, a touching childlikeness, that enchanted me. A very great woman, the late Mother Margaret Bolton; she would have seen at once that I was too deeply tangled in the adult infantilism of skepticism and paganism to achieve the directness and the sincerity a child needs.

The next morning, to my amazement, I was summoned to the Towers for luncheon. Mrs. Luce's secretary somewhat embarrassed, informed me, it was about the catechism, and it was urgent. Clare was the Editorial Supervisor but she had seemed most indifferent to the responsibilities implied in that impressive title. There was a rather formal luncheon for two set up in the living room and Clare in her most executive mood said she wanted to talk over something of vital importance. It was—it was about Holy Week.

She talked about her loneliness during this week, culminating in going to church alone on Easter Sunday. For her first Easter Sunday in the fold, she told me, she had bought a new hat. Everyone smiled at her as if they understood she hadn't anyone to go to church with and wanted her to feel at home, and she thought how much she liked Catholics. Then after church she walked across Fiftieth Street, and people turned around to look after her, smiling. And when she got home she found out there was a big gold tag hanging down the back of her hat, proclaiming in quite large letters, *MODEL—$27.50.*

"Now, Clare," I said, "you couldn't realize you'd come into a world of ten-dollar hats."

Anyway, I consented to be her companion for Holy Week services, filled with a sense of my own virtue at letting myself in for these great long devotions. But she refused to plan for me to go to Monsignor Sheen's famous Tre Ore sermons on Good Friday, for which tickets were needed, saying it was up to Monsignor, and she couldn't hold out much hope.

As we knelt together at various churches during Holy Week, her eyes were remote and she was quiet and at peace. The few things she said during these many hours had depth and insight. "We will die alone in hotel rooms in twenty years or so—possibly found by hotel maids—or in some hospital with a paid nurse beside us, because we have no children. The only thing that will give it meaning is because we've tried to find Him, to make Him a little less lonely and forsaken. And even if we forget and get lost again—maybe next Easter we'll both be doing some crazy thing—but just these few prayers now will help when it's all over."

"Never mind," I said, and I felt warmly affectionate toward her. "You won't get lost. For the first time in your life you've found something big enough to hold you."

Another time as we came out of church together, she said, "From midnight on Christmas Eve till Good Friday He's the Man-God, and we can love His humanity; and then the Church is so stupendous because from Easter Sunday He's the God-Man. In Lent we share His agony and do penance. In Advent it is our agony of unworthiness to prepare for Him. Pentecost is hard on humanity—that's when we have to stand on our own two feet. Do you think you can make it, Constance O'Hara?"

Holy Thursday there was the long solemn Maundy service at the Cathedral. I was by this time curious and intensely interested. I planned a morning of church-visiting by myself. The theatre, concerts, and church, are three places to which I like to go uncompanioned. I came home from a glut of churches to read Teresa of Avila's meditation on Gethsemani.

"Constance," came an imperious little voice on my telephone. "I'm afraid I will have to hire some Protestants as secretaries. Mine have gone off to pay court to Monsignor Sheen. I probably won't see them again till he leaves town. The mail is piling up and . . ."

"Look," I said, "I haven't a thing in the world to do. I'd love to help you."

"Oh, God bless you!" Her tones were ecstatic.

So I found myself in the Waldorf drafting cables and messages to the great while Clare sat with her feet up reading Robert Sherwood's *Roosevelt and Hopkins*, murmuring, "You'd think from this book Roosevelt won the war single-handed. I guess none of the rest of us ever did a thing."

I would read aloud the Easter messages on which I was expending every talent I possessed, and, if I do say so, some of my efforts were wonderful.

"Splendid, dear," she'd say, "that sounds exactly like me."

I drafted a telegram of beautiful piety to a priest.

"That," and her elfin grin flashed, "sounds most unlike either of us."

I came back to my hotel and reclined in a hot tub, aching a bit. There was one thing about Clare Luce, you never relaxed in her presence, she didn't allow a brain to lie fallow; if there weren't any odds and ends of work to do she got out one of the jig-saw puzzles she had made to order just so they would be really tough. I went sound asleep on my couch-bed in mid-afternoon. The phone cut through my needed slumbers and, cursing, I reached for it blindly.

"Welcome home, Constance O'Hara," said a well-known voice.

It was Holy Thursday, 1949, and Monsignor Fulton J. Sheen was on the phone. My sleep-fogged mind couldn't adjust itself to the gorgeous adjectives coming over the wire. The voice was warm with liking, rich in kindness. He made me feel as if my storm-tossed craft were in safe harbor, there would be no more darkness, but only gentleness and wisdom and security for the rest of my time on earth. The voice went on and the tight pressure around my heart eased, and tears streamed down my face.

He spoke of my father and the Seminary. He made it all come back. I felt like a child approaching my home, the lights streaming from every window and inside love and safety and all joy.

"How do you like Clare?" he asked.

"I like her very much," I said, "and it scares me to death."

In a second the tender, mocking friend was gone, and his voice was embarrassed, as if I had been too frank, too gauche.

"Ah! She's marvelous," he said.

His voice was theatrical, like an actor saying something intense. Antagonized, I retreated into my shell. My tears stopped. Was I being welcomed home to please Clare Luce?

"There's a card for you at my hotel for the Good Friday services," he said. "I'm at the Roosevelt. Can you come for it tonight?"

"Would the morning do?" I asked. I was, truth to tell, afraid of the visit.

"Yes." He sounded disappointed. "God love you."

I wondered if he had called me from the Waldorf; when Clare Luce called me a few minutes later I was sure of it. I decided to be coldly amused. After all, I was the grandniece of bishops, all my family were friends of archbishops and cardinals and I myself had been the beloved friend of the Right Reverend Monsignor Henry T. Drumgoole.

On Good Friday I went into St. Patrick's Cathedral a little before twelve, carefully fortified for my vigil by butter-thin crackers and tea. The Cathedral was packed, crowds lined the side aisles. I gave my card to an usher who looked, in his morning clothes, like an attaché at a British embassy. He put me in an end seat in the middle aisle, looked at my card, smiled, bowed and returned it. I saw then that it was autographed. I saw Basil and Ouida Rathbone right ahead of me. I saw in fact all of Catholic Broadway. Murrays and McDonnells were scattered all over the place. H. R. Luce with shoulders squared, head up, sat beside his demure wife. Purple-cassocked monsignors rustled up and down the aisles. In the side aisles people stood in masses—good, devout people. I felt a throb of shame for robbing the faithful of one good seat.

Christ had been crucified on this day, and here we sat like polite strangers at the funeral of someone we didn't know very well. It was "the thing" to be present, looking distinguished and expensive.

At last Monsignor Sheen stood in the pulpit. His face was agonized, magnificent in sorrow. His red-purple vestments gleamed and his voice throbbed.

"Father, forgive them for they know not what they do."

The effect was electrical. This was art, this was, for sheer competence, the most eloquent preaching in America. But it was something more, much more, it was living faith—and that is why the compassion of Christ lived in this vast cathedral. He spoke of the contradictions of the modern world and its sins: ". . . they know not what they do." This was more than spellbinding. These words satisfied your brain, rent your heart, cut your eyes with a vision of the dying Christ, played like fire on your nerves, satisfied every need. "Father, forgive them . . ." He was dramatic, this remote man on the high pulpit, with his deep, sorrowing eyes, and I was dramatic, and I couldn't breathe.

The slow, rich somber hymn filled the Cathedral. The splendor of it swamped my heart, and I could feel the coming of the sixth hour, and the pall of darkness covering the earth. I saw the red flash of Monsignor Sheen's vestment as he stood quietly with the crowd banked around the Sacred Heart altar but I did not see him return to the pulpit. I looked up as his voice rang out gently to announce the one joy of His bitter passion—the repentance of the good thief.

"Amen I say to you. This day thou shalt be with me in Paradise."

I could almost see the agonized eyes of Christ looking directly into those of Saint Dismas. This was gladness triumphing over sorrow. This was the first Saint opening his heart to Christ, renouncing his own self-centered will. It was Christ's belief in happiness that made Him show us even on the Cross that love which is gladness can touch us. And then that marvelous voice said astoundingly:

"I dedicate the second word of Christ to fallen-away Catholics."

Monsignor Sheen was saying exquisite things, born of such deep knowledge of the anguished human heart of traitors that I felt the tears sting my eyes. He told us how welcome we were at home, that we were needed in the world's most frightful hour. He spoke of us not as "those people" to be garbed in sackcloth and ashes. He uttered no warnings that in a timeless eternity we might look forever on what might have been our place in Heaven, if we had not forfeited it for the world's illusion. No man has ever wooed a weak faith in words of such tenderness. And then I heard phrases that seemed familiar, words like those I had won from that long, bitter night at Jefferson Hospital. I wondered if this man would cry my name aloud. I heard his voice filled with drama; "How divine it is to come home."

That evening I dined at Edith Meiser's—she had been one of the leads in *The Magnificent Heel.* We have to stand an awful lot of people to find a few friends, as I had learned by the time

I found Edith. My tension must have communicated itself, for she looked at me closely, and observed:

"Connie, this is awfully good theatre: this new trend toward the spiritual, with you in the starring role. Today was the climax. There's only a third act to go before the final curtain. Then Clare Luce will be gone. All of it will be over. If you let this hurt what you're trying to find in your Church you're a fool. None of this has a thing to do with religion."

So the central truth of that Good Friday was spoken by the descendant of a long line of German Lutheran pastors. Possibly the Augustinian good sense has never left the spiritual heirs of Martin Luther.

The next day I was preparing to go to lunch when the phone rang. A sweet little voice came over the wire. "This is Mrs. Luce's secretary. Could you come over to the Waldorf at once? Mrs. Luce has just a few moments and it's important for her to see you. She has—er—something for you."

I obeyed the summons, curious as to what had happened now. The hubbub that surrounded Clare Luce was both stimulating and nerve-racking. Dorothy Farmer, her secretary, came into the long living room of the Towers, with its many windows looking down on New York twenty-eight stories below. She was carrying a large package. A smile lit her face and she said, "A Happy Easter from Mrs. Luce," and put the ribbon bedecked present in my arms.

I felt as if Clare Luce had given me a gold brick, and it didn't seem to my Philadelphia soul that she had known me long enough to give me a present. I felt a stab of remorse; I hadn't even bought her a greeting card. I wondered what on earth she had given me, and then decided it was probably a religious statue—a madonna.

"And this, too," said Mrs. Luce's secretary, handing me a letter on pale blue stationery.

I scanned it hastily. It seemed that Father Patrick Peyton was giving me a job of some sort. It was not too explicit, but obviously I was being offered something in the writing line.

Clare Luce entered, and nothing in New York looked as lovely as she did that Holy Saturday. White orchids nestled at the high collar of her black suit that shone with satin coin dots.

"Now, Constance," she said kissing me, and her face fell at sight of the unopened package on the table before me, "would you like to go to Hollywood? Write and tell Father Peyton to wire your plane fare and expenses—perhaps next week would be a good time. No use putting it off till he comes East next month."

I stammered something about the as-yet-incomplete catechism, and reminded her that I had a mother in Philadelphia. I couldn't pick up and go to California without a little arranging here and there.

Her face clouded. "I thought you'd be so pleased. I called up California last week. I didn't know you liked your mother?"

I looked at her, too bewildered for speech. I had seldom mentioned my mother to her. But where had she got this extraordinary idea?

"Oh, you do like her, I can see." She pouted. "But you never said."

She held a dish with a sort of Easter rabbit made of ice-cream on it, which she was taking downstairs to a converts' luncheon, for all the world like a pretty child faring forth attired in all her best clothes and bearing a lavish gift. I could just see the faces of all her middle-aged contemporaries looking at her with tight lips. She was the little girl with the golden curls who liked to speak pieces in public, and share her candy. Well, being what we were, we'd take the candy, pull her curls and refuse to applaud her pieces. Who could blame us?

I got away somehow after assuring her I'd write air mail to Father Peyton, and opened my present. It was an opulent bag, loaded with gadgets, a present I could not possibly return in kind.

Amazed and a little angry, I called Brock.

"Keep it as a souvenir," he chuckled. "This time next week you two won't be speaking."

The telephone's ringing cut through my embarrassed thoughts. Clare Luce in trembling tones asked me to meet her at once.

(What on earth has happened to the converts' luncheon party, going on right this minute?) I disapproved of myself for responding to these demands, but I never knew that she might not have secret information that war would be declared in a matter of minutes or that the Pope had decided to take a vacation in Connecticut. On the corner of Fiftieth Street I met a petulant and shivering Clare Luce.

"I wasn't amused at that luncheon. No one had a thing to give me. I hate parties where I can't learn anything. I just got up and left."

We drove up to what looked like a reformatory, a gray-stone, forbidding building off Lexington Avenue. I decided we were visiting an orphanage. We ascended some steps and went into a little cell of some sort. Clare banged a bell on the table, and stood tapping her foot impatiently. A priest with a most wonderful face came in. He wore a shabby soutane bearing some sort of white insignia and his hair was wiry and cropped close. He was foreign and an ascetic. . . . Everything about him proclaimed, "Thou art a priest forever. . . ."

He glared at Clare Luce, and I got the odd feeling we were about to be thrown out.

"Constance, this is my father confessor. Father Thibodeau, here she is—"

He reminded me of what I imagined St. Francis de Sales to be like, a saint I love despite Léon Bloy; there was a stern masculinity about him that had no time for nonsense.

"Go to confession with Father Thibodeau," Clare ordered.

It was past lunchtime—life with Clare was a long series of doing without lunch, and feeling vulgar and earthy at eating at all. I decided I'd get some vitamin pills if it kept up much longer. But, hungry though I was, it was too early for Saturday confession. And who were we to demand special services of the Church?

"Come, my dear," Father Thibodeau said, reading my mind. There was sympathy and understanding on his face, and he begged for mine.

We went through a door, and to my amazement I was standing

in St. Jean Baptiste, the church I had gone to because of Mother Mary Agatha Scott that long-ago winter when I had lectured in New York. Why, Father Thibodeau was one of Cousin Fanny's beloved Fathers of the Blessed Sacrament! On that altar had been celebrated the hundred Masses for the repose of her soul. I remembered the afternoon I had sat before the confessional box trying to get courage to enter. I had just a moment to realize that Father Wilfred Thibodeau was leading me into the identical box.

He said things to me—wise, profound things—as if the struggle for faith were over, instead of only beginning. It was as if I caught hold of something strong and while I held it I was safe. He was filled with French common sense and he had no time for formal piety or parochialism, or narrow rules to hedge in the spirit struggling for the light.

I came outside and knelt saying my penance and felt exalted and good. The altar at St. Jean's was magnificent and ornate, the candles and the Easter lilies descending row upon row from the mighty monstrance that crowned the altar filled me with glory.

Once in the car, our devotions over, Clare said chastened, "He gives me hell. Father Thibodeau gives me hell."

I had an enormous respect for the gigantic effort it would take to curb a will that had never been crossed, to break desires that had never been thwarted, into the tremendous discipline of the Roman Catholic Church. It could satisfy every craving of her logical, fiercely acquisitive mind but to hold these imperious ways in subjection required a stupendous re-education of the will. But Clare Luce's will knows things about her that her mind has forgotten.

Easter Sunday we were going to Monsignor's seven o'clock Mass, then he would join us for breakfast at the Waldorf, and we'd go back to the Cardinal's Mass and Monsignor's Easter sermon. It was all fixed. . . .

"I'm always alone on holidays," she said. "Harry goes to visit his children. My friends have families. We'll have some fun tomorrow, you and I."

I looked forward to that breakfast with Monsignor. I went into the New Weston flower shop, and with left-over flares of resentment for the elaborate bag, selected two of the most ostentatious orchids I could find for Clare Luce. I stopped at the drugstore for sustenance, and went upstairs and read in Teresa of Avila's autobiography for the third time in one week. This woman had a spirit as modern as my own. She was a maddening woman, filled with neuroses, quarrelsome, sensitive—and yet she was our spokeswoman. Nothing in Teresa of Avila who was born over five hundred years ago is alien or remote from our own psychology. The war between self and God raged in Teresa's breast. This passionate and imperious spirit knew all our temptations. La Madre and I were at the start of our great friendship. . . .

The next morning, Easter morning, at seven I entered the Lady Chapel of the Cathedral. Monsignor said a beautiful Mass, filled with grace and holiness. I received Communion with a number of converts.

We stood outside the chapel, and Monsignor was gracious and tactful, his smile was warm, and his eyes turned from coal-black to blazing Irish blue. I was as nervous as a schoolgirl.

He joined the others, while I stood around feeling awkward.

"Clare," I said, "shall I wait here for you or meet you at the Waldorf?"

"We're not meeting," she said airily, with a flashing smile. "Harry's going with me to Mass. Isn't it terrific?"

The Monsignor wheeled around and objected to the change of plans, his face as stormy as Savonarola's, those uncanny eyes coal-black.

A bad little blond girl pouted at him. Mortified, I started for the door. Monsignor's back was stiff with outrage.

"Wait," he ordered me.

He spoke to someone and came over to me with a card, his shoulders moving in agitation. This man had a temper. I was ready to crawl under a pew and hide. I took the card, thanked him, and dashed out the door.

At the Cardinal's Easter Mass, I sat with some nice friends of Monsignor's. He mounted the pulpit and his living voice with its cadences now lowered in pathos, now lifted up with passion, had power as great as his words. He spoke of the Christ of Scars, and this was the Christ of my generation, a man of wounds and scars. Monsignor Sheen did not fall short of the Eagle of Meaux in gorgeous, soaring strength. He made Divine Agony live in the magnificence of Resurrection. Then his eye fell on me, in a pew practically beneath the pulpit, and I recognized a great actor aware of my response. I couldn't get that quick glance of Monsignor Sheen's out of my mind, and it broke the spell of the sermon. Yet I said involuntarily as he finished:

"Dear God, he's magnificent."

But it was my tribute to the artist—not to the priest.

I went into the crowded street after Mass and down to my hotel. On the opposite side of Fiftieth Street, Clare in her fabulous sable coat was accompanied by Harry Luce wearing a blue shirt and a mashed-down felt hat as if to proclaim he was still a Presbyterian barbarian. Between them, Elsa Maxwell trotted along happily wearing the orchids I had sent to Clare.

I decided to go home to Philadelphia and stay till the next morning. I needed Mother's mocking humor, her common sense, for I was about to lose my temper.

I heard those words of Monsignor Sheen's, "How divine it is to come home," and remembered they were the identical words Ethel Barrymore always used in her curtain speeches in Philadelphia.

## 2

> Mr. Pemberton's stable of glamor authors including Clare Boothe "The Women" Luce and Constance "The Magnificent Heel" O'Hara, are engaged in preparing a dramatized catechism to be called "The Way, The Truth, The Life," with a technical assist by Brock Pemberton. Mr. Bert Lytell who appeared in Mrs. Luce's hit-play "Margin for Error" and in Miss O'Hara's lamented "The Magnificent Heel" will take the lead role in the catechism as the Narrator. Mr. Emmet Rogers will enact the Christus.
>
> Mrs. Mary "Harvey" Chase and Miss O'Hara will both be in town for the third annual Tony Perry dinner and awards to be given in the Waldorf-Astoria ballroom on this Sunday . . .

THIS AMAZING BIT OF press drollery aroused no single misgiving in my mind as I sat in Barclay Street tightening the script against next week's recording. The artist beat time with a pencil, saying aloud, "Beep," as we hit the seventeen-second point. There were no customers and the wind beat the rain of that storm-shrouded Easter week against the plate-glass windows; the plaster statues, aesthetic monstrosities though they were, seemed warm and pleasing on this wild day. The steady sound of the artist's voice saying "beep" like a plaintive baby chick was halted as she spoke in the phone.

"It's about the imprimatur," she whispered, handing it to me.

"The imprimatur?" Oh, yes, Father Mullen had left the script with the Brooklyn chancellory, a mere routine matter. The doctrinal purity of our first play was such that Father Michael Mullen had inspected a comma for traces of heresy.

"Miss O'Hara," a fruity voice oozed disapproval. "I'm calling you from the Confraternity Office. Who was responsible for that piece I read in the paper this morning?"

I didn't have to be told my caller was a priest. I had heard these exact tones in my childhood, traces of brogue, and a belief in priestly omnipotence. They belonged to the class who always made the worst outcry over their physical upsets. Mother had lumped them together under the splendid title, "The Father Murphy's stomachaches."

"These names I read in the paper," the voice went, "are they Cath'lic people?"

"Why, no, Father," I replied. "I was told the religion of the actors was immaterial."

"Oh, you were, were you?" This voice foretold trouble. "Would anny of them now be DI-vorced people?"

How many divorces had dear Bertie to his credit? One, two . . . No, I was sure it couldn't be three.

"Mrs. Luce divorced her first husband," I informed him nastily, "but he died, you know."

"Now, look, Miss O'Hara," answered the horrified cleric from Brooklyn, "Mrs. Luce is one of our own people. I said nothin' at all about her marriage, nothin' at all. I don't understand it, but it's been vouched for. So we won't get into that question," he roared in the telephone, "for that would be disputin' the mind of the Church."

It was then I commenced to enjoy myself. I was up to Monsignor Drumgoole's favorite pastime, baiting the parochial mind.

"I'm askin' you to answer, and at once, who are these people whose names are in this Broadway story as bein' in the catechism? A catechism goin' to decent hard-workin' priests and nuns in parish schools? Could it be there's anny renegade Cath'lics among you?"

I had met this man by the dozens in my father's office, redolent of good cigars, crafty as Irish peasants and as narrow-minded.

"You'll answer my questions or there'll be no imprimatur. You're a woman of Broadway yourself from this piece in the paper?"

"I am from Philadelphia, Father." I trusted my tone was expressive of a state of mind as well as a geographical position.

"Oh, y'are? I'll just call Father John McFadden to give me a report."

"Well then, Father," I purred, "you will be told I am the grandniece of Bishop O'Hara."

That had him. All you had to do with these reverend gentlemen was drag in the hierarchy. That my bishop had been dead nearly fifty years was not important. The name O'Hara in recent times had literally become the cradle of bishops, and he would have to jump from north to south, from east to west, coming up in each place with a Bishop O'Hara, before he would be enlightened. And anyhow my bishop was a substantial ghost, the friend and patron of Denis, Cardinal Dougherty.

"W-which Bishop?" the voice had come down quite a few notes. "B-bishop Edwin of Kansas City, would it be, or B-bishop John of Buffalo? Ah! they're fine men both of them."

"Father McFadden will tell you exactly who I am, Father, and my status with His Eminence, Cardinal Dougherty." The woman artist was looking at me in genuine fright.

"I don't like this stuff in the paper," he said, chastened. "It was my duty to investigate. I d-do tell you," he tried to get back his splendid bullying tones, "that your story will have to be satisfactory in every detail or there'll be no imprimatur from Brooklyn."

"Perhaps not, Father," I lashed out, "but the imprimatur goes to the writer, and I am sure Cardinal Dougherty of Philadelphia will not deny me one," and I slammed down the phone through his sputters.

I was bluffing, of course. Father McFadden and I were in no sense friends. No doubt my record as a lapsed Catholic was horrifying to His Eminence. . . . I got home through the wind and the rain thoroughly soaked. I called Room Service and ordered a splendid dinner and took aspirin after a steaming tub while I raged at my first touch of Church discipline in long years.

"Ignoramus," I said to the startled waiter. "No, not you. A priest in Brooklyn."

He was French and violently anti-clerical and had a thorn in his side, too, a priest in the Bronx. He gave my dinner extra flourishes and ran back to the kitchen for hot rolls. I ate. I drafted telegrams in my mind to churchmen including the Papal Delegate. Father Michael Mullen, C. M., was in Woburn, Massachusetts, with his mother; in one splendid ten-word blast I informed him, "Denied imprimatur. . . ." It was enough to give that theological purist heart failure; for that most misunderstood term, the Imprimatur, only means that the doctrine is not contrary to the Church.

I paced the floor, debating what to do. I had no power left in the Church, no friends at court. Mrs. Luce, the wealthy convert, would be spared any shock; my name would be quietly dropped. "A renegade Catholic, you know . . ." The waiter appeared with a present for me, another pot of coffee.

"These priests!" He poured my coffee. "I think it is better to give up the Church."

I reached for the telephone book and searched for a number. I called Francis, Cardinal Spellman.

My hand shook and my voice was a mere thread when I asked to speak to His Eminence or, since I still had some grasp on practicalities, the secretary to His Eminence. I had a few priests on the wire to whom I identified myself and tried to explain my predicament. Then a nice voice came, "Tell me about it?"

"I am Constance O'Hara, perhaps I should say the grandniece of the late Bishop O'Hara of Scranton—"

"Are you the Constance O'Hara who was Monsignor Drumgoole's friend? I'm sure you are. I met you at Monsignor McMahon's. I was Father Francis Murphy, his assistant. Now I'm Monsignor Murphy and don't laugh. I know I don't wear the purple like my boss."

I remembered him now, the old firebrand's modest young curate. Out poured my story, punctuated by his chuckles. I haven't a doubt that later His Eminence, Cardinal Spellman, was advised of the whole situation, including my rattling of the bones of the long-dead Bishop O'Hara to confound a priest in Brooklyn, and that wonderful sound, clerical laughter, rang through the Cardinal's Madison Avenue house.

"Take it easy, Constance," Monsignor Murphy said. "We

don't treat Catholics that come back to the Church the way you seem to think. To get people like you back is the meaning of the priesthood. We'll even take your sassy tongue to keep you happy. Monsignor Drumgoole prayed you back and don't forget it. And don't you forget your daddy when you get mad at us. He knew how hard it was to be a priest. You'll get an imprimatur. There's nothing to worry about, though I'd worry if I were Mrs. Luce. You think there's a chance of you two making the Church 'the greatest show on earth'?"

The imprimatur was duly given to my script. Upstanding clergymen sat with me in the long room off the New Weston bar soothing the storm raging in my breast over "that fearful man from Brooklyn." There is no doubt that my little tempest was given more clerical attention than it would have otherwise warranted because of my friendship with Mrs. Luce. I was far too cynical not to realize this, as all my unpleasant memories from a childhood spent too close to the human element in the Church were revived.

My reaction against the menace from Brooklyn proved one thing. I was caught between two worlds and couldn't make the transition. No lapsed Catholic who returns to the Church should ever be taken out of his own world too soon. I stepped out and away into an abyss.

I went down to Maggie Perry's in this confused mood. Kurt Kasnar sat looking at me with his eyes hurt and faintly scornful. The conversation rattled on about Clare Luce and the catechism.

"It sounds like a new and wonderful sort of success story to me. The religion of the main chance." He was smiling in an elusive and intelligent way. "I was once a Catholic. I think I shall return. Will you take me to Mass?"

I could not join in the good-natured laughter. I was seeking something real in the Church; yet I loathed those aspects of it given me by the priest from Brooklyn. I loved the dramatic and the spectacular. Clare Luce fed that side of my nature. Wouldn't everyone say "the religion of the main chance"?

Then the month had gone. The first episode of the catechism was recorded. Everyone was flushed with accomplishment.

Father Mullen was like a pleased child. He, of all of us, was right for the catechism.

I was offered a job in New York writing scripts for audio-visual education, to which I promised a definite answer when I came through New York the following week, for I was going up to stay with Clare Luce in Ridgefield for a long week-end. It would be wonderful to lie fallow in the country for a few days; for Clare had assured me we were leading the quiet life with only walks in the fields and nothing to do but read and listen to records.

Neal, the Luce chauffeur, met me at the Branchville Station. We drove along a winding road with silver birch trees on either side; and then ascended a hill with the woods still surrounding us and came with abruptness on a driveway that led to Sugar Hill, a red-brick Georgian house.

I was ushered into a bedroom opening off a library study. I realized that I was to occupy the suite of H. R. Luce, then in Europe. It was a solid masculine type of room with books everywhere; and I found the poems of Charles Péguy and read for the first time, "I don't like the man who doesn't sleep says God." There was the gentle hum of a superbly run home of the very rich, where you never see the servants and it all has an air of deceptive simplicity. I amused myself going from the library study to my bedroom. I could order anything from the appearance of a valet to a Cadillac in the driveway. I wondered if I pushed something if a young man in horn-rimmed glasses and tweeds would appear from the Time office brief-case in hand . . .

During that week-end Clare and I went on a spree of confidences, bared our most private sorrows. There was no excuse for either of us. Extremely worldly people have a philosophy that in its view of human relations is precisely that of people of the deepest spirituality. The worldling's code is the wisdom of despair, to prevent damaged emotions. The spiritual person's, identical in its denying principle, is healthy and radiant because it proclaims that any absolute trust or liking given a creature, without detachment, is bound to end in disillusionment. We cannot love a friend unless we possess them in God. The worldly protect the "self" from degradation by never permitting themselves emotional dependence on another. The spiritual protect the "self" that is God's.

Yet I had no misgivings and came back to New York completely happy with my decision made about the audio-visual scripts. The new job would make me independent financially. I was not Clare's employee. I was her friend. An important distinction, to me. Warnings, many of them eminently sensible, rained on me like hailstones.

I arrived at the Grosvenor House on lower Fifth Avenue in full flight from Broadway with a taxi filled with books of profound spirituality, a typewriter, and all sense of reality submerged.

## 3

AND NOW EACH MORNING just before ten o'clock I crossed through Washington Square, where squat young women artists, who had never grown the right size for their big square feet, and willowy young men sat blinking up at the May sunshine. I turned into a narrow street and was in Little Italy. Often great brown paper bags of garbage lay in the narrow doorways, flies came, night fell, the bags burst open and the malodorous contents sprawled on the brick sidewalk. It was a street of little stores, and open fruit and vegetable stands lined the thoroughfare. Children two and three years old, as nimble as cats, dashed into the way of passing trucks, and escaped. They were hilarious and colorful children, and some of the boys at five were racketeers, who carried knives in their ragged pockets. On one corner stood a gloomy Mills hotel, and then I turned into Bleecker Street, and Vatican City.

My office was a cellar, impressive with a high-backed Renaissance chair and an ornate, carved walnut desk. The cellar was like the Catacombs; it led into mysteries, into vast storerooms filled with books, into a shop where Italian eyes bored into me when I appeared and there was silence. There was everything in the cellar, recording machines into which singers lustily roared Italian operas, sculptors carving religious statues, artists with pots of bright paint, printing presses, and a spiritual director Father Willy Fugello.

I sat at my desk writing publicity for an impressive list of audio-visual productions. Actually we had only one production in preparation—the catechism; but all I had ever actually seen of that was a sketch of a child with orange hair, wearing a bright red dress, lying on brilliantly green grass staring at one lone daisy. The master records had not yet been delivered.

"I don't want to hurry," said Father Mullen. "I like it this way."

When I think of the audio-visual catechism a knifelike wind blows through my memory, and I seem to freeze in an icy deluge of troubles. I have been asked on many occasions to explain the process for the dramatized catechism, and instead of the few concise words needed I am back in time to the week after week of crisis on Barclay Street, living through the maze of production difficulties, fuming at delaying actions, tempers exploding till some of us sounded like wild cats howling in the night. What was the catechism? Three double-faced records of actors speaking a brief and simple play for children, synchronized to still pictures, actually highly colored cartoons. The time limit consumed for the telling of this story was thirty minutes. That's all there was to it. How often I have been stopped in my too fulsome account by the thinly veiled disbelief and condescension on the faces of my interrogators. Why try to make something momentous of such a simple endeavor, their amused eyes seem to say. It was only a film strip with accompanying records, and yet the amount of human endeavor that went into this production was not unheroic.

The name of Clare Luce and her friendship for me was taken

in vain at least a thousand times a day. A bright blue banner on Barclay Street had her name emblazoned with her participation in the audio-visual catechism.

Often the phone would ring in my cellar to announce that Mrs. Luce and her entourage were motoring in from Connecticut and she would be pleased if I could join her at the completion of my duties; or it was suggested I join the homeward trek to Sugar Hill.

At the first showing of *Come to the Stable* Clare sat between Father Thibodeau and me, surrounded by the convert set, the new Catholics who were restoring the world to Christ. I was introduced to Carol Jackson, that strange, intense English girl who, as co-editor of *Integrity*, led the "Integrity set" to the prevue. Father James Keller led the Christophers who were contentedly parochial. All the editors from the Catholic magazines were there. All the Catholic intellectuals. Axes were being ground all over the place.

I looked into the wise eyes of Father Thibodeau and forgot to suffer while Kit Emmet, a young man who was going to put Christ in government by some sort of press campaign, talked to Clare. Down front sat Bernard Baruch, splendid, sane and benign, who seemed to know that truth has the power to slay a man when he has nothing but his reason. The God of Moses and Abraham looked from his splendid eyes, and the God of Paul and Augustine among the Catholic converts seemed obscured by their overwhelming convictions.

The lights went down and *Come to the Stable* was revealed as no more than a pleasant moving picture. Clare had meant it to be a tribute to contemplative nuns, an unseen force in a Connecticut town, with the convent bell sounding over the still countryside.

The film was over and the only person I wanted to talk to was Bernard Baruch, but I was hemmed in by Catholic intellectuals and the clergy. Perhaps the fact I had been a prodigal was interesting; everyone wanted to be most helpful in my spiritual development. Converts have no false humility, and they were quite ready to teach me the basic points of theology, even my prayers. The reverend clergy were kind, but a little suspicious of my motives. I looked after the towering height of Bernard Baruch wistfully, while someone who had been at the Trappists and seen Thomas Merton on top of a haystack told me all about it. The cultus of Thomas Merton was then at its height and if I had been told that the Holy Ghost in the form of a dove had rested on his shoulder while he was on the haystack I would not have been astonished. I stuck by Father Thibodeau, and escaped from my new-found friends.

Finally we were in the shelter of Clare's limousine. It was pleasant to drive Father Thibodeau to St. Jean Baptiste. Dear Father Thibodeau, in those days, represented all I hoped to find in the Catholic Church. We left him across the street from the monastery, because he didn't want his brother priests to see his return in a chauffeur-driven Cadillac. He gave us a gentle smile, as if he suspected both of us of vehemence and lack of restraint. Father Thibodeau had won the pleasures of the wise and as a penalty, for no pleasure is without pain, he had won the regard of two egocentric women. He looked curiously foreign and wistful as he crossed Lexington Avenue, and made his way down Seventy-sixth Street.

"He's a very holy man," I informed Clare Luce.

"He's too nice to see through us," said she, with her mocking grin.

I tried to go home to Philadelphia at least once in every week. I was filled with accounts of promises for the future; but Mother, serenely practical, reminded me that the present was being financed by an audio-visual producer in Little Italy for whom I wrote brochures on his dreams. Clare talked of books I would write, lectures I was to give, plays we were to co-author, editorial work, assured me I would never leave New York; her mind darted like a butterfly from project to project. I saw almost nothing of my friends in New York, and you can't put friends in a Deep-Freeze and expect them to thaw out when you need them. Yet I had no real idea what Clare Luce had in mind for me, and had enough intelligence even in my bemused condition to agree with Erasmus that "violent friendship is as little lasting as violent love."

It was at this time I found a source of strength. I went each morning to nine o'clock Mass at St. Francis Xavier's. I kept this a secret; it was soothing to walk up Fifth Avenue to Sixteenth Street and turn the corner. The bright gold dome of the church was somehow friendly on that dusty street. I liked the old brown church and the handful of quiet worshipers. It was pleasant not to be stared at, as always happened when Clare and I went to early Mass. I had no self-conscious feeling. I was alone in the silence and the peace.

I noticed one morning an old Jesuit with a silky fringe of pure white hair. His face was like porcelain, and he had an austere dignity as he came in from the sacristy with his acolyte. There was some quality in his Mass that reached me, that got below all the strange antipathies and withdrawals I felt for the Church. It was not just the splendid actions of the Mass, the beautiful prayers in the missal, it was the priest's concentration. It drew you to him, you were part of the mysteries.

He didn't hurry, but there was no waste motion; when he came to the Orate Fratres his stern old face was soft with invitation, his arms were thrown wide as if we were to be gathered in an embrace. There was a graciousness to his every gesture. And then came the Canon of the Mass. I remember at the Elevation watching his first genuflection. He came upright and one could almost see his leg muscles flexing, his arms coming up, as if he could barely lift the tremendous weight; as he held the Host aloft, every part of his body was straining. He was standing on his toes, his head flung back to look adoringly at the Host. . . . The exaltation and the agony of it tore through my body. He, a man, had lifted the Lord God of Heaven and Earth aloft over a few worshipers at St. Francis Xavier's. The golden chalice of the Precious Blood was lifted in the same way. It seemed then as if the old priest had tired. The glory of the Elevation carried you to the Pater Noster, and you knew he was asking his Lord to bless us all. We came up to the communion rail and he advanced toward us, his splendid face radiant. His old hands trembled as he gave us the Blessed

Eucharist; but he still had the manner of a host who wanted to be sure that in his house no guest went unfed. He stooped down over each one of us.

Once the Host fell from his fingers. It was the secret fear that had been planted in me in the Convent of Notre Dame. The old priest stooped and retrieved it. He laid it back gently in the ciborium, and he was half-smiling. You could almost hear him saying, "Sweet Jesus, I'm old now and my hands tremble. In another second I will have you safe in the heart of one of these good people."

I remember the bright scarlet of his vestment, and the red roses on the altar. I remember the happiness and the peace. This was Catholicism.

I used to kneel there in the stillness after Mass was over, not praying, not even thinking. I came out on Sixteenth Street so happy I could not believe it. Once a friend met me.

"Lord, you look young," he said. "What are you up to?"

It was true; these mornings at St. Francis Xavier's were making me young again. In my theatre days I would have gone mad with all the nervous tension, the baffling stupidity and stubbornness of my co-workers. I didn't mind, for I was so at peace. These mornings with the Lord were my secret. I had no intention of letting Clare Luce know, but she did, and with blessed tact never mentioned her knowledge to me. She had a Jesuit friend, Father Justin McCarthy, whom she called, "that rarest of all things—a humble Jesuit," and he sent her the report of my good conduct. Father Thibodeau was informed, but he was well aware it was going to take much more than a daily visit to Mass to spiritualize my nature. He knew I had to have a groundwork of discipline to reach the meaning of Communion. The saintly old Jesuit had made me take one tremendous leap forward, but my toehold on these heights was tenuous and Father Thibodeau tried to give me a grappling iron.

Among other things that happened to me at that time, while the historic and relentless heat wave of 1949 descended on the Eastern seaboard, was finding something I had lost in the secular world. It is a loss that all lapsed Catholics feel, driven as they are to spend their time in an earthly Hell, worshiping the suffering they have brought on themselves. It is the loss of affection and trust. We are familiar with bitterness and hate; more often than not we hate our neighbor as ourselves. We recognize treachery, because our souls are heavy with our own treachery.

Now my vision was clear. I liked and I trusted. I was not less intelligent, for I saw the human flaws in my new-found friends, but they did not disturb me. I saw the world as a child does or an artist; had I had a mature integrated love of Christ at the center of my being I might have lived that way a long time. The most adult discovery in the world is to learn how simple it is to be happy. I delighted in these new friends of mine, not as people who could help me accomplish a certain end, but just because they liked me.

It was a miracle to have no dislike in my heart for anyone, no bitterness. It was like living at the far-flung rim of the world where it is always morning.

Perhaps too, it was because I was financially secure, and it is amazing how beautiful the world seems, how easy it is to overcome anger, sail through emotional storms, when we are ballasted with even a little gold. But simple as the explanation for my joy may have been, I lived stimulated by the kindly wine of friendship in a Christianity where, because there was no Cross for me, I forgot the Crucifixion. Once I cried out to Father McCarthy:

"I'm happy. I'm not used to it. I'm not used to living without having to be assertive and aggressive. I'm afraid it will stop. I couldn't stand it, Father."

"It's not going to stop. It's your reward. Our Lord has some work for you to do, and He's put you here for a good reason. Clare and you will show 'em that everyone who believes in God just has to become a Catholic."

It wasn't so long after that conversation that I descended to the level of myself, and discovered that all these wonderful friends, who I serenely fancied loved me so much, were not altogether noble, nor altogether trustworthy, nor altogether consistent. All of us caught in the web of my outraged temperament were altogether human. A few of us lied to each other, and about each other; a few of us prayed for each other; a few of us wept, and time went on and only I could not realize that the bonds that unite another person to ourselves exist only in our mind. Memory as it grows fainter relaxes even that, and so it was that I made myself unhappy by being briefly happy.

My phone shrilled at all hours, heralding anyone from Mrs. Joseph Kennedy to the head of a religious order, or Dorothy Willard, Broadway's newest angel, but frequently it summoned me to deal with a crisis at the Waldorf Towers.

"Hello," said Clare's lilting voice on my telephone at the start of a red-hot day in June. "Constance, I want you to take a few days off next week and help me with *The Twilight of God.* You'll have to come out to the country. I'll want you to telephone all sorts of people . . . Arthur Krock—and oh, just everyone. I want you to start now and check every one of my quotes from Communist authorities. I have to be exact. I'll work you like a dog, and of course I'll give you a credit line, and a percentage of the royalties after publication. O.K.?"

I was off on the start of another adventure, which gave me an insight into Clare Boothe Luce's mental processes. She was a political thinker who dispensed with man the unpredictable.

I assisted Clare in tracking down quotations and it was a formidable task. She had given the giants of the Russian Revolution words that agreed with her damnation of them, but unfortunately she often gave Lenin words that Trotsky had written, or Marx the words of Stalin. I went among the old Bolsheviks in the Russian room of the New York Public Library, and with the manuscript of *The Twilight of God* before me, David Staub pulled down vast Russian language books and found the exact quotation.

The Grosvenor became host to a startling group of callers, the impoverished exiles from the second Russian Revolution. These were the men who had overthrown the Czar, the followers of Kerensky, all anxious to earn a little money from the Luce coffers. I had nothing to offer them, because I refused to accept recompense for my endeavors. Irish pride and Slavic patience before the inexorable laws of economics had a strange wedding, but I was immensely interested in my new assignment.

One day, following the trail of a flock of remarks Clare had attributed to Earl Browder, I appeared in the office of the *Daily Worker* on West Sixteenth Street. A taciturn woman with a deep bass voice assisted me in my search.

"Are you workin' for Mrs. Luce?" she questioned.

"Oh, no," I said brightly, "I'm just a friend of hers checking some copy."

"I kinda thought you were just foolish," she said with a wicked leer. "Want to see somethin' about your lady friend?"

She permitted me to see Mrs. Luce's file in the *Daily Worker*. They had missed nothing, from Clare's vacations on the Lido to her Hollywood sojourns. There was not a photograph that did not make her hideous. Trick photography had super-imposed the body of a bathing beauty—a virtually naked one—to her head. A mouth that was not hers hung open uttering incitements to class warfare in the halls of Congress.

"You still want to be her friend?" inquired the custodian of the files at the *Daily Worker*.

On the way up to Sugar Hill I commenced to wonder what the staff of the *Daily Worker* would say if they could see us now. Piles of Communist literature were heaped on the floor of the car. In the front seat Clare's maid, Gretel, was custodian of the silver fox cape, the sables and the jewel case. Tense with nerves from long hours at the typewriter, Clare was being soothed by the recitation of the rosary in Latin. It seemed like a revival of Catherine de Medici's court at the Louvre, and yet the Communists could not have produced a harder working human being than this intense little blond woman.

The hammering of all these intellectual excitements was stimulating; but I was still rushing back and forth to Philadelphia, keeping up my own work schedule, and I commenced to approach complete exhaustion. Mother was willing to join me in New York as soon as I had made a connection that would not explode in my face. I still had a haunting sense of insecurity, a wish that some opportunity would open up that would offer a fair prospect of permanence. Father Thibodeau, a man of the deepest spirituality, also had that practical good sense that is the sign of a great Catholic churchman. He realized that I was tiring, that often I was intolerably weary, and grew impatient of my pride. He thought I should take up my problems with Clare, and ask her pointblank what she had in mind. He loathed waste, and waste of talents awakened his scorn. Father Thibodeau could not realize how he was helping me with life. The things he said came back afterward, came back in dark days. When a priest can help you with life, he is holy enough to save your soul. Most contemporary priests make a vocation of passive resistance to the world; an active resistance would make the Gospels a living presence. Father Thibodeau would caution, "Live spiritually, my child," and then, knowing I was blind to the heart of things, deaf to the song of the spheres, recommend some books I might enjoy.

Most of them were published by Sheed and Ward. In them I found the Catholic Church I wanted. I found my old friend Gertrud von le Fort, and discovered meanings in her *Song to the Church* that had seemed impossible for me. I read Christopher Dawson. I read Frank Sheed's *Communism and Man;* and for the first time a Catholic exploded the doctrine of Communism for me, not by diatribes on atheism and materialism but by its own philosophical contradictions. I read *Theology and Sanity*, and felt the pulse of a precise intelligence that never stooped to emotionalism but had a sort of illumined sweetness when it came to man's relation to his Creator. I was too passionate and too irrational to appreciate thoroughly all that Frank Sheed represented, but I knew I was being drawn to his publishing firm as a solution to my muddled and confused life. My heart was set on the peace of a connection with these wonderful minds. This was not Catholicism that buried its head in the sand, it took up the totality of modern errors, extracted the good, the desperate yearning of minds to find purpose and faith. I did not speak of my desire to Clare, but I was childish enough to do a little praying about it.

On the anniversary of my father's death I had a long and

trying day, spent mostly in the stale heat of the New York subways. I had a heavy list of letters to be written, and when I laid my work aside shortly before midnight I wanted only to sink into a deep and dreamless sleep. Instead my mind flooded with memories of that tired man who had been my father. Could it be possible that twenty-three years had passed since that June night—twenty-three years in which I had frittered away a life in dreams and ambitions? Could I ever retrace my steps back to the mental and emotional safety of Catholicism as I had known it when I was the Doctor's daughter?

I had lived among non-Catholics and the shelter had seemed safe. But its subtle dangers had left me with no shelter, with a restless and divided soul. Could I go back? This haven with Clare Luce was wonderful, but perhaps it had no reality. Did I have strength to face the Catholic world of Philadelphia, to live among them the Catholic way of life? Was there any tangible hope of forgetting my conflicting loyalties? It is this poison of fear that keeps many thousands of lapsed Catholics for years on the threshold of the Church they have forsaken. No Catholic can leave the Church, as no Jew deserts Israel.

My phone rang. Clare had remembered this was my father's anniversary. There are few people who understand regret and remorse, but in those minutes while Clare and I talked she revealed an exquisite tenderness. Friends in this sorry world can become foes. The blades of calumnies can sever all bonds, and yet in any friendship that has meaning are memories that can blot out the bitterness, if we seek them.

Not long afterward the inevitable happened; the audio-visual project collapsed. The catechism for which I had written so many publicity brochures, so many letters, was apparently interred in the sound studio, with a preservative of Father Michael Mullen's idealism.

I decided to leave for Philadelphia in the morning, write Clare a letter once I was home—and my recall would then be her responsibility. The phone rang as I assembled my garments. Lady Inverchapel wanted me to tell Clare something. Dorothy

Willard called. I'd accepted an invitation for tomorrow night. Elia Kazan would call for me. None of these calls was prompted by a desire for my society. Everybody wanted something from Clare Luce. And I did too. . . .

It was another of those frightful days that beset New York in the last days of June, 1949, days that prepared the way for the inferno of July which made way for the sultry hideousness of August. I lay disconsolate on my narrow couch-bed. Dorothy Farmer phoned me, and had the story from me in no time.

"You mean you're going back to Philadelphia without a word to Clare! It isn't fair. Don't throw away her friendship."

"Dorothy," I said, "I'm a realist. Women like Clare don't want friends. They don't need them. This time next year she'll have forgotten I ever lived."

"Constance," the sweet little voice was horrified, "I don't believe you. People aren't like that. You two need each other."

"You will say nothing. Please. She's in the country. I'll write from Philadelphia."

"Oh, all right," she promised, "but it's not the way to treat a friend. We haven't helped you at all. You're still distrustful. Those rotten Broadway people. If only you hadn't left the Church and gotten yourself all mixed up. Constance, don't tell Brock Pemberton, at least not yet—"

Strangely enough Brock came to see me late that afternoon. I hadn't seen him for a few weeks, and he was nervous over the fate of his "nun." I put on my best blue dress and waited for him to say, "Philadelphia women!" He did, and we rode uptown and had dinner on a roof garden at a hotel somewhere near the Hampshire House. The prices on the menu were outrageous and I kept his affections by ordering the least expensive platter. New York was gorgeous from this vantage point, and I didn't even feel worried.

"I could get you on *Time*," said Mr. P. "I wouldn't ask Clare. I'd put it up to Harry, but I don't think you'd be happy."

I didn't dare confide in Brock my private dream about Sheed and Ward.

"Connie," he said, "you're a playwright. You'll never be happy till you've written that play. A high comedy. I'll finance you. I'll put it on too. . . ."

I looked away. We both loved the theatre. It was our common bond, this instinctive, unreasoning, unreasonable love for the theatre, a place of light and sound, of mystery and magic. We loved it blindly and foolishly, but with understanding. He had never lost faith in me. Why couldn't I keep my faith in him?

"I am a consistent pessimist," said Mr. P.

"I am an inconsistent Catholic," I answered. "Buy me some peach ice cream, it's sixty cents, and then I'm going back to the Grosvenor. I'm taking an early train."

I got in a taxi and said good night to Brock. In the hotel I learned Clare had been calling me. I assumed she was still in Ridgefield and peacefully got in bed. I kept going over Brock's words. "A high comedy!" Why not? I slept, seeing blazing electric signs proclaiming my name to the indifferent heavens, where they had my name, and number too. I saw box-office receipts in a great ledger. I'd live at Hampshire House. . . .

I was a very unstable character—or perhaps I was true to the way the Lord had made me.

## 4

My taxi pulled away from the Grosvenor, stirring up dust from the open excavation on the corner as we started uptown for the Cenacle of St. Regis. The sun was a blood-red palpitation flooding heat on the gasping city. Books on the publishing business stuck to the leather seat of the cab, my briefcase bulged with pages of notes, the advice of a young woman at Simon and Schuster, the pertinent observations of Aaron

Sussman, and a sheet of space costs from Schwab and Beatty, the advertising agency. The new advertising manager of Sheed and Ward, which was what I was unofficially, had had a week's intensive drill on the publishing business of which I knew virtually nothing, and was now on my way to make a private retreat at the Cenacle Convent on West 140th Street, from which I would emerge to meet Frank Sheed on his return from England and assume my responsibilities.

The heat shimmered in waves from the tall buildings, but I did not mind in the least. I lay back in the taxi, loving New York; soon night would fall, with that moment of miracle when the city's illumination taunted the skies. We turned up the West Side Drive. I wasn't going back to Philadelphia; I was staying in New York to write advertising for Sheed and Ward. Ebullient self-dramatizer that I was, and will always be, I was living the part. In deference to the distinguished minds with which I was to be associated, my manner had taken on a certain British decorum.

Days and days ago there had been the morning I planned to go home. Clare had called as I was leaving for the train, having just learned from Dorothy about the end of the audio-visual job. She had informed me Frank Sheed needed an advertising manager. He would be back from England in two weeks and she would arrange for me to take the job. The last candidate had been a young married Catholic man with five children who had to have twelve thousand a year, which was out of the question. She outlined my campaign, which was to originate and organize a plan to move the back log of excellent books that hadn't sold, a plan that must be unique yet not offend British sensibilities. She did not specify the exact salary but assured me that what with lecture engagements she'd arrange for me, and editorial work for her on the side, I would be able to take an apartment whenever I wanted, and bring my mother to New York.

The Vincentian Fathers, outraged by the audio-visual debacle, had retrieved the master-records of the catechism, and announced my selection as permanent writer of the series. From my point of view I was a capitalist.

The years had taught me one worldly precept: never leave the location where a job is pending, no matter how sure it seems, so I arranged to make a retreat at the Cenacle of St. Regis, in order to remain in New York and still conserve assets.

We were far uptown now, I could see the white, gleaming stone of St. Walburga's Convent. My luggage and books were carried through the double door of the Cenacle of St. Regis. Mother Mary Judge stood there, her eyes shining in welcome. Coolness and quiet and the plaintive melancholy of convent life enveloped me.

Mother Judge put me in St. Basil, a delightful room in the old mansion overlooking the teeming life of the Hudson River. She leaped over all the barriers, attentively lit my cigarette, briskly prodded into my spiritual state, provided me with the *Exercises of St. Ignatius*, and my meditation for the next day, then from her cape she drew forth several paper-backed, detective stories.

"You convert special!" I said in my mind, intensely amused at a nun who in her quiet convent is one of the most famous women in New York Catholic life.

I descended for supper and my place was set at the table of the summer-boarding nuns. There was one mammoth Sister of St. Joseph with twinkling dark eyes who was so much like my mental concept of Chaucer's nun that I loved her at first sight. A Mother of the Cenacle, who had the carefully modulated voice of the religious of my childhood, read from a dreary book an account of St. John of the Cross, who was suffering from eczema. The stout Sister of St. Joseph looked at me with a roguish smile, and we became conspirators against ascetical giants.

Mother Judge and I sat on the vine-covered porch after supper. I let her talk, for I was relaxing for the first time in months, away from, among others, converts who are not restful people. A handsome tomcat stalked the convent grounds and the little French lay-sister who baked the marvelous cakes and pies, called to him in a gentle patois; you could tell she doted on this arrogant cat who could have been Casanova reincarnated. In the best sense of the word Mother Judge is a superb gossip and I enjoyed her stories about leaders in the Catholic world. It was cool there on the porch and the sun went down caressing the Lourdes statue till it was molten gold and then left Our Lady in purple shadow as the long twilight embraced the Cenacle of St. Regis.

Mother Judge kissed me good night at the door of St. Basil and told me to read as long as I wanted. I slept like a child, dreamless, contented, on my first night in a convent in over twenty-five years.

Next morning someone knocked on my door, greeting me in Latin, and when I didn't respond, yelled right lustily, "It's time for Mass." The chapel of the Cenacle is the most prayerful convent chapel I have ever seen. It has a liturgical perfection. The chant of the Office was beautiful and unearthly. Through the grating I could see the nuns in their great white capes. The dialogue Mass started and the officiating priest had a strong masculine voice, and the responses from the nuns came clearly, unashamed of their feminine timbre. At the Communion of the Faithful my theatre sense took over, for the nuns came to the grating and all you could see were their white hands almost translucent in the gleam of the candles and the early sun; with infinite grace each recipient of the Holy Eucharist passed the golden paten to the next Sister. It was a pleasure in the sensible order, for the motion was as rhythmic and precise as the finest ballet technique.

My spiritual exercises consisted of two hour-long meditations each day in the chapel. I put aside the formal, assigned meditation impatiently and concentrated on learning the "Anima Christi," which proved that I had elements of spiritual common sense. The first day, when I had it letter perfect, I watched the sun from an aperture in the rear wall shine down on the monstrance, and thought about nothing in particular. I noticed Mother Judge come in for her hour of devotion. She knelt on the prie-dieu and was absolutely motionless. I was fascinated. I wondered if the Lord was telling her, "Love Me. Love yourself for Me. Love all others in Me." Probably . . . I commenced to feel rested, pleased with the tranquil day ahead of me.

That day at noon-dinner a laywoman was seated beside me.

My Chaucerian nun was in a state of suppressed excitement. Her eyes literally spoke to me; she kept jerking her head. My companion handed me a dish of boiled potatoes, and I looked into the roguish eyes of Peter Pan. Maude Adams was seated beside me: Maude Adams of the Empire Theatre! She held the dish of potatoes while I looked into eyes that didn't belong to a retired spinster, for this woman had loved deeply. She put down the dish firmly and smiled. It was sheer witchery. . . . Lady Babbie in *The Little Minister* was smiling at me. She lowered her head with its old lady toque ornamented with blue ribbons and gathered her Paisley shawl around her shoulders. I knew she hated to be stared at.

After dinner when the rule of silence was no longer in effect the nuns surrounded her, and she loved them. I crept away. Why destroy her solitude? She had given her estate at Ronkonkoma in the Catskills to the Mothers of the Cenacle, and now she lived in retirement. A Protestant with Catholic sisters. She had gone to their convent in Tours after Charles Frohman's death; somehow she had found peace in this sweetness and calm where the torment of time and ambition meant very little.

I commenced to love the convent, to feel like George Santayana with his nuns in Rome. I stood outside the kitchen door chatting with the little French lay-sister and the tomcat rubbed against me, his coat like velvet from the stroking hands of the Mothers, and all the fishheads saved for him. I talked to young Mother Symington who had the face of a Raphael madonna. The day ended with Benediction in the convent chapel and then Perpetual Adoration was over. Once when Clare telephoned me I missed Benediction and came to the chapel door just as the priest was lifting down the monstrance; an old nun with a face that was criss-crossed like fine leather stood in the door waving her knobby old hand. She was singing half to herself, "Good Night, Sweet Jesus." The miracle of this goodness in the midst of a corrupt world made me have no shame for my tears.

Mother Judge and I sat in the wisteria-shaded arbor and, with an ironic light in her eyes when I explained my tears, she said, "She's a wee bit senile you know."

So Mother Judge was accusing me of sentimentality? "Late have I found You," wrote St. Augustine; and a small child in a garden crying, "Take and read," had resolved all that great passionate spirit's questions. The old nun singing her sad little lullaby had touched me. I was tired of having to be complex and satiric and cold-blooded. I'd built up that personality and now I was being stuck with it.

I decided to get even with Mother Judge, who was bursting with curiosity as to why Clare had called, by not telling her that Clare had just given me a new job—to edit and get form out of her many scattered papers on the Negro, some of them in existence only on recording machines. Clare was filled with affection and concern for me this week. I did wish she could be more specific. I had been ordered to charge her for this work, and I was going to be sensible and do it, but I much preferred she mention an amount.

Mother Judge came up to my room later that night bearing a ream of expensive linen paper, her eyes dancing with mischief.

"This is for your book. Clare says, 'Start writing it tomorrow.' "

"Why, she hasn't even sent me the notes," I protested. "They're scattered all over New York. Buffy Cobb left some of them at St. Paul's Guild. Gretta Palmer has the sound recorder—"

"Oh," said Mother Judge sinking down on my bed, "this must be another book. Clare called because she wants you to start a book about your conversion, tomorrow morning."

"My—what?" I gasped. Then I remembered Clare wanted me to write a book about being a prodigal and coming back to the Church. Mother Judge and I sat on the bed howling in mirth. "I'll write a play about a convent and make you the lead," I promised. "We'll have Maude Adams play you."

"Indeed!" Mother Judge looked at me sternly. "Maude Adams hasn't the *umph* to play me."

"You can play yourself then. That would be news. A real live nun in a play. Why not? You could do it."

"I'm sure I could. I always thought I was going to be an actress. Never had a thing to do with a convent in my life.

Came here to this place, and in the chapel God claimed me. I took the order and the order took me. I still can't believe it."

Mother Judge then gave me a special treat, she had me called early the next morning to watch the nuns entering choir. She assured me she wanted me to get the scene in my mind so that I would have it done correctly for Hollywood.

I stood in an eerie summer dawn watching the slow, dignified procession down the cloister stairs; the Mothers' great white cloaks billowing like clouds of mist as they entered the long choir. It was still filled with shadows, the first daylight creeping through the long windows. The altar candles in the adjoining chapel cast weird reflections on the walls and ceiling. It was extraordinarily beautiful to watch the long line of white-garbed nuns file in, each bowing profoundly toward the altar seen through the grille. Mother Mary Judge was a regal little figure in a gorgeous choir robe. In the gloom, as the whole community assembled in long benches against the wall, it was like some strange mystic drama. A bell sounded faintly and the chant began. The sound rolled back the centuries. It had the wonder and ecstasy of Christians worshiping in the Catacombs. It had the grandeur and strength of the thirteenth century.

The next morning, after Maude Adams left for Ronkonkoma, Mother Judge and I invaded her first-floor rooms in Nazareth. Maude Adams had her own furniture, her little pink woolly things lay on the great Victorian bed. She was after all an old lady with aching bones who had chills even in this heat. It made a lump come in my throat.

"Constance," said Mother Judge as we sat on the porch, looking at the Hudson, which was almost an Italian blue on this day of intense heat, "you've been praying very hard lately. What for? Something you want Our Lord to give you?"

"Praying, Mother," I answered without pretense, "that this job with Frank Sheed will content me and I won't get tangled up in futility."

"I was afraid of that," she said. "Frank Sheed is not going to give you a job. Clare will not press it."

"Mother," I gasped, "it's settled. There's no doubt. Why . . ."

"Constance, listen to me. You're not strong—that dreadful operation," Mother Judge went on. "All the fretting you did about the play. I don't think you're going to live very long."

I was not going to let myself in for a lecture on death and judgment. I had to know about the job at Sheed and Ward.

"I cannot let you face another disappointment," Mother Judge's eyes filled with pain. "It may turn you away from Our Lord. Clare doesn't understand, because she can't, what you have been through. This friendship mustn't make you bitter."

I went into the kitchen after supper and helped the lay-sister with the dishes. I am not by nature domestic, but I wanted no more of Mother Judge's death-rays. The nuns were quietly going about their business of the Opus Dei. Outside the window the Hudson was flowing back to the sea. In one half hour I could make the shelter of Edith Meiser's. After all, I didn't particularly want this job with Frank Sheed. That was the real trouble. I wanted the theatre. I wasn't going to be happy in this life. I remembered that line of Chateaubriand: "In the day of our death it will be a matter of great indifference to us whether we have been happy or unhappy."

I went sadly to bed. I'd got myself all mixed up again. The heat of that infernal July came through the one narrow window of St. Basil's. This was the first night I hadn't felt sleepy. From where I lay I could see the red glow of the sign over Palisades Park, flashing on and off. It was like the lights going on over a theatre. I hadn't written a line since April, hadn't even discussed the play with anyone. It might have been ready by now. . . . O, Lord, why couldn't I stop longing for the theatre?

The Devil had not really had to bother about me for years. He didn't have to keep me on his side by swamping me with great temptations. He hadn't been annoyed when I came back to the Church; after all, he must have reasoned I didn't have enough character to persist. But perhaps he had now come up against something deep down, something solid.

The attack came lightly at first, for I put on my light and reached for Newman. I kept remembering as I turned the pages how badly he'd been treated in the Church, how little he'd been understood. There was that dreadful place in Birmingham. The failure in Ireland. Watching Manning's star ascend. The Church made every exceptional person miserable. I put down the book. Why stew over Newman? The man had a curious bloodlessness. I reached for the book of poems Mother Judge had left. Hopkins, the Jesuit. There were sentences of his that exploded in the brain like crimson bursts of fire. Newman and Hopkins, two of the finest souls in the Church in comparatively recent times, had suffered, victims of cruelty and stupidity. (I did not reason, because I could not then, that they had found the power and the sweetness and the infinity of Christ's love—a Christ who cried out at His own passion.)

"What are you doing in the Catholic Church?" a voice seemed to question. It whispered. It shouted. It came from all directions. I had visions of Catholic churches filled with smug people pointing a finger of scorn at me.

The small voice again sounded: "And what has any of this to do with the eternal truth of the Catholic Church?"

"Truth? Are you sure it's true," the rival voice questioned. "It's a life to be lived, not a creed to be believed. Where are your Catholics who radiate its doctrines?"

Soon the theatre season would open. I wanted to be back in that brilliant, restless life. I had to have a success in the theatre. I wanted those long intense hours and weeks of concentration. I'd get out of this convent in the morning. I was turning into a neurotic. I'd go to Mass on Sundays when I could, and the Sacraments a few times a year. It was my family religion, like the family nose and the family temper. . . .

I could hear it. It came from everywhere. *"GET OUT OF THE CHURCH. GET OUT OF THE CHURCH."*

And then the Devil brought out his big guns and attacked the Eucharist. I remembered Joris Karl Huysman's dreadful black Mass in *Là-bas*, and the narrow bed quivered with my uncontrollable shaking. I breathed a desperate "Salve Regina," and muffled my mounting hysteria in the pillow.

The next morning I stayed in the back of the chapel for Mass, and did not go to Communion. Mother Judge was worried and I gave some feeble excuse about feeling ill.

"Mother," I said, "when do your personal demons die?"

"Fifteen minutes after you do, dear," she said with a light of sympathetic understanding on her face.

I had to get out of this convent. Mother Judge knew I had reached a limit. Edith Meiser was at the door of the Sixty-ninth Street house to meet me and it was pleasant to sit again on the patio off the dining room while Helga brought long cool drinks. Edith called people on the telephone in that wonderful New York way and parties started.

"Connie's in circulation. She's a sinner again. I must say the Catholics are smart with their retreats, she looks as rested as if she'd had a trip to Bermuda."

The invitations piled up, and the din of sophists sounded in my ears and the pounding of orchestras. It seemed to me that everyone was unhappy, everyone was bitter. So was I.

"Connie," said Edith, always sane, "you're not a sinner. Go to Brooklyn and get the catechism straightened out, then go home to Philadelphia for a few days. These moods, with people like you, lead to bad trouble."

She was right and I took her advice. In Philadelphia I got in touch with Mother Katharine Drexel's Sisters of the Blessed Sacrament for Indians and Colored People who promised to send me all the material I wanted for the book on the Negro. I commenced to be interested. Clare telephoned in a joyous frame of mind.

"Frank will be here Monday," she said, "and I'll get everything fixed. And don't worry. I know something upset you. It takes an awfully long time to settle down in the faith."

Friends are facts. The trouble with me was that I had not dealt in facts for such long years that I could not believe in prodigiously solid things like people being fond of each other and helping each other. I returned to New York. The Grosvenor had a wonderful new room ready for me and express packages had arrived from Mother Katharine Drexel's Sisters. Jimmie, the friendly bellhop, arrived, his eyes looking anxiously over a teetering mountain of books he had stored for me, and soon reference books for *Twilight of God* were jostling the long and anguished story of the Negro in America. Father Mullen expected me at St. John's University in the morning. He had no talent for precise directions, and I kept getting on a subway train and in a few minutes arriving back where I had started. This weird little adventure might have been a heavenly commentary on my spiritual journey. I arrived an hour late.

"Aren't you coming back tomorrow?" questioned Father Mullen dolefully, when I said goodby.

"Father," I protested, "I'm to go to Frank Sheed's this week."

"You're not going to Sheed and Ward," he said, shaking his head portentously....

There it came again. I could feel the fear and the tension starting. Did he know something I didn't? I questioned him closely, but he seemed to have no foundation for his doubts. I came home, went to St. Francis Xavier's and prayed for a long time. The Sheed and Ward thing had to come out, I informed the Lord God, speaking to Him not so much as an equal as to a subordinate subject to my will.

When Clare telephoned that night she reported happily that Frank Sheed and his son Wilfred were sitting on the terrace with her, and I could feel the coolness and the night wind sweep over my parched body. Frank was coming down to New York and would see me in his office the next day at two. "Remember he's the boss," said Clare, hanging up the phone.

I worried over that remark, but consoled myself with all her previous assurances. I stayed awake most of the night studying my notes. I must have everything at my finger's end and be able to talk fast over any discrepancies.

Walking to Sheed and Ward's new offices on the corner of Sixteenth and Broadway the perspiration poured down my face, cascaded down my neck, it seemed to be dripping from my eyes when I stood facing Mr. Sheed, who was totally unlike my mental picture of him.

As I sat down and hopefully waited for the interview to commence, he smiled and pulled his ear.

"Now," he said, "I don't quite know what to say. Actually I haven't anything to say. It has seemed to me there are holes in my business, in bookstores perhaps, where our books are not selling. I have thought—er—vaguely that those holes must be plugged up."

"I understand I am to talk to you about a position as advertising manager," I announced.

"Oh, dear, no," Mr. Sheed was certainly surprised. "I have admirable people in that department."

Apparently Clare had put the whole matter up to the Holy Ghost and the Holy Ghost had got the wires crossed. Perhaps as a playwright she had run into the familiar bugaboo of a double story line, and had forgotten to provide us with dialogue.

The interview was over; it really had never commenced.

I went to see Father Thibodeau two days later when I realized that there were to be no explanations. I was aware that the tenor of my thoughts was dangerous if I wanted a faith to live by. I was torn with emotional conflicts, with outraged pride and fury at myself for having trusted Clare. That generous priest's kindness was like a caress on a tortured heart. He knew that I was starting the bitter folly of running like a child along a precipice, and the battle henceforth would be between God and myself; the unanswered question being whether He would in His infinite mercy bring me back before I fell over into the abyss.

I came home to the Grosvenor consoled, determined to leave for Philadelphia and not wait, in the face of a mounting hotel bill, for an interpretation of events, as it was obvious to me that they were to be ignored. The chambermaid met me:

"Oh, you're the nicest of my ladies, so I sneaked in and stripped your bed. You need fresh sheets every day in this weather and there's plenty of towels for your shower. That letter to Mrs. Luce on your desk, I stamped it and mailed it for you."

That was a sarcastic letter I had dashed off at the height of my miserable disappointment—and had had sense enough to leave on my desk unmailed. Well, it made no difference. Let Clare do a little smarting. I wasn't going to keep her friendship. I had better warn Father Thibodeau, for I suspected he planned to find out from Clare what had happened. I couldn't reach him by telephone. The next day I went back to Philadelphia, but told the Grosvenor I'd be there a few days the next week. I had arranged several appointments.

Mother was valiant. Mother has always been valiant. She had not been keen on the job with Sheed and Ward, she admitted; though it might have been a steppingstone. She did have hopes for that play Clare Luce and I were to write together. Fortunately she had not given up her apartment. I knew, as I looked at her, listened to her flashing wit, how blessed I was, and determined that these silly adventures with glamorous people were going to stop. I would discipline my life to real accomplishment. We could live through the branding of her ewe lamb as a failure again, and go on from there. Really go on this time. . . .

"I hate," said Mother, "Catholic publishers and Catholic this and Catholic that. The point of religion is to share, not build up sheltering walls. This whole affair is bewildering to me." She sighed, looking like Nana.

At the Grosvenor, on my return, I found a letter from Clare Luce. It said merely that she had hoped Frank Sheed would give me the position but had had no right to promise it to me, and did not think she had. Words leaped up at me defining what my attitude should be if I were to remain her friend. It was a letter which demanded a cold, logical, unimpassioned answer. I sat down before the typewriter and words dashed forth—"*How dare you presume. . . .*"

I was told my letter had not been given to her, so a few days later I called to say goodby, perhaps in expediency's name (I think it was more than that), for our names were linked together in connection with the catechism. With an adroit question here and there she established the fact that after all we did not know each other well. It was a wonderfully mannered and artificial performance.

I have never heard her voice again, save addressing great assemblies on the desperate wounds of the world.

# 5

FLOCKS OF SISTERS of the Immaculate Heart of Mary like restless blackbirds cast a shadow on the golden October afternoon as they fluttered toward the vast auditorium of the St. Francis de Sales Church in Philadelphia, where the dramatized catechism was, at last, to have its first showing. The air was filled with gentle chattering as new busloads of religious disembarked, the autumn winds whipping their long veils across their calm faces. The laity coming down the street in droves were sucked into the sober black and blue habits till they appeared to be circular splashes of color. A young man from the diocesan paper, *The Catholic Standard and Times*, had set up his tripod and camera on the top of the high steps, where he was jostled by sound experts calling down to the equipment truck which was blocking the way of impressive limousines. The V.I.P.'s among the Catholic laity stepped out; a Knight of the Cape and Sword gave a jovial greeting to a Knight of St. Gregory, and they turned to glare at a Knight of the Equestrian Order of the Holy Sepulchre of Jerusalem. Since the descent of every one of us was predominantly Irish, there was even the prospect of a good fight on an occasion this impressive. Catholic dowagers waved to me: "Constance, to think of you doing this. It's wonderful. Is Clare Luce coming?"

Clare Luce was at this moment winging her way to Rome where in a matter of hours she, reportedly, would ask Monsignor Francis Brennan of Philadelphia, an official of the Rota, "May I run right in and see the Holy Father?" and get this gallant response, "If I were the Holy Father I'd let you."

Like a frenzied mermaid I had thrown myself into the sea of Catholic life in Philadelphia; now I was swimming up top with the lordly fish. I had been entertained by leaders in lay Catholic society, who since I had been away from the Church had grown so rich that they owned Rittenhouse Square frontage, racing stables, old masters, country estates, and had so many Roman honors that they must have found it hard to decide which sort of Knight they were going to be on great Church occasions. One of them, if I had anything to do with it, was about to endow an audio-visual catechism.

Spurred on by my sense of guilt at having made a mess of things I had worked around the clock to make the audio-visual catechism a success. I sat on that barrel of dynamite, ecclesiastical conservatism, negligently scratching matches on the side, unaware of what I might be doing to the Church in Philadelphia, as I set off flares till the sky was bright with their gaudy glow. There was one trouble: I had never seen the catechism. I ranted in letters, I called long distance, I threatened. On Columbus Day I was assured it was ready, but no one could promise that the express company would deliver on a holiday; I screamed so loud it was a wonder the catechism did not come up the Delaware on Christopher Columbus' own ship, the *Santa Maria.* It arrived the night before the first showing and I ran it through the projector and rejoiced in an uncritical sense of elation. Why, there was the little girl in the red, red dress lying on the green, green grass, looking at the lone daisy! There was a splendid blue screen with white clouds and through them, shot in silver, appeared the magic name, Editorial Supervisor Clare Boothe Luce, and at that point the orchestration went into a few lovely bars of "Oh, Paradise." . . . There were several things that worried me, but when we got it down to St. Francis' auditorium with its superb acoustics, all the deficiencies would, I knew, disappear.

Through the side door of the hall came an impressive squadron of priests—the Bishop's palace guard in immaculate broadcloth, heads up, shoulders squared. The ranks parted and Father Michael Mullen, C. M., with his unruly lock of hair tumbling down, waved to me, his eyes shining in delight. This was triumph indeed, after those long sessions in the New Weston, on Barclay Street. This was his brain child, and it was *his* day. The nuns had subsided in that beautiful quiet which comes over dedicated women in the presence of the priesthood; it is a sort of quizzical silence in which thought is released, controlled. No mere individualist could understand the self-discipline of the composite facial expression of a female religious congregation being addressed by the clergy.

The introduction ran on, ending with these words: "The name Clare Luce among Catholics is a guarantee that here will be a big idea done with professional smoothness."

Then Father Michael Mullen took the rostrum. He regarded us all with a look of tender amusement. He believed the best of us. He leaned on the lectern, and he commenced to talk. He believed in audio-visual education, so did everyone in the early church. Father devoted much time to the rise of religious art. He talked to the end of the entire period allotted to us, and we were just in sight of the thirteenth century. I had never suspected it, but Father Mullen was obviously a pedagogical modernist; his theories on religious education must have been downright radical to judge from the gasps that were sounding in various parts of the hall. He seemed to be promulgating the view that the Fathers of the Council of Trent were a lot of old fogies who, because they couldn't think up a better idea than Martin Luther's Question and Answer Catechism, were responsible for religious laxity. Father, like the great Thomas Aquinas, always tried to demolish his own propositions. I grew a bit confused; so I think did the teaching Sisterhood. Finally he reached the catechism.

"Now, Sisters," he said, with that marvelous smile, "a child reads in the catechism, 'God is a pure spirit.' What's that mean? 'A pure spirit.' A child sees a piece of Ivory soap 99 44/100 per cent pure."

An old nun close by me, who had been listening with a cupped ear, whispered, "Has he compared my Merciful Redeemer to a piece of soap?"

"A little girl in Brooklyn told me," he went on, "God's a boy, twenty-one years old, in a pink dress, with red hair. And if that's the way she wants to see Our Lord, then I'm for it."

"This is too much," said the aging nun. "Outrageous."

"What do you want a little child to take out of religion classes? All a child needs is: God is good—God is love. And if you Sisters are good-humored and loving you'll save the faith. I'd rather toss the Baltimore Catechism out the window than fight a child for not studying all that dull stuff. It's not the words you make 'em memorize, all scared from a tongue-lashing and you Sisters sure can give 'em, it's the love you have for Our Lord, which makes you gentle and kind with little children, that teaches catechism. Love is the main ingredient. What kiddies remember from religion classes is what Sister was like."

Father Mullen's cheeks were pink, he was gesticulating, his earnestness was beautiful to see. He was on the side of the angels, and the joy in Heaven was profound. His statements were overwhelmingly true. It was Catholicism in its great sense. But Father Michael Mullen was in trouble with the girls. This, they said, is Revolution from Brooklyn.

The lights in the auditorium went down, through the loudspeakers came muffled voices. The recordings were not good. The figures in each unit did not correspond. The children grew big and became small again, and, as it wasn't *Alice in Wonderland*, it was baffling. This modern feature for which I had filled columns of newsprint resembled nothing so much as an old-fashioned magic-lantern show. Father Mullen did not give in to defeat, for at the conclusion he rose again and faced the audience. He was in love with the grotesque little figures in the film strip. He wanted to talk about them. The people were filing out of the auditorium, unaware that Father Mullen in defense of the catechism family was explaining any deficiency that might have been in it.

"I don't like slick, polished things, all weighted down by pride," he said, in splendid defiance.

The Bishop's palace guard were marching out, ignoring us. There was not even a mitigating word. One comment made to me was:

"How are you going to explain this to Mrs. Luce?"

A few of the nuns who were merciful surrounded Father Mullen, who saw nothing mean or ungenerous going on around him. My cousin Margaret, who had taught catechism for the Missionary Cenacle of the Trinitarian Sisters in the slums of Philadelphia, said sternly, "It is a big idea. The faults are minor compared to the value of the teaching method."

In the following weeks my resentment against authoritarianism was intense. I was up against the reality of living the Catholic life in a society which accepted clerical decisions without discussion. I felt that I was in stagnant intellectual waters, and openly rebelled.

"I hope Constance doesn't fight the catechism verdict to the Pope," said dear Aunt Francie with a smile, but she was worried.

I was taking stock of what it meant to live among my own. Catholicism is more than a faith based on the Apostolic succession. It is more than a study of the catechism and a ritual of prayers and laws. It is a way of life, a framework within which all other activities are encompassed. It is an exclusive society, cut off from much of the modern world. The charity of Christ may not have been an ever-present reality in the ornate homes of the rich Irish, but they were closer in spirit to the transcendence of the faith, than to the pinnacles of the world. They could and did reject in the name of the faith they professed the desirable errors of modern times. They did it simply, without struggle. To lose the faith was the ultimate loss.

I had become what all lapsed Catholics do become—a queer mixture of Catholic and Protestant. Out of place everywhere, at home nowhere. My thoughts and approach to life were more akin to what is called liberal Protestanism than Roman Catholicism. Yet a Catholic upbringing is always a clue to human character, so the Church always clung to me, as she does to all her children, in innumerable ways. In my return, I had only reached the outer edges of the Church; this clerical censorship and my antipathy to my own people were enormous obstacles. In the world I had often been swept by a feeling of being a stranger and an alien among Protestants. When we return to our own Church we have an exile's feeling of belonging nowhere.

One good sweet note in this savage symphony sounded—Father Michael Mullen, C. M. Father Mullen, with unbelievable courage, assumed I loved the catechism, kept me informed of every detail, although my resignation had been accepted. In the day when we are asked what helped us in a bitter struggle, we will not remember the eloquent sermon, the inspired book, but the simple, human kindness of a good priest, untouched by diplomatic considerations, the appearance of things, his only thought being, "Here's a troubled soul and Our Lord is troubled about such." Oh, the patience of the good Father Michael Mullen, who stood at my side a friend because he was God's friend.

I was still keeping up the habit of daily Mass, which meant little to me as I was far away; but one small pious habit will often win the battle. And what a battle it is. Dear God, what a battle!

Weekday Catholicism in action is a heartening thing. Each morning at St. Francis de Sales a handful of worshipers gathered on their way to offices and shops, mothers who had left their children in the near-by parochial school, old people whose lives had been prayers of sacrifice; nearly always there was an "innocent," one of those adults whose minds have not developed into the correct mold of bitterness and skepticism. Ecstatic holiness looked out of their clouded eyes, and if they ran up to light a candle while Mass was going on, or smiled and laughed aloud as they rattled their rosaries, it was not ridiculous or annoying. The priest celebrating the Mass on a weekday seemed to move more slowly. The strength of the liturgical year commenced to hold my restless and tormented heart. At Communion it was peaceful to kneel there with these people, divided from them and yet bound, to see their workworn faces touched with the beauty and youth and tenderness of the Blessed Sacrament.

It was at this time of conflict that Maisie Ward Sheed entered my life, when I wrote to inquire the publication date of Henri de Lubac's *Drama of Atheistic Humanism.* The paradox of Christianity did not touch my mind when we entered into friendship. In some way I knew she would include me in her prayers and in her life, and I was deeply grateful. I was only a little stunned by her gracious and interested response, and rather horribly aware that this would stop the gossip about the disgruntled job-seeker. I didn't pay too much attention to it then because I had real troubles; the time had almost come when it would have to be known that my mother's ewe lamb had got caught in the shambles of economic disaster again. The telling could be put off just long enough for me to enjoy the society of Brock Pemberton, who was trying out a new play in Philadelphia. Mr. P. was literally bowled over by my exuberant delight in seeing him again. I acted like someone who had been in exile for years and years. Paul Foley and Bill Sharon grabbed me one midnight and begged me to get to work on another play, for Brock had not done well with his latest, he had contracted that almost fatal disease for a theatrical producer—he had become dated. He sought in a play the glittering surfaces of the "twenties," which had been the period of his greatest success. The critics were brutal.

"Connie," said that drawling voice over my telephone the morning after the opening, "did you read what they said about me? I'm happy. This means you didn't fail with *The Heel.* I did. You're to come back with a success."

Who would not love the memory of a man like that? It was good to sit across from him at a table in the Warwick, though I thought how ill he looked. Then we said goodby, and Brock Pemberton was gone forever.

I had an appointment to keep the next morning with Dr. Thomas Shallow, one I had been putting off for a long time. The great ugly lumps were back on my neck. I had felt so wonderfully well, almost reborn after the operation. Dr. Shallow had been proud, as good doctors are with a fine result. Now, again, his face was grave, and I could feel those great hands on my neck, the authority and power and gentleness in those probing fingers.

"Sorry, Constance. It's all to do again." He looked at me, worried. "I'll call the hospital. These glands are quite serious, I thought you understood that. They're tubercular. Obviously you have been under a terrific strain." He smiled. "We'll lick it. Too bad to be in the hospital for Christmas."

It seemed as if only a few days had passed since I left Jefferson. The nurses who remembered me ran into my room, the young doctors. My operation kept being postponed. One morning Father Roul from St. John's came.

"They may operate in the morning. I'd like to give you the Last Rites of the Church. They helped before."

Once again the healing Sacrament was given me, and I ceased my bitter battle with the Church Temporal. This was the Church I wanted.

"No operation," said Dr. Shallow after days of indecision. "We're sending you to X-ray instead."

I remember it was the week before Christmas and there was a row of lighted trees in the long corridor leading to the X-ray section. The wards were filled, those long, dark wards. I came to an open door and heard:

"Too bad about Miss O'Hara, she's a poor operative risk."

That was that. One more blow. What was it going to mean? The nurses started to sing Christmas carols in the main lobby. While I waited the clerk from the post office rushed up to me.

"This just came. Look—"

I read in the left-hand corner in the familiar handwriting, "Clare Boothe Luce, The Waldorf Towers." It was the saddest looking package I had ever seen in my life. A torn piece of white paper held the box insecurely. A piece of twine was wound around it with two firm knots. Trust Clare for that! Inside the paper was a box marked, "Shaving Kit, $40.00. . . ." I commenced to laugh, so did the doctors. I pulled out newspaper twisted in protective shields, several covers of *Life* magazine, and a small white box labeled, "The Wishing Well." I opened it, and a porcelain lamb that fitted into the palm of my hand was revealed. I heard a voice saying:

"Now, Constance, do not dramatize yourself: you are not a black sheep; merely an unattractive, dirty gray."

Sister Julie du Saint-Esprit! And Clare had remembered. . . . I could see her with the mischief in her eyes, struggling with the wrappings of that package in fierce concentration. She was not going to ask for help; to have everyone chirruping about her Christmas spirit of forgiveness. This was between us. The lamb acquired a name after the hospital, Jefferson; and he represents to me the best thing there is in the souls of two women: the innocence of remembering childhood. I am very fond of Jefferson. After this, though Clare never telephoned, she commenced to send me letters and cards in her beautiful handwriting. Sometimes they revealed a flash of the old liking. . . .

I did not pull myself together after this illness, I was too tired. The pressures of life were not pleasant. Dependence is bitter. I knew that I could not undertake hard work, and to write another play was the work of years and a net to catch the wind. I tried to discipline myself to other forms of writing. It was not turning out.

On a gray Sunday in March, Mother looked up from the New York *Times*. "Brock Pemberton died suddenly yesterday," she said.

Much had been wrong in that professional association but my Kansas Hamlet was, nevertheless, a real part of my life; a man I liked so much that at his hands I accepted defeat without bitterness. When liking triumphs over a human situation, you have a friend. He was gone. It seemed impossible that he wasn't in the world.

Elaine Perry called: Tuesday morning I sat in Christ Methodist Church in New York. The music started, slow and solemn. They walked in, two by two; the theatre passing by. It wasn't real. It was a Pemberton production. Bert Lytell stood in the pulpit, you could see the faint trace of make-up, the old-school actor. Bertie would give this his *all*.

"It's knowing a man in failure that counts," he said, and he was very simple and direct. "I was with Brock in a beautifully written play of tremendous power—a play that failed."

"A play that failed." Dear Bertie! Wonderful artificial theatre! Place of the tall corn. The children's corner of the world.

Lawrence Tibbett sang the "Our Father," and it was over.

Later we sat at Sardi's. Brock would never come in the door again. Everyone talked about his crazy, wonderful luck, going at the peak of his form without a pain or an ache. Lucky, lucky Brock!

"Stop grieving, Connie," I was ordered. "Don't look so sad. Dear old goat, he had a scrumptious time."

The actresses were on display at Sardi's. The managers were talking about plays. All I had to do was bring them one. This was the theatre, so gay, so bright and shining. But if you come close you'll smell the tired sweat, you'll see the tears. At that table Tony Perry used to sit holding court: "Constance, will I see God?"

In some way I'd lost peace and health again, but Father Thibodeau, whom I would see in the morning, would fix it. He always had. He would understand that returning to the Catholic Church in Philadelphia had only meant going back to the past and not belonging there any more; like looking at houses where you'd once lived, schools you'd gone to, and finding everything had changed.

I sat in the visitors' cell of St. Jean's and waited for his coming. The priest who entered was almost unrecognizable. He wore a new shining black silk soutane and there was an onyx ring on his finger. I thought of Fénelon, a character I could never abide. His eyes, which had always bulged a trifle, now seemed dark and mysterious behind rimless glasses. His almost white hair was well cut. He moved toward me with an easy grace I did not remember. Since I had seen him last he had been made Father Superior.

We talked of T. S. Eliot's play, *The Cocktail Party*. He had brought me Father Garrigou-Lagrange's *Three Ages of the Interior Life* and a small volume with the horrid title, *Why Not Be Happy?* The one person I did not want to discuss was Clare Boothe Luce, but Father Thibodeau was not letting me off that easily.

"Oh, Father, why pretend. We're not friends. Those letters, books, mean nothing."

"No," he answered, with a remote smile, "they mean nothing.

You'll have to stand on your own two feet. These things happen. It's no one's fault."

"It was as unfortunate for Clare as it was for me that we ever met," I said.

The priest beside me commenced to laugh.

"You find me amusing, Father?"

He looked at me, honestly puzzled. He had no idea what was wrong.

His laughter led me down the streets of New York, it walked beside me. This, I said, is the answer of my Church to my desperate need—a laugh.

Ridicule is a shaft that pierces through and through, and my wound was the more painful because I knew I was not only reacting to that casual laugh in an absurd manner, but I was being unjust. I knew that Father Thibodeau, the gentlest of men, was incapable of unkindness, and what was more had credited me with intelligence and an adult personality. Only a man of prayer like the good Father could ever have forgiven a friend he had trusted, who so carelessly made a fool of herself. He has forgiven me.

## 6

My suffering was real, even though ridiculous, for I was proving, among other things, that self-centered people create Hell for themselves.

It is true that it had been good to live in an atmosphere of trust and friendship however briefly; but I knew, as every woman must, there are no deep roots to feminine friendship, for it is not within our capacities. It is not realistic enough for our bread-and-butter natures. It wilts under our insistence that all human relations are valueless unless they can be fondled and caressed and subjected to sentimentalities. In all history there is no record of a great feminine friendship, save the mother and daughter-in-law idyll of Ruth and Naomi. The lack of knowing what friendship means seldom disturbs women.

Therefore, the end of my friendship with Clare Luce would not have been disturbing if my pride had been unscathed. But because my pride was stung I would not and could not let her go until she knew I too had strength, bitterness, the capacity to hurt. St. Augustine has written truly that for the sword of hate to reach our enemies it must first pass through us.

On a warm Sunday in May, as a gesture of defiance, I decided to go to Vespers at St. Clement's Anglo-Catholic Church. But knowing myself to be only a bedraggled pretender seeking an intellectual night's lodging, I turned away from the beautifully simple façade of St. Clement's. I remembered the grave courtesy of Father Gorgas, Monsignor Drumgoole's friend. There was no solution for me among the Anglo-Catholics, and I could not insult them by bringing them the baseness I knew was in my own heart.

I would not, I told myself, ever return to the Roman Catholic Church. My legs were trembling, had been for many days, so were my hands, I was ill and too indifferent to seek cure. At times my eyes did the most astounding tricks, I thought I was walking in the center of the street and found myself crashing into something on the extreme left or right. I looked into a face, and was horrified when it became two faces. This double vision was almost continuous.

I found myself, this Sunday, walking in the Tenderloin, not even on a bright May afternoon a safe place for a stroll. The wretched people I passed gave me new fuel in my war against the Roman Catholic Church. Where were the churchmen working in the name of Christ in order that poverty and destitution should be merely melancholy memories in society? Where were the priests who tried to bring joy and human decency to these abandoned people? They were all too busy in their pathological warfare against Communism, I told myself, to bind up the wounds of society.

There is a moment in every human life when we must hear, however dimly, the footfall of Christ walking beside the most undeserving of His children. Shaking with nerves, I saw a small shining new church: a Catholic church. There was an asphalt yard with an iron railing around it. People were going in the gates, I saw folding chairs set up, and I knew I would fall down in a faint if I could not rest. No one would know me here and I'd go in and watch for a cruising taxi. Most of the people entering were Chinese. Then I knew I was in the churchyard of the Church of the Holy Redeemer, built by Cardinal Dougherty's Jubilee purse for the Chinese Catholics. Cardinal Dougherty! I could see Monsignor Drumgoole's heartbroken face, hear my father's cough. . . .

I sat down on a folding chair and commenced to feel stronger. The Trinitarian Sisters were shepherding Chinese children in their native dress. I realized it was to be a May Procession. A huge limousine drove up to the side of the church. I watched His Eminence, Cardinal Dougherty emerge, a tired old man dragging his great bulk up that long flight of stairs. I felt to my amazement the sting of tears. There was something heroic about him, like a stern old soldier. Yet I had no admiration for His Eminence, no kindly sentiment toward him.

"Dear old soul," said one of those good women who attend all Catholic affairs.

"I don't think I would call him just that," I answered.

"Don't heed all the priests tell you," she whispered. "They need a strong hand like the rest of us."

The music started, and the hymns. The little Chinese children appeared in their colorful costumes, carrying blue banners for the Mother of God, and nodding Chinese lanterns. The tiny ones were helped along by Trinitarian Sisters, courteous babies who made no whimper if their uncertain footsteps made them fall away from Sister's grasp; as they hit the hard asphalt their eyes seemed to say, "Who did this to me?" It seemed most unkind of

God to let these enchanting children hurt themselves honoring His Mother.

At the top of the stairs stood His Eminence Denis, Cardinal Dougherty, Archbishop of Philadelphia, wearing the regal ermine, the cappa magna. He had refused to don these trimmings for the Drexels, who at their famous reception for His Eminence had run the red velvet carpet to the curb, where there stepped forth from the limousine a lonely figure in plain black broadcloth. But in the slums of Philadelphia, a Prince of the Church gave honor to his children. The priests rushed to his side to assist him down that steep flight of steps. He pushed them aside and, not even touching the hand-rail, his crimson cloak billowing around him, he descended the long stone stairs in majestic solitude. Reminding me of Queen Victoria, he sailed at the rear of the May Procession.

Along the iron railing outside stood wretched men, the scourings of a vast city. They looked like hungry scarecrows, a painting by Hogarth; they were like the lost and the damned seeing Paradise. I remembered a little girl at St. Charles Seminary being told a story by Bishop Dougherty from the Philippines. I hadn't let him finish the story.

"Who are you?" It was spoken in an old voice that quavered, but still had the ring of iron in it.

"I asked your name, madame?" The Cardinal was standing looking at me, a stern expression on his face.

Why had he singled me out? I would give my name and be insulted. So be it! His Eminence had not been gentle, and I would not be gentle. I knelt to kiss the ring, conscious of his eyes.

"I am Constance O'Hara," I said, as I came upright. "Your Eminence would not know me. My father was doctor of the Seminary, so was my grandfather."

"Yes, yes," his tone was almost impatient, "and why did you come here?"

"My father had much admiration for Your Eminence, which I have come to share." I was stunned by my own words. "I am here because when Your Eminence believes in a cause he does something about it. Your church for the Chinese Catholics is an actuality, not a sermon. 'Words are the daughters of earth, deeds the sons of Heaven,' Eminence."

I certainly was going all out. I thought I heard the silvery giggle of Monsignor Drumgoole, Monsignor who could never harbor a resentment, from the far ramparts of Heaven.

"That is kind of you, Constance." He was smiling like a pleased child. "I was almost sure you were an O'Hara when I saw the face. Something came to me. Father Sheridan had Bishop O'Hara recommend me to the Seminary, and your grandfather the elder Doctor O'Hara turned me down. He said I wasn't strong." Amusement overcame him. "I went to Canada, but two years later I was in Overbrook. Bishop William O'Hara called me to Cardinal Satolli's attention when I went to Rome. I've known the O'Haras for sixty years. You favor your dear grandmother O'Hara, with whom I was especially acquainted."

The May Procession was approaching the outdoor altar and the startled clergy brought it to a halt. I kept looking into the wonderful eyes of Cardinal Dougherty. They did not reject me. They drew all the hurts out of me. I backed away so the procession could continue.

"Come here, Constance O'Hara."

He had said the identical words to me on the porch of St. Charles Seminary, nearly forty years ago.

"I would like to see you. I know and like all your family. We are old friends. I like to talk of old days with old friends. I have such esteem for the O'Haras."

So, in the courtyard of the Chinese Church of the Redeemer, the old Cardinal gave me my welcome in the name of my family.

The procession continued. I saw the Cardinal ascend to the throne on the Gospel side of the outdoor altar. Those old hands did not dare hold the monstrance at Benediction; he knelt there, his great full cloak a splendid dash of scarlet. A man looked out of an open window in one of those Tenderloin houses where wretched men find lodgings for the night. This man's face was hideous with all the vices. He made great jerking signs of the cross, as he looked down at the altar; once he fell over on the window sill sobbing drunkenly. The Cardinal's eyes never left the awful apparition that had once been a living, believing man. This old Prince of the Church did not reject any one of the Church's desperate children. This was the bricklayer of God.

Father Roul preached on the Prodigal Son, and still those magnificent eyes looked toward the window into that dreadful face, watched an abandoned man make the sign of the cross. It was the miracle of the Church that one prayer might reach that heart and transform that man.

And I could think of leaving a Church that could bring before my eyes such a reality?

Again, I went back to confession. I stood outside the box in St. Francis de Sales where the priest had made the tirade against me long years ago. Why? I think in my folly I was daring God to bring more abuse on me, so I could brand it all as a religious obsession. In the darkness of the box I looked at the dim image of the crucifix, and I knew what I had done to the priceless gift of faith which had been handed back to me. Oh, yes, I had been acted upon, certainly I had seen dismal manifestations of materialism in the Church, compromises with the world, the catering to great wealth, the theatrical surges, bleak unkindness, but that was no excuse. My absurdities, my contradictions, my mortal sins were shortly to be before the Judge.

A voice spoke and into the darkness and sadness and evil came the radiance of Christ. There was no compromise in this man. He cared nothing for the intellectual Catholic as such, or the gifted, or the rich, or the favored. He left those things in the realm of economics and biology. He knew only St. Paul: "Beggars enriching many, paupers possessing all things."

"God alone," he said.

This priest was buried in God. And yet he was a simple parish assistant. His business was souls, and our complexities bothered him not at all. He drove out the demons with blessed endurance. He had the gentleness of all strong people. There is only one quality that can save the world, and that is personal holiness. There is no argument against it.

So it was that I found Father William Flatley and started my journey once again to find a Christ who had not yet really touched my heart.

There is a folksaying, "Too mad to see straight." That was my trouble in the spiritual order, and my trouble in the physical order. The Lord, knowing my stupidity, may have had to make certain things manifest. I could no longer read print for it slipped away in all directions, lines tilting into each other.

Dr. Thomas Shallow gave me the benefit of the doubt that I was not a nerve case with psychosomatic symptoms, and took me to Jefferson on his service, for a possible thyroid operation. In desperate anguish I wrote to the old Cardinal, and he responded in the letter of a great churchman promising me that in every one of his Masses and his prayers I would be remembered. I know he kept his promise.

It was a grim time. There were many specialists. A famous doctor stood at my bed. "Pick up that paper and read. *YOU CAN READ*," he scoffed. . . .

Now they were accusing me of fantasies. After his visit massive sedation was ordered. One night Dr. Shallow and his staff came in late. I was too weak even to notice him, though I usually rallied to say something cheerful. The overhead light shone into my tortured eyes. Voices came from a great distance.

"Call our endocrinologist," Dr. Shallow ordered one of his assistants. "I'll stay here till you get him."

Medicine is still a glorious profession, victorious, despite its critics, over callousness. Dr. Shallow, one of the giants of modern medicine, waited through his dinner hour with a patient whom he was not going to charge a fee. Miss Lewis, the head nurse, that testy, magnificent woman who has made nursing an art and the sixth floor of the old building at Jefferson a miracle of order and competence, came back and forth. Dr. Shallow munched on an apple, his keen eyes studying me, as I sank into shadows, and then rose and looked at distortions like those comic mirrors in an amusement park.

A slender figure entered my room. He had a cornflower in

his buttonhole. He bowed, he clicked his heels. A Teutonic voice overlaid with Oxonian English said, "I am Dr. Karl Paschis."

He had been a blond Austrian in his youth. He resembled no one so much as the philosopher in one of those long second acts of a Sam Behrman play. Fog drifted across his face and suddenly he was two doctors standing against my bureau.

"Doctor," I was begging now; "I do not imagine it. I can't see straight. I see double."

"No." He folded his arms. "You don't imagine it. Your trouble is entirely real." He came over, felt my eyeballs which were hardening, ordered me to follow his finger. "Have you had lately an emotional shock?" He sat in the big chair beside my bed and with scientific precision drew the story from me. "You are a neurotic. Who is not? Even the cows have turned neurotic in our time."

There were more days of tests. This doctor knew I was harassed by financial anxiety, that I had no personal resources. On those terms I became the patient of one of the greatest doctors I have ever known. My doctor and my friend.

He came into my room one night, "Now I am ready. You have a rare nervous disease of the eyes, stubborn, hard to treat. The reason for this disease is because, like myself, you have a pre-1914 mind. Our infant memories are of order, stability; that is, those of us of the middle and professional classes. Then came the First World War and the nightmare. You are not European as I am, so you did not get the full impact of change. We seek to return to our lost securities. You, a complex woman, went back to find your childhood's God. Only someone born prior to 1914 could do that, and yet also possess a subtle, disillusioned mind." He smiled at me, and I saw myself not alone, but part of a world. "That yearning to retrace our steps, to find our lost security is the great neurosis of modern times. I wish that to face the cause would be the cure."

The Benedictine Fathers, who had taught at the Gymnasium where he had been till he was eighteen, had marked this doctor, who is a great individualist, with their sanity, touched him with the mystery of pity. He would be amused to realize that the Holy Rule has exercised a profound influence on his character. He knows that the present state of the world and the whole of life is diseased. He lives in it, frightened as only brave men can be; and in a research laboratory, night after night, he fights that men may live, even in the pestilential climate of intellectual death. Such is the way of a great doctor!

And now I had two friends for the hardest sixteen months of my life—one a humanly wise priest, Father William Flatley, whom I seldom saw face to face, who has mentioned but one book to me—Hilaire Belloc's *Reformation;* and a brilliant, subtle European who has read everything, knows every nuance of a play, a ballet, a symphony, who has toyed with all philosophies. There was a fundamental likeness between these two men; they lived to save. The priest was perhaps the more profound.

I was in a strange world of half-sight. I could not see to read. The beam of an autombile headlight at night could throw me into a world of optical illusions, and I would lose all sense of direction. Outwardly, for the sake of my mother, I remained calm. Religion, which I practised with a dreadful persistence in its outer form, though I could not pray, was as dry as dust. It only took on meaning in Father Flatley's confessional box.

He and I fought the war in Korea through my anguished eyes, we offered them for the soldiers in that tragic war. We went over the rocky terrain inch by inch. We offered my pain and my torment at being deprived of the world of print for the screaming Chinese Communists caught on barbed wire and dying in this agony; for American boys in the bestial business of war. We went to the Yalu River, back to the Thirty-eighth Parallel.

"Don't waste this suffering, someone needs it," he begged.

Father William Flatley, with his patience, his kindness, had the compassion of his Christ; and proved over and over the infinite resources of his Church. He did not preach, "Offer it to God"; he did not say, "These things happen. It's His will. Meditate." He said, "Let us make use of this suffering. Let us not waste it."

Dr. Paschis would look at me, his long slender fingers twining around each other. "I hate suffering. I can let you have more sedation."

I thought of Father Flatley and I stuck to the minimum dose.

Dr. Paschis kept the world of ideas before me. The plays of Christopher Fry who enthralled him. The ballets we both had seen. The books we had read. The embattled cause of liberalism and freedom.

And then Dr. Paschis, like Father Flatley, made demands on my courage. My disease was unique; I was a case history. He brought me before his students at first. Then he took me to the Pit at Jefferson to discuss my disease and its treatment before a group of doctors. I stood outside that narrow door, unprotected, cringing. I entered, looking up at tier after tier of seats directed at a circular pit. The lights were agony, but I saw doctors looking down at me—men of my father's profession, my grandfather's. Lights commenced to blaze down on my head. A young doctor impersonally discussed my disease, the glandular involvement, my body as if it were a mechanical thing gone wrong. I saw lights over a theatre: "Brock Pemberton Presents."

"We believe the patient may see to read. It is doubtful if the eyes will ever resume their normal appearance." The young doctor held my head steadily forward. "You see the stare—that will remain."

My eyes that had been the one beautiful feature I possessed!

"A provocative case." Dr. Paschis was leaning forward. "This patient is a writer, a woman artist with all that means in the way of temperament. She has gone through this with enormous patience, as obedient as a docile child. Because of her there may be a better cure for a hellish disease."

My sufferings had been used, not only in the anonymity of a confessional box, but in a scientific laboratory.

But there was still no sweetness or joy in my heart toward Christ, I was still unmoved. Humanly I was wretched among Catholics, and in no way did they try to make it easier. Dr. Paschis once told me of a long-anticipated return to Vienna. He had looked forward to a visit that would make him part of the good, familiar things again, but commenced to feel sad and restless the first hour after his arrival. There was his old Gymnasium. His ears heard the familiar bells of St. Stephen's Church. Here was the house where he'd lived, the University where he'd got his medical degree. All the great experiences of his life had been lived through in Vienna—artistic, emotional, intellectual. And now he returned and he didn't belong. It wasn't his life any more. He was a ghost tormented by the past, memories reviving which he had long forgotten. His friends came to his hotel, even before he'd ordered breakfast. There were joyous reunions, but then something stirred, hostilities from the past. He was two men—a young Viennese, and an assured, aging American. German was his language, but he kept speaking it slowly. It was not till he was safely out of Vienna, away from the past, that he realized what a terrific emotional impact it had had on him, how it had cut into his new life, how frightened he'd been.

That was what being a Catholic in Philadelphia was like for me. I was middle-aged, yet I seemed to be the sensitive girl who had left the Church. The past would not let me go. I had a curious young-mindedness, my emotions surfaced at the slightest provocation. I was an alien at home.

I struggled on, but religion was all dryness. Nothing moved in my heart.

"The faith is there," said tired Father Flatley. "You would not be here if the faith was not in your heart. Try again. It is not impossible to love God. Remember He loves you. It will happen. He will touch you with such charity and such love that all this will vanish like the mist. I promise, but you must not dwell on bitter things."

There came a day when they took off the sheltering black glasses, stripped away the patch, and I saw print again. It was a day of glory. Books, books . . . I could scarcely bear it. Week by week passed and the eye muscles held and the vision kept at a peak. Father Flatley gave up Asiatic wars, and it seemed as if now I could get about the business of living.

Then illness struck me down again.

There were no longer any protective, sheltering walls. The fearful expenses of a woman unable to work, and too nervously ill to concentrate on writing, kept up. I refused private rooms. I was grateful for the hospitalization that paid those staggering bills. The first time I went in a room-ward I cringed; it would be worse than the physical illness. I thought of all the sordid traits of human beings; close to them no detail of illness or loathsome personal habits would be spared me.

In a few days it was I who was ill, retching and agonized, unable to pull close the sheltering curtains. I fought to keep back groans of pain. I turned my head and in the bed next mine an elderly Jewess was weeping. My shame was dreadful, for she was in great agony and was a dear, considerate woman. I gasped out an apology, begged her to get a nurse to pull close the curtains.

"It is not myself," she said, incredulous that I had such an idea. "It is you. I cannot bear to see you suffer like this."

I had never had a stranger revelation. In this cruel century we can still weep for each other. I was glad that the human family of Jesus had brought this knowledge to me. Tears for me! This was Gospel love for each other. That they were the tears of Israel made me proud.

How can I describe those years of illness, of debt and worry, the years that had the shape of gaunt gray wolves? I fought against self-pity and that was the best I could do. Sometimes I sat at St. John's where the Blessed Sacrament is daily exposed and looked up imploring help, but it did not come. There came to me a haunting idea, almost as if someone had spoken, "Give in." What could it mean? No, I would not give in, I would struggle on, outwardly with courage, inwardly with rebellion. "Give in." There was a strong, sweet, impelling comfort to this idea. What could it mean? "Give in. . . ."

I see myself coming into Jefferson Hospital, time after time, remembering my valiant mother saying goodby with no trace of drama. Her courage is so strong that we seem almost cold with each other.

"Give me a call," she says at the door, "when you can. Don't worry. I'll be all right."

The little inconsequential words that break your heart; the

wonderful attitude of people who can discipline their deepest emotions and weep their tears alone.

The porter who knows me well, all the Jefferson porters know me well, makes a grab for my bag. I am assigned to a room by the clerk who is like someone at a summer hotel greeting a season-after-season guest. It is one steady procession of greetings till Miss Lewis looks up and growls:

"What, you here again?"

Lew-y tips her battleflag to only one enemy, the enemy she respects, death. But till he wins, she's his most formidable foe. There are no hours for Miss Lewis. There are just sick people, and nurses to discipline, and doctors to keep in line. You come to know that when it's bad the doctors try to get you on Lew-y's floor.

I give the old bear a hug and she shakes with laughter. We're pretty good friends.

I've cast myself in the role of the gallant, laughing lady. I've got so I believe in it myself. Dr. Shallow's resident looks up from his chart.

"For Pete's sake—Scarlett O'Hara."

A nurse who knows me nearly drops the thermometer tray. "Not you, again? What have you got now? Here, stick one in your mouth. Might as well get back in the old routine."

That's Jefferson. The doctors come. Dr. Eberhardt with his lean, dark taciturn face sits on the side of my bed and broods over me, explaining to his resident, "It started with lymphatic glands. See here—" He draws a pencil down my long incision. "There hasn't been a single thing this woman hasn't cooked up for us since."

There's Dr. Paschis coming down the hall, accompanied by one of his brilliant young scientists.

"Did you see her the day I had her on television? That was quite a symposium. I made it with the eyes, but the damned thyroid went into goiter. It's the next step, yet if I take it—the eyes . . . Oh, here," he tosses an English review on my bed. "The piece on Christopher Fry." Then to his assistant, "I need a new pituitary in the lab. Any posts scheduled?" In the same breath he says to me. "Ah! last night I saw a magnificent play. Superb. . . ."

Perhaps I'm not putting up too good a fight. It's all become too much the endless struggle, the torment of worry, the gray shape of the future. He dismisses his young doctor.

"Constance, I tell you a doctor cannot do what you must do now. It is not the time to appeal to your subconscious, your conscious mind must find out what is within you even if it is the last of your reserves. I need it. I must have it. It is an order."

These are the true tests of Catholicism; this is where you find out if you're in the state of grace.

Dr. Shallow looks in at me: "Operation, Tuesday. I'll clean up some more lymphs before John goes to work."

Dr. John Montgomery stands there, that mild and gentle man. "I'm sorry I hurt you yesterday. I'd operate in a minute, but—"

I am the great question, the imponderable. Kitty, the nurse's aid, bustles in with the biggest tray in the hospital, looks like three desserts. Kitty, Monsignor Cunney's convert with her medal of St. Jude and her wonderful smile.

It's not so bad. No, it's not so bad. There are the nights when screams ring through the corridors, and then they cease and the silence is vocal and terrifying. The meaning comes closer. Living in the sight of death we can no longer push back the certainty that we must die. Will we survive death? Can we become extinct? No one believes that in his heart.

There comes a day when I am helpless, the hospital faces me again. No human being can help me now. It's a day in Lent and I sit in church, my heart a stone, scoffing at myself for believing that help can come from this source. God is pitiless. I get up like an automaton to make the Stations of the Cross. I observe these customs. I have built them into a routine.

I stand at the First Station: Christ before Pilate. The humanity of this journey commences to move within me. Pilate washing his hands, and the Saviour of the World is one with all men who are judged unjustly. But Jesus is perfect and He feels no hate, but in His clean heart are all the hurts of all mankind judged unjustly. The Second Station: the Cross is placed on His shoulders. He carried it for us even till the end of the world. What is this Cross but an "I" crossed out? And then He falls and it is the Third Station. A God falls stunned under the weight of the Cross, just as we do. Mary waits at the Fourth Station to look at Her Son. Mary, the symbol of women looking on a man's sacrifice. In Mary's eyes, in Mary's anguish, a woman can make the perfect Stations of the Cross. But this is more than heartbreak for the humiliation of a Son, this is mystical adoration of her God.

And here, now, are the Stations of the human consolations. . . . Simon who has come to Jerusalem with his sons is called from the crowd to share the Cross, and is reluctant. He is a respectable man, who was standing there to watch a criminal pass by; but because he must, his strong hands help this pitiful Jesus. What must have happened to Simon of Cyrene! The Station of the good Simon, compassionate human goodness–so will each of us touch the Christ when we help Him bear the Cross. And now Veronica steps forward to wipe His face of the blood and sweat and the marks of those who have spat upon Him. He gives to her the image of His sorrowful face. His sorrowful face–that is still the gift He gives to those who truly love him. . . . O, Christ, you are coming to my heart.

The Second Fall . . . there is such loneliness in that fall, such pleading that speaks to those who follow Him. . . . "This is your Fall."

The Weeping Women come to Him, and now the strength of Jesus shines forth. He utters no weak words, but, "Daughters of Jerusalem, weep not for me, but weep for yourselves and your children."

And I heard again, "Give in."

He falls the third time, and now He is abject, anguished, broken.

These are the lonely Stations, for He moves to death and Resurrection in the most forlorn, the most cruel circumstances in all history. He is stripped of His garment, the garment Mary wove. There is no vestige of human dignity left in this Christ. He is nailed to the Cross. The hammer, sounding on the still air of a Friday in Jerusalem, rings down the centuries to our ears.

I hear, "God so loved the world . . ." Love, in this most fearful death?

Christ dies on the Cross, crying, "My God, my God, why hast thou forsaken me?"

A mother holds the broken, bleeding body of a Son. Jesus and Mary . . . Jesus and Mary, the cry of the Church.

Jesus is laid in the tomb. Ah, here is Nicodemus, that man of large affairs, the concealed follower of Christ, bringing ointment to preserve the dead flesh of God. . . . There is even irony in this most human story of the Redemption.

I approach the altar and kneel there in the stillness. The Tabernacle is the Fifteenth Station. The meaning of love. . . .

And I, being what I am, could have nothing left but my need, to know at last the meaning of the sublime love story of the Redemption.

It was not mystical union, there were no tremendous transports, but my tabernacled Christ had claimed me. I was at the heart of love. I had been denied, to find His love. I had been impoverished, to be enriched. I had been rejected, to be claimed. Sickened, to be healed.

A few moments in a city church, worth all of life . . .

THE END